Colonialism, Modernity, and Religious Identities

Colonialism, Modernity, and Religious Identities

Religious Reform Movements in South Asia

Edited by

GWILYM BECKERLEGGE

OXFORD

UNIVERSITY PRESS

OXFORD

UNIVERSITY PRESS

YMCA Library Building, Jai Singh Road, New Delhi 110 001

Oxford University Press is a department of the University of Oxford. It furthers the
University's objective of excellence in research, scholarship, and education
by publishing worldwide in

Oxford   New York

Auckland   Cape Town   Dar es Salaam   Hong Kong   Karachi   Kuala Lumpur
Madrid   Melbourne   Mexico City   Nairobi   New Delhi   Shanghai   Taipei   Toronto

With offices in
Argentina   Austria   Brazil   Chile   Czech Republic   France   Greece   Guatemala
Hungary   Italy   Japan   Poland   Portugal   Singapore   South Korea   Switzerland
Thailand   Turkey   Ukraine   Vietnam

Oxford is a registered trademark of Oxford University Press
in the UK and in certain other countries

Published in India
by Oxford University Press, New Delhi

© Oxford University Press 2008

The moral rights of the author have been asserted
Database right Oxford University Press (maker)

First published 2008

ISBN 13: 978-0-19-569214-3
ISBN 10: 0-19-569214-4

Typeset in Agaramond 10.5/12.5
by Sai Graphic Design, New Delhi 110 055
Printed at Ram Printograph, Delhi 110 051
Published by Oxford University Press
YMCA Library Building, Jai Singh Road, New Delhi 110 001

Contents

Preface

This volume is the third collection of essays largely based on the work of the panel on 'Religious Reform Movements in South Asia from the Nineteenth Century to the Present' which has met regularly at the biennial European Conference on Modern South Asian Studies. Comprising papers originally presented at the conference hosted by the University of Heidelberg in 2002, the volume contains contributions from members of this panel and cognate panels.

Certain themes and topics, which have been central to the ongoing work of the 'Religious Reform Movements' panel, ensure a measure of continuity between this volume and its predecessors. Such concerns include patterns of political interaction and, more particularly, the changing relationship between religion and the socio-political context, the roles of specific religious movements, and the lives and contributions of individuals. As colonialism has shaped in various ways all the movements and historical personalities covered in this volume, a number of authors continue the panel's exploration, at its previous meetings, of the experience of South Asian religious groups and movements during the period of British rule. Other authors have centred their attention upon more recent developments, drawing in one case upon substantial fieldwork. The issue of gender in religion, which similarly has provided a recurrent topic for the panel's attention, is here addressed through studies of both Hinduism and Islam. Other topics in this volume include the interpretation of religious texts, proselytism, the apologetic use of art, and Hindu constructions of East and West. The 'Introduction' initiates a wider consideration of the study of South Asian religious reform movements. Acknowledging novel aspects in the redefinition of South Asian religious identities during the nineteenth century and subsequently, it discusses the relationship between the past and modernity implied by religious reform. The uses of functionalism, orientalism, and syncretism as analytical concepts are examined subsequently in different chapters as part of the book's reflection on methodological issues in the study of religious phenomena.

Each of the preceding collections of essays produced by the panel has covered a variety of religious movements while highlighting certain focal points in their study; identifying paradigms and parameters (Copley 2000), and religious values in relationship to Hindutva (Copley 2003). This latest collection of essays is not organized in the same way around any one factor that has impinged upon the religious life of South Asia in the intervening years. Unlike the panel's two earlier volumes that dealt largely with Hinduism, this collection offers a more extensive treatment of Islamic movements, and thus a more balanced representation of scholarly work on South Asian religious reform movements.

The timing of the last volume brought out by the 'Religious Reform Movements' panel understandably led to interest being concentrated on the ideology of Hindutva and its impact upon India (Copley 2003). This is an apt illustration of the way in which commentators upon recent Indian history, like other scholars, occupy shifting vantage points. These can open up new vistas, obstruct others, and leave some things in shadow, if only temporarily. In re-examining the processes that have shaped the development and place of religious reform movements in South Asian society since the nineteenth century, the contributors to this volume attempt to capitalize on the differences between their historiographical vantage points and those accessible to earlier scholarly commentators.

REFERENCES

Copley, Antony (ed.) (2000), *Gurus and Their Hlowers: New Religious Reform Movements in Colonial India*, New Delhi: Oxford University Press.
——— (2003), *Hinduism in Public and Private*, New Delhi: Oxford University Press.

Introduction

GWILYM BECKERLEGGE

SHIFTING VANTAGE POINTS

Historical scholarship on India underwent significant developments during the last quarter of the twentieth century. The pervasive influence of Socialist, and more specifically Marxist, perspectives in the historical and social sciences until well into the 1970s created a somewhat negative climate for the reception of studies primarily dealing with the role of religion in society, other than as a superstructural element (Robinson 2000: 1–2). It was the collapse of socialist regimes, the Iranian Revolution, and evidence of the global impact of religious resurgence, Francis Robinson suggests, that brought the study of religion back to centre-stage. To this we can now add the heightened interest in global Islam since 2001. This is not just a consequence of 9/11 but also because of ensuing debates about multiculturalism, in which the status and nature of Muslim organizations have been scrutinized by observers as never before, not least the Tablighi Jama'at, said by Dietrich Reetz in Chapter 4 to be considered by many standards the 'largest living Islamic movement in the world' (cf. Robinson 1988: 14–15). The Ahl-i Hadith, discussed in Chapter 6 by Martin Riexinger, with their historical roots in the same region as the Deobandi school, similarly have a considerable outreach beyond India, including countries where Islam has become established only relatively recently as a substantial religious presence. The increasing global influence of these South Asian Islamic movements underlines the importance in the contemporary climate of understanding the sources of their dynamism (cf. Robinson 2000: 20). Interest in the connection between religion and India's politics has continued to be sustained by the fortunes of the Bharatiya Janata Party (BJP), which governed India in coalition until the spring of 2004. The rise of coalition politics in India, which assisted the BJP's rise to power following the decline in the electoral performance of the Congress from the mid-1980s, gave fresh weight to religious, as well as regional and caste, identities in the political arena (see, for example, Zavos *et al.* 2004: 2). Beyond India, the continuing vitality of the Hindu diaspora has fostered the growth of 'transnational' expressions of the Hindu religious tradition, pre-eminently the Swaminarayan sect (Williams 2001), which is the subject of the essay by Heinz Werner Wessler. The emergence of such global Hindu movements gives rise to important questions about the boundaries of 'Hinduism'.

Like histories produced under British imperialism and later by Indian nationalists, Marxist histories too were 'shaped by notions of "progress" and what was seen as an inevitable progression towards presumably already known models of "modernity" that included economic development and democracy' (Metcalf and Metcalf 2006: xv). These 'old narratives' were challenged by Indian historians, and, particularly from the 1980s, by the Subaltern Studies Group (Metcalf and Metcalf 2006: xvi). The direction taken by its members has been criticized by other historians, not least by one of its former associates (Sarkar 1997: 82ff., 358ff.). The dominant concern of this group, however, with challenging 'statist' historical narratives and listening to a wider range of 'voices', including the 'small voices' in civil society (Guha 1996: 1–3), remains influential, and is no less relevant to historians other than those who work largely on Indian nationalism.

Participating in a panel on religious reform movements at a conference on modern South Asia cannot but raise significant conceptual problems specific to this topic, in addition to long-standing, definitional problems relating to 'religion' and 'South Asia'. The use of 'reform' to characterize certain South Asian socio-religious movements has increasingly invited more explicit and nuanced analyses of the relationship of the 'reformist' stance to the past, and so to tradition, and contemporary needs and circumstances. Kenneth Jones (1989: 14), for example, emphasized, in his influential study of socio-religious reform movements in British India, the emergence of such movements as dissenting forces, although he also acknowledged the 'dual role' played by religion of 'sustaining . . . the established social order while also providing an instrument for challenges to that order'. Such socio-religious movements, Jones states, called for the creation of a more egalitarian society and attempted to redefine the role of women and to modify customs.

In a discussion of Swami Vivekananda, often classed as a Hindu 'reformer', however, Amiya Sen (1993: 341) refers to 'serious theoretical problems' in the use of terms such as 'reformer' and 'revivalist'. He judges such categories to be unhelpful in reaching an adequate understanding of complex figures like Vivekananda, for example, whom Sen (1993: 341–2) describes as exemplifying 'the limits to bhadralok radicalism'. Extending this discussion in a later work, Sen (2003) makes a series of points about nineteenth-century Hindu 'reform', which are no less pertinent to understanding Islamic movements, not least that the 'world of reform' was neither homogeneous nor united in its objectives (p. 5). 'Reform represented a specific reading of the need for change', Sen argues observing that reform and change did not always intersect because not every matter considered from this perspective 'gained the status of a social reform issue' (p. 8). He also notes that defining the self in the face of external challenges was undertaken by Hindus in a more critical and self-conscious way over the last two centuries than it had been by Hindus previously (p. 6). Inherent in this act of self-definition is the use of the past as a cultural resource. While acknowledging that prominent Hindus made different judgements about the degree to which they would draw upon the past, Sen (2003: 16–17) makes the point that if social reform involves what is held to be a positive modification of social customs and thus a break with the past, those who pursue this path have to decide how far to deviate from the past and what constitutes 'the past'.

Questions about the limits of an acceptable degree of change, and about what should provide the touchstone (here, at least in part, 'the past') for often fiercely contested judgements on the need for change, are by their very nature sensitive and difficult to resolve. This is even more so in the realm of religion. Such modifications affect the individual at an existential level by requiring change in a world view that typically may lay claim to a vision of ultimate and unchanging truth, and which may refer to a conviction in sanctified moments or even an ideal period in the 'past', paradigmatic for later ages. A further complication arises from the internal differences that characterize religious traditions. The philosopher of religion, Ninian Smart (1973: 20–5), has likened different strands within the same broad religion to different arrangements of pictures in a gallery. While one school might recognize the continuity of the pictures, thus expressing solidarity with all the pictures in the gallery, another might make a radical selection, foregrounding some pictures, perhaps viewing other pictures in their light, and discarding others.

Individuals and groups conventionally thought of as unified by an overarching religious identity, rather than differentiated by their respective positions under this broad umbrella-term, all too often do not share one view of their 'past', which is in any case inevitably coloured by the way it is understood in whatever 'present' its heirs and interpreters occupy. (See, for example, Copland's description of Islam in India during the 1940s in Chapter 1, of this volume.) It is, perhaps, for these reasons that we find evidence of a deep and often troubling sense of ambivalence about the relationship between the past, present, and future often voiced by those caught up in the process of religious and social reform. If, as has been argued above, notions of both 'reform' and 'the past' are far from homogeneous and have depended upon different readings of India's past and current condition, this would reinforce the importance of listening to as wide a range of 'voices' as possible in order to construct as rich and comprehensive a historical narrative of the nature and passage of religious reform movements in South Asia as sources permit. The 'voices' heard in this volume, through the work of an international, multidisciplinary group of scholars, include those of religious, social, and political movements in various regions of South Asia, women in a family setting, Hindu teachers addressing a global audience, and, by extension, the medium of Indian painting and debates surrounding it.

The reworking of 'the past' has also been central to the formation of nation-states, often involving claimed roots in remote antiquity. Ranajit Guha (1996: 1) contends that the 'historic' is determined by the dominant values of the state, which thematize and evaluate the past. This kind of reference to an understanding of the 'past', Barbara and Thomas Metcalf (2006: xvii) suggest, underlines the relative newness of identities in South Asia, such as 'Hindu', Muslim, and 'India'—'new meanings infused into old terms', which in part was a consequence of the highly self-conscious processes of definition and redefinition that took place in India under the pressures of colonialism. They argue that this recognition must replace 'common sense notions of continuity, fostered by nationalism'.

Notions of continuity can also be imposed by historical accounts of religious reform movements in South Asia, not least during the period of colonialism because of their association with the cultural resurgence in India that nourished campaigns for independence. To accept such an understanding uncritically, however, would be to risk ignoring the kinds of questions that Guha has raised about the historiography of Indian nationalism, some of which are no less relevant to understanding the dynamics of religious reform. For example, is the impetus for religious change entirely driven by the elite, or by the leadership of charismatic religious thinkers and organizers who appear to pass the baton of reform from one to another? A narrow focus on leaders and institutions, such as formally constituted organizations, may lead to the 'small but heroic sagas' of families and individuals remaining 'unsung' (Sen 2003: 7). Similarly, it is important to recognize that a wide range of factors—environmental, political, and socio-economic, as well as those internal to the religions under discussion—may impact upon human value-systems, leading to changes that conventionally come to be held as 'reformist' in nature. Religious reform, moreover, has sometimes been pursued during this period in conscious reaction against pressures to accelerate the transition into 'modernity', here no longer regarded as an ideal but a concept so contested as to lead to alternative visions of the future to be realized through reform.

The essays in the first part of this volume, 'Competition, Institution-building, and the Formulation of Religious Identities', offer insights into the varied ways and circumstances in which groups in South Asia have defined their religious identities through socio-religious change. In so doing, they illustrate the complexity of, rather than the continuity between, events and outcomes later held to be parts of a historical process of 'reform'.

COMPETITION, INSTITUTION-BUILDING, AND THE FORMULATION OF RELIGIOUS IDENTITIES

The period of British colonial rule in India has been described as 'an age of definition and redefinition initiated by socio-religious movements that swept the subcontinent' (Jones 1989: 1). Sensitivity over matters relating to religious identity, and the ensuing competition between groups more sharply demarcated by religious difference, has been attributed to the increasing impact of Christian missionaries, the introduction by the British of a decennial census, and successive policies adopted by the British to encourage different religious groups to support British rule. The emergence of the Arya Samaj, Muslim *anjumans*, and Sikh *sabhas* exacerbated inter-religious and emergent political rivalries, even though intended in part to act as bulwarks against these same competitive forces. They were indicative, Avril Powell (2000: 128) suggests, of the crisis that India might be thought to have entered under British and Christian rule. As the campaign for independence intensified, so did pressures leading to a greater sense of separation between religious groups, by then also characterized, in many respects, by competing political agendas.

Ian Copland begins his contribution to this volume by noting the fluidity in manifestations of religious identity in his examination of evolving Muslim loyalties in Princely States. He concedes that the 'religious factor cannot be discounted', because some Muslims in the Princely States clearly desired to make common cause with other Muslims in India and were inspired by the vision of creating 'the new Medina'. He argues, however, that historians are nevertheless confronted with the problem of trying to explain how and why in a relatively short period Muslims at the elite and mass levels came to think of themselves as a community, in spite of many real differences between them. Commenting on attempts by 'primordialists' and 'mobilizationists' to explain national-consciousness raising among Muslims, Copland observes that, in spite of important differences in their arguments, scholars such as Francis Robinson and Paul Brass have assumed that this has taken place vertically, ideas emanating within the elite and filtering down to the masses. Copland, however, argues that there is evidence that communal tendencies among Muslims (and Hindus) also spread laterally, within and across geographical regions. He suggests that this in turn raises the question as to why the communal violence associated with these tendencies did not spread evenly during the colonial period. Copland argues that distance and communication regulated the spread of communal consciousness, the effects of isolation being reduced through the introduction of rail and road links and being increased by the absence of these or the presence of geographical or political barriers. His chapter tests this thesis by examining the increasing number of communal riots in the 1930s in the light of the reduced isolation of Princely States, following the development of transport and communication networks, including publishing, internal political changes, and the promotion of the ideal of a Muslim homeland.

In setting out his thesis, Copland touches on a number of issues to which other contributors to this volume return in exploring the rich complexity of South Asian religious reform movements. The first of these is the importance of historical and geographical contextual influences, which enable us to appreciate the distinctive manner in which religious identities came to be formulated in different regions of South Asia, and how these expressions have changed over time. The second is social position and its importance relative to other factors, such as membership of a common religion, in the shaping of identity. More narrowly, Copland also touches on the problems of how to describe the intersections between popular Muslim and Hindu culture, including the contentious use of 'syncretism'. The use of this concept is revisited later in Chapter 3 of this volume by Heinz Werner Wessler on nineteenth-century Hindu reform movements.

In Chapter 2, Diego Abenante explores the dynamics of Muslim religious identity in another region, Multan in south-western Punjab. Like Copland, Abenante also emphasizes the influence of changes in the physical surroundings, here, irrigation, upon religious identity and outlook, which, he argues, has not been sufficiently appreciated. In assessing the way in which the colonial presence, by inducing change in the ecological and social configuration of the territory, influenced the development of Muslim religious identity in the district, he draws particular attention to the evidence of change in 'marginal' territories, as in Multan. Abenante suggests that, with the gradual advance of settlement and cultivation in the territory of Multan, at the expense of the previous living patterns of pastoralism and limited trade, the social functions of the Sufi saints and their shrines also changed. Tracing the growth of religious controversies, which had their roots in rivalry between the Makhdum Qureshi and the *mahant* of Prahladpuri, the representatives of the two most important holy places in Multan city, Abenante suggests that these arguments were indicative of the changed atmosphere in Multan in the 1880s. The religious communities of Multan were in a process of identity-building, which was centred on the places of religious devotion. While acknowledging that the controversy also revealed the extent to which reformist discourse had entered the local environment, emanating from schools such as Deobandi and Ahl-i-Hadith, Abenante concludes that the transformation brought by the irrigation projects, and its consequences in terms of social dislocation, constituted a possible cause of the violent communal tensions that surfaced in the district in the 1920s.

In Chapter 1 of this volume, Copland refers to the problem of how to describe the many intersections between popular Muslim and Hindu culture. He points out that the extent of this phenomenon had led many scholars to question the helpfulness of referring to 'syncretism' as some kind of distinct cultural phenomenon, preferring instead to speak of 'composite culture'. In fact, historians of religion in other fields have questioned whether the term 'syncretism', apart from its pejorative overtones, refers to anything other than the process through which all religions develop through interaction with other systems of beliefs and practices with which they are brought into contact (see, for example, Pye 1994).

In Chapter 3, Heinz Werner Wessler grounds his discussion of syncretism and anti-syncretism in Hindu reform movements in recent debates about the concept of syncretism, which locate its use within religious discourse, bringing with it a sense of 'own' and 'other'. Wessler begins his study with reference to Dayananda Sarasvati, the founder of the Arya Samaj, who refuted a long list of Hindu and non-Hindu religious movements prevalent in India at that time. All these were judged by Dayananda against 'his monolithic concept of *satya* ('truth') . . . beyond discussion and beyond historical religion'. His exclusivist position and intolerance of pluralist theological positions, Wessler emphasizes, were strikingly different from the inclusivism now associated with neo-Hindu movements. Dayananda's attempted 'destruction of the diverse creeds' thus leads Wessler to consider, in the light of Dayananda's anti-syncretism, what would constitute an adequate hermeneutics to detect syncretism. Arguing that this cannot simply mean the application of a classification relating to another region, for example, as used in discussion of Hellenistic religions of the ancient world, Wessler urges caution before simply adopting the meaning attached to this term by authors such as J.N. Farquhar and Paul Hacker. He notes, for example, the difficulty of translating the term syncretism into an Indian language. Having examined the attitudes of Ram Mohan Roy and Sahajananda Swami to the worship of images, in the light of Dayananda's criticism of their theologies, Wessler concludes that there is no evidence of either functional or intentional syncretism.

Wessler's reference to the characteristic outlook of neo-Hindu movements is pertinent to another issue explored in this volume. Ram Mohan Roy's Brahmo Samaj and Sahajananda Swami's Swaminarayan Hinduism were reformulations of Hinduism that, in the first case, intellectualized and anglicized the tradition and, in the second, created the base from which would later develop a powerful, worldwide Hindu movement. In both, we see the beginnings of the reshaping of tradition into forms that would directly and indirectly contribute to more globalized expressions of modern Hinduism in the twentieth century. Speaking specifically of Swaminarayan theology, for example, Wessler suggests that its ascetic character, its restraint over identifying devotees with Krishna's *gopis*, had contributed to its reputation for morality and thus standards compatible with other modern religious movements. We shall consider other examples of modern Hindu movements in the next section.

The Tablighi Jama'at is another movement that has been affected by the activity of the Arya Samaj, being one of several Muslim movements that has resisted the Samaj's attempts to reclaim what it has classed as Hindus lost to Islam. Created in 1926, the Tablighi Jama'at has continued to grow and is now considered by many to be the largest Islamic movement in the world. Its preachers are to be found in all regions where Islam is present. Based on fieldwork conducted in 2002, Dietrich Reetz tests, in Chapter 4, claims by the movement that its lay character has not given rise to any new organization and thus that it is not 'in the modern fashion' a new group. He argues that comparing the group's functioning with that of a bureaucracy is apposite because of the association of this concept with modernity, following Max Weber. Reetz later concludes that the Tablighi Jama'at offers lower middle-class Muslims in South Asia a moralistic vision of modernity. He begins by noting that the conduct of the movement is closely governed by an unwritten constitution, although followers are commonly associated with the movement for the length of a preaching tour. Reports on progress are submitted to the local centre on return from such a tour. Reetz places particular emphasis on the operation of 'mosque groups', which keep the work alive after preaching tours have ended. The rigidity of this scheme, he suggests, is reminiscent of other mobilizationist ideologies, and the movement is controlled by a command structure that is hardly visible to outsiders and those not at the heart of the movement. The growing size of the movement has increased the need for centralized record-keeping and filing, which Reetz attributes to the dynamics of the movement's expansion, rather than to any policy on the part of the leadership.

The impact of British rule is the starting point for Maruti Kamble's account of the transplantation of the Ramakrishna movement from Bengal to Karnataka. This study reminds us that, although indissolubly linked to Kolkata in the popular imagination, Swami Vivekananda initially gathered much of his support from south India. Kamble thus offers a distinctive regional perspective on both the growth of the Ramakrishna movement and its reception as a perceived vehicle of reform. When Vivekananda visited Belgaum in 1892, Kamble notes that he found Karnataka politically disintegrated and generally agrarian and backward. While parts of the region were under direct colonial administration, others were under independent rulers. The political circumstances in the region were thus very different from those in Bengal where the earliest institutions of the Ramakrishna Math and Mission were located. Kamble argues that Vivekananda's visit resulted in the transference of the values of the

Bengal renaissance to Karnataka where the creation of branches of the Ramakrishna movement stimulated wider socio-religious reforms. Kamble shows how Vivekananda's impact upon local rulers and prominent intellectuals led eventually to the creation of Ramakrishna centres in Karnataka, including the influential Ramakrishna Institute of Moral and Spiritual Education (RIMSE), which developed out of retreats conducted in the 1960s. No less important, he argues, is the extent of Vivekananda's influence over the minds of a number of prominent poets and scholars of Karnataka whose influence has extended far beyond the institutional base of the Ramakrishna movement in this area.

As a prelude to introducing the second part of this book, 'Responding to Colonial Modernity', we examine below the interplay between notions of modernity and understandings of religious reform movements.

RESPONDING TO COLONIAL MODERNITY

Just as the term 'reform' offers a particular reading of the need for 'change', so too Partha Chatterjee (1999: 265) reminds us that the use of the term 'modern', with its implication of progressive continuity, may well be an epithet retrospectively applied to what those in an earlier age recognized more simply as the 'new'. In the context of India, however, it is clear that the advent of British colonialism did constitute for many social commentators another watershed in Indian history. What has come to be recognized by historians and social scientists as increasingly problematic is the relationship between this intervention and what has sometimes been characterized as India's entry into 'modernity'. Although it is still common to find India's increasing contact with the West being referred to as inaugurating the 'modern' period of Indian history, both the concept of 'modernity' and the nature of India's engagement with it continues to be reconsidered. If, as Vasudha Dalmia (1998: 77) prefers, 'modernization' refers to altering and improving existing institutions and systems, then this would suggest an ongoing transformation, which, although possibly taking place at different rates over time, could not be anchored in one distinct historical period, far less be the basis for the definition of one such period.

In addition to the problem noted earlier about the constructed nature of notions of the 'past', conceptualizing the start of a 'modern' period in India through reference to increasing exposure to European influence may seem to imply a radical discontinuity between the early nineteenth century and the preceding century. Arjun Appadurai (1996: 3) has spoken of the legacy of Western social science, which has reinforced the sense of a single moment that 'by its appearance creates a dramatic and unprecedented break between past and present'. It may also be taken to imply that the developments, which accelerated in Western Europe from the eighteenth century, constituted something akin to a universal model of 'modernity', thus raising the problem of the relationship between 'modernization' and 'westernization'. This kind of crude identification of 'modernization' with 'westernization' and the placing of 'modernity' in opposition to 'tradition' (Western societies against non-Western ones) has long been challenged by scholars (for example, Rudolph and Hoeber 1967). Thus, David Ludden observes that, if the 'juggernaut of Western modernity' rolled over traditional communities that were mauled, transformed or shocked into rebellion and resistance, there were nevertheless significant continuities of belief and practice, not least religious identity (cited in Smith 2003: 26).

More specifically on Islam, David Waines (2002: 192) refers to the 'long nineteenth century' of modern Islamic history, symbolically beginning in the late eighteenth century with Napoleon's invasion of Ottoman Egypt. He cautions that the use of a Euro-centric model of modernity can 'lead to important eighteenth-century religious developments in non-European cultures becoming obscured or ignored altogether' (p. 84). He argues that the influence of eighteenth-century Muslim religious reform thought on the following centuries has not been sufficiently appreciated. The artificial nature of attempts to insert such a wedge between the nineteenth and preceding centuries is aptly illustrated in this volume by Martin Riexinger's discussion in Chapter 6 of the Ahl-i-Hadith with roots in the puritan trends of the eighteenth century. Where continuities between the eighteenth and nineteenth centuries have not been given due recognition, Waines suggests that Islamic movements in the nineteenth century have often as a consequence been interpreted simply as 'anti-Western' and therefore 'anti-modern', rather than being understood as part of an ongoing process of seeking to provide responses to 'perceived problems of internal moral and spiritual decay in Islamic societies'. They were part of what John Voll (1983: 34) described as a 'renewalist tradition' with deep roots in Muslim historical experience. The 'modernist' agenda was thus as much about addressing the internal state of Islam as responding to Western perceptions of Muslim societies, although as the nineteenth century progressed these two strands became increasingly entwined for some thinkers. The growth of the influence of

Islam in some countries during the last two centuries, moreover, has increased just as these countries have undergone certain structural changes that are frequently associated with the process of modernization.

Waines urges that it is necessary 'to become sensitive to observing and imagining modernity-as-tradition' when referring to the non-European world. To illustrate this point, he asks how best to characterize a many-sided movement such as the Deobandi school, using labels such as 'traditionalist', 'fundamentalist', 'modernist', or 'secularist'. Conceding that it is frequently dubbed 'fundamentalist', Waines argues that it shares features from all these categories, in that 'tradition and modernity' in this movement 'seem in league with one another' (Waines 2002: 195). Acknowledging the problematic nature of the label 'fundamentalist', Waines proceeds to make a broad distinction between 'modernist' Muslims, who seek to modernize Islam, and 'Islamicists', who seek to Islamize modernity. In Part One of this volume, Reetz speaks of the 'skeletal modernity' of the Tablighi Jama'at, with its reliance upon pre-modern forms of communication, a movement of 'reformist' tendencies, which has contacts with the Taliban. Similar problems of categorization could be said to arise over the Swaminarayan sect, whose standards and morality, Wessler argues in Chapter 3, make it compatible with other modern religious movements. As Raymond Williams (2001: 31–2) has pointed out, Sahajanand, the founder of the Swaminarayan movement, could be described correctly as both the 'last of the medieval Hindu saints and the first of the neo-Hindu reformers', making him the 'best early representative of neo-Hinduism'. His world view was in continuity with the medieval saints of India, while his reforms 'met the needs of the Gujaratis during the period of modernization and Independence' (p. 32). Jones (1989: 3–4) acknowledged that the difference between his typological distinction between 'transitional' and 'acculturative' movements of socio-religious dissent was 'primarily at their point of origin', because of the duration of some of the former and the roots of the latter in 'the general high cultures of South Asia and the specific subcultures of a given religion'. The problematic relationship between tradition and modernization, including the impact of colonialism, suggests that even this distinction might tend to imply a rupture in India's history, which overshadows important continuities.

We noted above the allusion in Metcalf and Metcalf (2006) to the persistence in imperialist, Marxist, and nationalist historiography of assumptions concerning 'already known models of "modernity"', including characteristics such as economic development and democracy. Even while criticizing analyses of social and political change that have placed modernity in opposition to tradition, Lloyd and Susanne Rudolph (1967: 3–4) nevertheless acknowledged that they had found certain contrasts 'heuristically' useful. 'Modernity' assumes among other things, they suggest, a more cosmopolitan outlook, giving precedence to reason, greater individualism, and greater participation in government. It would appear that although it is no longer assumed that all societies will follow the same route to modernity as that taken by the West, the nature of 'modernity' remains problematic. David Smith, in *Hinduism and Modernity* (2003: viii), emphasizes that 'modernity' refers to the 'theorization of modern times', not modern times. He elects to treat 'modernity' as 'Western modernity', against which Hinduism is juxtaposed, in order to understand the parts played by India and Hinduism in the formation of the ideology of modernity and further effects that Hinduism might have upon it (p. 5). Sceptical of modernity and postmodernity, Smith distinguishes his approach from those who, like Breckenridge and Appadurai, treat modernity as a varied, global experience, created by national societies each with 'its own ways of playing with modernity', including the means of 'modernity' of which the advanced capitalist counties are no longer the 'gatekeepers' (quoted by Smith 2003: 7). Chatterjee (1999: 269–70), who is persuaded that forms of modernity will have to vary according to context, concludes that, insofar as there can be a universally accepted definition, 'by teaching us to employ methods of reason, universal modernity enables us to identify the forms of our own particular modernity'.

It is perhaps in the critical reflection on the predicaments arising out of tensions between notions of the 'past' and a sense of a 'present', illuminated and heightened by an awareness of existing in a less parochial context with multiple points of reference, that we can locate one characteristic of 'modernity', that has been central to both the legacy of the Enlightenment project in Western Europe and formulations of modernity in other cultures. In colonial India, reflection on the significance and implications of the encounter with the West for the present and the future might be said to have contributed a strand to a form of 'modern' critical reflection shaped by that distinctive context, whether articulated by Syed Ahmed Khan or Ram Mohan Roy. This was expressed in a heightened preoccupation with questions of identity, and, questions about fidelity to tradition, the changing nature of society, and what adaptations of value systems, if any, would be an appropriate response to this theorized understanding of the socio-political context and its existential dimension. Thus, for example, although David Kopf (1979: 46) has argued that even though intellectuals in Bengal during the nineteenth century could only 'participate intellectually' in the modern movements of the time emanating from Europe, because India had not been 'modernized' along the lines of the European path of social and material development, it is evident that this 'intellectual participation' was in itself an expression of modernity: a theorization about a present, informed by readings of the 'past', which was far from untouched by awareness of the transformation taking place in the West and its possible implications for Indian society and beyond. As Waines has emphasized, such reflection itself was a manifestation of 'modernity-in-tradition', and change where it was embraced was frequently accompanied by ambivalence and a determination not to abandon tradition.

Examples of ambivalence about modernity and of determination not to abandon tradition are to be found in Daniela Bredi's study of women of the Tyabji family (Chapter 7). Bredi refers to 'women . . . increasingly becoming the symbols of the reformers' hopes and fears', and draws attention to the complexity of Atiya Fyzee's personality: 'Alongside her attitudes, which suggested a rupture with Indian and Muslim tradition and which might lead one to consider her a champion of change, there was the firm desire to maintain a strong link with Islamic culture, a continuity she thought necessary in order to preserve Muslim identity.' Women in the same family, Atiya and Raihana, as Bredi shows, also drew upon the resources of Islam, European cultures, and even Hinduism in strikingly different ways. In his examination of Swami Vivekananda's criticisms of the artist Raja Ravi Varma, Gwilym Beckerlegge (Chapter 9) similarly refers to the 'delicate balancing act performed by those who openly put Western techniques and knowledge to use in their attempts to reshape Hindu tradition' and the criticism they faced from others as a consequence. Beckerlegge suggests that Vivekananda's treatment of Raja Ravi Varma hints at the former's ambivalence about his own role as a self-appointed cultural mediator between India and the West.

The relationship between religious traditions and a society's capacity for socio-economic development, frequently presented as a characteristic of modernization, has attracted the attention of many scholars, writing on vastly different historical and cultural contexts. For his study of the Ahl-i-Hadith Martin Riexinger takes as the starting point Ernest Gellner's contention, based on North African evidence, that puritan Islam, as distinct from intercessionary Sufism, leads believers to systematize their lives in a way at least compatible with modern social organization. Taking the Ahl-i-Hadith as his example, Riexinger questions the applicability of Gellner's thesis to Islamic movements in South Asia, and in particular the affinity that Gellner claims to exist between puritan Islam and urbanity, while locating intercessionary Sufism in rural society. Riexinger concedes that existing studies have frequently characterized the Ahl-i-Hadith as an upper-class sect with urban roots. He argues, however, that in the Punjab sources show that the first people converted to their teaching were in the rural areas surrounding urban commercial and administrative centres, a pattern that has continued to the present day and is to be found in other regions of the subcontinent. Riexinger also argues that factors other than ideology may also account for the prominence of officials and traders among the Ahl-i-Hadith. The part played by individual Ahl-i-Hadith in the promotion of secular education is said by Riexinger to contrast with the more limited involvement of other Sunni groups. In testing whether this should be taken as testimony to the Ahl-i-Hadith's inclination to modernity, Riexinger balances this against a view of the world that was far from 'disenchanted' and a generally highly conservative attitude by Ahl-i-Hadith scholars to the role of women and their education. In a closing reflection on the 'puritan tradition' more widely held in Islam and claims concerning its positive inclination to modernity, Riexinger notes the emergence from this source of the Taliban, the most 'anti-modernist' movement in recent Islamic history. This would appear to be yet a further illustration of the complex nature of the factors, influences, and transformations, which may, but do not necessarily, play a part in the process of modernization.

The education of Muslim women is examined in greater detail in Daniela Bredi's study of women of the Tyabji family in Chapter 7, which analyses a response to the challenge of western-style education, shaped by gender and a very specific location in the class and community structure of Bombay. Her work also offers further insights into the 'very circumspect' advocacy of education for women during the last years of the nineteenth century by some Muslim men (cf. Powell 2000: 136). Bredi's case study illuminates her initial observation, which is relevant to this volume as a whole, that in British India even the components of various communities comprising Indian society responded to modernization in different ways. The challenge of the West and the Hindu revival in India, itself at least in part a response to this same challenge, shaped the context in which Muslims in the subcontinent, according to Bredi, felt the need to elaborate 'a model of woman that should respond to the needs of the times'. At the heart of debates about the most appropriate model lay questions about the education of women who became symbolic, Bredi argues, of reformers' hopes and fears. As Bredi shows in her study of one family, the Tyabji family, by this time reference points in the debates included not just competing Muslim opinions but also the experience of women members of the Muslim elite who had been sent abroad for the purposes of education. Such women, Bredi observes, were unlikely to resume *purdah* and remain within the domestic sphere, becoming instead involved in political and social issues. Bredi presents three women from the Tyabji family as examples of different outcomes of encounter with the process of modernization, thus refining generalizations about responses to the challenge of modernization in South Asia that tend to operate at the level of communities, if not entire religious traditions and nation-states.

As scholars have explored more closely the phenomenon of globalization and its definition, it has become increasingly difficult to maintain a rigid geographical boundary to area studies. Unlike Islam, Hinduism prior to the late nineteenth century had been almost entirely confined to India, with some outreach into South-East Asia. The tracing of relocations from South Asia in the nineteenth century by migration and diaspora studies has been supplemented by an awareness of the new level of connectedness now possible between not just intimates but also large numbers sharing a common sense of identity based on religious or political values, or those drawn to a religious philosophy now made accessible through an increasingly global exchange of ideas. Distinctions, once commonly drawn, between the 'universal religion' of Islam and the 'ethnic religion' of Hinduism have to be reconsidered in the light of the blurring of Hinduism's boundaries during the last century.

For several prominent nineteenth-century Hindu thinkers, some degree of involvement in apologetics, whether for specifically religious or broader political ends, was almost inevitable when striving to secure a sympathetic hearing for what many Europeans had dismissed as an idolatrous and immoral religion, and a region debilitated by its adherence to this religion. In the process, the initial steps were taken towards presenting Hinduism as a 'world religion'. This in turn led to Westerners being attracted to modified versions of Hinduism and the creation of a receptive English-language audience and readership. In the latter half of the twentieth century, several of these forms of Hinduism also came to serve the needs of English-educated, Hindu communities of Indian descent living in the Hindu diaspora. Hiltrud Rüstau's discussion, in Chapter 8, of Pravrajika Vivekaprana's lectures to women's groups and others in the United States and Europe is illustrative of a new global constituency wishing to engage with those contemporary manifestations of the Hindu religious tradition that now function like a 'world religion'. The Ramakrishna Math and Mission, which figures in this volume, is but one example of a number of movements with roots in the Hindu tradition, which nevertheless reach out to a worldwide following, and in so doing, challenge earlier assumptions about the boundaries of Hinduism.

Hiltrud Rüstau offers another perspective on the contribution of women to their respective religious traditions in her examination of different interpretations of the *Devimahatmya* by Pravrajika Vivekaprana of the Sarada Math, and the *Saundarya Lahari* by Nataraja Guru, co-founder of the Sree Narayana Dharma Paripalana Yogam (SNDP). Both these interpreters may legitimately be said to have participated in global Hinduism. Vivekaprana's ideas, for example, are derived from lectures given to women's groups and other sympathizers in the United States and Germany. Nataraja Guru, however, internationalized the message of Sri Narayana Guru, a teacher revered by low-caste groups in Kerala (see also Chapter 5).

For Rüstau, attempts to interpret ancient scriptures to meet changing circumstances add to the authority of these texts. She notes, however, that their interpreters have attempted simultaneously to demonstrate that their new interpretations have conformed to the 'eternal wisdom' of these texts—a blend of detachment from, yet continuity with, the past comparable to that noted by Bredi in her study of the Tyabji women. Vivekaprana is said by Rüstau to have broken new ground in taking a special message for women from the *Devimahatmya*, which has generally been used by men in the worship of the female divinity. Nataraja Guru, however, was determined to maintain that Shankara was the author of the *Saundarya Lahari* and that it thus contains pure Advaitic philosophy, rather than being a *tantra shastra*. Consequently, he found no special message for women in this poem. In explaining how these two interpreters came to their different understandings of the 'true meaning' of these two texts, Rüstau points to the importance of gender and social background. She also draws particular attention to the significant increase in the influence of feminist thought, which is so marked in Vivekaprana's hermeneutics, during the three decades or so that separated these two expositions.

The increasing preoccupation of Hindu thinkers since the early nineteenth century with the place of Hinduism both within the world and the 'East', and thus its challenge to those not born Hindus, is also the subject of Gwilym Beckerlegge's study, in Chapter 9, of Swami Vivekananda's appreciation of the art of Raja Ravi Varma. Beckerlegge argues that Vivekananda's judgements shed further light on his position within late nineteenth-century Hinduism, and more particularly within the process of interaction between Indian and Western intellectual, religious, and aesthetic traditions, which provided the backdrop to his mission and for which to some extent he consciously acted as a mediator. It is argued that the transformations of Indian art, which took place during the late nineteenth century and led to the emergence of new styles of art, reveal certain parallels with the development of Neo-Hinduism. This is evident not least in the ways in which critics have questioned the authenticity and worth of these modern forms of art and religion. Although both Vivekananda and Raja Ravi Varma in different ways were hailed as representatives of India at the Chicago Exposition of 1893, Beckerlegge draws attention to the ambivalent nature of Vivekananda's judgements on the art of Raja Ravi Varma. He links this to Vivekananda's determination to promote an 'Eastern' style of art, and to Vivekananda's declared hostility towards Indian 'reformers' and those who copied Western styles, which arguably masked his own mixed feelings about his role as a self-appointed conduit between the East and the West. Vivekananda's occasional polemical statements about Western art and his glorification of Eastern art are shown to parallel elements of his apology on behalf of Hinduism, now being presented on the world stage.

Just as Hindu thinkers have devised typological classifications of East and West, so too scholars and other commentators on South Asia have drawn upon constructions of the 'Orient' when interpreting this region's history and culture. According to Ashis Nandy (1983: xii), 'The West has not merely produced modern colonialism, it informs most inter-pretations of colonialism.' It is appropriate, therefore, that this volume concludes its section on 'Responding to Colonial Modernity' with an extended discussion of 'orientalism', the increasingly contested concept at the heart of the multi-disciplinary debate stimulated originally by Edward Said. Peter Heehs' contribution in Chapter 10 of this volume brings together a study of one prominent Hindu thinker's attitudes towards 'orientalism' with an extended examination of different types of orientalism found in Indian historiography. He identifies six styles of orientalist discourse about India, understood here as heuristic devices and not essential types, ranging from the precolonial to the postcolonial period. More recent examples include studies influenced by Edward Said, who has had a profound impact on the study of Hindu culture through the work of scholars such as Partha Chatterjee and Ronald Inden. Heehs regards 'Saidian' treatments ('reductive orientalism') firmly as another form of orientalist discourse. He also traces the emergence of 'reactionary orientalism', which is determined to restore India to its ancient glory. Within his typological classification of types of 'orientalism' Heehs examines at greater length the work of Sri Aurobindo, a proponent of 'nationalist orientalism'. Highlighting Aurobindo's resentment at the handling of India's heritage by colonial scholars, Heehs acknowledges that Aurobindo, like other Indian nationalists of his day, believed India's culture to be superior to that of Europe (compare Beckerlegge's study of Vivekananda's views of art). He examines five topics still debated by historians in order to test which of these competing styles of orientalism has opened the way to a more accurate understanding of India's past and suggests that it would be profitable to subject other orientalists to a similar 'triage'.

In conclusion, this volume offers the reader not simply a varied and useful collection of historical case studies. Like the earlier collections of essays from the panel of the European Conference on Modern South Asian Studies, it also provides on overview of current lines of enquiry within the study of South Asia, and more specifically its socio-religious movements, as represented by the ongoing work of one international group of scholars from their various vantage points.

BIBLIOGRAPHY

Appadurai, Arjun (1996), *Modernity at Large: Cultural Dimensions of Globalization*, Minneapolis and London: University of Minnesota Press.

Chatterjee, Partha (1999), 'A Possible India: Essays in Political Criticism', in Partha Chatterjee, *The Partha Chatterjee Omnibus,* New Delhi: Oxford University Press.

Dalmia, Vasudha (1998), 'The Modernity of Tradition: Harishchandra of Banaras and the Defence of Hindu *Dharma*', in William Radice (ed.), *Swami Vivekananda and the Modernization of Hinduism*, New Delhi: Oxford University Press, pp. 77–92.

Guha, Ranajit (1996), 'The Small Voice of History', in Shahid Amin and Dipesh Chakravarty (eds), *Subaltern Studies IX: Writings on South Indian History and Society*, New Delhi: Oxford University Press, pp. 1–12.

Jones, Kenneth (1989), *Socio-religious Reform Movements in British India*, Cambridge: Cambridge University Press.

Kopf, David (1979), *The Brahmo Samaj and the Shaping of the Modern Indian Mind*, Princeton: Princeton University Press.

Metcalf, Barbara D. and Thomas R. Metcalf (2006 [2001]), *A Concise History of Modern India*, Cambridge: Cambridge University Press.

Nandy, Ashis (1983), *The Intimate Enemy: Loss and Recovery of Self under Colonialism*, New Delhi: Oxford University Press.

Powell, Avril A. (2000), '"Duties of Ahmadi Women": Educative Processes in the Early Stages of the Ahmadiyya Movement', in A. Copley (ed.), *Gurus and Their Followers: New Religious Reform Movements in Colonial India*, New Delhi: Oxford University Press, pp. 128–56.

Pye, Michael (1994), 'Syncretism versus Synthesis', in *Method and Theory in the Study of Religion*, Vol. 6, No. 3, pp. 217–29.

Robinson, Francis (1988), *Varieties of South Asian Islam in Britain*, Warwick: ESCR/ University of Warwick.

———— (2000), *Islam and Muslim History in South Asia*, New Delhi: Oxford University Press.

Rudolph, Lloyd I. and Susanne Hoeber (1967), *The Modernity of Tradition*, Chicago and London: University of Chicago Press.

Sarkar, Sumit (1997), 'The Decline of the Subaltern in *Subaltern Studies*', in Sumit Sarkar, *Writing Social History*, New Delhi: Oxford University Press, pp. 82–108.

Sen, Amiya P. (1993), *Hindu Revivalism in Bengal, 1872–1905: Some Essays in Interpretation*, New Delhi: Oxford University Press.

———— (2003), *Social and Religious Reform: The Hindus of British India*, New Delhi: Oxford University Press.

Smart, Ninian (1973), *The Phenomenon of Religion*, London and Basingstoke: Macmillan.

Smith, David (2003), *Hinduism and Modernity*, Oxford: Blackwell.

Voll, John O. (1983), 'Renewal and Reform in Islamic History: *Tajdid* and *Islah*', in John Esposito (ed.), *Voices of Resurgent Islam*, New York and Oxford: Oxford University Press, pp. 32–47.

Waines, David (2002), 'Islam', in Linda Woodhead (ed.), *Religions in the Modern World*, London and New York: Routledge, pp. 182–203.

Williams, Raymond B. (2001), *An Introduction to Swaminarayan Hinduism*, Cambridge: Cambridge University Press.

Zavos, John, Andrew Wyatt, and Vernon Hewitt (eds) (2004), *The Politics of Cultural Mobilization in India*, New Delhi: Oxford University Press.

Part One

Competition, Institution-building, and
the Formulation of Religious Identities

1

From *Communitas* to Communalism
Evolving Muslim Loyalties in Princely North India

IAN COPLAND

THE 'PAKISTAN' DEMAND

Quaid-i-Azam Mohammad Ali Jinnah's presidential address to the annual session of the All-India Muslim League (AIML) at Minto Park, Lahore, on 22 March 1940, is renowned for its forceful articulation of the view that Muslims in India formed a separate national group, distinct from the Hindus and the other 'minorities'. Hinduism and Islam, the Quaid-i-Azam insisted, were 'different and distinct social orders'.

The Hindus and Muslims belong to two different religious philosophies, social customs, literatures. They neither inter-marry nor inter-dine together and, indeed, belong to two different civilizations . . . based mainly on conflicting ideas and conceptions. Their concepts on life and of life are different. It is quite clear that Hindus and Mussalmans derive their inspiration from different sources of history. They have different epics, different heroes, and different episodes. Very often the hero of one is a foe of the other and, likewise, their victories and defeats overlap. To yoke together two such nations under a single state, one as a numerical minority and the other as a majority, must lead to growing discontent and final destruction of any fabric that may be so built up for the government of such a state (Gwyer and Appadurai 1957: 441–2).

On the basis of this nationality claim, the 50,000-strong assembly voted unanimously, two days later, to press the British government to commit to organize the impending transfer of power in India in such a way as to provide for the establishment of 'Independent States' in the areas of the subcontinent where Muslims constituted a majority of the population. Thus was born what history knows as the 'Pakistan demand'.

The Lahore demand was a brilliant political initiative. It put the Indian National Congress (INC) on the defensive, and galvanized what had been, until then, a rather impotent party. Outside of League circles, however, most contemporary commentators found Jinnah's 'two-nation theory' unconvincing;[1] and scholars looking back on the period have largely echoed their scepticism. It is difficult to disagree with them.

Objectively, the notion that the Muslims in the 1940s (or at any other time, for that matter) constituted a monolithic community, separate from the rest of Indian society, is impossible to sustain. Islam (like Christianity) is divided along doctrinal lines, notably over the issue of the succession to the leadership of the Muslim community after the death of the Prophet. In India, the Muslims are split, in this way, into no less than four sections—the Sunnis, Shi'ias, Ishmaelis, and Ahmadiyyas—and relations between them are often acrimonious. During the late colonial period the annual Muharram festival, which commemorates the martyrdom of Imam Ali's son Hussain at the hands of the Umayyads, witnessed repeated bloody clashes between the Shi'ias, or 'partisans' of Ali, and the majority Sunnis. In 1953, brutal attacks on Ahmadiyyas in Karachi were followed by a call from the Sunni *ulama* for the courts to declare them non-Muslims and for the government to ban members of the sect from holding public office in Pakistan. Likewise, the South Asian Muslim community is divided racially and by class. Muslims of Arab, Central Asian, Persian, and Afghan descent (the *ashraf*, or 'noble' ones) have always been disparaging towards those Muslims whose ancestors converted from Hinduism (the *ajlaf*) and who remain, for the most part, trapped in the same menial occupations, and accompanying social servitude, their ancestors sought to escape from by converting to Islam. Except during Friday prayers, the two groups do not interact socially. Nor, specifically, do the ashraf take brides from among the ajlaf. The Hanafi ulama have dubiously defended this un-egalitarian practice by a generous interpretation of the doctrine of *kafa'a* that holds that marriages should be contracted between partners of more or less equal status. And language too divides Indian Muslims. They have no *lingua franca*. Arabic, the language of the Qur'an, is understood only by the learned, while Urdu, now the national language of Pakistan, was until recently spoken mainly by the Muslims of Uttar Pradesh. Jinnah's presidential speech of 1940 was delivered in English, which probably made it unintelligible to many in his dominantly Punjabi-speaking audience. Ironically, Jinnah himself, several years later, as good as admitted the force of these objections in his first speech to the Pakistan Constituent Assembly, when he noted that the Muslim population of the new Dominion would comprise 'Pathans, Punjabis, Shias, Sunnis and so on' (Jinnah 1962: 8). Indian Muslims were definitely not a homogenous group.

Nor were they, contrary to what Jinnah asserts in his address, so very different from Hindus. Of course, Hinduism and Islam expound very different conceptions of the divine and make very different ritual demands of their adherents. That much goes without saying. But at least at the margins—that is to say, among the rural-dwelling, poorly educated Muslims who make up the aforementioned ajlaf—significant traces of older Hindu values and beliefs survive. In Malerkotla, 'people of all castes and creeds', but '[e]specially Hindus and Sikhs', revere the tomb of the Sufi warrior-mystic Hazrat Sheikh Sadarul Din Sadar-i-Jahan. In Patiala, Hindu women sometimes take their ailing children to the local mosque, it being widely believed that the touch of a Muslim who has recently offered *namaz* has the power to heal. At Pandiayat in Kotah district, Muslims and Hindus celebrate the onset of the rains with a joint procession. Muslim guards protect the shrine of Bikaner's patron deity, Karni Mata; and in Jaora, Muslim peasants make offerings at shrines of the smallpox goddess. Around Indore, Muslim Patels and Mirdhas dress exactly like their Hindu neighbours; while the Momins of Cutch, nominally Shi'ias, do not eat flesh, or practise circumcision, or keep the fast during Ramadan.[2] Syncretic adaptations are widespread and endemic in South Asia amongst both Muslims and Hindus, especially in rural areas—so much so, that some commentators prefer to talk, not of syncretism, but of 'composite culture' (Alam 1994: 30). But cultural intermingling is not just a phenomenon of the villages. During the period of Mughal rule (sixteenth to eighteenth centuries), Hindu elites, especially in north India, adopted and assimilated numerous elements of *nawabi* courtly culture: the custom of *purdah* or seclusion of women; *ghazals* (songs, a traditional genre mainly associated with Muslim artists); the long frock-coat or *sherwani*; Hindustani/Urdu, with its Arabic script and Persianized vocabulary; the *pillau* and the *biryani*. As late as the early twentieth century, this legacy still cast a long shadow.[3] Premchand, generally regarded as the century's greatest exponent of Hindi prose, wrote his first stories in Urdu. Jawaharlal Nehru, scion of a Kashmiri Pandit family whose fortunes were laid in the service of the Mughal imperium, was brought up to regard Urdu as his native tongue; and as an adult he proudly wore the sherwani (the 'Nehru jacket') on formal occasions, in the manner of his forefathers. Jinnah, ironically, favoured suits tailored on Savile Row.[4]

As for the League's demand for a homeland, this seemed, at the time, quite chimerical. How many areas would be involved? Would they each constitute separate sovereign states or would they form part of a single confederacy? If 'Pakistan' was to consist only of areas in which Muslims were in a numerical majority, what fate awaited the millions of Muslims living in the so-called 'minority provinces', such as United Provinces (UP) (which was then the League's principal, indeed only real, stronghold) and Bombay (which was Jinnah's stomping-ground)? Where and how should the boundaries of the new state(s) be drawn: with reference only to religious demography, or with regard also to other elements such as communication links and hinterlands? How could *any* partition not fail to sever important economic arteries? Surely, a state so lacking in large towns (apart from Lahore) and industry would be struggling to pay its way? If Islam was to be the prime determinant of citizenship, why stop at the northwest frontier? Would not a pan-Islamic state extending across West Asia make just as much (or little) logical sense as the one outlined in the League resolution? The editors of the English dailies shook their heads.[5] Congress at first refused to take the Lahore demand seriously. The British Cabinet Mission, which visited India in 1946, pronounced the proposal unviable. Historian Ayesha Jalal (1985: 2) concludes, having closely investigated surviving documents pertaining to the League's adoption of the Lahore scheme, that the initial reaction of the INC was sound—that the Pakistan demand was never intended to be translated into constitutional reality but was put forward, rather, as a 'bargaining chip', with a view to extracting better terms from the Congress and the British.

Nevertheless, against the odds, Pakistan came into being as a full-fledged state just seven years later. Moreover, although most nationalist historians think that Jinnah blackmailed the British and the Congress into conceding Pakistan by evoking the spectre of civil war if the demand was not met, there is substantial evidence to support the Pakistani view that by 1947 the homeland idea had the backing of most Indian Muslims. In the 1937 elections, the AIML did quite poorly, winning only 109 of the 482 seats reserved for Muslims, including just two in the Punjab, the fulcrum of the Lahore scheme for a future Muslim state. In the 1946 polls, however, running on the single plank of Pakistan, it won a 'famous victory' (Hardy 1972: 236), sweeping the Muslim reserved seats and destroying its non-Congress opponents. In Punjab the League won 75/ 86 Muslim reserved seats, in Bengal 113/119. In the Central Assembly it captured *all* the Muslim seats. Of course, in the absence of exit polls in those days one cannot say for certain that all of the Muslims who cast their votes for Pakistan did so solely or primarily on the Pakistan issue; nor, as Sumit Sarkar (1983: 427) points out, does the election provide a window into the minds of the Muslim masses who were excluded from the franchise. Nevertheless, the result is suggestive. It suggests that, despite the objective differences between them (of sect, class, and language) and notwithstanding the many points of intersection between 'Hindu' and 'Muslim' culture in South Asia, both at the elite and mass levels, the generality of Indian Muslims had come to think of themselves as a community or—if you prefer—a proto-nation. Accounting for this sea-change in consciousness remains a major preoccupation of historians of modern South Asia.

'PRIMORDIALISTS' AND 'INSTRUMENTALISTS'

Scholarship on nation-formation falls broadly into two schools. One, sometimes known as the 'primordialist' school, holds that nations are essentially natural artefacts, defined by inherited ethnic markers such as race, language, and religion and by the circumstances of geography and historical development. The other, sometimes called the 'instrumentalist' school, acknowledges that shared ethnic characteristics may assist in the emergence of nationality, but puts the main emphasis on external agency. According to the instrumentalists, nations are first born in the minds of elites through an act of selective imagining, then purposefully 'sold' to the putative membership of the national group through consciousness-raising propaganda and active political mobilization of the masses. As Benedict Anderson perhaps the most celebrated exponent of this view, puts it: 'the convergence of capitalism and print technology on the fatal diversity of human language created the possibility of a new form of imagined community, which in its basic morphology set the stage for the modern nation' (Anderson 1991: 46).

Broadly speaking, these two interpretations constitute the theoretical poles around which the modern scholarly debate about Muslim 'separatism' in India—leading ultimately to the founding of Pakistan—has been waged. American political scientist Paul Brass (1974) triggered the debate with his *Language, Religion and Politics in North India,* written unapologetically, and in the circumstances of the time fairly provocatively, from an instrumentalist viewpoint. For Brass, Muslim separatism was not about religion, but about class and power. He suggests that the Muslim elites of UP in the late nineteenth century chose deliberately to distance themselves from their Hindu neighbours—by emphasizing the core religious differences that separated them, to the exclusion of the many social similarities that bound them together—because it suited their interests to do so (Brass 1974: 124). Closely argued and richly documented, Brass' book received hearty acclaim. But almost at once a young scholar, Francis Robinson, then at Cambridge, rose to the challenge. Robinson offered what almost amounts to a defence of the primordialist Jinnah–Pakistani position, but written with a degree of theoretical sophistication hitherto lacking in Pakistani historiography, and with the benefit of his own doctoral research into the politics of the UP Muslim elite.[6] Elites, Robinson (1985: 344) suggests, 'are not wholly free to select aspects of a group's culture, attach values to them, and [then] use them to mobilise the group, being constrained only by the culture of the group they . . . [wish] to lead. . . . Elites are also constrained by their own culture'. North Indian Muslims possessed a culture that was deeply impregnated by Islamic beliefs and practices, by frameworks of ideas rooted in the Qur'an and the *Hadith*, and by a sense of mystical brotherhood promoted by 'such Muslim observances as communal prayer, communal fasting in the month of Ramazan, and the shared experience of the Haj' (Robinson 1977: 219). When the UP Muslim elite felt threatened, he concludes, their visceral reaction was to activate this latent Islamic network, even as, more consciously, they realized its powerful potential as a vehicle for the organization and mobilization of the Muslim masses (Robinson 1985: 348). Brass, in his turn, penned a riposte that accused Robinson of failing to distinguish between:

a community of believers, united by a common relationship to a deity and sharing in sets of ritual practices and laws of daily life, and an ethnic community joined together on the basis of its religious distinctiveness for the purpose of social and political action (Brass 1977: 231).

Neither since has given much away. But somewhat unexpectedly, more recent scholarship from the likes of Farzana Shaikh (1989), Javeed Alam (1994, 1995), and David Gilmartin has tended to add weight to Robinson's reservations. Gilmartin's work is especially germane to the present discussion in that it brings out the important contribution that Islamic professionals, notably the *sajjada nashin*s, or guardians of Sufi shrines, made to the League's election victory of 1946 and thus to the establishment of Pakistan (Gilmartin 1979, and 1988: 189–233). It now appears fairly clear that many Muslims were induced to vote for Pakistan in the belief that they were helping to bring about not just the creation of a Muslim homeland, but what Deoband *alim* Maulana Sabbir Ahmad Usmani in his *Hamara Pakistan* (Mushir-ul-Haq 1985: 420) had called the new Medina—an Islamic state where the *shari'a* would be law.

COMMUNALISM AND GEOGRAPHY

Yet all this writing, primordialist and instrumentalist alike, shares the assumption that political mobilization for purposes of national consciousness-raising occurred exclusively along a vertical axis. Robinson stresses the missionary efforts of nineteenth-century 'Wahabis' and of twentieth-century *tablighi* preachers such as Maulana Ilyas; Brass puts greater emphasis on the role of secular leaders such as Sir Saiyyid Ahmad Khan of Aligarh. But they agree that the idea of Muslim separatism originated with the *ashraf* elite in the cities and filtered downward to the *ajlaf* masses in the villages. Javeed Alam, too, accepts that this was the way it happened, though for him the downward penetration of orthodoxy is a matter of regret, since it spelt doom for what was left of rural India's unique 'composite culture': 'Once the orthodoxy felt the danger [from revivalist Hinduism] and began intervening from above, they... succeeded... in pushing back or defeating most of these [syncretic] tendencies in social life' (Alam 1994: 30–1). However, there is substantial evidence that communal tendencies among Muslims (and Hindus) also spread laterally, within and across geographical regions. Consider the closely linked phenomenon of 'communal' riots. Riots between the two groups became progressively more frequent and severe as the colonial period wore on. But their increase was not evenly spread. Some areas succumbed quickly; others—including, inexplicably, towns with large Muslim minorities—appear to have remained virtually riot-free through-out the colonial period and beyond. Bijnor, for example, situated in the heart of strife-torn western UP, managed to defy the odds until October 1990 (Jeffrey and Jeffrey 1994: 551). This raises the interesting question of what kept some regions of India during the nineteenth and early twentieth centuries relatively immune from contagion? The hypothesis advanced in this chapter is that the spread of communal consciousness was regulated primarily by two factors: distance and communications. Places that were far from existing centres of communal tension and conflict (which, by the early twentieth century, included most of UP and Bihar, the provincial port-capitals of Bombay and Calcutta, and Ahmedabad, Delhi, and Lahore) were shielded by the simple fact of their remoteness; but beyond this a great deal depended on how easily people and ideas from the communal core areas could reach them. Distance was less of a buffer when there was a main-line railway connection, or a good road. Conversely, its impact was reinforced by an absence of good communication links and by the existence of intermediary physical barriers— geographical or political.

However, physical isolation was likely to be a diminishing asset— vulnerable to the march of modernization. In the early twentieth century, the north Indian Princely States, Hindu- and Muslim-ruled alike, were well situated to reap the benefits of the aforementioned buffers. They were located, for the most part, in regions outside the old Mughal heartland, and remote from the big port-cities. Communications between them and the provinces of British India were generally poor. No railway line connected Cutch with the rest of Kathiawar; and the desert kingdom of Jaisalmer could be accessed only by camel-train. Tripura was linked to Agartala in Assam by a single phone line, which was often down. To get to Loharu, visitors from south-east Punjab had to negotiate a 42-mile sandy track that was impassable in the wet seasons. Baoni in central India was six hours drive from the nearest cantonment town of Nowgong. More importantly still, the Princely States, being largely autonomous, had borders that could be policed to exclude troublesome outsiders. When an agitation was got up in Tonk in 1919 in support of the Khilafat movement, the Nawab nipped it in the bud by the simple device of issuing orders 'for the expulsion from the State of 4 pleaders, one school-master and a local merchant'.[7] The rulers, and—it must be said—many of their subjects too, prized this relative seclusion, and did all they could to preserve it. But it was doomed not to last.

COMMUNAL CO-EXISTENCE IN PRINCELY INDIA IN THE EARLY TWENTIETH CENTURY

In the 1941 census, the population of the Princely States is recorded as 93.2 million, that of the provinces as 258.8 million. All other things being equal, therefore, the provinces should have suffered about two and three-quarter times more carnage, as a result of communal conflict, than the states. In fact, depending on whether injuries or deaths are counted, they suffered 12–13 times more (see Appendix 1.1). Furthermore, insofar as the two sets of figures are closer together in respect of incidents than in respect of casualties, one might conclude that communal violence was not only more general in the provinces than in the states, but on balance more severe. Comparing the provinces and the states is, of course, of itself, a crude measure, and it is hoped that in time more sophisticated inter- and intra-regional studies of the geographical spread of communalism will be undertaken; however, it suffices to make the point.

But that is not all. Riots were not only infrequent in the states in the early twentieth century, but all the archival evidence seen by this author suggests that the states' subjects at that time went to great lengths to prevent, or at least minimize, disagreements arising from religious difference. Hindus in the state of Jodhpur agreed that 'Mussalmans need absolute silence when they offer their prayers',[8] and were prepared to divert their religious processions away from mosques and regulate their hours of religious worship so as not to coincide with Islamic prayer times. In Muslim-ruled Mangrol, 'the ancient practice' was for Hindus to refrain from playing music 'while passing by mosques . . . in deference to the religious beliefs of their Mohamedan brothers'.[9] In 1928, in the Nabha town of Bawal, Muslims worshipping at a mosque came out to remonstrate with a passing Hindu marriage party that was playing loud music, pointing out that they were about to start their evening prayers. The Hindu celebrants 'quietly consented to their request', and afterwards the town's Muslim and Hindu leaders met with officials to assure them 'that there was not the least chance of any fracas'.[10] To be sure, incidents did occasionally occur; the states were not, even in the 1920s, totally free from communal violence. Yet for the most part these outbreaks were quickly contained and defused by apology and recompense. In 1923, four Muslims threw a handful of animal bones into a Hindu temple at Phagwara in Kapurthala. The culprits were tracked down by the police and arrested; but before they could be brought to trial, the Hindus leaders of the town, in a concerted effort to 'avoid [further] communal bickerings', successfully petitioned the authorities to pardon them.[11] Ten years later, in the same state, someone set fire to the door of a mosque in the village of Sultanpur Lodi; it was assumed that the perpetrator was a Sikh. Far from condoning this act of vandalism, the elders of the Sultanpur Sikh community publicly apologized and collected money to repair the damage.[12] The way of life at the grass roots revealed in these documents brings to mind Robert Redfield's concept of the rural Little Tradition (Redfield 1960); however, it appears to involve far more than just an inheritance of syncretism. It speaks of an experience of 'lived' community, of a moral order based on economic interdependence, and an acknowledgement of the functional necessity—given that people in Indian villages and urban neighbourhoods live in very close proximity to one another—of some form of agreed coexistence. We have here, it seems to me, a perfect example of the spirit that Victor Turner called *communitas*.[13]

RISING ANIMOSITY AFTER 1930

By the 1930s, however, documentary records indicate that the spirit of communitas in the Princely States of north India was starting to diminish. Specifically, the number and scale of Hindu–Muslim communal riots rose steeply during the decade (see Appendix 1.1). More generally, British onlookers observed, particularly in the Punjab, the 'growth of a communal feeling hitherto unknown' in princely India.[14] For our purposes the interesting thing about this communal upsurge is that it typically followed upon provocative acts of public religious assertion by Muslims, who (outside of Kashmir, Bahawalpur, Khaipur, and Kalat), constituted a very small demographic minority—smaller by far than in British India.

Shortly after the Lahore Muslim League session of 1940, Muslims in the capital city of Charkhari 'ceremoniously brought a cow into the street and killed it'.[15] In August 1940, Muslim butchers in a Jodhpur village smashed an idol. The following month, stone-throwing Muslims attacked Bhaironji's temple in the Jaipur town of Ramgarh. And in March 1942, Muslims in another Jodhpur town, contrary to time-honoured practice, refused to allow a Holi *ghair* party to pass by the Jama Masjid.[16] Hindu *darbars* feared the worst, that of Gwalior lamenting that its Muslim subjects seemed to have been 'taken for a ride' by Islamic 'groups from outside'.[17]

Inevitably, this uncharacteristic Muslim behaviour incited Hindus to hit back. The result was not only, as noted above, an overall increase in the intensity of communal conflict, but a shift in the pattern of its distribution. While as far as can be ascertained, by 1930 only a handful of north Indian states had experienced overt communal conflict in the form of riots, during the 1930s and early 1940s the number of affected states multiplied. Two that succumbed for the first time in this period were Gwalior in central India and Kotah in Rajputana. The next section looks closely at how and why these outbreaks occurred.

THE UJJAIN RIOT OF 1942

The first link in the chain of events that led to the Gwalior outbreak was the arrival in Ujjain, in August 1942, of a prominent Bohra Muslim from Cambay named Mullaji. To celebrate his coming, local Bohras took out a procession, which was punctuated by loud cries of 'Pakistan Zindabad' and 'Quaid-e-Azam Zindabad'. Ujjain Hindus later claimed that this was the first time these highly charged slogans had been heard in the town. Shortly afterwards, came news of the passage of the INC's 'Quit India' resolution on 8 August, and the arrest of its members the following morning. A number of mostly Hindu shopkeepers at once closed their premises in sympathy; and the same evening the Gwalior Praja Mandal called a mass meeting to discuss what if anything could be done locally by way of support for the Quit India movement.

The meeting opened in an atmosphere of tension and excitement, but there was no hint of violence in the air. Then, just as the president of the Mandal rose to speak, a group of Bohra 'youngmen' burst in 'and demanded that the . . . meeting be postponed, as it was the time of Namaz'. This was agreed to albeit grudgingly. The demand had no precedent and many left the meeting mouthing curses at the Muslims for their lack of patriotism. On 13 August, some of the latter, mainly students, marched through the city's central commercial district, remonstrating with proprietors, mainly Muslims, whose businesses were still open. 'It is said that [when] these students [reached the vegetable market they] began to compel Boheras [*sic*] to close their shops.'[18] Forewarned and perhaps forearmed, the Bohras poured out on to the street and attacked the students with sticks. Although 500 strong, the student militia fled. But they soon returned with reinforcements in the shape of some 'Hindu strongmen' from the nearby Patni Bazaar—and on this occasion, the Bohras found themselves on the receiving end. By the time the police arrived on the scene, two had been killed, dozens wounded, and scores of Bohra shops looted.

Outwardly, peace was soon restored. Another small affray erupted on the 15th, but it did not result in any casualties. However, the incident left a bitter legacy. A couple of days after the second riot Muslims held a mass meeting at which allegations of atrocities were levelled at the Hindus; and every 13 August thereafter, down to 1947, the Bohras of Ujjain observed *hartal* in memory of the event. For their part, the Gwalior Praja Mandal leaders concluded that the whole thing had been set up:

'these riots were intentionally devised by Muslim Leaguers to disrupt [the] August Movement'.[19] One of the tragedies of bloody communal riots is that it is very difficult for the participants, and especially the relatives of the victims, to expunge memory of the riots—even when it is not kept alive artificially as it was among the Ujjain Bohras. Once the communal peace of a town or region has been broken by a major riot, the odds are that further outbreaks will occur. Ujjain would be no exception.

THE KOTAH RIOT OF 1943

The Political Department's post-mortem on the savage Kotah riot of March 1943, which found that Muslims were principally to blame, caused some puzzlement at the India Office: 'It is unusual for a community so small a minority to act aggressively', opined former Political Officer Sir Courtenay Latimer.[20] However, Muslims comprised 15 per cent of the city population, considered by some scholars such as Gopal Krishna (1985: 65), to be enough to constitute a quorum for action. More importantly, Latimer seems to have not appreciated the extent to which the outlook of the state's Muslims had become infused with separatist ideas and their resistance stiffened by League propaganda. As recently as six years earlier, Kotah Muslims had joined in the annual Holi festival procession, which in 1943 occasioned the riot. Since then, they had 'kept away more and more' from Hindu affairs.[21] By the early 1940s, the state's Muslims had become fiercely anti-Congress.

Still, it took the Quit India movement to transform an attitude of implacable hostility into a zest for active confrontation. Even more than in other places, Kotah Hindus allied with the local Praja Mandal embraced the Congress 'Quit India' call enthusiastically. They paraded, went on strike, walked out of classrooms, blocked roads, and cut telephone lines. For several days in mid-August, the Praja Mandal effectively controlled the town. Moreover, to an extent unparalleled in other states, the 'rebellion' in Kotah city attracted support from above. Putting Maharaja Bhim Singhji's tenure on his throne at considerable risk, the state executive council resisted until the last moment British advice to call out the troops.[22] The Kotah Muslims, who as in other places had very publicly dissociated themselves from the Quit India agitation, felt betrayed by the darbar's partiality towards the movement; and this added to their concern about its manifestly Hindu character, as reflected in the composition of the bureaucracy. To drive their point home, in November

1942 they staged a highly publicized meeting to celebrate the Allied victory in North Africa. The meeting was harangued by, amongst others, the son of Qazi Kasimuddin of Delhi who said that

the Muslims should . . . be pleased at the victory of the British Empire, the defeat of which would again enslave them for over 100 years. They should also fight for the scheme of Pakistan and try to bring it in[to] force.[23]

At the end of the meeting, a vote of loyalty to the Raj was carried with acclamation. Meanwhile Delhi-based Muslim papers took up the charge, publishing a spate of vitriolic attacks against the ruler and his officials. The *Mussalman* was especially inventive, on one occasion likening the condition of the Kotah Muslims to that of the Jews in Germany, on another suggesting that 'the Congressite goondas' at large in the state had 'made it difficult for Muslims to live there'.[24] Muslims would later explain the riot of March 1943 with reference to these proceedings. Specifically, they would allege that 'Hindus were looking for a chance to avenge Muslims for their loyalty to the British Government on account of [the fact that] they took no part in their hooliganism . . . after the arrest of Gandhiji and other Congress leaders'.[25]

The allegation has considerable force. Certainly, extremist elements among the Kotah Hindus, as represented by the leaders of a newly formed ginger group, the Mahavir Dal, became increasingly agitated at the provocative behaviour of the Muslim community. Posters attributed to the Dal accused the Muslims of putting obstacles in the path of freedom, and urged retaliation. Dal President Shyama Narain Saksena, a former *darbari* filing clerk dismissed for his role in the 14 August disturbances, fired off a similar broadside from the public platform.[26] What is more, there is evidence that some Hindu elements were planning revenge. Police reports record 'drilling' by members of the Dal and a shadowy group called the Azad Sangh; and in early March 1943 the authorities got wind of an invitation to visit extended to 'well-known communal agitator' and veteran riot-captain Thakur Tej Singh Bhajnik of Bulandshahr. But Kotah's Muslims, too, appear to have resolved upon a show of force. On Bakr'Id day 1942 they taunted the Hindus by parading a herd of garlanded goats through the main city bazaar; and police information indicates that from the beginning of the new year, perhaps in anticipation of the Holi festival coming up in spring, the city's Muslim *kabaris* (scrap-iron dealers) were kept busy filling orders for *dharias* (swords) and other sharpened metal weapons.[27]

As with all riot narratives, the story of what actually took place in the Kotah capital on 22 March 1943, and who was responsible, is confusing and often contradictory. All versions of the event are in agreement though that in 1943 the procession, which always climaxed the town's Holi celebrations, was larger than usual with perhaps 5000 Hindus taking part; that 'contrary to established usage', slogans of a political nature were chanted by the Hindus; that the procession was ambushed, near the main city bus depot, by a substantial body of Muslims; and that this assault triggered a 'free fight with sticks, spears and stones' that rapidly enveloped the Muslim quarter, and led to the deaths of three of the rioters from skull-fractures, and the hospitalization of 200 others, mainly Hindus. What remains unclear, and in dispute, is the extent to which the Muslims were provoked into launching their attack. The Muslims claimed later that members of the procession were chanting 'Qur'an murdabad' and 'Pakistan murdabad'; and that stones were thrown into a mosque. The darbari version, however, rejected these claims. There were no stones, and no provocative slogans, except for a 'few . . . non-communal "Jais"'. Indeed, the official version went further, describing the riot as a 'premeditated act' by Muslims anxious to 'teach the Hindus of Kotah a lesson'.[28]

Probably neither account is reliable. The Muslim version is clearly self-serving while the official version is so shot-through with prejudice towards Muslims in general that one can readily understand why the *dewan*, S. N. Mehta, a loaned Indian Civil Service officer from the Central Provinces, was quietly removed by the Political Department later in the year. Yet the Kotah government's contention that Muslims were mainly responsible for the riot seems basically correct. The casualty figures bear it out. One hundred and sixty Hindus injured as against forty Muslims suggests, as the Kotah darbar's police reports assert, that the Muslims were better prepared, better armed, and in the last analysis more brutal. To return to Latimer's enigma: here a minority clearly had the gall to tackle a majority, and what is more with gusto and ruthless efficiency. In the Kotah riot, as they had the year before in the Gwalior affray, Muslims living in the 'Hindu' states served notice that they were no longer prepared to submit to majoritarian hegemony.

HOW AND WHY MUSLIMS IN PRINCELY STATES BECAME
MORE ASSERTIVE OF THEIR RELIGIOUS IDENTITY

In 1920, Muslims living in the Princely States of north India were not politically distinguishable as a group from other sections of the population.

Although nothing seen so far by this author indicates that they were any less pious, or dutiful to their religious obligations as Muslims, than their brethren in the provinces, the pride that they undoubtedly felt in belonging to the tribe of Islam was only one strand of their identity and probably, in most cases, less important to their sense of who they were than things such as family and ancestry, the physical environment of the neighbourhood, and the fact that they were each and all residents of discrete kingdoms: loyalty to the throne and the person of the ruler ran deep in those days within all communities. Twenty years on, Muslims in the states were showing signs of identifying with their co-religionists elsewhere in princely India and in the provinces, of imagining themselves as part of a community bound together not just by a shared faith but also by common political, social, and economic interests. One indicator of this has already been noted—the increasing tendency of urban Muslims in the states to stand up for themselves in street confrontations with Hindus (or to seek out such confrontations, even where, as in Kotah, they were locally outnumbered). Another was the proliferation from the late 1930s of Muslim social clubs—*anjumans*—and the establishment in the early 1940s of a network of state-based AIML branches (though their memberships, except in Kashmir,[29] remained fairly small). Yet a third was the defiant decision of many of Baroda's urban Muslims to return their language as Urdu instead of Gujarati in the census of 1941.[30]

Accounting for this sea-change in the mentality of the states' Muslims is no easy matter; and a great deal more research will be required before anything like a final account can be rendered. What follows is no more than an interim report, based on a larger work in progress. Still, the main elements seem clear enough.

First and foremost, their physical and political environment changed. Although the Princely States had never been completely cut off from the rest of the subcontinent, they had remained, for the most part—for the reasons indicated above—somewhat isolated. Over the twenty years 1925–45, the number and quality of railways and roads linking the states and the provinces rose dramatically, which made ingress physically easier. Meanwhile, a mushroom growth took place in British India in all areas of vernacular publishing. This made it harder for the darbars to keep out everything potentially seditious. Last but not the least, the princes began, with cautious imperial encouragement, to take a larger and more active interest in all-India affairs, especially in their role as putative communal leaders. As the states opened up, outsiders came in, bearing a variety of communal messages and understandings.

Some of these were politicians. In the early twentieth century, the provincial-based political parties, by common consent, largely ignored the states; they felt that they had no business interfering where their writ did not run. However, during the early 1930s this self-denying ordinance was separately broken by the Majlis-i-Ahrar and the All-India Hindu Mahasabha, whose leaders saw an opportunity of profiting from insurrections in Kashmir and Alwar. After much agonizing, the Congress followed suit in 1938, launching a widespread *satyagraha* movement in the states in alliance with the All-India States Peoples' Conference (AISPC) with the aim of compelling the princes to introduce responsible government. Only the Muslim League hung back, fearful of antagonizing the rulers it hoped would take its side against the Congress in a future federal government. These interventions in turn accelerated the growth in the states of local political parties—Hindu Sabhas, and the so-called *praja mandals*, or 'people's organizations'—which exposed the people there, for the first time, to the dynamics of political mobilization. However, for the most part, states' Muslims shied away from joining these bodies for fear of antagonizing the governments they relied on for legal protection. When the Congress and the AISPC jointly launched their satyagraha in 1938, Muslims were conspicuous by their absence; and the pattern was repeated during the Quit India movement four years later. For instance, except for a few labourers, the Muslim community in Indore 'abstained totally'—the Sunnis reportedly because of 'Muslim League principles', the Shi'ite Bohras because of their business interests.[31] Needless to say, the reluctance of the generality of Muslims in the Princely States to get involved in what was perceived by most of their Hindu neighbours by this time as a national struggle put a strain on communal relations.

Others, far more numerous, were economic migrants, attracted by the economic opportunities that were opening up in the states through rural development (for example, the new canal colonies of Bahawalpur and Bikaner), industrialization, and targeted bureaucratic recruitment as in the case of Bhopal, which filled 80 per cent of its public service vacancies during the 1930s with men from the Punjab and the Frontier.[32] Unlike the politicians, they did not come to sell a specific ideology; nevertheless, their cultural baggage contained much that was foreign and potentially damaging to the states' social culture, as this Jodhpur district officer recognized:

General conditions in British India and the strained relations between Hindus and Muslims everywhere outside Marwar are likely to have a bad effect upon the people [of] Marwar. It is therefore necessary to see that unsocial elements do not infiltrate and preach violence and hatred to members of either community. Makrana being the biggest town in this district, with a large industrial population, a large number of bad characters and a Muslim majority, is likely to take up this infection if precautions are not taken at an early stage.[33]

Moreover, in the case of the northern Princely States, the disruption caused by in-migration was exacerbated by the fact that while the states were predominantly Hindu, the migrants were mainly Muslim. During the decade 1921–31, the Muslim population in Jaipur increased by nearly 20 per cent (and over 25 per cent in Jaipur city), and in Bikaner by a massive 89 per cent. In the following decade, the Muslim population in Indore increased by over 18 per cent, and in Bhopal by 27 per cent. Why so many of the migrants who came to try their luck in these states were Muslims is hard to say, though chain-migration was probably a factor, the fact that they were is of crucial importance. On the one hand, the Muslim influx had the effect of altering the communal balance. The shift was not, to be sure, a very large one, but it was sufficient to cause a flurry of concern and dismay among some locally dominant Hindu communities when the full extent and rapidity of the change became known with the publication of the 1931 Indian census. Echoing a refrain first heard in the provinces in the 1920s, Bhopal's Thakur Lal Singh declaimed forlornly in 1938: 'the Hindus are dying out'![34] On the other hand, the intrusion of Muslims into previously Hindu-dominant localities increased the potential for religious conflict by pushing Muslim numbers closer to, or beyond, the nominal demographic threshold for violence and by creating additional arenas for religious disputation. For example, the immigrant Muslims not unreasonably expected to be able to attend Friday namaz in a proper mosque; so there was unleashed a spurt of new mosque-construction, which did not always take account of local Hindu susceptibilities.[35]

Secondly, there was a change in the political environment within the states. Imperial pressure on the princes to 'reform' their administrations— especially after the debacle of 1938–9—led to the progressive intro-duction, particularly in the larger states, and particularly in the first instance at the municipal level, of representative institutions filled partly by means of election. The advent of elections required aspiring candidates to connect with constituencies—what would these days in India be called vote banks—and the form of constituency that proved easiest to mobilize was in most cases one that was fashioned by religion: community. Moreover, although the object of the exercise was principally to rally support, rather than to set one community off against another, the mere fact of a candidate standing on a communal platform tended to colour the politics of the contest. In Bhopal, this was so widely understood, and accepted, that Hindu and Muslim candidates were routinely issued with yellow and green electoral symbols respectively by the darbar's electoral officials.[36] Inevitably, therefore, these electoral contests became arenas for communal confrontation.

Nevertheless—as earlier in British India—Muslims and Hindus in the Princely States reacted very differently to the challenges posed by this new quasi-democratic order. The Hindus mostly welcomed it; the Muslims embraced it fitfully and unwillingly because it put them at an inherent numerical disadvantage, especially where the electoral rules prescribed, as they did almost everywhere, that there should be single-member territorial constituencies. Although Muslims comprised a substantial minority of Sirohi's urban population, particularly in Abu Road town, they were nowhere sufficiently concentrated, geographically, to carry even a single ward in the state's first municipal poll of 1940.[37] For the Muslims of Princely India, elections were a recipe for permanent exclusion from political power. Hence, when it became known that the states were planning constitutional reforms, Muslims everywhere rallied to press on the authorities the same demand their provincial cousins had made of the British thirty years before—for separate electorates. Even the Kashmiri Muslims, who were in a large majority, opted to have separate electorates incorporated in the state's constitution. However while many important states agreed to reserve seats for minorities, almost all were unwilling, for perhaps self-interested reasons, to depart from the democratic principle of joint electorates. This rebuff left the Muslims feeling dissatisfied and vulnerable. Many vented their frustration by boycotting the electoral process altogether.[38]

This brings us to the third thing that appears to have radically transformed the outlook of the states' Muslims. It was an external factor, and on the face of it, a most unlikely one, in the form of the resolution passed at Lahore calling for the establishment of a Muslim homeland. Not only was the Lahore resolution itself well received by Muslims living in the states; the idea of Pakistan at once took hold of their imagination.

Note the spontaneous cry of 'Pakistan Zindabad' raised in August 1942 by the Muslims of Ujjain; note how the Muslims of Kotah city rose to the anti-Pakistan taunts of the Holi revellers in March 1943; note the proliferation of violent communal acts involving Muslims from other Princely States in Rajputana and central India in the twelve months immediately after the historic Lahore session (see above p. 31); note the continuing upsurge in state Muslim League membership;[39] note how states' Muslims turned out in their thousands in answer to the Quaid-i-Azam's call for a day of 'Direct Action' on 16 August 1946 in furtherance of the Pakistan scheme.[40] Had the Muslims of the states been able to vote in the 1946 election, there seems little doubt that most would have chosen to cast their ballots for the League and its homeland policy.

MINORITY PROVINCE AND PRINCELY STATE MUSLIM SUPPORT FOR PAKISTAN—A PARADOX

Yet the proposed Pakistan was slated in the Lahore resolution to occupy territorial space in the north-west and north-east corners of the sub-continent—a long way from where the bulk of the Princely States were clustered (in Rajputana, central India, and Kathiawar). Most Princely States' Muslims cannot have anticipated migrating to Pakistan, and, in fact, very few outside of the east Punjab states did so in 1947. Why, then, all this enthusiasm? Why did the Muslims of the states embrace, and give active support to, a scheme that, on the face of it, looked largely irrelevant to their situation?

Mushir-ul-Haq has investigated this question with respect to the Muslim minority provinces of British India. He asks, 'Why did Muslims of the minority provinces . . . vote for Pakistan? Did they not know that their home and hearth could not be included in the geographical territory of the future Pakistan?'[41] (Mushir 1985: 414). Mushir concludes that they did so in a willing spirit of sacrifice, in the hope that their vote might help to create a genuinely Islamic state. 'The great majority of Muslims,' he declares, 'chose what they thought would be the "Kingdom of God"' (Mushir 1985: 420.) This recalls the emotional speech by the Central Provinces League leader, Syed Abdur Rauff Shah, in support of the homelands resolution at Lahore, in which he pleaded with the assembly 'not to worry about Muslims living in the minority provinces' who would put their trust in God.[42]

This explanation is, however, somewhat unconvincing. For one thing, Mushir offers no direct evidence for it, beyond quoting the pro-Pakistani propaganda put out by some of the Barelvi and Firangi Mahal ulama, which begs the question of why the charismatic pronouncements of this group registered more than the equally charismatic counter-appeals of the majority Deobandis and the Jaamiat-al-Ulema-i-Hind. Indeed it is hard to see, given the absence of opinion polls and the paucity of political memoirs for the period, where such evidence might be found. For another, those minority provinces' Muslims who did, indeed, cast their votes in 1946–7 with the intention of helping to create an Islamic state, ruled by the shar'ia, could not have done so with any great confidence that it would come to pass. The AIML had remained steadfastly coy on this point, and its leaders were men who pretended, at least, to be secularists. Jinnah's first speech to the Pakistan Constituent Assembly—arguably the clearest statement of a secularist vision that has ever been uttered by a South Asian politician—would certainly have left many in this group of voters feeling deceived and betrayed (see Jinnah 1962: 8–9). Again, while it can be argued that many Muslims chose Pakistan literally in 1947 by migrating there, it is also true that, outside of Punjab and Bengal, the majority of the community stayed put—and not just because they had no real choice. Many simply could not bring themselves to abandon the familiar props that defined and structured their lives—the neighbourhood, their friends, the local mosque, and the nearby shrine—for the unknown terrain of far-off Pakistan. Some who went (albeit half-heartedly) such as the Meos of Gurgaon and eastern Rajputana, quickly became disillusioned and returned.

The religious factor cannot be discounted, of course. But almost surely it does not constitute the only explanation for the strong support that the Pakistan scheme garnered both in the minority provinces of British India and in the Princely States. Let me suggest, by way of conclusion, several possible alternatives.

TOWARDS A RESOLUTION

Firstly, it is probable that many of the states' Muslims who embraced the Pakistan idea in 1940 fully expected to be part of it. Several homeland scenarios were doing the rounds at that time, and one, authored by Dr Abdul Latif, contemplated a homeland squarely situated in the Deccan, based on the state of Hyderabad. As we have seen, the Lahore resolution itself was ambiguous on the issue of exactly how many homelands there would be, and their precise location. Moreover, by retrospectively adopting the popular name Pakistan for the homeland scheme voted on at Lahore, the League encouraged the perception that the latter was essentially the same as Choudhury Rahmat Ali's 1934 version, which specifically included Kashmir in its ambit, and which he occasionally stretched to include Cutch and Kathiawar (Sayeed 1968: 39). Although later repudiated (the official line that the League took to the voters in 1946 was that the Lahore resolution referred just to the 'six Muslim provinces': Bengal, Assam, Punjab, Sind, North West Frontier Province (NWFP), and Baluchistan), this view refused to die—and was given some support from the comments of people like League council member Chaudhuri Khaliquzzaman, who told the Gwalior Anjuman-i-Islam in 1942 that the Muslims of India were 'one and united' and 'could not be separated and segregated' by artificial boundaries;[43] and by the controversial and much debated tour of Kashmir by Jinnah himself in 1944.

Secondly, a related point, the political implications of Partition were little understood until after the event. As Mushirul Hasan (1997: 128) explains, the notion of 'India' and 'Pakistan' as wholly separate and sovereign countries, divided by borders, was something most people in the lead up to 1947 had great trouble grasping—or perhaps did not want to grasp, because the implications were so overwhelming. Anecdotal evidence, such as the raising of the Pakistan flag by Aligarh Muslim University students on 15 August, Independence Day, indicates that, almost to the last, some Muslims living in the provinces entertained the illusion that bits of Pakistan might be allowed to flourish in the middle of India. So, too, it would appear, did a sprinkling of their co-religionists in the Princely States. In late 1946 and early 1947, mass meetings were held with the object of establishing a new, ethnically Meo (that is, effectively Muslim-controlled) province or state embracing Bharatpur and Alwar and the district of Gurgaon. In August 1947, Leaguers in the UP Princely State of Rampur launched an abortive coup in an attempt to force the Nawab to declare for Pakistan. On 13 September, the Muslim ruler of Junagadh, in Kathiawar, infamously negotiated an Instrument of Accession with the Karachi government.

Thirdly, it is possible that some Muslims in the states lent their support to the Pakistan scheme even though they knew, fairly certainly, that they would never be part of it. Why? Because they felt uplifted, ennobled, by the daring, glamour, and potential world-significance of this national project, and because, more specifically, they believed that Pakistan would act as a guardian of their religious and secular interests. As Robinson (2000: 199) points out, one of the meta-themes of Indian Muslim discourse in the 1940s is 'fear of Hindu domination', fear that without direct access to power they 'would not be able to survive as proper Muslims'. A Pakistan nation promised to serve as a check on this dire possibility, not simply because of the diplomatic pressure that it would be able to invoke as a powerful neighbour, but because of the 'hostage' factor: India would be forced to treat its Muslim minority generously for fear that if it did not, Pakistan might crack down on its Hindus and Sikhs.

All these finely balanced calculations depended, however, on the AIML being able to make good its claim for the six provinces. This dream was shattered by the settlement imposed by the British—and reluctantly agreed to by Jinnah—on 3 June 1947, under which the putative Pakistan was shorn of Assam, the eastern half of the Punjab, and the western half of Bengal, including the city of Calcutta. The 'moth-eaten' Pakistan that emerged from Viceroy Mountbatten's surgery in June 1947 was by a considerable order of magnitude weaker than the original conception would have been; it also lacked a useable hostage population of Hindus and Sikhs. As Pakistan shrank, so did the hopes of the Muslims marooned in the Hindu heart of the subcontinent.

NOTES

1. See, for example, Bombay Liberal leader Sir Chimanlal Setalvad's withering critique as reported in *The Times of India* (Bombay), 25 March 1940.
2. Nawab of Malerkotla to M.R. Bhide, Regional Commissioner, PEPSU, 11 January 1950, P[unjab] S[tate] A[rchives, Patiala], Patiala, Dharam Arth, 564/103; Verma 1992, I, 267; interview with Jaswant Singh, Kota, 17 February 1998; Mujeeb 1967: 11, 15–17.
3. The enduring importance of this Persian 'husk culture' in Uttar Pradesh is eloquently outlined by Anthony Low in his editorial introduction to *Soundings in Modern South Asian History* (Low 1968).
4. There is a famous photograph of Nehru and Jinnah walking side by side during the Simla conference of September 1945—the former in a sherwani and the latter in grey suit and spats(!)—which brings out this sartorial irony very nicely.
5. See, for example, the editorials in *The Times of India*, 26 and 29 March 1940.
6. Actually, Robinson's thesis, which was published around the same time as the Brass book (Robinson 1974), contained much evidence that could be said to support an instrumentalist interpretation of nineteenth-century UP politics. Indeed, Robinson was criticized by several reviewers for not giving enough attention to religion (see, for example, Eugene Irshick's comment, in a review of a related Robinson article in 1975, that 'Robinson looks on religious feeling

[merely] as a cover for the changing economic and social conditions in which Hindus and Muslims find themselves' (Irshick 1975: 464). But Robinson avoids making this connection in his critique, and later distanced himself from some of the claims made in the monograph.

7. P[olitical] A[gent] Tonk to Assist[ant] A[gent to the] G[overnor] G[eneral], Rajputana, 8 May 1919, in Muhammad (1983: Vol. 6, 13).

8. Petition from 'the Beldars of Jodhpur' dated 7 November 1938. R[ajasthan] S[tate] A[rchives] B[ikaner], Jodhpur, Social, C 2/21 of 1939–45.

9. Petition from 'The Hindu Subjects of the Mangrol State Trading in Bombay' to the Sheikh of Mangrol dated 15 July 1933, [Br. Lib.] I[ndia] O[ffice] R[ecords], R/1/1/2595.

10. Gurdial Singh to J.W. Johnston, Administrator Nabha, 17 July 1928, PSA, Nabha, P[rime] M[inister]'s Office, 2349/2503E.

11. Chhajjumal Bhabra, presdt, Phagwara Municipality, to chief minister, Kapurthala, 28 June 1923, and chief minister to Bhabra (teleg.), 29 June 1923, PSA, Kapurthala, Sadar Office, M/3-27-23.

12. Chief Minister Kapurthala to the Sec[retary] to the AGG, Punjab States, 9 March 1932, PSA, Kapurthala, Sadar Office, E/5-1-32.

13. Turner (1974: 45, 169, 174–5).

14. This was a comment about Faridkot. 'Resumé of Events in the Indian States for the Fortnight Ending 31 May 1934', IOR L/P&S/13/1375.

15. Press statement by Hindu Mahasabha, n.d., N[ational] A[rchives] of I[ndia], CI Agency, Confdl., File 70-A of 1940.

16. Supt. Police, City, to I[nspector]-[General of] Police, Jodhpur, 25 August 1940, RSA, Jodhpur, Social, file C 2/21 of 1939–45; Fort. report on Rajputana for period ending 15 September 1940, IOR L/P&S/13/1406; and Chief Minister, Jodhpur, to PA Western Rajputana States, 6 March 1942, IOR L/P&S/13/1417.

17. *Jayanti Pratap*, 6 August 1942, M[adhya] P[radesh] S[tate] A[rchives], Gwalior.

18. Ibid.

19. Unsigned report by an officer of the Gwalior Praja Mandal on the 'Hindu-Muslim Riot at Ujjain', AISPC, File 60 of 1946–7; and *Jayanti Pratap*, 20 August 1942.

20. Note by Latimer dated 26 May 1943, IOR L/P&S/13/1425.

21. G. V. B. Gillan, Res[i]d[ent]t., Rajputana, to Sir K. Fitze, 23 April 1943, recounting a conversation with the Maharaja of Kotah, IOR L/P&S/13/1425.

22. Bhim Singhji's son recalls that his tutor in the 1940s 'was a very nationalistic man' who proudly sported a Gandhi cap in the palace. Apparently the resident recommended the Maharaja's deposition, but Delhi eventually gave him the benefit of the doubt after Ganga Singh of Bikaner intervened with the viceroy on his behalf. Interview with H.H. of Kotah, Kota City, 18 March 1998.

23. Fort. report by IGP, Kotah, for the period ending 30 November 1942, RSA, Kotah Confdl. File 26.

24. *Mussalman*, 2 and 13 November 1942, RSA, Kotah Confdl File 49.

25. 'Full Report On the Recent Hindu-Muslim Riot Of Kotah State' by the 'Muslims of Kotah', [?] April 1943, IOR L/P&S/13/1425.
26. Fort. report by IGP, Kotah, for the period ending 15 December 1942, RSA, Kotah Confdl. File 26; and Sir Mohammad Yamin Khan to Sir K. Fitze, 3 June 1943, IOR L/P&S/13/1425.
27. Fort. report from IGP, Kotah, for period ending 31 December 1942, RSA, Kotah Confdl. File 26; and G. V. B. Gillan, Resdt. Rajputana, to Sir K. Fitze, 23 April 1943, IOR L/P&S/13/1425.
28. S. N. Mehta, PM Kotah, to PA Eastern Rajputana States, 3 April 1943, IOR L/P&S/13/1425; *Lok Sewak* (Kotah), 5 April 1943, RSA, Kotah Confdl File 34; and 'Full Report on the Recent Hindu-Muslim Riot of Kotah' by the 'Muslims of Kotah' dated [?] April 1943, IOR L/P&S/13/1425.
29. By 1939 the Sheikh Abdullah-led Jammu and Kashmir Muslim Conference, which had evolved out of the Srinagar Muhammadan Youngmen's Association of the early 1930s, had become, in all but name, allied to the INC. To signal that change, the name of the party was changed from 'Muslim' to 'National'. In 1942 hardliners led by Abdullah's lieutenant Ghulam Abbas broke away and set up the Muslim Conference, a branch of the League in all but name.
30. *Census of India 1941*, 17, Part I, paragraph 2.
31. Memo. by I-G Police Indore dated 5 October 1942, MPSA, Indore, Foreign Dept, File 28 of 1942.
32. Bhopal actively recruited Frontier Afridis and Pathans for its army. By 1941, 9 per cent of the population of the state was born outside. AISPC, I, File 20, Part II of 1947.
33. Hakim, Parbatsar, to Sub-Inspector of Police, P.S. Parbatsar, 19 October 1946, RSA, Jodhpur, Social, File C 1/1 of 1944–9.
34. Address by Thakur Lal Singh to the Bhopal Hindu Conference, 27 May 1938, AISPC, I, File 18, Part II of 1938–42. On the genesis of the 'dying Hindus' thesis, see Thursby (1975: 123–4, 135–6); and Datta (1993: 1305–25).
35. Interestingly, these constructions were opposed by and large by Muslims long resident in the localities. Their stated motive was that they did not want to antagonize the dominant community with which they had always had good relations. See, for example, the report by Hakim, Barmer, dated 26 February 1947, RSA, Jodhpur, Social, C 2/21 of 1945–8.
36. Press statement by Sayer Zaheer Hashmi, general secretary, and Govind Prasad Srivastava, publicity secretary, Bhopal SPC, 6 January 1946, AISPC, Part I, File 19 (2) of 1945–8.
37. *Sirohi Administration Report 1940–41*, 78–9.
38. This happened, for example, in Sirohi in 1942 and in Gwalior in 1945. Yet even in Kashmir, where they had the advantage of separate elections, Muslims remained much more suspicious of the political process than the Hindus and Sikhs. In the second (1938–9) general elections, the average voter turnout was 40 per cent for Muslims and 54 per cent for non-Muslims. Likewise, Jaipur's Muslims refused to take comfort from the fact that the reforms introduced

there in 1944 gave them an allotment of seats in excess of their population share. 'Report on the Working of the Constitutional and Administrative Reforms Introduced In[to] the States For the Six Months Ending 15 May 1942', IOR L/P&S/13/993; fort. report on the Gwalior Residency for the period ending 30 September 1945, IOR L/P&S/13/1192; and *Dawn* (New Delhi), 13 January 1944.

39. Membership of the Jaipur League branch, for example, grew from about three score in 1940 to 11,500 in 1944 and to almost 30,000 in 1947. PM Jaipur to PA Jaipur, 9 September 1943, Home Minister Jaipur to PA Jaipur, 4 April 1945, and PM Jaipur to PA Jaipur, 2 January 1947, IOR R/2/150/123.

40. See, for example, fort. report on the Central India Agency for the period ending 31 October 1946, IOR L/P&S/13/1181; and fort. Report on the Gwalior Residency for the period ending 31 August 1946, IOR L/P&S/13/1197.

41. The full sentence includes, interestingly, the phrase 'and Princely India'. It is hard to know what he means by this since the article does not mention the states' Muslims specifically. Of course the latter never got to 'vote' for Pakistan directly at all: either in the elections of 1946 or via the referenda held in the NWFP and Assam.

42. *The Times of India*, 25 March 1940.

43. *Hindustan Times*, 3 April 1941.

APPENDIX 1.1
Major Hindu-Muslim Communal Clashes in India, 1920–1940

Year	Incidents		Killed		Injured	
	P	S	P	S	P	S
1920	1	–	–	–	–	1
1921	4	2	8	1	29	6
1922	4	–	15	–	172	–
1923	13	2	21	6	518	7
1924	23	3	88	5	849	32
1925	20	–	25	–	987	–
1926	33	8	292	3	1878	80
1927	41	3	199	9	1510	35
1928	14	3	167	1	975	163
1929	12	3	186	6	1020	66
1930	14	2	66	–	347	3
1931	27	4	360	12	2645	20
1932	6	9	235	28	2726	363
1933	6	7	10	16	59	52
1934	6	5	16	21	80	71
1935	8	5	71	14	223	110
1936	6	1	99	–	791	–
1937	22	5	30	19	180	115
1938	24	3	59	7	540	203
1939	39	8	306	18	1331	78
1940	5	5	10	6	31	42
Totals	322	79	2273	172	16891	1447

P = provinces   S = states

Sources: Coupland (1943) pp. 11, 35, 47n, 48–9. 69–70, 130–1, 131 n; Indian Statutory Commission Report, 1930, Vol. 1, 27–8, 253, Vol. IV, 108–20, Vol. VI, 586–99, Vol. VII, 233-8; Home (Pol.) file 249/XI of 1924; IOR R/1/1/1404, R/1/1/1448, R/l/1/1570, R/1/1/2035 (1); PSA, Patiala, Ijlas-i-Khas, file 2051; RSA, Bikaner, Home Dept, file 67/1932; RSA, Jodhpur, Social, C 2/21 of 1928–46; The New York Times 1920–40; The Times (London) 1920–40; The Times of India 1920–1940.

BIBLIOGRAPHY

Alam, Javeed (1994), 'Tradition in India Under Interpretative Stress', *Thesis Eleven*, Vol. 39, pp. 19–38.

———— (1995), 'Composite Culture and Communal Consciousness: The Ittehadul Muslimeen of Hyderabad', in Vasudha Dalmia and Heinrich von Stietencron (eds), *Representing Hinduism: The Construction of Religious Traditions and National Identity*, New Delhi/Thousand Oaks/London: Sage Publications, pp. 338–57.

Anderson, Benedict (1991), *Imagined Communities: Reflections on the Origin and Spread of Nationalism*, rev. edn, London/New York: Verso.

Brass, Paul R. (1974), *Language, Religion and Politics in North India*, Cambridge: Cambridge University Press.

———— (1977), 'A Reply to Francis Robinson', *Journal of Commonwealth and Comparative Politics*, Vol. 15, No. 3, pp. 231–4.

———— (1979), 'Elite Groups, Symbol Manipulation and Ethnic Identity Among the Muslims of South Asia', in D. Taylor and M. Yapp (eds), *Political Identity in South Asia*, London: Curzon Press.

Coupland, R. (1943), *Indian Politics 1936–1942*, London: Oxford University Press, and Indian Statutory Commission [Chairman, Sir John Simon], Vol. 1, London: HMSO, 1930.

Datta, Pradip Kumar (1993), 'Dying Hindus: Production of Hindu Communal Common Sense in Early 20th Century Bengal', *Economic and Political Weekly*, Vol. 28, No. 25, pp. 1305–25.

Gilmartin, David (1979), 'Religious Leadership and the Pakistan Movement in the Punjab', *Modern Asian Studies*, Vol. 13, No. 3, pp. 485–517.

———— (1988), *Empire and Islam: Punjab and the Making of Pakistan*, Berkeley: University of California Press.

Gwyer, Sir Maurice and A. Appadurai (eds) (1957), *Speeches and Documents on the Indian Constitution 1921-47*, Vol. 2, Bombay: Oxford University Press.

Hardy, Peter (1972), *The Muslims of British India*, Cambridge: Cambridge University Press.

Hasan, Mushirul (1997), *Legacy of a Divided Nation: India's Muslims Since Independence*, London: Hurst and Company.

Irshick, Eugene F. (1975), 'Interpretations of Indian Political Development', *Journal of Asian Studies*, Vol. 34, No. 2, pp. 461–72.

Jalal, Ayesha (1985), *The Sole Spokesman: Jinnah, the Muslim League and the Demand for Pakistan*, Cambridge: Cambridge University Press.

Jeffrey, Roger and Patricia Jeffrey (1994), 'The Bijnor Riots of October 1990: Collapse of a Mythical Special Relationship', *Economic and Political Weekly*, 5 March, pp. 551–8.

Jinnah, Quaid-i-Azam Muhammad (1962), *Speeches as Governor-General of Pakistan*, Karachi: Ministry of Information and Broadcasting, Government of Pakistan.

Krishna, Gopal (1985), 'Communal Violence in India: A Study of Communal Disturbances in Delhi—I', *Economic and Political Weekly*, Vol. 20, No. 2, pp. 61–74.

Low, D.A. (1968), 'Introduction', in D.A. Low (ed.), *Soundings in Modern South Asian History*, Berkeley: University of California Press, pp. 1–24.

Moore, Robin (1983), 'Jinnah and the Pakistan Demand', *Modern Asian Studies*, Vol. 17, No. 4, pp. 529–61.

Muhammad, Shan (ed.) (1983), *The Indian Muslims: A Documentary Record*, Vol. 6, Meerut: Meenakshi Prakashan.

Mujeeb, Muhammad (1967), *The Indian Muslims*, London: George Allen & Unwin.

Mushir-ul-Haq (1985), 'The Authority of Religion in Indian Muslim Politics', in Mushirul Hasan (ed.), *Communal and Pan-Islamic Trends in Colonial India*, Second edn, New Delhi: Manohar.

Redfield, Robert, (1960), *The Little Community and Peasant Society and Culture*, Chicago: Chicago University Press.

Robinson, Francis (1974), *Separatism Among Indian Muslims: The Politics of the United Provinces' Muslims, 1860–1923*, Cambridge: Cambridge University Press.

——— (1977), 'Nation-Formation: the Brass Thesis and Muslim Separatism', *Journal of Commonwealth and Comparative Politics*, Vol. 15, No. 3, pp. 215–30.

——— (1985), 'Islam and Muslim Separatism: A Historiographical Debate', in Mushirul Hasan (ed.), *Communal and Pan-Islamic Trends in Colonial India*, Second edn, New Delhi: Manohar.

——— (2000), *Islam and Muslim History in South Asia*, New Delhi: Oxford University Press.

Sarkar, Sumit (1983), *Modern India 1885–1947*, Madras: Macmillan India.

Sayeed, Khalid bin (1968), *Pakistan: The Formative Phase, 1857–1948*, London: Oxford University Press.

Shaikh, Farzana (1989), *Community and Consensus in Islam: Muslim Representation in Colonial India, 1860–1947*, Cambridge: Cambridge University Press.

Thursby, G.R. (1975), *Hindu–Muslim Relations in British India: A Study of Controversy, Conflict, and Communal Movements in Northern India 1923–1928*, Leiden: E.J. Brill.

Turner, Victor (1974), *Dramas, Fields and Metaphors: Symbolic Action in Human Society*, Ithaca: Cornell University Press.

2

Islam, Irrigation, and Religious Identity
Canal Colonies and Muslim Revivalism in Multan

DIEGO ABENANTE

The roles of Sufi saints in the formation of local communities' identity in the subcontinent has been one of the main preoccupations of recent scholarship on Islam in South Asia (Gilmartin 1984; Ansari 1992; Liebeskind 1998; Rao 1990, 1999; Eaton 1984; Sikand 2000). In the Punjab, this line of research has often interacted with the study of colonial rule and its connections with the rural power structure (Gilmartin 1988; Talbot 1988a, 1988b). This article aims, firstly, to emphasize the connections between the Muslim shrines and the territory in the region of Multan, in south-western Punjab, and secondly, to assess the way in which the colonial presence, by inducing change in the ecological and social configuration of the territory, influenced the development of Muslim religious identity in the district. We wish also to suggest that the overall effect of British policy on the rural structure in the Punjab was not only one of protecting and safeguarding existing institutions, as has often been assumed. It can be argued that in more 'marginal' territories, as in Multan, the process of change was particularly evident. The reasons lie basically in the peculiar ecological and social conditions that made the rural society in Multan different from what the British considered ideal. The role of irrigation as a factor of social and economic change in the Punjab has been emphasized by existing studies (Ali 1988; Gilmartin 1994, 2003). The influence of such processes on religious practice, however, has not received sufficient attention. Factors such as expansion of cultivation, settlement by agriculturists coming from different districts, sedentarization of pastoral tribes, and their effects on the models of religious styles still require historical analysis.

THE SETTING

The rich tradition of Sufi shrines of Multan must be understood in the light of its pre-Islamic history. The city has been for centuries a centre of Hindu pilgrimage, due to the presence of two famous *mandir*s, the 'Temple of the Sun' and the Prahladpuri temple. Two of the main shrines, those of Shaikh Bahawal Haq Zakariya (d. 1262) and Shah Rukn-i Alam (d. 1335), were built near the mandirs, the holiest places of the Hindu town. This indicates not only the Islamic tendency to occupy symbolically important sites in the conquered territory, but also that the Muslim shrines partly recaptured the Hindu religious tradition that made Multan a place of pilgrimage.

During the reign of the emperor Aurangzeb (1658–1707), Multan was the capital of one of the main *subah*s (provinces) of the empire, comprising southern Punjab, part of eastern Baluchistan, and northern Sindh. Among the many Sufi traditions of Multan, three *dargah*s (shrines) stand out for their social and historical roles. Two of them belong to old established Sufi lines: the Suhrawardiya, represented in Multan by Bahawal Haq, but also by the numerous smaller shrines of disciples and relatives of the founder saint spread over the surrounding territory (Chand 1884: 62–84; Multani 1980); the Qadiri line, descended from Muhammad Ghaus of Uch (d. 1517), embodied in Multan by the shrine of Musa Pak Shahid Gilani (ca. 1534–92). The third tradition was represented by a saint, Shah Yussuf Gardezi (d. 1136), who was not apparently connected to any specific Sufi line. Still the memory of the saint was important for the religious identity of the Muslim population, being traditionally considered the first saint to have settled in the place. The Muslim quarters of the city were supposed to have been built around his tomb, near the old bed of the river Ravi.

Two shrines in particular, those of Shaikh Bahawal Haq and Musa Pak, stood out for having connections beyond the limits of the district, the former's influence extending towards Sindh—where Bahawal Haq had most of his disciples—and the latter having mainly a Baluchi and Pathan audience, gathered around the traditional Qadiri stronghold of Uch, and north-west in the Derajat.[1,2] These two shrines consequently attracted most of the disciples from outside the district, and it was due largely to them that Multan had acquired its importance.

A distinction must be made, however, between two models of religious style (Eaton 1984: 335–6). While the sajjada nashins in Multan continued to initiate disciples into their respective *silsilas* (the 'chain' of succession of a Sufi brotherhood), a parallel style developed that placed the giving of amulets and the cure of disease, at the centre of the ritual religious mediation. This model was centred on the belief that the *barakat* (divine blessing) of the dead saint did not disappear after his death and transferred to his tomb and his living descendants. The blessing of the saint was not homogeneously distributed among his family, but concentrated in certain individuals, the custodians of the shrines, who were also the representative of the saint on earth, the sajjada nashins. Therefore, in Punjab as in many Muslim societies, folk Islam was connected to a set of beliefs in the embodiment of barakat in human beings.[3]

Another important point relates to the connection between the shrines and the ecology of the region. The territory of Multan was characterized by a pattern of human settlement profoundly influenced by the course of the rivers. Most of the villages and the settled world were situated in the riverain areas (*hithar*), while the so-called *bar* or *rawa* lands (the arid highlands at the centre of the *doabs*) were, in the pre-colonial era, largely uncultivated and used for grazing and pastoralism. The interdependence between the settled and nomadic worlds was a prime reason for the relevance of the saints and their shrines (Eaton 1984: 342). The interaction of the nomadic pastoral tribes of the bar with the settled population was motivated by the need to exchange the products of pasturage, as well as by the pilgrimages to the dargahs. As nineteenth- and early twentieth-century sources testify, the *urs*—the celebrations in memory of a deceased saint—were particularly relevant for the interaction between these social groups in the district. In the second half of the nineteenth century, forty-six Muslim festivals were recorded by a local historian (Chand 1884: 513–14). Besides those of Multan city, there were important celebrations at Sher Shah, Makhdum Rashid, and Jalalpur Pirwala; here the religious nature of the event coincided with secular and commercial functions. There were festivals that had become famous as places where 'young camels from Bikanir (sic) and Bahawalpur' could be purchased (*Gazetteer of the Multan District*, 1923–4, 1990: 139; henceforth. *GMD*). The shrines' festivals, therefore, were particularly important for the pastoralists.

Such a role must have been functional in turning the territory of Multan from Hindu to Islamic. Connections between the dargahs and the tribes of the region, represented by traditions of conversion to Islam through the preaching of Muslim saints—generally identified with Baba

Farid, Shaikh Bahawal Haq, Shaikh Musa Pak, or Shah Gardezi—are frequent in the popular biographies that are sold to this day around the shrines of Multan (Chand 1884). Historical evidence shows that it would not be correct to regard these traditions as merely symbolic. There is ample evidence indicating the relevance of the saints for the religious identity of the rural population. The connections between the tribes and the holy families were crystallized in the toponymy of the villages. Between 1885 and 1900, Edward Maclagan (n.d.) observed that the Sufi saints were frequently recorded in local memory as founders or even as purchasers of villages, a fact that he correctly interpreted as a representation of spiritual authority rather than proprietary right.

However, the *pirs* of Multan were not to be considered as purely spiritual leaders. In south-western Punjab, the figure of the sajjada nashin tended to show a particular emphasis on the political aspect, as compared to other South Asian contexts. This is symbolically indicated by the local traditions in which the saints of Multan are depicted as having a spiritual but also a political control over the territory. Sometimes the pir appears as the 'patron saint' who saves the city from plunder through intercession, as in the case of Bahawal Haq, who apparently protected the city from the Mongol invasions in the thirteenth century. In other cases, the figure of the pir can be seen leading an army in battle or fighting against dacoits to protect his own disciples, as in the case of Musa Pak (Chand 1884: 81–3; *GMD* 1990: 32). But besides hagiography, substantial historical records testify to the activity of many pirs in politics. The most relevant example is that of the Suhrawardis, who played a role in the medieval period (Nizami 1957). The roles continued until more recent times also. In the Indus Valley, Sufi leaders frequently tended to transcend the spiritual field to fill the political vacuum left by a distant Muslim state (Ansari 1992: 9–35; Gilmartin 1988: 39–46).

The mixed political–spiritual authority of the saints of Multan was also evident from their emphasis on religious and 'caste' hierarchy. All the long-established Sufi traditions of Multan belonged to *sharif* families, generally Sayyid, Qureshi, or, in the case of the more recent Chishti Nizami, Pathan. These families, together with the Baluchis, represented the upper level of Muslim society, in Multan as elsewhere. They came to develop a distinctive culture, through the adoption of a lifestyle that emphasized a 'high' Islamic standard. The saint in the Indus Valley maintained his spiritual authority also by 'keeping the distance' from his *murids* (Ansari 1992: 46).

As is often the case, Muslim high culture in Multan had a strict connection with the Law. The sharif families declared to follow the *shari'a*, particularly in the matter of family law. Interestingly enough, the only point on which they all declared to follow the 'customary law', was the field of succession. Women usually did not receive their share of the assets; moreover, the person who became sajjada nashin would normally receive a larger share of the land—one-third to half—than his brothers (Emerson 1924: 13, 54, 74). This practice was generally justified with the sajjada nashin's need to maintain an image that emphasized the divine blessing. A further point was the adherence to strict marriage rules, which characterized mainly the Sayyid families, who followed a policy of intermarriage. For example, the Gilani Sayyids of Multan and the Sayyids of Sher Shah, sajjada nashins of the shrine of Shah Ali Muhammad, were connected through both spiritual and marriage relationships. But strict links existed also between the Pathans and the sajjada nashins. In this case, as usual, marriage symbolized political and religious submission, and went frequently together with spiritual affiliation. *Piri–muridi* links were established in the fifteenth century between the Makhdum Gilani and the Nawab Langah of Multan, and more recently between the Gilanis and the Saddozais, who were Nawabs of Multan between 1752 and 1818.[4]

As noted above, pirs were not the only members of the 'high' Islamic society in Multan. Baluchi presence in Multan went back to the mid-fourteenth century, and was connected to a long-term interaction between Baluchistan, the Derajat, and the Indus Valley. Moreover, an ancient and stable Afghan presence in Multan was connected to the trade route that passed through the city, which was used by Afghan merchants, mainly Rohilla. Apart from this community, the Afghan settlement in Multan originated with the Pathan tribes that had migrated in the sixteenth and seventeenth centuries, following the many Turko-Afghan warriors who invaded India.

At the other end of Muslim Multani society were Hindu tribes and castes, mainly Jat and Rajput, who had converted to Islam. Many of these were tribal groups of Sindhi origin that had established themselves in south-western Punjab, as had the Siyals who dominated the territory on the lower Ravi, between Jhang and Multan. Further south, in the bar lands of the Mailsi and Kabirwala *tehsils*, Langrial, Hirraj, and Singana were the dominant nomadic or semi-nomadic tribes, and the Joyas on the southern course of the Sutlej. Langah, Thahim, and Traggar were present along the Ravi in the Shujabad tehsil. While many of these tribes in the nineteenth century appeared to have settled in great numbers, founding the riverain villages, the tribes inhabiting the bar, although converted to Islam, had not yet made, or not completely, their transition to a settled way of life.[5] Therefore, almost to a large extent, the difference between hithar and bar or riverain and highlands corresponded to one between settled and nomadic or semi-nomadic worlds. This pattern was maintained largely unchanged, despite pressures from the British, until the end of the second half of the nineteenth century (Abenante 2002: 25, 2006: 104–6).

THE BRITISH AND THE CONTROL OF THE TERRITORY

The British annexation of Multan in 1849 brought, here as elsewhere, the colonial attempt to order the structure of landownership. With the Land Settlement, however, the British did not merely record land rights and collect revenue, but also tried to modify the local rural structure. The idea of 'village community' was soon to become the key concept in Multan (Gilmartin 2004: 9–13. Also see Abenante, 2004: 104–12). This idea was considered important not only because the officials who were sent to the region came from the North-Western Provinces, where the concept had been put into practice (Douie 1930: 8), but also because, since the early Summary Settlements, the British were convinced that in Multan the ordinary peasants and the bigger zamindars lacked the necessary spirit to become the backbone of the province, as was the case in the eastern and northern districts of the Punjab. According to Edward Maclagan, Settlement Officer in Multan between 1885 and 1900, the Multani peasant was:

. . . more self-centred and, at the same time, less alert and less industrious than the ordinary Punjabi. The Multani peasant lives on a well and not in a large village, and he marries a neighbour and not a woman from a distant district. He never enlists, and sees nothing of any district but his own. He has therefore a distrust of strangers.... He has little public spirit, and seldom looks at any one's interest but his own.... The richer men have no idea of spending money on works of public utility.... The inhabitant of Multan, though capable of exertion for a time, is, as a rule, easily discouraged. His efforts are by fits and starts; long continued energy is unknown to him; and he has not the instinct of discipline which mark (sic) the Jat of the Central Punjab (*GMD* 1923–4: 142).

The concept of village community, therefore, was not merely an administrative procedure intended to improve the revenue of the district. It was a way to build a 'community of interest'. Despite the fact that the villages in Multan were present only in the riverain areas, apart from a few collections of scattered houses in the bar near the wells, the view that the British administrators had of the lower Bari Doab was that there should be 'village communities', and that these should form the basis of the revenue administration in the Multan region.

The village communities in the Punjab were defined by Richard Tupper at the end of the 1890s as 'groups of families bound together by the tie of descent from a common ancestor' (Roe and Rattigan 1895: 8). The idea was that the population residing in a certain territory was bound by blood ties and common interests. Therefore, the people had to be made collectively responsible for the collection of revenue. The land was thus divided into artificial units, called *mauzah*, to which a collective responsibility was attributed. However, the existence of these communities in Multan was more imaginary than real, due to the ecological characteristics of the region. The Commissioner, G. W. Hamilton, in 1860, warned the provincial government of 'the non-existence of village communities, and the incoherent nature of the subordinate fiscal divisions'.[6] However the government, while admitting the non-existence of these communities, emphasized the need to create them.

I am glad to find that along the rivers, where population and cultivation have attained a large degree of permanence, 'common land' exists and regular communities: here we have proof, that there is nothing in the physical features of the country, or in the customs of the people, to render this development impossible. As we retire from the River and approach the Bar, or barren dorsal ridge, we lose all trace of these communities. Each well has its separate owner unconnected with its neighbour interest, or homestead, no ties of race, religion, or kindred.[7]

There was a sense that the creation of the communites had to be the 'natural' evolution of the Multan society. The individualistic stage at which the rural people of Multan lived was for some a sort of first step on the way of civilization. The Financial Commissioner R. N. Cust in fact wrote that:

. . . these people are the pioneers of civilization, the squatters in the primeval forest. Gradually, however, the ramparts of a municipality will be formed round them; we have now given them a defined village area, and a joint property in the jungle, to the exclusion of others . . . the ties of fellowship and mutual advantage will draw them together; the law of joint responsibility will bring with it the right of preemption. As cultivation, population, and wealth extend, these infant

communities will develop themselves on one of the well known types.... Such
has been the mode by which in the old settled tracts of the Gangetic valley, the
village community has come into existence....[8]

However, trying to define a territory in terms of common property
for a community 'to the exclusion of others' in an area where grazing
areas were so scanty that the cattle had to 'wander over wide tracts in
search of food' (Douie 1930: 76), did not only go against any evidence
of the lifestyle and ecology of the area, but also entailed the danger of
creating conflict in the society. It was a situation similar to the Kashmiri
context analysed by Aparna Rao (1999: 64–5), where common access to
resources was restricted by the colonial intervention.

In any case, despite the government's wishes, the village communities
did not become the characteristic of the Multan territory. The communities, apart from the riverain, where the villages had existed since precolonial times, remained only a revenue administrative subdivision,
without creating a community of interest, or a common identity, as the
British had hoped:

In the tracts near the rivers ... are found regular village communities.... Away
from the rivers the villages are generally merely a collection of wells, which have
been sunk in the neighbourhood of a canal or in the more favourable spot in the
high lands (*GMD* 1990: 231).

It is interesting to note, however, that, in the colonial mind, the Sufi
shrines could become an instrument to build 'common identities' in the
localities. During the administrative processes with which, in the late
nineteenth century, the British recorded the confirmation—or resumption—of *jagirs* or *muafi* attached to the shrines, particular attention was
given to the social life of every institution. The British tried to assess if
the shrine was in fact at the centre of the local villagers' or pastoral tribes'
life. This would confirm the tendency by the British to see the dargahs as
the nucleus of local identities (Gilmartin 1988: 49), but would also suggest
a long-term process towards the 'secularization' of the shrines under the
colonial government (Ewing 1997: 49).

TIRNI AND JAGIRS: THE BRITISH AND THE ENCOURAGEMENT
OF SETTLED LIFE

While the attempt to create village communities was not successful, a
further attempt to modify the rural social structure was made through

the claims to revenue-free grants that after annexation were forwarded to the government. Apart from the various cases of exemption from the payment of land revenue—known as jagir or muafi—a further model of patronage was exemption from *tirni* (grazing tax). These grants were usually quite old, many of them originating from Mughal *sanad*s, and testified to the relevance of pastoralism in the south-western Punjab economy.

Between the 1850s and the 1880s, the British had to analyse a great number of claims for the confirmation of tirni grants. The tendency was towards a reduction of the grants. The official reasons were usually the lack of written evidence or the possible falsification of the documents by the claimants. Although interviews with witnesses were part of the process, and these often confirmed the claims, little value was given to them; oral testimony always succumbed to written evidence. For example, in the 1850s, cases were recorded for two Hindu families—entered as 'nomads' (*khanabadosh*)—both of whom claimed tirni grants for various numbers of camels. Both grants, according to the claimants, had been conceded by the former Diwan Sawan Mal (1821–44), and this was confirmed by the witnesses. Nevertheless, both were resumed due to lack of the original sanad. In another case, the Langrials, one of the most powerful semi-nomadic tribes of the bar in the Mailsi tehsil, applied for the confirmation of a tirni grant for more than 300 animals. Even in this case, the British seemed reluctant to concede it. Although the incumbents had documentary evidence of the grant, the Deputy Commissioner proposed the resumption of the grant, on the basis of the rather strange argument that the grant was 'not in favour of a shrine or temple'. However, in this case the influence of the tribe led the Commissioner to go against his subordinate's view and confirm the grant for the life of the incumbent.[9]

From the 1880s onwards, the British authorities in Multan tended to confirm the grazing grants only for the life of the incumbent, and in case the importance of the family suggested confirmation in perpetuity, to resume the tirni grant and to replace it with a grant in land.[10] This policy cannot be explained in terms of a decrease in the importance of pastoralism. Instead, the high number of tirni grants enjoyed by landed—not nomadic—families confirms that in Multan the modes of subsistence were mixed to a considerable extent. The Khakwani Pathans, who since their migration to the Punjab had led a sedentary life and had become one of the most important landed Muslim families in south-western Punjab, enjoyed a tirni grant conceded in Mughal times for pasturage of a hundred camels. Many saintly families also enjoyed grants for pasturage of their cattle. The offering of animals by the murids to the shrines' custodians was customary in Multan.[11] In this case there were different strategies; some pirs kept the cattle, while others sold them to the market. The family of the Makhdums of Sher Shah, for example, were denied by the British the confirmation of their grant on the basis that they used to sell the animals received by the murids after a few months, instead of keeping them.[12]

Moreover, in the early twentieth century, about 48 per cent of the territory of Multan fell under the category of 'uncultivable waste'. In the uplands, according to the official records, land was 'a grazing ground for sheep and a browsing ground for goats and camels' (*GMD* 1990: 144; Douie 1930: 76). Furthermore, we have enough evidence to suggest that different sectors of the society tended to maintain pastoralism as a favoured activity. Between 1917 and 1921, the British recorded the high incomes derived from the selling of animals and their products, a fact that led a British observer to note that 'the people have evidently a considerable fund of untaxed resources in their cattle and other stock' (*Settlement Report* 1921: 14). If, therefore, pastoralism and breeding were so important in the life of the district, we would argue that the reduction of grazing tax benefits by the British to the families and tribes of the district signalled the colonial interest in reducing the access to resources for pastoral nomadism in the district, encouraging instead settled life and agriculture. In any case, the permanence of a 'pastoral spirit' in the character of the Multani peasants was something about which the British kept complaining throughout the period under consideration. According to one Report for 1921, the Multani tenants were 'in general ... but poor cultivators: their hearts are still given to their cattle rather than to their crops' (*Settlement Report* 1921: 2). This difficulty faced by the British in enforcing a different pattern of economic activity will be part of the background of the large-scale irrigation projects of the late nineteenth and early twentieth centuries.

THE BAR AND THE IRRIGATION PROJECTS

As we have seen, the Multan bar was a high and mostly arid region, which extended from the southern part of the Jhang and Montgomery districts to the confluence of the Sutlej and Chenab rivers, south of Multan city. It was a region that was populated mostly by nomadic or semi-nomadic tribes judged by the British to be generally 'unreliable' and 'predatory'. The area had not significantly changed despite previous attempts at artificial irrigation made during the Mughal period (Abenante 2002). In the early eighteenth century, cultivation in Multan was still limited to the fertile hithar lands. A partial extension of the cultivation towards the bar began many years later under the Nawabs of Multan and Bahawalpur in the mid-eighteenth century, probably due to the political autonomy enjoyed by the Nawabs with the passage of the sovereignty from the Mughal to the Afghan kingdom (*GMD* 1990: 187–202; Durrani 1981: 165–8).

The canals can be divided approximately into two categories: one, those from the Chenab, in the north, were generally constructed by Pathan chiefs for irrigating the lands of their own jagirs; and second, the canals from the Sutlej were almost all excavated by the Daudpotras of Bahawalpur, except for the Ghulamwah, constructed by Ghulam Muhammad Daultana, the Diwanwah, by Diwan Sawan Mal, and the Hajiwah, by Ghulam Mustafa Khan Khakwani. In general, the pre-colonial canals did not have the scope to irrigate the bar lands but rather to improve the cultivation along the villages that were too much dependent on the natural floods. Two relevant exceptions were the said Diwanwah and Hajiwah. With these two canals, for the first time, a partial cultivation into the bar was introduced. But in these cases the canals created tensions with the nomadic tribes of the area reached by the water.[13] Despite the canals of the mid-eighteenth century, the ecological structure of the territory did not change. At the beginning of colonial rule, it was still possible to distinguish the fertile strips of irrigated areas along the rivers, mostly inhabited by settled Jat tribes, and the arid, basically uncultivable lands at the centre of the doabs, inhabited by nomadic or semi-nomadic tribes (Douie 1930: 76).

The uncultivated areas were not economically profitable for the British: the lands paid little as revenue and the grazing tax paid was considered 'insignificant' by a British officer in the early nineteenth century. Furthermore, the tribes of the bar were not useful for the military needs (Wikeley 1915). This was an important cause of complaint by the British against the Multani population in general, and at the same time marked an important point of difference between the south-west and the other districts of the Punjab, where the peasants were the backbone of the colonial army. The only tribes that in the early nineteenth century were entered for recruitment were those Pathan tribes, as the Khakwanis and the Badozais, with which the British had had close connections since the

1849 war.[14] However, the members of these tribes used to enlist as officers of élite Cavalry and Camel corps, not as infantry troops. The hostility of the British towards the tribes of the bar was expressed clearly during the Mutiny, when British officers feared that the tribes could join the insurrection. According to a British officer, 'the predatory clans inhabiting the Bar . . . from time immemorial had been addicted to robbery and cattle-lifting, and under former Governments had repeatedly broken out in insurrection'. During the Mutiny some of the chiefs were detained as de facto hostages by the Deputy Commissioner in Multan, in order to avoid the feared insurrection (*Mutiny Records* 1911: 9–10).

As already noted, British criticism was strong not only against the nomadic tribes, but in general towards the rural Multan society, including the zamindars. These were considered to hold too large areas of land, and as being generally less efficient than those of the rest of the Punjab. To be fair, some British observers admitted the peculiar conditions of the frontier regions. Malcolm Darling (1925: 95), for example, wrote that in Multan 'insecurity dominates everything'—insecurity of the crop, insecurity of the property. Only persons with strong economic and military means would be able to protect their holdings. This fact had favoured the concentration of land rights on vast territories in the hands of few families, generally belonging to high strata of the society (Hunter 1886: 2–13). The criticism of the zamindars also involved their lifestyle, which was criticized for being 'careless' and 'extravagant'.

To sum up, the motives behind the decision by the British to colonize the bar in the Multan territory in the late nineteenth century were various: improving the revenue by putting new land into cultivation; settling the tribes inhabiting the lands; and integrating the indigenous peasants with cultivators coming from more 'efficient' Punjabi districts.

Before starting the project of the Canal Colonies, the British had begun, since the mid-nineteenth century, to amalgamate the existing canals. In the 1860s, there were 34 canals in the district: 20 from the Sutlej and 14 from the Chenab. These had become 13 in 1880, and were further reduced to 9 in 1900. The declared aim was that of having a more regular flux of water but 'the net result was to benefit the small rather than the large owner who has had to economize in the use of water' (*GMD* 1990: 189). In this case, apparently, a first step was made towards reducing the power of the bigger zamindar over the smaller landowners.

The Sidhnai Colony, the first large-scale irrigation project to be realized in Multan, was excavated on the Ravi river between 1883 and 1886, and covered an area of about 250,000 acres (*GMD* 1990: 196; Ali 1988: 14). The project was based on plots of land of 90 acres each, which were still relatively large compared to the pattern of land prevalent in the northern and eastern districts—of around 5–6 acres—as well as compared to other colonies like Shahpur and Lyallpur (Darling 1925: 117, 121). It is likely that the British in the late nineteenth century did not want to break too radically the existing pattern of landed property, while acknowledging the need for its gradual revision. Of these plots, about half went to colonists from other districts, generally Jats and Rajputs from Amritsar and Jullundur.

With the Lower Bari Doab Colony, realized between 1914 and 1924, about 60 per cent of the land went to colonists from outside and from the same Multani population, while 8 per cent was sold by auction and 32 per cent was reserved for 'special objects'. The Lower Bari Doab Colony extended over the districts of Multan and Montgomery for a total area of about 900,000 acres, partly irrigated from the Ravi and partly from the Chenab (*GMD* 1990: 201; Ali 1988: 29–30). Later these two districts also accomodated the Nili Bar Colony, started in 1926 and completed in the 1940s (Ali 1988: 38).

The colonization projects brought great changes in the district in the late nineteenth and early twentieth centuries. From an economic point of view, as in other regions of the Punjab, the extension of irrigation generally brought a benefit for those who owned land. There was a sharp increase both in the value of the crops and that of land. According to the data for 1917–21, the average rise in the crops' price was between 33 and 42 per cent (*Settlement Report* 1921: 20). The same happened for land: sales prices more than doubled in the Multan district between the 1890s and the 1920s. In the Multan tehsil alone it grew four times from the level of 1896 (*Settlement Report* 1921: 4). However, these benefits did not go to all. They went in particular to those fortunate enough to be able to buy—or to obtain as jagirs—lands in the new irrigated area in the doabs. The picture was different for the lesser zamindars and peasant proprietors who owned lands in the riverain areas, the hithar territory that in south-western Punjab had been the most fertile lands, where most of the Jat tribes of the district had settled. Now these lands would enjoy a much reduced quantity of water to grow their crops. Paradoxically, it was just in the few lands of Multan that resembled the small 'peasant proprietor' British ideal that the negative effects of the irrigation projects were mostly felt. According to S. S. Thorburn, in a few years 'for a depth of thirty miles on either side of the canal-irrigated country, wells were abandoned'. Many were forced to leave their land and migrate towards the newly irrigated land to work as 'farm-labourers, artisans, and menials' and 'numbers of previously well-to-do peasants and yeomen families were reduced to want' (Thorburn 1986: 283). There is evidence of British anxiety over the problem, and the complaints against the government were not slow to come.

The problem emerged, for the first time, with the construction of the Sidhnai in 1884, when the zamindars of the riverain villages on the Ravi complained to the government about the effects of the canal on the irrigation of their land. Though the British tried to play down these complaints they admitted that the complaints were well founded and that 'the prosperity of the villages concerned would be affected by the emigration of the cultivators to the more favoured tracts commanded by the new canal ... it was undesirable that these villages, which were not at their best in a very flourishing condition, should be reduced to greater straits by the opening of the Sidhnai canal' (Thorburn 1986: 197).

The government reacted by excavating three minor canals between 1890 and 1891, in order to improve the irrigation of these areas (Ibid.: 197–8). Nevertheless, the negative consequences of the opening of the canals kept coming to the surface in many areas of the Punjab. In 1899, the Financial Commissioner of the Punjab wrote that 'the complaints of failure of Sailab[15] ... come not only from Gujranwala and Jhang, but also from Shahpur, Mooltan and other Districts bordered by the great rivers.... The popular idea is that the diminution of Sailab is due to the canals'.[16] In the south-west, the complaints appeared to be serious. In May 1900, J. Wilson, Settlement Commissioner of the Punjab, admitted that the opening of the canals was in fact reversing the old pattern of cultivation and pasturage and that the old inhabited villages were 'rapidly falling into decay'. Wilson went straight to the problem:

besides stopping the flow of the rivers which was the main source of their prosperity, we have also given over to colonists from a distance the great stretches of waste land which from time immemorial have formed grazing grounds for the cattle of the riverain villages, and because the greater advantages of canal irrigation in the uplands have tempted anyway large numbers of their tenants and thrown their wells out of work and their lands out of cultivation.[17]

The Punjab government seemed more concerned to avoid the possibility that the zamindars would attribute the diminished sailab to the government canals, by giving them a credible explanation, rather than really improving the irrigation of the riverain.[18]

There appeared to be a growing dissatisfaction among the Muslim tenants' and smaller zamindars' community in the last years of the nineteenth century. Many of them had to leave their villages and move up to the *rawa* and bar lands in search of jobs. Many of the bigger proprietors too were dissatisfied because they were losing their cultivators who moved to the more favourable tract in the newly irrigated lands.[19] However, in the irrigated lands the immigrants would find colonists from the central and eastern districts of the Punjab, the ones the British considered 'the most industrious castes and tribes' of the province (Ibid.: 282). Here there would be more competition for jobs among cultivators. It is no surprise, therefore, that in the second decade of the twentieth century the statistics for the density of population in the cultivated areas of the district show higher numbers for the irrigated uplands, than for the riverain. Of course, this is not to say that the configuration of the bar had changed completely. In fact the hithar still had a much superior density of population in absolute terms (196 persons per square mile against 22). Still the number of residents per square mile of cultivated land was superior in the bar (635 to 565).

We might reasonably argue that here lies a basic contradiction of the British policy of irrigation in the south-western Punjab. Aimed at creating 'communities of the best Punjab type' and reforming rural society in Multan by building a new cooperative identity, it had the consequence of making the local communities increasingly fragmented socially and weakened economically. It also dangerously spread dissatisfaction among the same landed classes that it was aimed to protect. If this were not enough, the tensions deriving from this movement of people from the riverain to the uplands was reinforced soon afterwards by the problem of rural debt. Although the position of the influential landed families was protected by the colonial government with the allotment of land reserved for 'Landed gentry', this did not prevent many of these families from falling into debt. Between the late nineteenth century and the 1920s, for example, some of the Sayyid and Qureshi families in Multan fell into debt and their properties were ultimately taken under the administration of the Court of Wards.[20]

FROM SOCIO-ECONOMIC CHANGE TO RELIGIOUS CHANGE

The period under consideration witnessed a process of monetarization of the rural economy in Multan, and the sajjada nashins themselves, as zamindars, were changing with it. With the greater value accorded to land, the position of the sajjada nashins tended to change from an informal position of authority to one of power. The religious families were encouraged to invest increasing sums of money into irrigated land. There was, it seems, a clear imbalance between lands in jagir or muafi and those in proprietary rights. The branch of the Gardezi family of Salarwahan, for example, which was taken under the management of the Court of Wards in the early twentieth century, in 1910 had more than 6,000 acres of land in the district, paying more than Rs 5,000 as land revenue, but had no jagirs.[21] Other families had considerable jagirs, such as the family of Makhdum Hassan Bakhsh Qureshi, that of Makhdum Shah Ali Muhammad of Sher Shah, or that of the Gardezis of Hamidpur, but in all these cases the value of the land held in proprietary rights was considerably superior.[22]

As the position of the sajjada nashins as zamindars became increasingly marked, also their relationship with the tenants could change. An example is given in the controversy between the Makhdum of Sher Shah and the cultivators of his land. In the case of this family, whose property had been taken under the management of the Court of Wards in 1900, the administration was characterized by a relevant arrears of rent. Apparently, the Makhdum had given the management of the lands to middlemen who had asked for excessive rents, creating a situation of conflict with the population. This case was an eloquent indication of the process of change in the sajjada nashin's authority vis-à-vis the local villagers, from spiritual leadership to economic power.[23] However, the most serious signals of religious change in the district became visible in the 1880s. In these years, the relations between the religious communities in Multan became very tense. In 1881 and 1882, serious riots broke out in Multan city. No doubt, the emergence of communal violence in the late nineteenth century was not unique to Multan nor to the Punjab. However, the peculiarity of these events was the presence of the sajjada nashins at centre stage. Even more significant was the fact that, before this period, there was no evidence of the sajjada nashins in Multan acting as leaders of a single, unified religious community, given that the popular religious culture of the shrines was shared by Muslims and Hindus.

We would suggest that with the gradual advance of settlement and cultivation in the territory of Multan, at the expense of the previous living patterns of pastoralism and limited trade, the social functions of the saints and their shrines changed. While the public rituals of the shrines where largely aimed at mediating the interaction between the settled and the nomadic worlds, this function became less relevant in the late nineteenth and early twentieth centuries. While the relationship between the sajjada nashins and the pilgrims was, for the most, centred upon the pastoralists' needs, from the late nineteenth century onwards the sajjada nashins had an increasingly sedentary audience, made up of villagers, agriculturists, and town dwellers. A consequence of this was a change in the religious significance of the shrines. Urban people were less interested in the traditional *ta'wiz* writing and thaumaturgical activities, and more concerned with a symbolic approach to Islam—a universal and homogeneous approach to religion that transcended the local spiritual traditions.

In the late nineteenth century, some of the sajjada nashins of Multan seemed less interested in behaving as traditional 'mediatory' leaders, while approaching their religious role as Muslim leaders vis-à-vis a homogeneous religious community. Moreover, while the pirs were accumulating a considerable amount of land, their concerns were increasingly those of the zamindars. It was, therefore, not surprising to see the emergence of a growing tension with the Hindu community that—as customary in the Punjab—comprised for the great majority the moneylending class. The pirs were now commonly perceived no longer as the heirs in a chain of succession that went back to the founder–saint and, through him, to the Prophet, but as the embodiment of a common Muslim identity vis-à-vis an aggressive Hindu community. Paradoxically, while the British had been trying to build a sort of collective identity, or 'community of interests', in Multan, this had now indeed come about but in religious–symbolical terms.

The controversies emerged initially as a rivalry between the representatives of the two most important holy places in Multan city: the Makhdum Qureshi, custodian of the two dargahs of Bahawal Haq and Rukn-i Alam and the *mahant* of Prahladpuri.[24] Although the actual controversy took place between July 1880 and October 1881, its roots were inherent in the post-war settlement that had taken place in Multan after the annexation by the British. During the siege of the city, in 1848–9, the buildings had been severely damaged. Therefore, after the war, Makhdum Qureshi had asked for permission to repair the two shrines and for the government to contribute financially. The former request was accorded, while the latter was eventually refused. On the same occasion, the mahant of the nearby temple, Narain Das, had addressed an analogous request to the British authorities. This provoked the opposition of the Makhdum. The final decision of the British authorities, after a complex consultation between civilian and military authorities, and a summary survey into the history of the two buildings, accorded permission to rebuild both the edifices 'to the condition in which they were in the time of Maha Raja Ranjt Singh (*sic*)'. This vague statement would cause further troubles.[25]

Thirty years later, the mahant of the temple requested the British for permission to build a pinnacle over the temple, raising the total height of the mandir. This request was also vigorously opposed by the Makhdum. The final decision by the British was in favour of a compromise that in fact left both parties unsatisfied and frustrated, as the facts would demonstrate later.[26] Both complained that they had been mistreated by the authorities and there is no doubt that all this formed the background for the new and more serious riots that occurred a few weeks later. In April 1881, the controversy in Multan acquired a new, and more symbolic, significance with a question concerning the selling of beef meat in Multan, which provoked serious incidents between Hindus and Muslims, with damages to various mosques and Hindu temples.[27]

The feelings of the Makhdum were evident in a Memorial he wrote to the government in January 1882:

... I suffered much at the hands of the Hindus of Mooltan in connection with the Prahladpuri Mandir. The followers of the deceased Bahawal Haq have become ill-disposed towards me because I silently submitted to the orders of Government raising the height of the temple to 33 feet. This has caused me a great loss in my income. I have no other means, in the shape of a jagir ... to maintain the honor and reputation of my family.[28]

In other words, the Makhdum resented the pressure being exerted on him by his disciples in order to maintain a 'hard line' in the face of the requests of the Hindus. These arguments are an eloquent indication of the changed atmosphere in Multan in the 1880s. The religious communities of Multan were in a process of identity-building that was centred on the places of religious devotion.

The arguments put forward by the Hindu representatives during the disputes are also very interesting. In a long memorial written in July 1881 to the Indian Government, in order to complain of the behaviour of the local authorities, the representatives significantly challenged the legitimacy, in religious terms, of the cult of the saint Bahawal Haq, and in general of the whole cult of Muslim saints, in fact, taking up the argument put forward, in those years, by the Islamic revivalist movements that were taking firm foot in Multan itself:

> ... The temple of Pehladpuri (*sic*) is held by the Hindus of India as an object of great veneration. . . . On the other hand, Bahawal Haq and his tomb have no connection with Muhammadanism (*sic*) as a religion, which does not encourage tomb-worship. The knowledge that such a personage existed a few centuries ago is confined only to a very limited space on this side of India, and had it not been for the fact that his memory is preserved by those who make their living out of it, the name of Bahawal Huq (*sic*) would have, perhaps, long been forgotten.[29]

The tone of the memorial reveals the extent of the penetration of the reformist discourse in the local environment. In fact, the representatives of the 'Panchayat', which represented the Hindus, challenged the legitimacy of the cult of saints, saying that Islam does not accept saint-worship, and charging the sajjada nashin of maintaining the memory of the saint for 'making a living out of it'.

In the following years, Multan continued to be characterized by communal tensions. In September 1922, during Muharram celebrations, riots exploded that continued for various days and were only suppressed after the intervention of the army.[30] In this case, the incidents took place during the passage of a *taziya* procession through a Hindu quarter. It gave way to assaults by Muslims to the residences of Hindu *sahukars* (moneylenders), betraying the economic background of the tensions in the city.

The basic question here, in our view, is how much these developments may be seen as a response to external influences—as with the spread in the district of movements of religious revival and reform—or whether it may be considered a response to local pressures. In this chapter we have suggested, as a possible cause, the transformation brought by the irrigation projects and its consequences in terms of social dislocation. However, we do not want to deny that other elements must be taken into account, as, for example, the development in the region of religious traditions born in reformist environments like the UP or the larger urban Punjabi centres, such as the schools of Deoband and Ahl-i-Hadith. The diffusion of reformist ideas may have influenced the religious atmosphere in the city. The extent of this influence in Multan appears, in particular, from the analysis of the biographies of local *ulama*. In the nineteenth and twentieth centuries, a growing number of ulama appear to have studied in reformist madrasas or to have had contacts with reformist religious centres. The most important school for the Deobandi view was the madrasa Nu'maniya, founded in 1905 thanks to a donation by Nawab Ahmad Yar Khan Khakwani (Kamal Khan 1984: 44). Some of the leading ulama of this school had studied at the Dar-ul-Ulum of Deoband, such as Maulana Faizullah and Maulana Muhammad Ibrahim.[31] Between 1870 and 1880, the Ahl-i-Hadith also extended their influence to Multan. In 1875, a Maktab-i-fikr-i-Ahl-i-Hadith was founded by Maulana Sultan Muhaddith Derwi (d. 1909). His son Abdul Haq Muhaddith Multani (d. 1945), founded in 1910 a Jamiat-i-Ahl-i-Hadith, Multan and, at the same time, reorganized the existing madrasa, renaming it Arabiya Dar-al-Hadith Muhammadiya (Kamal Khan 1984: 51–3). Many of these ulama, such as Maulana Abdul Haq, had studied in the madrasa Ahl-i-Hadith of Delhi (Kamal Khan 1984: 53–4). Moreover, we would argue that the process that saw the pirs acting as leaders of community is to be placed in a context where the pirs actually acted not only as the spiritual 'alter-ego' of the king, but actually as 'little kings', as their titles—Makhdum, Gaddi nashin—clearly indicate.[32] In the comparison between different figures of holy men, therefore, the pirs of Multan never resembled the purely spiritual Sufi saint of other regions of the Muslim world. Their tradition of leadership can help us to explain their readiness to take part in political struggles against any perceived threats.

NOTES

1. The religious influence of the Bahawal Haq shrine on the Sindhi population was so important that, at the time of the provincial elections of 1946, the Muslim League was induced to ask the support of the sajjada nashin, Makhdum Qureshi, for its campaign. The Suhrawardi order had a tremendous importance in the islamization of Sindh. It is considered to be the first Sunni order to challenge the Ismaili dominance over the region (Ansari 1992: 19).

2. The Derajat is the region to the West of the Indus, lying approximately between the British districts of Dera Ismail Khan and Dera Ghazi Khan.

3. Clifford Geertz (1973: 74–8) has defined this model of spiritual intercession as the 'sayyidi complex'.

4. Around 1456, Muhammad Ghaus Gilani became pir of Sultan Qutbuddin Mahmud Langah and married his daughter (Chand 1884: 81–3; Kamal Khan 1995: 165; Zahid Khan 1981: 121).

5. The peculiarity of the pattern of conversion and its connection with sedentarization in Multan have been suggested by Karin De Vries (2001: 9). I have myself reached similar conclusions (Abenante 2002: 25; 2006: 104–6).

6. No. 175, 16 July 1860, G. W. Hamilton, Commissioner and Superintendent, Mooltan Division to Financial Commissioner, Punjab, 'Report of the revised settlement of the Mooltan Division', pp. 13–14.
7. No. 776, 23 August 1860, R. N. Cust, Officiating Financial Commissioner to Secretary to Government, Punjab, Ibid., p. 5.
8. Ibid.
9. 'Register of rent-free holdings for the District Mooltan', 1852–5 ca., File T/ 13, Multan District Record Room (hereafter MDRR).
10. Ibid.
11. For example, Chand (1884: 85–100) writes of offerings of animals and breeding products for the dargahs of Pir Ghaib Bukhari at village Halalvaja, and of Qazi Muhammad Issa at Khanpur, both in the Shujabad tehsil.
12. 'Register of rent-free holdings for the District Mooltan', p. 17.
13. This is true in particular of the Hajiwah, which had been given in administration to the Khakwani family (*GMD* 1990: 193).
14. For details, see Edwardes (1986). In fact, Herbert Edwardes was a staunch supporter of the creation of this relationship between the British and some leading Muslim families of Multan.
15. Under the category *sailab* were classified the lands subject to natural irrigation; in this case, the reference was to the riverain lands along the Chenab, Sutlej, and Ravi.
16. Financial Commissioner, Punjab, 'Review on the Departmental Report of the Direction of Land Records and Agriculture, Punjab, for the year 1898–9', File A-19/42, MDRR.
17. No. 924, 14 May 1900, J. Wilson, Settlement Commissioner, Punjab to W. S. Hamilton, Senior Secretary to Financial Commissioner, Punjab; File A-19/ 42, ibid.
18. Financial Commissioner, Punjab, 'Review', File A-19/42, ibid.
19. Of course we are referring to the small and medium proprietors, those who were not considered 'influential' enough to receive 'landed gentry' grants in the Sidhnai and Lower Bari Doab Colonies. This was the position of some of the most influential sajjada nashins. For example, the Gardezi, Qureshi, and Gilani families obtained respectively 193, 275, and 262 acres in the Lower Bari Doab Colony (Ali 1988: 106).
20. Punjab Government, *Reports on the Administration of Estates Under the Court of Wards in the Punjab*, Lahore, annual publications.
21. Ibid., 1907, 1928.
22. Ibid., 1894, 1919.
23. Ibid., 1915, 1916, 1919.
24. Besides the archival sources, a detailed account of the Multan riots of 1881–2 can be found in Roseberry (1988: 238–70).
25. No. 2380, 16 July 1852, C. Allen, Officiating Secretary to the Government of India to: Board of Administration, General Department ('B') Proceedings, 31 July 1852, no. 62–3, Punjab Secretariat Archives, Lahore (hereafter PSA).

26. The compromise included the construction of a pinnacle of 33 feet instead of 45 feet as requested by the Mahant, and the donation of a nearby well as a compensation to the Makhdum.

27. Among the buildings damaged were the Prahladpuri mandir, the Wali Muhammad masjid, and various 'minor Hindu shrines' (see *Civil and Military Gazette*, Lahore, 24 October 1881; File G-37, October 1881, 'Grants to Religious Shrines', MDRR).

28. 'Petition from Bahawal Bakhsh, Priest of the Bahawal Hak tomb ... dated 28th January 1882', File No. 4, 'Construction of a spire to the Prahladpuri temple at Mooltan', Home Department Proceedings, April 1882, p. 39, P/1818, Oriental and India Office Collection, The British Library, London (hereafter IOL).

29. 'Memorial of Hindu Raises ... to Viceroy', File No. 4, 'Pehladpuri Temple in the fort at Mooltan', Home Department Proceedings, July 1881, p. 501, P/1618, IOL.

30. *Paisa Akhbar*, Lahore, 6–9 September 1922.

31. Maulana Faizullah was a pupil of Maulana Anwar Shah Kashmiri, himself a student of the famous Hadith scholar—and future rector of the madrasa at Deoband—Maulana Mahmud Hasan (1851–1920). Muhammad Ibrahim was a pupil of Maulana Hussein Ahmad Madani (1879–1957), one of the most eminent ulama of Deoband in the twentieth century and nationalist leader (Kamal Khan 1984: 45; Metcalf 1982: 108–10, 133; Robinson 1993: 422).

32. Aparna Rao (1990) has emphasized the role of the pir as a mobilizing figure for the formation of a community.

BIBLIOGRAPHY

PRIMARY SOURCES

Civil and Military Gazette, Lahore, 24 October 1881.
Multan District Record Room, Multan: Deputy Commissioner Files.
Paisa Akhbar, Lahore, 6–9 September 1922.
Punjab Secretariat Archives, Lahore. Punjab Government Proceedings: General Department ('B') Files.
India Office Library and Records, British Library, London: Punjab Government Proceedings: Home Department, 1881, 1882.

SECONDARY SOURCES

Abenante, Diego (2002), 'Cultivation and conversion in Multan', *International Institute for the Study of Islam in the Modern World Newsletter*, Vol. 9, p. 25.

—— (2004), *La colonizzazione di Multan: Islam potere, istituzioni nel Panjab Sudoccidentale* (1848–1922), Trieste: E.U.T.

—— (2006), 'Islamizzazione e "sociologia coloniale": il Panjab tra ottocento e novecento', in Diego Abenante and Elisa Giunchi (eds), *L'Islam in Asia meridionale: identità, interazioni e contaminazioni,* Milano: Franco Angeli, pp. 91–114.

Ali, Imran (1988), *The Punjab Under Imperialism, 1885–1947,* Princeton: Princeton University Press.

Allami, Abul Fazl, 1949 (1891), *Ain-i Akbari,* (Eng. tr.) Calcutta: The Royal Asiatic Society of Bengal.

Ansari, Sarah (1992), *Sufi Saints and State Power: The Pirs of Sind, 1843–1947,* Cambridge: Cambridge University Press.

Chand, Hukum (1884), *Tawarikh-e-zilla-e-Multan,* Lahore.

Copies of Certificates and Testimonials of Makhdum Pir Syed Mohammad Sadr-ud-din Shah, Chief of Gilani (& his ancestors), Sajjada Nashin, Darbar Piran Pir Sahib and Viceregal Darbari, Multan city (n.d.) (private library, Gilani family, Multan).

Darling, Malcolm Lyall (1925), *The Punjab Peasant in Prosperity and Debt,* Lahore: Vanguard.

De Vries, Karin (2001), 'Pirs and Pastoralists Along the Agrarian Frontier of Multan', *International Institute for Asian Studies Newsletter,* Vol. 24, p. 9.

Douie, James M. 1930 (1899), *Punjab Settlement Manual,* Fourth edn, Lahore: Government Printing.

Durrani, Ashiq Muhammad Khan (1981), *Multan Under the Afghans, 1752–1818,* Multan: Bazme Saqafat.

Eaton, Richard Maxwell (1984), 'The Political and Religious Authority of the Shrine of Baba Farid in Pakpattan, Punjab', in Barbara Daly Metcalf (ed.), *Moral Conduct and Authority: The Place of Adab in South Asian Islam,* Berkeley: University of California Press, pp. 333–56.

Edwardes, Herbert B. 1986 (1851), *A Year on the Punjab Frontier in 1848–49,* Vol. II, New Delhi: Nirmal Publishers.

Emerson, H. W. (1924), *Customary Law of the Multan District,* Lahore: Government Printing.

Ewing, Katherine (1997), *Arguing Sainthood: Modernity, Psychoanalysis, and Islam,* Durham: Duke University Press.

Gazetteer of the Multan District, 1923–4, Lahore: Sang-e-Meel Publications, 1990 [1926].

Geertz, Clifford (1973), *Islam observed* (ital. tr.), *Islam: analisi socio-culturale dello sviluppo religioso in Marocco e Indonesia,* Brescia: Morcelliana.

Gilmartin, David (1984), 'Shrines, Succession and Sources of Moral Authority', in Barbara Daly Metcalf (ed.), *Moral Conduct and Authority: The Place of Adab in South Asian Islam,* Berkeley: University of California Press, pp. 221–40.

——— (1988), *Empire and Islam: Punjab and the Making of Pakistan,* Berkeley: University of California Press.

——— (1994), 'Scientific Empire and Imperial Science: Colonialism and Irrigation Technology in the Indus Basin', *The Journal of Asian Studies,* Vol. 53, No. 4, pp. 1127–49.

———— (2003), 'Imperial Rivers: Irrigation and British Visions of Empire', Paper Presented at the Conference on 'How Empire Mattered: Imperial Structures and Globalization in the Era of British Imperialism', 4–5 April, Center for South Asian Studies, University of California, Berkeley, (*http://ias.berkeley.edu/SouthAsia/metfest.htm*).

———— (2004), 'Migration and Modernity: The State, the Punjabi Village, and the Settling of the Canal Colonies', in Ian Talbot and Shinder Thandi (eds), *People on the Move: Punjabi Colonial and Post-Colonial Migration*, Karachi: Oxford University Press, pp. 3–20.

Griffin, Lepel H. and Charles Francis Massy, 1993 (1911), *Chiefs and Families of Note in the Punjab*, Vol. II, Lahore: Sang-e-Meel Publications.

Hunter, William Wilson (1886), *Imperial Gazetteer of India*, Vol. X, Second edn, London.

Jamali, Muhammad Salim (n.d.), *Zohur-e-Jamal*, Multan: Jamal Library.

Kamal Khan, Umar (1984), *Fuqaha-e-Multan*, Multan: Bazme Saqafat.

———— (1995), *Multan Langah dur men*, Multan: Bazme Saqafat.

Kozlowski, Gregory (1985), *Muslim Endowments and Society in British India*, Cambridge: Cambridge University Press.

Latif, Syad Muhammad, 1997 (1891), *History of the Punjab: From the Remotest Antiquity to the Present Time*, Lahore: Sang-e-Meel Publications.

Liebeskind, Claudia (1998), *Piety on its Knees: Three Sufi Traditions in South Asia in Modern Times*, New Delhi: Oxford University Press.

Maclagan, Edward D. (n.d.), 'Notes on Village Names and History' (manuscript, ca.1900, Multan District Record Room).

Maclagan, R. (1848), 'Fragments of the History of Mooltan, the Derajat, and Buhawulpoor, from Persian MSS', *Journal of the Asiatic Society of Bengal*, Part II, Vol. 17, November, pp. 559–72.

Metcalf, Barbara Daly (1982), *Islamic Revival in British India: Deoband, 1860–1900*, Princeton: Princeton University Press.

Morris, J. H. (1860), *Report on the Revised Settlement of the Mooltan Division*, Lahore: Government Printing.

Multani, Farhan (1980), *Awliya-e-Multan*, Multan: Aiyaz Publications.

Mutiny Records, 'Reports', Part II, Lahore: Government Printing, 1911.

Nizami, Kaliq Ahmad (1957), 'The Suhrawardi Silsilah and its Influence on Medieval Indian Politics', *Medieval India Quarterly*, Vol. 3, Nos 1–2, pp. 109–49.

Reports on the Administration of Estates Under the Court of Wards in the Punjab (annual publications), Lahore: Government Printing.

Rao, Aparna (1990), 'Reflections on Self and Person in a Pastoral Community in Kashmir', in Pnina Werbner (ed.), *Person, Myth and Society in South Asian Islam*, Special issue of *Social Analysis*, No. 28, July, pp. 11–25.

———— (1999), 'The Many Sources of an Identity: An Example of Changing Affiliations in Rural Jammu and Kashmir', *Ethnic and Racial Studies*, Vol. 22, No. 1, pp. 56–91.

Robinson, Francis, 1993 (1974), *Separatism Among Indian Muslims: The Politics of the United Provinces' Muslims, 1860–1923*, New Delhi: Oxford University Press.

Roe, Charles Arthur and H. A. B. Rattigan (1895), *Tribal Law in the Punjab*, Lahore: Civil and Military Gazette Press.

Roseberry, Royal (1988), *Imperial Rule in Punjab: The Conquest and Administration of Multan, 1818–1881*, Lahore: Vanguard.

Sarwan, Ghulam, 1987 (1959), *A Descriptive Catalogue of the Oriental Manuscripts in the Durgah Library, Uch Sharif, Bahawalpur State*, Bahawalpur: Urdu Academy.

Schimmel, Annemarie (1975), *Mystical Dimensions of Islam*, Chapel Hill: University of North Carolina Press.

Settlement Report of the Multan District (1921), Lahore: Government Printing, 1921.

Sikand, Yoginder (2000), 'The Sufi Shrines of Jammu', *International Institute for the Study of Islam in the Modern World Newsletter*, Vol. 5, p. 4.

Talbot, Ian (1988a), *Provincial Politics and The Pakistan Movement: The Growth of The Muslim League in North-West and North-East India, 1937–47*, Karachi: Oxford University Press.

——— (1988b), *Punjab and the Raj: 1849–1947*, New Delhi: Manohar.

Thorburn, S. S., (1986), *The Punjab in Peace and War*, New Delhi: Nirmal, [1904].

Wikeley, J. M., 1991 (1915), *The Punjabi Musalmans*, New Delhi: Manohar.

Zahid Khan, Ansar (1981), 'The Role of the Qadiri Sufis in the Religious Life of Sind', in Hamida Khuhro (ed.), *Sind Through the Centuries*, Karachi: Oxford University Press.

3

Idolatry, Syncretism, and Anti-syncretism in Hindu Reform Movements of the Nineteenth Century

HEINZ WERNER WESSLER

ABOUT SYNCRETISM

In his introduction to the study of Hinduism, Axel Michaels (1998: 60ff.) divides the history of Hinduism into six periods. He argues that during the fifth (*ca*.1100–1850) and the sixth periods (since *ca*. 1850), Hinduism is characterized by syncretism, first Islamic–Hindu and then Christian–Hindu. This interpretation follows a common pattern, appearing to be self-explanatory, since Muslim and later Christian administrative and religious domination through the ruling elites must have made some impact on the historic situation, and this impact could not have left classical Hinduism intact. Standard Hinduism, so the interpretation has it, is pre-1100, implying that pure (and antique) forms of Hinduism and mixed forms are historically distinct from each other.

The big divide may be dated sooner or later, but the pattern remains the same. Slaje (2003), for example, is not in favour of the syncretism model for Islamic India before colonization by the East India Company and the impact of English education. He uses the picture of a 'path cut through' (German *Schneise*) to describe the limitations of the impact of Islam before the advent of the British. Osmotic effects between Islam and Hinduism prior to the British conquest do not fit into the picture. On this understanding, they become marginal. In his view, the tradition had remained undisturbed prior to the British presence.[1]

Michaels' interpretation implicitly contains an understanding that the normative phase of Hinduism ended somewhere between Mahmud of Ghazni's series of raids early in the eleventh century and Qutbuddin Aibak's foundation of the Delhi Sultanate in 1206. According to Michaels' scheme, the fifth period begins a little less than a century after Mahmud started raiding the Indian Doab, and the sixth period a little less than a century after the battle of Plassey (1757), marking the East India Company domination in Bengal. The construction of this interpretative pattern of post-classical Hinduism, so characteristic of the indological interpretation of the history of Hinduism, remains obscure.

The *sant* tradition and its opposition to image worship have often been interpreted as an indicator of the Islamic impact on Hinduism. 'The early sants, we have been told, brought together popular Hindu and Sufi religious currents—sometimes in a highly revolutionary way' (Gold 1987: 4–5).[2] While such general statements are difficult to prove in detail, in nineteenth century neo-Hinduism it might be much easier to prove dependencies and relationships, and the relatedness to the encounter with European and Christian conceptions. This chapter contributes to this debate.

This chapter focuses on how far the discourse on the personhood and the image of God, with or without attributes, in the theology of nineteenth-century India can be related to the present discourse on syncretism and anti-syncretism (Stewart and Shaw 1994).[3] The chapter examines theological conceptions chosen by eminent, but very different religious spirits—Ram Mohan Roy and Sahajanand—towards the end of Michaels' (1998) fifth period in the early decades of the nineteenth century.

Recent research has focused on the background of syncretism in the context of the dynamics of religious change, in which it forms one aspect within a wider range of patterns in the interaction of the 'own' and the 'other'. In other words, syncretism has to be 'seen as part of the religious discourse' (Van der Veer 1994: 208) in a given situation. Van der Veer (1994: 209) points out that the discourse on multiculturalism in the contemporary United States has something in common with the debate on syncretism: 'They both try to give answers to situations of civil strife seemingly caused by insurmountable differences in religious or cultural identities. Both terms belong to a discourse of tolerance and communal harmony. This is also true for the Indian case.'

DAYANAND'S CONCEPTION OF THE OTHER

Dayanand Sarasvati's (1824–83) famous *Satyaarthprakaash* (2nd edn, 1883) (henceforth *SP*) consists of the refutation of a long list of Hindu and non-Hindu religious movements prevalent in India in its author's time.[4] In his true *summa contra gentiles*, Dayanand minutely argues against fictive opponents and their heretical arguments in the traditional *puurva-paksha—uttarapaksha* manner (refutation of the opponent), refusing traditional beliefs of all sorts in favour of his own, and revolutionary conception of authentic Vedic religion. While preparing a course on tradition and modernism in Hindu reform movements, it struck me how closely the Brahmo and Prarthana Samaj follow each other in the text— they are analysed and refuted almost immediately after the Swaminarayans in the eleventh chapter of the *SP*, the 'bible' of the Arya Samaj.

The long eleventh chapter is devoted to the merciless examination of sectarian Hinduism against the background of Dayanand's monolithic concept of *satya* (truth). For him, satya is beyond discussion and beyond historical religion. Dayanand opposes satya to *matmataantar*, a pejorative term used to characterize the situation of his contemporary Hinduism, 'the diversity of opinions'. Within the text, the survey of the Swami-narayans and the Brahmo/Prarthana Samaj are separated only briefly by a short glimpse of two southern traditions, the Madhvas and the Lingayats. Of course, the two movements are quite different, one middle class and Anglophone, the other speaking a more or less traditional language, at least in its public appearance and its theology. It is interesting to contrast the position of the founder of the Brahmo Samaj, Ram Mohan Roy, with the position of the early Swaminarayans, founded by an immediate contemporary of Ram Mohan Roy, Sahajanand, far away—seen from the Calcutta perspective—in a restless province on the Western coast. The follow-up within the eleventh chapter of the *SP* does not always conform to an obvious systematic order. Nevertheless, for Dayanand, the two reform movements may have had something in common, at least because they were relatively recent foundations during the lifetime of Dayanand.

Even though the practising parish of Ram Mohan Roy's (1772–1833)[5] Bengali Hindu reformism and his Brahmo Samaj (established in 1828) was confined to very small circles (cf. Killingley 1993), they mark the starting point of the neo-Hindu reinterpretation of Hinduism as an intellectual movement and its deep repercussions on the public discourse on religion in India. The Brahmo Samaj served as an intellectual elite group, while Swaminarayan Hinduism was a popular movement in Gujarat, attracting followers from a diversity of social backgrounds, turning later into a worldwide movement among non-resident Indians in the age of globalization. In other words, the Swaminarayan form of Hinduism 'has become one of the most successful of the neo-Hindu reform groups' (Williams 2001: 2).

The mainline neo-Hindu discourse is only distantly related to the Swaminarayans. Ram Mohan Roy and Sahajanand (1781–1830) were very different contemporaries. The impact of the East India Company's colonialism, of English and Western culture, was much less felt in Gujarat and the Kathiawad peninsula in particular, where Sahajanand travelled and preached, accompanied by a fully armed trail of *sadhu*s and laymen on foot and horses, the usual entourage of important persons of public life in a region where the *pax britannica* was not yet fully secured. Bishop Heber's description of his meetings with Sahajanand still provide us with a vivid impression of how Sahajanand's entourage used to look like and how a meeting of two religious leaders used to take place. Roy and his successors were based in nineteenth-century Calcutta, the administrative centre of the East India Company's colonial administration. They were well versed in Bengali, and English as well, on par with the East India Company officers and their female company, well educated, intellectual, and cosmopolitan. Anyone based in Calcutta in the nineteenth century would have regarded Sahajanand as provincial and backward. He was at the periphery, at home in the small towns and the villages of Gujarat, the charismatic founder of a distinct, somehow obscure *sampradaay* and its theological basis in some odd *Krishna bhakti* theology. Sahajanand did not know English and had only few meetings with some high-ranking East India Company officers and other Englishmen, such as the Governor of Bombay, Sir John Malcolm, and the Lord Bishop of Calcutta, Reginald Heber.

Sahajanand, nonetheless, was a reformer, and the growth of the Swaminarayans was somehow related to the increasing influence of the reign of the East India Company in Western India. As is well documented, the collector of Ahmedabad offered land to Sahajanand in 1820 for the construction of the first of the six large temples built during Sahajanand's lifetime (cf. Williams 2001: 29). In the sectarian iconography, Sahajanand's meeting with Sir John Malcolm, then Governor of Bombay, figures as a prominent subject. These two examples prove the reputation of Sahajanand and his early movement for the colonial power. The relationship between the colonial administration and the early Swaminarayan movement served mutual interests.

Sahajanand's social agenda had something in common with that of his uneven contemporary on the other side of the subcontinent, Ram Mohan Roy, which can be outlined only briefly here. Both were opposed to suttee and positive on the status of widowhood (*Shikshaapatrii* 163–72), in favour of the promotion of women and of education in general. Both found pragmatic solutions to questions relating to low-caste and outcaste members/devotees. Neither Sahajanand nor Roy were 'anti-casteist' in the sense of some twentieth-century reformers.[6]

Perhaps the most appealing opposition appears to be in their theology in the strict sense, particularly in the case of image worship. One was a prominent fighter against idolatry and the other was promoting the worship of Krishna images made of stone or metal, or a *shaaligraama* stone (*Shikshaapatrii* 56). A careful reading of Sahajanand's sermons however reveals that his concept of god as *saccidaananda* is not entirely opposed to Ram Mohan Roy's conceptualization of monotheism. Roy and Sahajanand were innovative reformers and at the same time exponents of ecumenical Hindu theological traditions.

THE IMAGE WORSHIP ISSUE

'The idolatry of India . . . has for the object of its worship the material substance itself', says the famous A. Dubois (1906: 548), explaining his opinions about the origin of temple worship in the cult of the elements— a typical approach in nineteenth-century interpretation of Hindu religion. Image worship had been a focus of the early Hindu–Christian confrontation in India, and was often used in anti-Hindu polemics.[7]

At the same time, the discourse on image worship has indigenous sources. The polarity of *nirguna* and *saguna bhakti* has its own history in the Hindu tradition. In the mysticism of someone like Kabir (traditionally 1398–1518 CE) and the sant tradition, the criticism of image worship already reflects the Islamic challenge to image worship. The inclusivist model, which defines image and non-image worship as the two poles of one and the same tradition, is the most common interpretation of the underlying theological dichotomy within this discourse.

The nineteenth century, with its Christian and Western enlightened challenge, gave a new impetus to the debate on image worship. The criticism of 'Hindu idolatry' was taken very seriously and was a major issue for the nineteenth-century Bengali Hindu renaissance movement, particularly for Ram Mohan Roy with his outspokenly deistic reading of Hinduism. The early Bengali reformers put much energy into proving that image worship was not an original feature of Hinduism as such, but a symptom of decadency and an abominable practice. The history of Hinduism was, therefore, interpreted as a continuing decay from Vedic (and normative) origins. Consequently, reform was understood in the original sense as a return to the origins.

Roy, however, refused to be called a reformer: 'In none of my writings, nor in any verbal discussion, have I ever pretended to reform or to discover the doctrines of the unity of God, nor have I ever assumed the title of reformer or discoverer....'[8] Beyond the demonstration of courtesy considering his own role, this statement illustrates Roy's understanding of the nature of Hindu monotheism as the uncovered and authentic essence of the great tradition. The authentic textual sources are, therefore, to be found in the Vedic texts. The sanctity of the Vedic texts is thus related to their theology—and this is what relates Ram Mohan Roy to Dayanand Sarasvati.

Roy is indeed opposed to image worship, but a closer reading reveals a less rigorous approach to idolatry than expected, as Killingley (1993) has demonstrated. Moderate and inclusive elements are not simply absent in Roy's understanding of reform Hinduism. To sum up, Roy argues much from inside the Hindu tradition and his reading of the tradition has an *advaitin* inclination. In the case of image or non-image worship, the dividing line is between pure and less pure forms of worship. Even though non-image worship is better, there is a certain licence to less pure forms of worship. The underlying conciliatory position towards image worship is more obvious in Roy's Bengali publications than in his works written in English, as Killingley (1993) has demonstrated. Even though Roy advocates 'an invisible Supreme Being', he does not condemn 'the worship of Idols' categorically, since 'those what are competent for the worship of the invisible God, should disregard the worship of Idols'.[9] This means that there is a clear hierarchical and inclusivist order of the forms of worship: the dividing line is between 'those what are competent' and those who are not. This is a clear reference to Shankara's theory of two levels of truth, permeating the neo-Hindu interpretation of worship until Sarvepalli Radhakrishnan. Of course, true religion does not give a licence to idol worship, but Roy interprets it as a 'last provision' (see Killingley 1993: 76ff.)

Sahajanand, founder of the Swaminarayan movement, considered himself a follower and representative of the one Lord, and many of his followers declare themselves as monotheists. On the background of the Vaishnava theological tradition, the existence of a multitude of gods is however never explicitly denied in Swaminarayan's writings. Much of the Hindu pantheon is represented in temples, even though it may be argued that the pantheon is mostly functionally insignificant for Swaminarayan believers. Some features of Swaminarayan theology are clearly inclusivist (Hacker 1983; compare Halbfass 1988: 403ff.). Reform is interpreted in terms of return to the Vedic tradition: for example, the unity of Naaraayana and Shiva is—according to Sahajanand's teaching—Vedic (*Shikshaapatrii* 47). Dayanand's, but also Roy's, rhetoric is often quite outspoken, even polemic. Sahajanand, however, is hardly polemic at all, but his theological position in favour of a personal God is outspoken.

SCEPTICISM AND REFORM

Dayanand's polemical rhetoric is well known. The eleventh chapter of his *SP* does not spare the Swaminarayans and Brahmo Samaj (and Prarthana Samaj). He treats the Swaminarayan movement after the Vallabhaacaaryas (p. 352ff.), which falls under Dayanand's strict moral condemnation, particularly because of the commercialization of religious practices by the Gusaaiims. 'Such people are responsible for the decline of *aaryyaavartt* [that is the Indian subcontinent].'[10] The next question in the learned dialogue, in which Dayanand explains his positions, is on the Swaminarayans.

For Dayanand, the Swaminarayan movement was identified as a Vallabhaacaarya reformist movement.[11] He did not, however, take its reformist agenda seriously and argued that the Swaminarayans were like the Gusaaiims, since their behaviour concerning the stealing of wealth etc. was exactly the same.[12] Besides, they used the same basic *mantra*—a strong argument for Dayanand.[13] His historical account of how the Swaminarayans gained prominence is extremely polemical, almost sarcastic.[14] Nevertheless, Dayanand was well acquainted with Swaminarayan doctrines, as is demonstrated particularly in his anti-Swaminarayan pamphlet *Shikshaapatriidhvaantanivaarana* (1876), a critical analysis of the basic text of the Swaminarayans.[15]

SAHAJANAND'S IDENTITY

The most striking and defining feature of Swaminarayan belief, the identification of Sahajanand as a historical personality with the personal God *purushottama naaraayana*, stresses the traditional character of the Swaminarayan doctrine. Purushottama naaraayana, residing in his eternal abode (*aksharadhaama*), comes down on earth in the person of the *guru* and founder of the movement. This doctrine was already developed in Sahajanand's lifetime and was present in the earliest surviving treatise of the Swaminarayans, the *Yamadanda* from 1804. It is also present in the *Shikshaapatrii* (written in 1826), a condensed account of Swaminarayan belief, and is referred to on numerous occasions in the *Vacanaamrita*, a collection of Sahajanand's sermons. The origins of this basic dogma of Swaminarayan belief are mysterious. They may be dependent on Ramanuja's philosophy of the identity-relationship between Naaraayana and Shrii. Like many other details of Sahajanand's theology, this issue needs further research.

The *Vacanaamrita* reports not only Sahajanand's sermons, revealing his theology, but also the reactions of the audience at certain dates and certain places to his overwhelming and miraculous charisma. Over and over again, the mixed audience of Sahajanand's sermons realizes that he is a manifestation of the one and ultimate god in human form (for example, Vartal 18 etc.). To describe the divine revelation the physical presence of Sahajanand reveals, the terms *svaruup* or *arcaa* (images) are mostly used. These terms can also be used in connection with temple images. Theologically, they are open to interpretation. They do not indicate the mode and the intensity of divine–human identity.

In the theology of the Swaminarayans, however, the mode of identification of Sahajanand as Swaminarayan goes beyond what is traditionally explained as the difference between *anshaavataara* ('manifestation of a part') and *puurnaavataara* ('full manifestation'). The classical doctrine of divine manifestations in human form is the background of the Swaminarayan theology of the Sahajanand–Naaraayana identity. Therefore, Sahajanand is unique among men. His status is based on the identification with the Lord himself. The traditional terminology of the *avataara*, used to describe the relationship between the divine Lord and his incarnations, is not used in the context of the Sahajanand–Naaraayana identity. The usage of avataara is restricted to the ten avataaras of Krishna (*Shikshaapatrii* 115). Placing the divine–human identity categorically above the avataara is perhaps the most striking innovation Swaminarayan theology has introduced—a theological argument that, as far as is known, was never used before.

Already during Sahajanand's lifetime, his charisma was interpreted by his immediate disciples and by the guru himself as different from the charisma of a common ascetic Vaishnava Guru, a Mahaaraaj, or Gusaaiim. Sahajanand is interpreted from early on as a manifestation of purushottama, the highest god, governor and originator of the world. Following this theological statement, transcending the theological range of sectarian Krishnaism, some of Sahajanand's immediate associates are equally interpreted as manifestations of divine persons or institutes in the theological realm, mirroring the Swaminarayan heaven and its theological hierarchy in a historically concrete set-up.

The identification of some of Sahajanand's immediate followers and his relatives with divine persons or institutions (such as Dharmadev and Bhaktimaataa as his parents) characterize what Williams (2001: 71) termed the 'theanthropic sphere' of the Swaminarayans. On the other hand, the *Shikshaapatrii* (115) explicitly forbids using human beings as objects of meditation. This commandment may have contributed to the theanthropic character of Swaminarayan belief and theology, since such an identification could be seen as the licence to worship images besides the image of Sahajanand–Swaminarayan himself.

This identification of the human and the divine has been gradually extended over the years and continues to be innovative until today.[16] It has been the reason behind several, severe internal controversies over the divine status of historical persons. Pramukh Swami, the present head of the *Bochaasanaavaas Akshar Purusottam Sansthaa* (*BAPS*) for example is identified with *akshar*, which is—according to *BAPS*-theology— eternally existent, together with purushottama who places his lotus feet at aksharadhaama (akshara's abode). This akshara is also to be identified with Gunaatiitaanand (1785–1867), whose relationship to the historical Sahajanand is considered as the earthly representation of purushottama to aksharadhaama (see Williams 2001: 85).[17] Pramukh Swami is the most dynamic Swaminarayan leader, and his *BAPS* and its strictly disciplined monk community has been continually expanding, particularly overseas— first among overseas Gujaratis in East and South Africa, and consequently in Britain and North America. The *BAPS*, however, is the result of an internal split, and for the more traditional Swaminarayan branches, *BAPS* is a somehow illegitimate aberration from the mainline. Traditional

Swaminarayans certainly do not accept the identification of Pramukh Swami with akshar.

KRISHNA AND MODERNITY

Swaminarayan theology is largely dependent on Ramanuja's theistic Vedanta and the Vishishtadvaita tradition. The souls and the world are different from God, and they are real separate entities. Even though God dwells within the individual souls (*jiiva*) as *antaryaamin*, he is unaffected by them. At the same time, God resides in his images (arcaa) and his divine manifestations (*vibhaava*). There is, however, a certain reservation about the traditional identification of the *gopiis* in their eternal play with their adulterous and divine counterpart Krishna, a typical feature of the Pushtimaarga and other bhakti movements.[18] The ascetic character of Swaminarayan doctrine seems to prevent the identification of individual believers with certain gopiis (the adulterous Krishna's girlfriends) in the divine play (*liilaa*) in the heavenly world (*vaikuntha, goloka, devaloka, paramadhaama*), where God resides in his highest form as *paraa*. In practical and in theological terms, the Swaminarayan tradition is rather reserved towards the mystic eroticism and transsexualism of the earlier traditional Krishna-bhakti, particularly in the context of the Pushtimaarga in Gujarat. This feature makes the Swaminarayans compatible with modernist moral standards for religious movements, particularly in contrast with the notorious sex scandals of the Pushtimaarga Mahaaraajas. The modern success story of the Swaminarayans, particularly of the *BAPS* is closely related to its moral reputation.

Modernity is not really compatible with certain aspects of the traditional Krishna-bhakti, particularly when it comes to Krishna's wickedness and his erotic relationship to the gopiis of Vrindaavana. This is probably one of the reasons why it was Rama and not Krishna, who was to serve the interests of political Hinduism better. Nevertheless, Krishna-bhakti is not without an ascetic undercurrent. Strict celibacy of its monks and inner-worldly ascetism of its lay people contribute much to the attraction of the Swaminarayans to this day. The scriptural tradition is based on Krishnaism, and Ramanuja's commentaries on the Bhagavadgitaa and *Bhaagavatapuraana* are considered authoritative (*Shikshaapatrii* 100), even if the Swaminarayans produced much of their authoritative scripture on their own. Even though Sahajanand's intention was reform, he did not like to argue on purpose with representatives of other opinions on matters of religion. His homiletic rhetorics were most of the time somehow softer than Dayanand's and less polemical. An important text like the *Shikshaapatrii* (81–81) refers to Vallabhaacaarya and his son Vithalnaath in venerative terms, and prescribes the days of *vrats* according to the prescription of Vithalnaath.

Like Ram Mohan Roy, Sahajanand is in 'Defence of Hindoo theism', the first being an advaitin referring back to Shankara and his tradition, the second a Krishnaite referring back to Ramanuja. Theologically, the crucial point of reference for Ramanuja is the question of whether God has attributes or not (see Carman 1974: p. 73ff.). Sahajanand's explanations on this point are quite outspoken. His argument is clearly anti-syncretistic and follows the traditional and polemical pattern in theist Vaishnava theology. He clearly takes sides against classical Advaita. The Lord (*bhagvaan purushottama*) always has attributes. God is never formless, he eternally is 'with form' (*bhagavaanto sadaa saakaaramuurti che*) (Vac 135/Prathama 71). This credo is repeated over and over again in the *Vacanaamrita*. On certain occasions, Sahajanand goes further: One who says that the Lord Purushottama is formless, does not understand him.[19] In Prathama 71, Sahajanand speaks about the question of whether there are sins that are not forgiven by the Lord. In this context, he states that it is a serious sin (*moto aparaadh*) to *criticize* the orthodox opinion that God actually has form. This statement clearly marks the limitations of the doctrinal tolerance of Sahajanand. Monism is wrong.

The manifestations of God on earth are for the purpose of the well-being (*kalyaan*) of the individual souls—the purpose of incarnation[20]—even though the souls may not recognize divine manifestations as such because of the evil effect of the power of illusion (*maayaa*). The manifestations are identical with the divine forms, they are not illusionary.[21] Heavenly and earthly manifestations of the divine are somehow parallel to each other. According to Sahajanand, illusionary (*maayik*) manifestations are clearly distinct from the divine (*divya*). This becomes clear, for example, in Sahajanand's explanation of Advaitic statements that the Lord does not have hands and feet. According to Sahajanand, this statement simply means that the Lord does not manifest himself as an illusion, but according to his divine form—which means, the Lord does indeed have hands and feet! But the hands and feet He has are simply not to be considered as maayik. This is not the style of theological treaties, but homiletic. To understand this statement, one has to keep in mind the popular polemics of Kabir and other nirgun bhakti traditions against image worship and the saguna bhakti. For

Sahajanand, meditation on Krishna, his avataaras and his images is central for any believer (*Shikshaapatrii* 115).

The concrete manifestations within time and space are the real ones, they are the divine forms. The real and the transcendental are one (Vac 303/Loya 18), even though the perception of the luminous form (*tejomaymuurti*) of the Lord is mystical and dependent on the devotee's facilities, his subjectivity. On the other hand, there are non-personal aspects of the divine in Swaminarayan theology, particularly God as all-pervading and inborn agent in any being (*antaryaamin*), and his function as akshara, the dwelling place of the one Lord.

DAYANAND'S VIEWS

After his polemical examination of the Swaminarayans, Dayanand's *SP* critically examines the Brahmo Samaj and the Prarthana Samaj respectively (SP 357ff.). His first observation in this context is the inherent Christian, and, therefore, in Dayanand's view, antipatriotic impact displayed by them. For him, the mixture of the Brahmo Samaj and Christianity is— unlike his evaluation of image worship and the temple practices in nineteenth-century India—not negative *per se*, at least not in this part of the *SP*. He can be sharper in the thirteenth chapter, which is devoted to the Bible and *krishciinamata*, Christian religion. In the eleventh chapter and particularly in Dayanand's interpretation of the Brahmo and Prarthana Samaj, the Christian impact is not necessarily considered negative, as far as 'small-minded people' are 'saved'. He also respects the reform movements' criticism of idolatry. They also serve by saving people before they get lost in the bindings of 'net books' (that is, books that bind those, who read them).[22] Otherwise, patriotism (*svadeshbhakti*) is weakened because of the impact of the behaviour of Christians, particularly in respect of eating and marriage. It is regretted that they criticize the ancestors, having their stomach filled.[23] Instead of this, Christian and other British are praised in their stories.[24]

Dayanand explicitly rejects theologically pluralistic positions (*SP* p. 360ff.). The question for Dayanand is whether the truth is to be found in the Vedas as well as in the Bible, the Qur'an, and any other religious book. He does not accept the opponents' argument that they are equally true, that there is nothing like *asatya* in holy books. To some extent, he argues, they do contain asatya, as he understands them—except the Veda, which is nothing but pure satya.

Dayanand's position towards the pluralism of *mat* is made clear already in the introduction of his *SP*. As the chapter on the Christian and Islamic eras shows, the term mat can be translated as 'religion' or 'confession', but also in the sense of what is usually called sampradaay, 'school tradition' (or 'sect'). Dayanand is far from the neo-Hindu consensus on the ecumenical unity of Hinduism, even though he states that the puranic religion (*puraanii*) is one of four religions (together with Christianity, Jainism, and Islam), into which the multitude of traditions (sampradaay) fits (*SP* 363). He is well aware that Hinduism consists of a plurality of mats, which cannot be simply put together as a conclusive whole, and is critical of them all. The polarization of mat and satya is dominating in the *SP*, somehow reminiscent of the Theosophical Society's slogan, 'no religion higher than truth', which Siv Ellen Kraft (2002) so convincingly analyses as anti-syncretistic in character.[25] At the same time, Dayanand perceives mat as a mixture of satya and *mithyaa*, truth and its opposition, which leaves open a possible positive judgement on certain features of the individual mats under his examination, relating Dayanand's approach to the neo-Hindu approach. *Dharma*, in modern Indo-Aryan often semantically completely Westernized in the sense of 'religion', and *panth* (equivalent to sampradaay, 'school tradition') are also occasionally used in Dayanand's early Modern Standard Hindi prose in that sense. 'The position taken in this book is that any true issues any creed contains, is accepted, because it is not opposed against them, but whatever false issues are contained in the different creeds, are critically analysed.'[26]

SP 363 discusses the issue of whether all the dharmas are one or manifold. Responding to a query, Dayanand writes that, if they are different from each other, they are fighting each other, because otherwise there would be no reason to remain different. This position is Dayanand's methodological preamble. With this rather radical statement Dayanand refuses any form of syncretism or inclusivism. The different creeds are not fulfilled in his conception of Vedic religion and his Arya Samaj, but they stand in opposition to it. This exclusivist position is clearly different from the advaita-inspired inclusivism of neo-Hindu mainstream theology.[27]

On the other hand, Dayanand evaluates religions from other world regions (*desh*, that is, regions outside the subcontinent) in the same manner as those from the region of aaryaavartt (that is, the Indian subcontinent, Hindu traditions) itself, as Dayanand explains in the following sentences. In a particularly modernist understanding, transcending the traditional exclusivist perception of non-Indian religion and philosophy, he explicitly refuses any systematic division between Indian and non-Indian religions and their believers. *SP* chapter 11 is devoted to the examination of the situation among the creeds in aaryaavartt (that is, Hinduism), which he characterizes as 'the destruction of the diverse creeds' with its explicitly anti-syncretistic zeal.[28]

RAM MOHAN ROY'S VIEWS

Roy, Dayanand, and Sahajanand developed their own religious persuasions on the folio of a criticism of other religious doctrines not shared by them. The diversity of religious beliefs was not simply imagined, it was a reality of everyday life. Hindu reformism naturally had to cope with the fact of the multi-religious situation in India under foreign rule. Theological reform developed out of a positive knowledge of the doctrines of the other, reflecting a conscious choice of belief.

The belief in the one Lord is a prominent feature in the reform theology of Swaminarayan, Dayanand, and Ram Mohan Roy. The belief in the one Lord can be interpreted on the folio of its own resources in the scriptural tradition, but also against the background of the Islamic and Christian challenge. In Dayanand's perspective, Roy's theology contains one substantial, positive feature—that his approach was useful to avoid conversions of Hindus to non-Indian religions, that is Christianity and Islam.

Like Dayanand, Ram Mohan Roy occasionally could be a polemical author, and his constant criticism of sectarian Hinduism was often perceived by his compatriots as too radical and somehow elitist as well.[29] Rajnarain Bose of the Adi Brahmo Samaj, an ardent defender of the Brahmo Samaj and its reformist agenda, wrote in the 1860s that 'Ram Mohan's catholicity had to be corrected by a more Hindu aspect' (quoted in Kopf 1979: 68).

Killingley (1993: 22), summarizing the research on Ram Mohan Roy, remarks that he '...stands no longer alone between Western enlightenment on the one hand and Indian chaos and darkness on the other.' Roy understood himself as an exponent of tradition—even though a controversial one. He was at home in the Advaita Vedanta tradition. He understood himself and was interpreted as an exponent of the Shankara school of advaita (Killingley 1993: 92), and his understanding of Hinduism was finally apologetic. In his own perspective, he was not so much innovative, but rather a fighter in 'defence of Hindoo theism'.[30]

ANTI-SYNCRETISM

Both Ram Mohan Roy's and Sahajanand's treatments of the question of image worship are clearly within the range of traditional arguments. Roy, with his *Gaudiiya Vaishnava* background, turned to a Shankara oriented reformist theology, using Advaita arguments. Sahajanand came from a Sarvariya-Brahman and Hindi-speaking family. He probably had some Advaita training at an early age during his spiritual vagrancy, when he took the name of Niilkanth, an epithet of Shiva 'with his blue throat', indicating yogic and shivaitic affiliation. He finally proved to be a charismatic and effective organizer of a new, and more ascetic than emotional, sampradaay with a Krishna-bhakti background in Gujarat.

In a way, Ram Mohan Roy and Sahajanand continued the traditional dispute on the nature of God and his true worship, between saguna bhakti and nirguna bhakti and the Shankara and Ramanuja traditions. Both were well aware of traditional counter positions, and Sahajanand could occasionally argue as polemically as the very polemical Dayanand—one against 'idolatry', the other against the Advaitins. They began institutional reform movements, but at the same time their reference was a selective choice of tradition.[31] This does not exclude the possibility of Christian or Muslim impact on their ways of thinking. While the discourse itself may have been motivated by Christian or Muslim arguments (or both), this thesis still remains to be substantiated in detail. This leads to the question of the demand of adequate hermeneutics to detect syncretism.

This finding is reminiscent of Van der Veer's social-anthropological analysis of a Sufi saint cult in Gujarat. Sufi saint worship is often understood as syncretistic. Hindus do participate in some form as tomb worshippers in the Rifa'i cult in Surat, but they do not take part in the 'playing' with swords (a self-immolation practice). Muslim saint worshippers argue that the saint worship is an integral part of orthodoxy. They do not argue that saint worship is syncretistic and therefore tolerant (Van der Veer 1992, 1994: 210). It may well be that Muslim saint worship leads to more tolerance in the religious pluralism in India, but this is a side effect and not the immediate purpose of the religious practice of Muslim saint worship. One could continue saying that Muslim saint worshippers are confessing anti-syncretists.

'Syncretism' as a technical term is always arbitrary. In theology and comparative religions it has often been used as a classificatory term for a variety of phenomena. It is used with either negative, neutral, or sometimes positive connotation for phenomena otherwise called mixing, assimilation, inculturation, integration, inclusivism, or synthesis. Any meeting of cultures or religions different from each other sets free a dynamic process of assimilation and reassertion of identity. Conversion or explicit assurance of one's religious identity is embedded into this process; they are aspects of it, but they do not govern and rarely dominate it. Similarly, religious pluralism of any degree sets free processes of syncretism and anti-syncretism as well. Stewart and Shaw (1994) demonstrate this structural interrelatedness of syncretism and anti-syncretism: they are not mutually exclusive, as has often been argued, but complementary. Whenever one of the two is detected, the other is not absent.

Within the Christian discourse, indigenous churches such as the Kimbanguist church in the Congo have been labelled as 'syncretistic', but Christianity as a syncretistic religion *per se* has occasionally been used as an *argumentum fidei*, that is, positively in an affirmative sense. Nevertheless, the discourse on syncretism of the Christian creed and its scriptural basis in particular is usually perceived as a challenge to its theological identity. The question of the impact of or interaction with other (oriental) religions concerning elements of creed, cult, liturgy, high theology, sacral architecture, etc., was generally perceived as threatening the essentials of one's religion. The question of the emergence of Israel's so-called monotheism and the relationship of Jahwism to other religious phenomena in the Palestine region and the modern discourse on 'mythology' in the New Testament might be referred to in this context as typical examples of how this discourse was dominated by the perception of an ultimate dichotomy between identity and syncretism in religion.

Detecting syncretism in the South Asian context of intellectual theology cannot mean simply an application of a classificatory scheme that was developed in another context, namely the ancient near east and in relation to the historic epoch of Hellenism. South Asian syncretism, if it exists, cannot be without repercussions on the theoretical model itself. The term syncretism, which was often used to categorize developments in the history of Hinduism of the nineteenth and twentieth centuries, may ultimately turn out to be misleading. From Farquhar (1924) to Hacker (1983) and Halbfass (1988) it has often been argued that recent developments in Hindu reform movements are due to the Western and particularly Christian impact and the colonial background, in which the Hindu reform grew. Individual personalities, particularly Vivekananda and Mahatma Gandhi, interpreted the presence of Christianity as

functionally complementary or corrective for Hinduism. This is
particularly true in terms of the development of a Hindu social agenda,
but also in relation to the question of the 'rediscovery' of Hindu
monotheism.

Others, like Dayanand Sarasvati, strongly refused any ambiguous
interpretation in terms of what could be qualified as syncretism or perhaps
hybridity. According to his own understanding, Dayanand was a true
reformer of the Vedic religion and a radical advocate against any form of
syncretism. His clear dualism of satya and mithyaa (and mat), with its
obvious parallel in the discourse on truth in Madame Blavatsky's
Theosophy, may be considered as parallel to the discourse on syncretism
and anti-syncretism, assimilation and identity.

As regards the question of image worship in the theology of two
eminent early nineteenth century, Hindu reformers Ram Mohan Roy
and Sahajanand, the findings are somehow similar to Van der Veer's
analysis of the Rifa'i cult in Surat. Roy and Sahajanand come to opposite
conclusions, but neither of them refers to anything like the term or the
concept of syncretism. There is no evidence of any intentional or
functional syncretism. Some people argue that Roy was possibly trying
to link Christian unitarianism with Advaita. Killingley (1993: 160) has
contributed another interpretation of Roy's insight into Hinduism, Islam,
and Christianity: '... in the *Tuhfat* he speaks from within the Islamic
tradition, although he does not appear there as a Muslim in any strict
sense. In his Hindu expositions and controversial works he speaks within
Hinduism, and in much of the *Precepts* controversy he speaks within
Christianity.' It has to be mentioned here that it is already difficult to
translate the term 'syncretism' into an Indian language,[32] and equally
difficult to explain the Western conceptualization in Hindi, Gujarati, or
Bengali, avoiding superficial communalist misunderstandings.

The desire of reform is evident in the movements started by Roy and
Sahajanand. A desire to bridge the gap between Christianity and Hinduism, however, cannot be detected directly from textual sources, neither
on the level of the system as a whole (as a syncretistic system like Madame
Blavatsky's Theosophy) nor on the level of elements.[33]

ABBREVIATIONS

SP	*Satyaarthprakaash*
BhG	Bhagavadgiitaa
BhP	*Bhagavatapuraana*

Vac   *Vacanaamritam*
BAPS   *Bochaasanaavaas Akshar Purusottam Sansthaa*

NOTES

1. 'Anders als die islamische Präsenz, von der sich sagen läßt, daß sie im Grunde bloß eine politisch-religiöse Schneise in die gesellschaftliche Landschaft Indiens geschlagen hat, hat die britische Epoche quantitative Durchdringungs- und qualitative Sättigungsgrade erreicht, mit denen sich die muslimische Vorgeschichte sich nicht vergleichen läßt. Das erst führte ja zu dem tiefgreifenden Bruch mit indigenen Ideen und darauf beruhenden Traditionen', Differing from the Islamic presence, which can be said to be merely a political-religious cutting through India's social landscape, the British epoch has led to degrees of quantitative pervasion and saturation, which are completely incomparable to the Muslim prehistory. This only led to the deep reaching disruption with indigenous ideas and the traditions based upon these' (Slaje 2003: 325).

2. Compare also Gold (1987: 207ff.).

3. The use of the term syncretism as an analytical category in the modern Indian context leaves open the question of whether the meeting of Hindu and Christian features in Hindu religious reform movements is to be understood derogatively as a 'mixture' of religions, patchwork model, or even some form of religious synthesis as the specific mode of interaction between the two.

4. *Satyaarthaprakaash* (vide bibliography).

5. See Killingley (1993: 1ff.) on the question of Roy's correct birth date.

6. *Shikshaapatrii* 44–5 allows *satshuudra* Krishna devotees to wear a necklace and a tilak mark like the twiceborn. The kumkum mark on the forehead is slightly different (lacking a sandalwood dot in the middle). For Roy, see, for example, Robertson (1999: 30): 'The system of their subdivisions in each caste ... is also a modern introduction....'

7. The arguments were usually quite explicit then, as in the case of Abbé Dubois, who argues on 'the extravagant and barbarous idolatry which forms the religious system of the modern Hindus' (Dubois 1906: 555).

8. *A Defence of Hindoo Theism*, introduction (1827), in Robertson (1999: 70).

9. Preface, Translation of the Ishopanishad (1816), in Robertson (1999: 23).

10. 'Such people have made this land of the Aryans declining.' (*aise-aise logomne is aaryyaavartt kii adhogati kar dii*, p. 352).

11. Swaminarayan literature occasionally refers formally to the Vishishtadvaita and the Vallabh–tradition (for example, *Shikshaapatrii* 121) as predecessors of the Swaminarayan movement. A detailed analysis of the relationship of the Swaminarayans to the Vallabh–sampradaay is still lacking.

12. '... as the Gusaaiimjii acts in a strange way in looting wealth, so does Svaamiinaaraayan also.' (*... jaisii gusaaiimjii kii dhanaharnaadi mem vicitr liilaa hai vaisii hii svaamiinaaraayan kii bhii hai*, p. 352).

13. *shriikrishna.h sharanam mama*, p. 356.

14. Characteristic of Dayanand's polemic interpretation of sectarian Hinduism, his account contains accusation of fraud. Dayanand's account is as follows: Some pupils of Sahajanand had reached an agreement that their Sahajanand was an avataar [*sic*] of Naaraayan himself and his appearance in his four-armed form was a proof of his being the incarnated Lord himself. Sahajanand's pupils produce a fraud of a living four-armed form of Sahajanand by placing somebody exactly behind him waving his arms, additional to the two natural arms of Sahajanand. Since this was done in the twilight, it appeared real to some people. This fraud, continues the ridiculous story, was particularly successful with a simple-minded landowner from Kathiawad called Daadaakhaacar whose support for the movement was crucial for its continued spread. Daadaakhaacaar was a rich zamindar living in Gadhdaa and a close follower of Sahajanand. In the introduction of many of the sermons in the Vacanaamrita Gadhdaa-madhyaprakaranam, it is mentioned that they were given in Daadaakhaacaar's house opposite the Vaasudevnaaraayan temple in Gadhdaa. In the second part of his analysis of the Swaminarayans, Dayanand explains how a strange practice of self-mutilation became prominent among the Swaminarayans after Sahajanand's death. Having one's nose cut, explains Dayanand, was believed to be a means to achieve the vision of the four-armed lord Naaraayan. On the folio of Dayanand's refusal of the Vaishnava avataara theology, this ridiculous account of the Swaminarayans in the *SP* can be read as an anti-*darshan* tract, meant to make fun of the importance given by many of the Vaishnava bhakti traditions to the ecstatic vision of the divine person, relating to his representation in stone in the temple.

15. 'The method used in this work [Dayanand's Shikshaapatriidhvaantanivaarana] is the favourite one of the Swami when dealing with any religion: it consists in writing a scathing commentary on its principal sacred text' (Jordens 1978: 150).

16. See Michaels' 'identifikatorischer Habitus' (Michaels 1998: 371ff.).

17. See Williams (2001: 85). It does not concern this analysis that this teaching accompanied the split between mainstream Swaminarayans and the *BAPS*.

18. Sahajanand teaches the existence of a beautiful heavenly world of the gods (*sundar devaloka*), where a *bhakta* may remain as a reward for his performance on earth, but he has to return to go through many births on the way to reach *moksha* (comp. Vac 380/Gadhdaa 16).

19. *je niraakaar kaheche teto samajhtaa nathii,* (Someone claiming him to be formless, does not understand him) (Vac 80/Prathama 45).

20. See the *locus classicus* of this belief, Bhagavadgiitaa 4,7–8.

21. *divya che pan maayik nathii* (They are divine, but they are not illusory) (Vac 80/Vartaal 45).

22. *iisaaii mat mem milne se thode manushyom ko bacaaye aur kuch-kuch paashaanaadi muurttipuujaa ko ha.taayaa, anya jaal granthom ke phand se bhii kuch bacaaye.* (By changing over to the Christian religion, only few people are saved and some are led away from the veneration of demoniac idols, and from the charms of other tricky books some have been saved.)

23. *pet bhar nindaa karte haim.* (They fill their stomach and complain afterwards).
24. *iisaaii aadi angrezom kii prashansaa.* (The praise of Christians, and other British).
25. 'There is, according to the quasi–official slogan 'no religion higher than truth' and fragments of this truth can be located in all religions. This project of ancient wisdom-recovery was, however, basically intolerant towards contemporary diversity' (Kraft 2002: 153). Kraft's analysis is very close to Paul Hacker's analysis of inclusivism in Hinduism, which is unfortunately not referred to in her paper.
26. '*Is mem yah abhipraay rakkhaa gayaa hai ki jo-jo sab mat mem satya-satya baatem haim ve-ve sab mem aviruddh hone se unkaa sviikaar karke jo-jo matmataantarom mem mithyaa baatem haim, un-un kaa khandan kiyaa hai*' (*SP* 5).
27. Compare, for example, Radhakrishnan's statements on the pluralism of religions, going back to the deistic undercurrent of his theology.
28. *matmataantar kaa khandan mandan*—compare the Sanskrit subtitle of the chapter: *athaa 'ryyaavarttiiyamatakhandanamandane vidhaasyaamah.* (In the following, we will demonstrate the destruction of the creeds of Hindu-creeds.)
29. '. . . We may say that nearly all Ram Mohan's work on religion is in the form of controversy' (Killingley 1993: 65).
30. Consider book titles of 1827, *A Defence of Hindoo Theism*, etc.
31. The relationship of certain Hindu reform movements to tradition is always a question of hermeneutics on a highly abstract level. Beckerlegge (2000: 52ff.) points out the opposing interpretations of the Ramakrishna Mission as either a 'religious reform movement' or as a '"full defender of the old religion" with some unnatural Christian borrowings (service to humanity)'.
32. Syncretism is difficult to translate into a Sanskrit neologism. My informants with Hindi-speaking background suggest *dharmamishran* or *panthmishran*, both far from being easily intelligible. Raghu Veer's famous dictionary (1960) of technical terms does not contain 'syncretism', neither do the common dictionaries from European language into Hindi.
33. See Berner (1982: 96–109) on 'Synkretismus auf System-Ebene' and 'Synkretismus auf Element-Ebene'.

BIBLIOGRAPHY

Beckerlegge, Gwilym (2000), *The Ramakrishna Mission: The Making of a Modern Hindu Movement*, New Delhi: Oxford University Press.

Berner, Ulrich (1982), *Untersuchungen zur Verwendung des Synkretismus-Begriffs*, Wiesbaden: Harrassowitz (Göttinger Orientforschungen: Veröffentlichungen des Sonderforschungsbereiches Orientalistik an der Georg-August-Universität Göttingen: Reihe Grundlagen und Ergebnisse; Band 2).

Carman, John Braisted (1974), *The Theology of Ramanuja: An Essay in Interreligious Understanding*, New Haven, London: Yale University Press.

Dayanand Sarasvati, *Atha Satyaarthprakashah: Vedavivividhaasacchaastra-pramaanaih samanvitah shrimatparamahansaparivraajakaacaaryya mahaarshidayaanandasarasvatisvaami iviracitah sarvatha rajaniiyame niyojitah*, Aajmer Samv. 2007 (ca. 1950): Vaidika-Yantraalaya [30th edn]. (Reprint: Ajmer 1971, 35th edn).

Dubois, Jean Antoine (1906), *Hindu Manners, Customs and Ceremonies*, (3rd edn), Oxford: Clarendon Press.

Farquhar, John N. (1924), *Modern Religious Movements in India*, London: Macmillan (repr. New Delhi 1977).

Gold, Daniel (1987), *The Lord as Guru: Hindi Sants in North Indian Tradition*, New York, Oxford: Oxford University Press.

Hacker, Paul, (1983), *Inklusivismus: Eine indische Denkform*. Edited by Gerhard Oberhammer. Wien, pp. 11–28.

Halbfass, Wilhelm, (1988), *India and Europe: An Essay in Philosophical Understanding*, Albany, NY: State University Press.

Jordens, Joseph T. F. (1978), *Dayananda Sarasvati: His Life and Ideas*, New Delhi: Oxford University Press.

Killingley, Dermot (1993), *Rammohun Roy in Hindu and Christian Tradition: The Teape Lectures 1990*, Newcastle upon Tyne: Grevatt & Grevatt.

Kopf, David (1979), *The Brahmo Samaj and the Shaping of the Modern Indian Mind*, Princeton: Princeton University Press.

Kraft, Siv Ellen (2002), '"To Mix Or Not To Mix": Syncretism/Anti-syncretism in the History of Theosophy', *Numen*, Vol. 49, pp. 142–77.

Mahaaraajaajna, Ajendraprasaad (ed.) (1985), *Vacanaamritam*, Surat: BAPS.

Martin, Luther H. (2000), 'Of Religious Syncretism, Comparative Religion and Spiritual Quests', *Method and Theory in the Study of Religion*, Vol. 12, pp. 277–86.

Michaels, Axel (1998), *Der Hinduismus: Geschichte und Gegenwart*, München: Beck.

Radhakrishnan, Sarvepalli (1969), *Eastern Religions and Western Thought*, 2nd edn, London: Oxford University Press.

[Raghu Veer 1960] Raghu Vira, *A Comprehensive English-Hindi Dictionary of Governmental and Educational Words and Phrase*, New Delhi, 1960, 2nd edn.

Robertson, Bruce Carlisle (1999), *The Essential Writings of Raja Rammohan Ray*, New Delhi: Oxford University Press.

[Roy, Ram Mohan], *Dialogue between a theist and an idolater: an 1820 tract probably by Rammohun Roy*, Edited with an introduction by Stephen N. Hay. Calcutta: K. L. Mukhopadhyay 1963.

[Shikshaapatrii] Nitya vidhi tathaa shikshaapatrii. (arth sahit.) Amdaavad 1983.

Slaje, Walter (2003), 'Was ist und welchem Zwecke dient Indologie?: Tractatus irae', *Zeitschrift der Deutschen Morgenländischen Gesellschaft*, Vol. 153, pp. 311–31.

Smith, David (2003), *Hinduism and Modernity*, Malden: Blackwell.

Stewart, Charles and Rosalind Shaw (eds) (1994), *Syncretism/Anti-syncretism: The Politics of Religious Synthesis*, London: Routledge.

Van der Veer, Peter (1992), 'Playing or praying: a Sufi saint's day in Surat', *Journal of Asian Studies*, Vol. 51, No. 3, pp. 445–564.

—— (1994), 'Syncretism, Multiculturalism and the Discourse of Tolerance', in Charles Stewart and Rosalind Shaw (eds), *Syncretism/Anti-syncretism: The Politics of Religious Synthesis*, London: Routledge, pp. 196–211.

Wiedenhofer, Siegfried (1991), 'Methodologische Vorüberlegungen zur theologischen Synkretismusrede', in Hermann P[ius] Siller (ed.), *Suchbewegungen: Synkretismus kulturelle Identität und kirchliches Bekenntnis*, Darmstadt: Wissenschaftliche Buchgesellschaft.

Williams, Raymond Brady (2001), *An Introduction to Swaminarayan Hinduism*, Cambridge: Cambridge University Press.

4

The 'Faith Bureaucracy' of the Tablighi Jama'at

An Insight into their System of Self-organization (*Intizam*)

DIETRICH REETZ

Ham ne is kam ke liye ko'i anjuman nahin bana'i, na is ka ko'i daftar hai, na rajistar (register) *hai, na fand* (fund) *hai, yeh sare hi musalmanon ka kam hai, ham ne murawwaja tariqa par ko'i 'alahida jama'at bhi nahin bana'i hai.*[1]

Muhammad Yusuf, second *Amir* of the Tablighi Jama'at

The Tablighi Jama'at, a movement of Muslim lay preachers, has recently attracted increasing attention, as the ranks of its followers seem to be increasing continuously. The term 'tablighi jama'at' is derived from Urdu and means 'preaching movement' or group, where *tabligh* denotes the activity of propagation, applied here to the theology and practice of Islam. It is considered to be part of the more general task of *da'wa*, marking the obligation of all Muslims to propagate the faith. The movement came into existence in India in 1926 and has since spread all over the world where Muslims live. While its creed and basic structure have been discussed in a number of recent research works, its internal functioning has so far been largely obscured from public view. The Tablighis forcefully assert, notably at the leadership level, that there is no special organization or administration involved, emphasizing the lay character of the movement. A closer look at their manner of operation reveals that this is far from true. This can hardly be surprising as by now they are directing a movement which by many standards is considered the largest living Islamic movement in the world, drawing into its fold Muslims in their millions, and especially so in South Asia. Its internal administration has become strong and robust. The movement is highly hierarchical and in many instances appears to be rather rigid. The movement is judged here not by its religious agenda but as a sociological phenomenon. From the latter perspective it is understood as a sociologically relevant group with clear in- and out-group distinctions. It forms a social group inasmuch as its members are marked by 'relatively stable patterns of interaction' (Marshall 1994: 207) through shared group norms and institutions where the density of the interaction varies (Fuchs-Heinritz *et al.* 1994: 255). Its members share not only common religious goals, but also many social views and cultural practices. While the movement knows no formal membership it is marked by a distinct internal culture, which influences all members and their mutual relations.[2] The group ethos is even more relevant for the regulars who dominate decision-making and set the rules. They form a minority of 10–25 per cent of the followers, fulfilling the requirement of spending at least three days per month in preaching tours (cf. p. 115).

Derived from the travelling practice as its main form of activity, arrangements are kept deliberately provisional and temporary. Yet there is an unwritten constitution of the movement that determines in great detail what issues are confronted in what way and how the work, such as organizing the preaching tours, is to be conducted, how new members should be attracted, and how issues of leadership and guidance are to be resolved. Comparing their conduct of business to a bureaucracy is an analogy that highlights its rules and procedures, structure, and decision-making. The analogy of the group's functioning with a bureaucracy is also sought here because of the association of this term with modernity. The German sociologist Max Weber argued that the formation of a bureaucracy conducting the affairs of society became a feature of its modernity, moving away from arbitrary and personalized decisions to impersonal and law-based rule, developing specialization and differentiation (Weber 1972: 551ff.).

After briefly introducing the movement the argument will be made that many of its features resemble the functioning of a bureaucracy and de facto contradict the claim by Muhammad Yusuf that the movement is not a group or party in the established sense. Many references are based on field research in India and Pakistan in 2001–2, where informal structured interviews were conducted with respondents in two selected context situations: the universities of Aligarh and Lahore and the annual congregations of the movement (*ijtima'*) at Bhopal and Raiwind in India and Pakistan. Several of the respondents were involved in decision-making at the local and national levels and could provide unique insights into the functioning of the movement. Most of them requested anonymity for purposes of publication as they felt that discussing such issues openly would undermine their standing in the movement.[3] The practical dimensions of the tabligh work have so far been rarely documented in academic publications. Previous analysis was mostly based on the hagiographic and propagandist literature of the movement (Anwarul Haq 1972; Masud 2000). Though the movement has for long successfully deflected investigative attempts by non-Muslim scholars, lately however, the number of case studies has increased (Faust 2001; Zainuddin 2001; Sikand Yoginder 2002).

The philosophy of the movement is summarized in the famous six points, demanding to focus attention on (i) the confession of faith by reciting the *kalima*, (ii) praying regularly and correctly (*salat*), (iii) acquiring religious knowledge and remembering God (*'ilm, zikr*), (iv) respecting fellow-Muslims (*ikram*), (v) reforming one's inner self through pure intentions (*niyyat*), and (vi) spending time on the propagation of Islam through tabligh work, making oneself a servant of God (*nafr*) (Faridi 1997: 114–16). The movement's self-declared objective is the so-called internal mission, to make Muslims better Muslims, as the Tablighis say. It strongly denies any political ambitions. Yet its efforts to 're-islamize' large numbers of Muslims cannot but have political consequences if only by providing a fertile ground for the activities of Islamic political parties and radical or militant groupings. The movement is predominantly male-oriented, although it does organize women's activities on a limited scale in ways strictly conforming to prescriptions of dress and modesty as derived from Islamic law. Women's activities may partly be regarded as emancipatory, if compared with traditional gender roles in South Asia or in other Islamist movements (see Metcalf 1999; Masud 2000).

TRAVELLING PREACHERS

The Tablighi movement came into being in 1926 when Muhammad Ilyas (1885–1944) started preaching correct religious practices and observance of rituals to Muslim tribes in the region of Mewat around Delhi (cf. Mayaram 1997). In doing so, Ilyas joined other Muslim activists and groups who confronted the preachers of the reformist Hindu movement Arya Samaj since the beginning of the century. The area had become a battle ground for the souls of the local tribal population whose ancestors had converted from Hinduism to Islam. Since then the tribesmen had retained a number of earlier non-Islamic customs. The Arya Samaj aimed at reclaiming these tribes for the Hindu faith into which they would be readmitted after ritual 'purification'—*shuddhi*— the name by which the campaign became known. Contacting local elders, Ilyas aimed at reorganizing the religious and social life of the tribes, creating new facilities for religious education, and improving social ﾨommunication through regular council meetings in villages. His main ʿ. ɔvation, however, pertained to the introduction of travelling lay pₓeachers who were being dispatched to other Muslim regions in India. Their objective was twofold: the participants should reform themselves on these tours and they should carry the faith to other fellow-Muslims who so far had remained passive or disinterested in the observance of religious practices. Those preaching tours became the hallmark of the Tablighi movement. Today Tablighi lay preachers practically traverse the entire world.

The groups are formed at the local Tablighi centre, which is usually attached to a Deobandi mosque or *madrasa*. Starting with Ilyas' personal association with the *Dar al-'Ulum'* of Deoband, the movement has been supported by its religious scholars, *'ulama'*, propagating the purist teachings of this seminary located in the north Indian state of Uttar Pradesh (UP) (Metcalf 1982). The Tablighi movement also kept close contact with the Nadwa seminary from Lucknow, the capital of UP (Malik 1997). The association of followers with the movement is mostly a temporary one, lasting for the duration of the particular preaching tour.

At its destination the travelling groups would usually head for a local, mostly Deobandi, mosque. There they would stay for two to three days and sleep inside the mosque—which is a practice not fully accepted by all *'ulama'*. The Tablighis try to give it legitimacy by presenting it as some form of *i'tekaf*, the ritual seclusion for prayer in the mosque during the fasting month of Ramadan. They are always self-sufficient with their bedding and cooking utensils, which they carry with them. After prayer they go out and tour the local Muslim community. They knock on doors of most houses to invite people to attend the next prayer at the mosque. While responses vary, between 2 and 10 per cent of those approached may turn up, of which some might have come anyway to say their regular prayer there.[4] After a joint prayer they are given an inspirational religious talk (*bayan*), narrating religious principles, events discussed in the Qur'an, and the Prophetic traditions (hadith). Its prime objective is motivation (*targhib*). Usually a session of religious education follows (*ta'lim*). This consists of reading from a book written by one of its founding fathers, Maulana Muhammad Zakariya (1898–1982), 'The Virtues of Good Deeds' (*Faza'il-e A'mal*), which the movement has adopted as standard educational reference material (Zakariya 1994). It represents a compilation of religious texts, mainly drawn from Prophetic traditions. Then those present are called upon to volunteer for future preaching tours (*tashkil*). People stand up and give their name and local association, which are noted down in a special register or book kept at the mosque. Later the new volunteers will be taken up on those pledges and reminded to live up to them. As pointed out by Yusuf, the target is to get out one person per house for three *chillas* (Hasani 1982: 772)—a demanding task indeed. When the groups return to their home base they will report to the local Tablighi centre either in oral or written form (*karguzari*) about the progress achieved.

CONGREGATIONS

Next to the preaching tours, its congregations (ijtima') constitute the most well-known feature of the Tablighi movement. They are of various scopes: local, regional, national, or international/global. On one side, they take up the tradition of the weekly Friday prayer congregation at the local mosque, on the other they represent a kind of community 'orientation' meeting, which perhaps has grown out of the initial local community meetings in Mewat with religious scholars and tribal elders. Their programme closely follows the itinerary of the preaching tours, consisting of joint prayers, inspirational talks, readings from the Zakariya volumes, and calls for volunteers to register for future preaching tours. A concluding prayer of supplication (*dua*) is added here. The ijtima' is held regularly on fixed days at the local tabligh centre, usually once a week. It convenes around prayer times to induce the faithful of the area who come to the mosque for prayers to participate in the tabligh meeting as well. The ijtima' also facilitates social communication and networking among followers.

The grand national meetings stand out in a category of their own. The annual congregations of the Tablighis in Bangladesh, India, and Pakistan are remarkable for the huge numbers they attract and the amount of publicity they generate among the local population, but also on a wider scale in national newspapers and the international media. Tablighis used to stress that these meetings represent the second-largest congregation of Muslims after the Hajj. Reports assume that up to two million people participate in the Bangladesh meeting in Tongi, and between one and one-and-a-half million in India and Pakistan each. In Pakistan, the meeting usually takes place at Raiwind, the location of the Pakistani centre of the movement near Lahore. In India, major annual congregations were held at different places, although now they seem to have settled on the longstanding Bhopal ijtima'. For about fifty years the congregation was held at its huge mosque *Taj-ul-Masajid* (crown of the mosques) but has shifted recently to open fields outside the city for want of space. The congregations seem to be important venues for mobilizing support not only among Muslims, but also among non-Muslims and secular elites, notably politicians. The Presidents and Prime Ministers of Bangladesh and Pakistan have repeatedly used the occasion to rub shoulders with the praying millions on occasions that are bound to attract mass media attention.[5] The former head of the Afghan Taliban regime, Mullah 'Omar, was also reported to have attended the Pakistan congregation. In India, cooperation with state authorities is smooth and traditional, although less publicity-oriented. Tablighi leaders seem divided over the merits of such huge meetings. Muhammad Yusuf (1917–65), second Amir of the Indian Tablighi Jama'at, had already emphasized that the regular work in propagating Islam was more important than the meetings (Hasani 1982: 756). There are attempts made in India nowadays to scale back the national congregations in favour of the regular work.

At the national congregation, local Tablighi centres (*markaz*) are represented by formal delegations squatting on the prayer ground behind signboards indicating their place of origin. Also attendance from other countries is a regular feature now as the movement has become truly global. The increasing social function of the movement is displayed in staging mass marriages (*nikkah*), celebrated by prominent elders of the movement. The concluding act, the prayer of supplication (dua), apparently holds an enormous social importance. It is this prayer, which attracts huge additional crowds from among the local population seeking blessings (*barakat*). It is they who swell the participating numbers to the millions; the actual number of participating Tablighis is significantly less than generally assumed. The congregation winds up with sending off all participants on their respective tours, having recharged their motivation and energy.

DEMANDS ON FOLLOWERS

Travelling in preaching groups is the core activity of the movement. It generated a demanding roster of regular commitments differing mainly in the amount of time spent by the Tablighis:

• Three days per month on a full preaching tour to another locality in their home region;
• Forty days per year, called by the Sufi term chilla, generally a longer period of withdrawal or seclusion for contemplation and prayer, which could be a tour to other states or provinces of their country, but also to other countries;
• The 'grand chilla,' consisting of three consecutive chillas, once during their lifetime, which equals four months (120 days);
• For the ardent there are even longer chillas, mostly when going abroad, for a period like seven months or one year, or on foot across the country for a whole year (*paidal* jama'at) (cf. Hasani 1982: 772).

Since the 1980s Tablighi activists have devoted growing attention to a scheme that has slowly but steadily evolved over the past decades, the formation and operation of a local 'mosque group' (*masjidwar* jama'at) in addition to the travelling preaching group, the Tablighi Jama'at. It considers the local mosque as the basic unit of operation. It is meant to keep the work of tabligh alive after returning from the preaching tours. The details of this scheme have been fixed in a rigid grid of demands that are made on its participants on a daily basis. It rests on the understanding that every potential follower of the movement is always and first a member of his local mosque group. This makes the scheme somewhat akin to ideological structures of mobilization, such as the basic units of the Communist movement. In reality, it is only the regulars who are involved in it. It requires doing five 'good deeds' (*a'mal*) every day:

• Attending all five prayer sessions at your local mosque which are also used to fulfil specific functions for the movement;
• Forming a council (*shura*), which meets daily, and to attend its sessions at one of the prayer times;
• Spending two-and-a-half hours daily of dedicated tabligh activities in meeting fellow-Muslims and inviting them on to the path of Allah in a one-to-one meeting (*mulaqat*);

- Conducting two educational sessions (*t'alim*) daily by reading from the Zakariya volumes for about 30–45 minutes, one at the mosque and one at home;
- Making two rounds of preaching walks (*gasht*) per week, around the immediate neighbourhood on one day—which is fixed for every local mosque—and around the adjacent mosque area on their fixed day.

The three-day preaching tour (*seh-roza*) promises to earn the performer thirty days of reward (*thawab*) on the path of Allah. If it is observed every month for a whole year, the individual's lifetime account for paradise will be credited with a reward of one year. The reward system works like collecting rebate points. Different actions promise different amounts of time earned for the afterlife. The idea of specific amounts of time as reward is derived from Prophetic traditions. However the Tablighi Jama'at has uniquely adapted it to its own requirements based on point six of its mission goals, calling upon followers to spend time on the path of Allah. The rewards of varying sizes are mentioned in the Zakariya volumes *Faza'il-e A'mal*. Various Amirs kept developing the system. Detailed time rewards for specific preaching activities of the movement are frequently mentioned in Yusuf's writings. They constitute an arithmetic challenge for individuals to keep track of their faith record, but Yusuf had a rule of thumb for this as well. Calculated on a 24-hour basis, individuals should aim at spending not less than one-third of their time on tabligh. Only then could they be reasonably sure to break with old habits and defeat the devil, really to change in the way required for a pious life. It means that the above-mentioned obligations would not be sufficient. The task for the more advanced regulars or 'old comrades' (*purane sathi*, cf. p. 115 1982: 772) would, therefore, be to make arrangements for spending four months on the path of Allah every year in addition to all the other obligations. Otherwise the ways of humankind on the social level could not really be mended and falsehood (*batil*) rooted out. If the regulars do not undertake at least one proper grand chilla without coming home in between, the spirit of their lives cannot really be changed (Hasani 1982: 772).

Committing to these activities—travel, mosque, and congregation—puts a heavy burden on the shoulders of every regular, especially as these tasks do not present alternatives but are cumulative and have to be followed one in addition to the other. It is not uncommon that those doing so tend to neglect their worldly engagements. At the same time, the mobilizing efforts can also have affirmative results. A survey made at Aligarh Muslim University in India was said to have shown that the academic achievements of Muslims students who were Tablighi regulars significantly surpassed those of their co-students.[6]

Yet a regular can hardly pursue his predilection for tabligh work, if he does not make it his lifetime occupation and does not count the hours. This also entails social consequences with regard to Tablighi family life. Several informants suggested during interviews that those families where both partners were actively involved in tabligh work tended to have fewer children. They would have more simple marriage ceremonies—because they shun ostentatious expenditure—and easier divorces—because they do not ask for bride money, both under the influence of reformist teachings.[7] Occasionally, young Tablighi activists seek out the advice of their elders for finding suitable marriage partners tolerant of the demanding tabligh work.[8]

LEADERSHIP AND COUNCILS

In its self-representation, the movement stresses its egalitarian character. Outgoing preaching groups (jama'at) elect a leader (*amir*) from among themselves whose orders would be obeyed unquestioningly. Obedience (*ita'at*) to the amir is a cornerstone of the movement. Yet he could be any of them, and more important, he is expected to lead through his personal example in his devotion to preaching, praying, religious education, but also in his humble demeanour towards other members of the group, in his readiness to take over ordinary daily chores of cooking or cleaning. Beside this leader of the basic preaching group, the only other leader who is well-known in public is the national leader of the Tablighis in India or Pakistan (or any other country). The middle rung of leadership is hardly visible to outside observers and not even to irregular participants. Yet the movement is ruled by a clearly defined command structure at every level, being both flexible and rigid in turns. It is based on the principle of consultation as gleaned from the Qur'an and the Hadith (shura, *mashwara*), led by an amir or a responsible person of varying designation. It is assumed that the Prophet's practice of consultation with his companions is the example. Council is held in the open, accessible to all members or interested people, at least in theory. In practice though, there is a selection of those attending and not all business of the movement is conducted in public. While most of its business is limited to its own followers, there definitely is a closed or secret part of business of the movement, which is deliberately kept away from the public eye.

These councils were originally meant to serve as temporary and flexible arrangements, allowing the leaders of groups, local and national centres to take the right decisions. Yet the swelling numbers of followers led to growing requirements for decision-making. Councils over time became more permanent and a regular leadership feature. The shura derives some of its prestige from the amir as and when he presides over the council. It is interesting to note that the councils have some autonomy and permanence, cementing the strong hierarchical order of the 'faith bureaucracy'. While in the lower ranks their composition is shifting and rotating in fairly short intervals to involve as large a number of volunteers as possible, the councils appear fairly stable from the level of the local markaz upwards. Members of these councils are generally endorsed, if not appointed, by higher-standing councils. They often enjoy a life membership. They are mostly not religious scholars, but often academics and professionals who belong to the group of the 'old comrades'. Treated with great reverence and respect, they are next to the amir in enjoying a more or less privileged position. Serving on a council is demanding with sessions held every day and a seemingly endless amount of business to be enacted. The endorsement of outgoing, and the reports of incoming, groups are done on fixed days. Other days are devoted to the congregations, local and national, to settling differences among followers or lower-standing council members where they act as an internal court of appeal on discipline, mission goals, methods, and conflicts.

Maulana Yusuf laid down detailed principles for mashwara in a letter to departing preachers.[9] He specifically warned that in council, participants should not insist on their opinion and push through its implementation, as this would cancel out Allah's support for the movement. If an opinion is required it should be expressed from one's heart and put forward gently (narmi), not in competition (taqabil) with others (Hasani 1982: 777). One should remember that one's opinion is coloured by evil (shurur). If a decision is taken in favour of some other opinion one should be glad to have been saved from this evil, and if one's opinion is accepted one should be filled with fear and pray to God. 'Majority opinion is not our basis of decision and it is not necessary to ask everybody's opinion on every issue' (ibid.) Everyone should have the desire to be kind to the others. After taking opinion there will be discussion in a manner that different temperaments are considered and weighed, after which the amir will then decide. These instructions are obviously meant to take care that council sessions do not give rise to leadership ambitions and power struggle. These are general principles of consensual management, adapted for a religious movement but by no means specific to it.

Taking India as an example, where the movement started and its global headquarters are located, the leadership structure comprises the following levels:

• The lowest level is the travelling preaching group, the Tablighi Jamaʿat. Leadership here is a temporary assignment for the duration of the tour. As the size of the groups rarely exceeds 10–15 people, there is no shura formed here. At this level, an amir is always selected, or sometimes appointed.

• Next comes the mosque group where a shura is formed and in operation. But its composition varies. The regulars of the locality take turns in sharing responsibilities. Its leader would be the 'decider'— *faisal*. While his appointment may be confirmed by higher-standing authorities in the movement, the assignment rotates, even at short intervals such as two to three months.

• The next higher-up level would be the locality where one or more local shuras are in operation. In Aligarh, there are two Tablighi centres, one in the university area at the Sir Sayyid Hall Mosque and the other at the old town mosque. The shura has four to five members. Its composition and more so the function of faisal is usually confirmed by the higher up Tablighi leaders, either at the state/provincial level or even at the national level. In the case of Aligarh's university shura, due to its eminent status in the Tablighi movement as a centre of learning and the seat of the most prominent Muslim university it was confirmed by the very leaders of the Tablighi movement in India, the Nizamuddin shura at Delhi. The shura members often keep their post until they die. Age in the Tablighi understanding only adds to authority. This shura would also meet every day, but hold council on the more important affairs of the movement in the locality on the day of the ijtimaʿ, which for the university area was Sundays.[10]

• There are also shuras in operation at the level of the Indian states. Some of their leaders were formally designated amir. They conduct the affairs of the movement in their state or province fairly independently. Nowadays the new heads of the councils are preferred to be called by the less formal and presumptuous title faisal (decider).

• Then there is the central Tablighi shura at Nizamuddin. This name is applied to the current collective leadership and also to a larger ruling council. Ilyas was succeeded as amir first by his son Muhammad Yusuf and then by his grandnephew In'am al-Hasan (1918–95). After the latter's death, a collective leadership took over, as the movement could not decide on a single successor. It consisted of the Maulanas Sa'd al-Hasan (b. 1965, grandson of Yusuf and great-grandson of Ilyas), Zubair al-Hasan (b. 1950, son of In'am), and Izhar al-Hasan (related to Ilyas). In'am al-Hasan himself was reported to have contributed to the 'democratization' of the movement as he moved to strengthen the role of the shura against the amir and the role of the daily work (within the mosque group) against ostentatious congregations. After Izhar died, this collective leadership or small shura now only consists of two persons. Among those it is Maulana Sa'd who seems to have moved to the centre. He is seen as the new theoretical, spiritual, and symbolic head of the movement. He seems to be immensely popular with followers as could be judged from reactions to his appearance at the 2002 Bhopal congregation. Maulana Zubair apparently concentrates more on the internal structure and organization of the movement.[11]

Beside the small circle of collective leadership there is a larger shura in operation at Nizamuddin which consists of elders (*buzurg* or *bare*) from all over India and counts approximately fifteen members. While it meets daily it holds open council on Thursdays on the occasion of their version of the weekly ijtima'. Not all its members attend all its sessions. There is a rotation and sharing of responsibilities at work, guaranteeing that issues concerning the reception of incoming or preparation of outgoing preaching groups are not left undecided.

PRINCIPLES AND RULES

The approach of the Tablighi Jama'at to the administration of its movement has remained contradictory. As indicated, in the beginning Yusuf and his successors as Amirs asserted that the movement did not keep an office (daftar), or any kind of administration. He strongly urged not to rely on 'customary' (*riwayati*) means used by other Islamic groups, as they would only strengthen the grip of 'custom'. By this he understood newspapers, other media, established offices and branches, or the collection of donations (*chanda*). He was quoted as having angrily intervened when a tabligh group intended to build a local centre or house of Tabligh. The group wanted to finance it by selling printed tracts and collecting contributions. This would go against the spirit of the movement, he thundered (Hasani 1982: 750–51). At the same time it was Yusuf who more than anyone else contributed to setting up a strong internal administrative system. It made sure that new entrants would quickly and reliably learn the ways of the movement. Thus uniformity and coherence of purpose and practice was to be kept. It worked like a modern franchise system running on a strong motivational basis. In fact he was quite conscious of the innovative character of his approach, as he predicted that scholars would come one day to study its principles.

Formulating sets of rules for guiding behaviour in all situations became a key leadership instrument. Yusuf was reported to have given detailed instructions to departing preaching groups at congregations (ijtima‘).[12] They were aimed at spelling out how to fill the time while on tour. Since he regarded the devil and personal inertia to be the biggest enemies of good missionary work, he insisted on not leaving time for them to catch up with the preachers. He, therefore, considered it essential to keep them busy 24 hours for which a detailed plan was laid out. He formulated several sets of four points, covering the basic tasks, things to do, not to do, etc. These were broadly based on the philosophy of the six mission principles. As the four basic tasks he highlighted preaching (da‘wa); [religious] education (ta‘lim), based on the Zakariya volume Faza’il-e A‘mal, and reading other religious literature, in particular the Qur’an; remembering God through prayer (namaz, zikr); and making oneself his servant by serving others (khidmat) (Hasani 1982: 788–90).

Other sets of principles for guiding behaviour while on tour included the four things to do only as much as absolutely necessary, such as eating and drinking; following your needs (going to the toilet); sleeping; and mutual conversation (Hasani 1982: 790). There were four things to stop doing at all, such as asking questions or making personal demands; asking these questions in the heart; making unnecessary expenses; and taking things from others without express permission (Hasani 1982: 791). Six hours of sleep was considered sufficient by Yusuf, more was excess. Tablighi activists were to observe four things to avoid in relation to fellow preachers: rejection (tardid); criticism (tanqid); competition (taqabil); and pride (tanqis) (Hasani 1982: 13). Respondents reported that there were more sets of rules in circulation.[13]

These rule sets had several advantages. They were easy to memorize. Sometimes they even rhymed on alliteration, that is on the first letter, as mentioned above (tardid, tanqid, taqabil, tanqis). They ensured that behaviour was guided uniformly, maintaining the coherence of its practices. This approach apparently resulted from the deliberate and rapid expansion of the movement started under Yusuf. When a part of the movement relocated to Pakistan as a result of partition the need for strategic thinking on how to expand and secure the movement was born. Decisions were formulated as to where to put new centres, who was going to aid in their formation, and what were the geographic areas most in need of attention (Hasani 1982). Respondents confirmed that this thinking prevails until today. Policy for internal and external (international) expansion of preaching is formulated on the basis of the evaluation regarding whether a particular area or region is in need of religious renewal. Such need is expressed through demands from local religious scholars and leaders who send in requisitioning letters for preaching groups (*taqaza*). It can also result from reports of preaching groups (karguzari) dissatisfied with the state of religion in particular areas or countries. The same approach is also taken for evaluating the internal soundness and viability of the movement. With reference to the five a'mal (see above) the question is asked as to how many of them are alive in that area or centre (markaz) or local mosque. Thus a huge map of religious activity and performance is imagined of the country and the whole world. It is not unlike the target map of a huge global corporate enterprise, setting course on expansion.

The traditional form of letter-writing became an important form of relaying messages, orders, and reports within the movement. Yusuf's famous letter to a departing group of preachers became a sort of rulebook for the movement (cf. fn. 9). Letters written by the leaders to lower-standing leaders, preaching groups, or important elders became a regular form of administration. The new Amir introduced himself to the local centres through such a letter. Nowadays, in Pakistan for instance, regular meetings of the national shura are summarized in letters, sent out to all markaz where they are read out on fixed days in the ijtima' of the local centre. Letters are used to request the dispatch of preaching groups to certain areas (taqaza), and also to report about the progress of some preaching tours, particularly to foreign countries. Letters are written to request the endorsement of expenditure from higher-standing centres, where the conformity of material changes or expenditure with the mission goals of the movement is carefully evaluated. For instance, it was related to the author that the extension of ablution facilities at the Raiwind Pakistan Ijtima'gah had to be sanctioned by the Nizamuddin Centre in Delhi, which in such cases acts as a regional and even global centre of reference and authority.[14] Such an approach invariably led to a growing bureaucratization of decision-making.

The letter-writing in turn creates the need for offices to write and file the letters. It is the tradition that letters from close or trusted comrades have to be faithfully answered. Thus a need for a chancellery is created, at least at the national centre of the movement, called *sho'ba-e khutut* in Raiwind. The ever-increasing size of the movement demanded further specialization in bureaucratic functions of its centres. Respondents narrated to the author that there were thirty-eight specialized departments in operation at the Raiwind centre.[15] Beside general departments it is primarily the offices for the formation, dispatch, and return or arrival of preaching groups that have become increasingly important. Huge offices of *tartib-o-tashkil* are maintained at the Bhopal and Raiwind congregations and also at the national centres at Nizamuddin and Raiwind. The role of *Chhote Sayyid Bhai* ('the younger Sayyid'), a Maulana from Nizamuddin who was in charge of coordinating travel routes for outgoing preaching groups, may serve as an example. He also was a member of the preparation team for the Bhopal ijtima' 2002, attended by the author. While he explicitly denied any role of regular administrative work in running the movement, he was reported to have his own permanent office at Nizamuddin where he kept a huge oversize chart of all possible desti-nations of preaching tours in the world, complete with names and addresses for the mosques of destination, and bus and train connections.[16] With the national centres functioning like mini 'holy cities' recreating a religious social utopia, a common kitchen (*matbakh*), facilities for electricity (*bijli*), a post office, and even a mortuary (*murda khana*) came into existence there.

Other administrative business relates to tracking outgoing and incoming preaching groups (jama'ats). Long lists of its members are kept at national but also regional centres under the names of the amirs designated for those groups. This practice has apparently been necessitated by incidents of families searching for relatives who had gone missing but had in fact joined a preaching group.[17] The preaching groups themselves are reported to keep detailed written accounts of their expenditure so that nobody should feel cheated. As the author was told, these are usually destroyed after reporting back to the centre and accounting for the funds and expenses. It is not uncommon that some Tablighis take notes during council sessions or at congregations, which they then share with others or which are used to instruct lower-standing councils or groups. Tablighi elders try to discourage this practice, deemed to go against the 'spirit' of the movement, although the habit seems to be resilient and popular.[18] Another type of business relates to the requirement of making reports (karguzari). There exist separate departments at the larger centres such as Raiwind to process those reports. They discuss the experience of the groups when preaching to local Muslims, whether they met with a good response or not, what arguments were most effective, or whether the observance of Islamic rituals was good or lacking. The more sophisticated ones would also discuss the programmatic targets of the movement, such as how many of the five prescribed 'good deeds' were alive in the local mosque communities.

ELITE GROUPS

A closer look at the functioning of the movement reveals that its egalitarian pretensions did not prevent the emergence of specific elites in it. Over time, groups have emerged enjoying a special status. They enjoy certain privileges in terms of their impact on the movement. Ilyas had called on followers—and Yusuf had confirmed this—that members should give due respect to religious scholars and mystics— 'ulama' and masha'ikh. By spreading religious education and revival some followers felt apparently sufficiently empowered to look down on clerics outside the movement, some of whom did not seem to be as well versed in Prophetic traditions or as articulate as Tablighi activists. Both Ilyas and Yusuf repeatedly warned against this folly, particularly as several 'ulama' had—and still have— some reservations about the movement and its alleged externalism. Yusuf pointed out that because of their inherent connection with religious knowledge and devotion ('ilm, zikr)—two of the main principles of the movement—the 'ulama' and masha'ikh should occupy a special place in the movement. Yet they seem to be less then ever before involved with the executive side of the movement. Four 'career' paths suggest themselves to gain a special status in the movement: an ancestral connection with the roots of the movement; a 'career' of tabligh; service in the faith 'bureaucracy'; and becoming a pious and erudite 'foot soldier'.

The ancestral connection seems to have benefited the offspring of the two family branches from Kandhala that were related to Muhammad Ilyas and Zakariya. They have fashioned themselves in the Sufi tradition as members of the Kandhalawi family order or silsila. The amirs of the Tablighi Jama'at in India and key shura members have since been selected from their fold. Another such root connection relates to the early companions of Ilyas, particularly to those from Mewat. They are still seen by many as representing a particularly genuine and authentic tradition in the movement.[19] At annual congregations both in India and Pakistan the Tablighi activists from Mewat hold special meetings always attended by the elders of the movement.[20] Maulana Saad is today seen as the worthy successor of the Shaykhs of the Mewatis, as the Tablighi Amirs have sometimes been called.

The Tablighi Jamaʿat has also succeeded in establishing a rather modern career path in its 'bureaucracy'. Its various levels are measured in preaching time spent in the service of the movement. As indicated, the regulars stand out from the chance followers by at least spending three days in preaching per month, the seh-roza. Several respondents agreed that this is the first significant threshold to take. This is also borne out by the instructions from Maulana Yusuf. The next level seems to be the grand chilla or four months. It tallies with the desired pious one-third of the year level of tabligh time that Yusuf suggested as a necessary minimum for rectifying the ways of society. Those who accomplish it are called the 'old comrades'—purane sathi. Their privileges and obligations are significant. Separate congregations are held for them as a sort of elite gathering (puranon ka jor). The author learnt from respondents that being counted as an 'old comrade' is also a qualification required to become eligible for certain leadership positions such as being selected for specialized leadership jamaʿats or particular councils (see below). From respondents in Lahore we know that comrades who give time to the movement every day form yet another higher level, the 'daily comrades'—rozana ke sathi. They would typically have done a 'grand chilla', thus belonging to the 'old comrades'. In a city such as Lahore they man most of the zonal committees (halqa jamaʿat).[21] The next higher-up level is that of a resident preacher (muqim), residing permanently or repeatedly for extended periods of time at one of the centres, mostly at the national level but also at various other centres. In Pakistan, respondents related that the decision had been taken at the leadership level that those giving more than four months to the movement every year would be considered eligible for being called a muqim. They lead a life marked by asceticism and full-time devotion to the movement in prayer, preaching and organizational work, not unlike Hindu sanyasins at a temple or Christian monks in a monastery. Officially they are supposed to support themselves financially, which some do through family resourses or by running their businesses on part-time basis when they go home on leave from the centre for a limited number of days per month, like once per week. Others have taken full residence there and are kept up by community resources where personal donations are pooled. Assumptions also persist that outside donors from Arabic countries may contribute.

Service in the 'faith bureaucracy' partly overlaps in terms of status with advancement on the Tablighi 'faith career path', the second category. It includes those who serve on the various councils, run the specialized departments, and support the functioning of the markaz, particularly at the centre. Council members, particularly from the local, more formal centres (markaz) upwards, will most likely be from among the 'old comrades'. Evidently also many of the *muqimin* holding trusted positions in running the affairs of the centre gain greater importance by running a particular department (*sho'ba*). A prominent example of those would be Masih-uz-Zaman, a former civil bureaucrat who has long been responsible for foreign connections at the Pakistan centre. His two sons, Arif and Iftikhar, have followed in his footsteps and also occupy prominent positions at different levels.[22] A number of religious scholars ('ulama') are also involved in directing the affairs of the movement on a permanent basis. They are attached to the *madari*s of the Tablighi centre at the national level or at the local level. In Pakistan, for example, the Maulanas Muhammad Ahmad Bahawalpuri, Muhammad Ahsan Sahib, Nazirur Rahman, and Muhammad Jamshed have gained much prominence on this count.[23]

The administration also employs a number of full-time volunteers who could be called religious interns, who have decided to give service (khidmat) to the movement for weeks, months, or sometimes a year and longer. The author talked to some who had graduated from universities and now took time out from their civic life supporting themselves on contributions from family members or sharing meagre resources with other Tablighis to be able to devote their full time to the movement.[24] The less sophisticated among them work as ushers at the centres, ensuring that every incoming or outgoing Tablighi or visitor finds his group or stays in touch with his programme. They also shield the centre's core activities from stray visitors, particularly non-Tablighis and non-Muslims, foreigners, and journalists. Those going on longer preaching tours of four months and above would typically also spend part of that time, either at the beginning or at the end giving service (khidmat) to the movement at one of its centres.[25]

Rank and file Tablighis who seem to embody a particularly pious and God-fearing lifestyle represent a fourth, more informal option to acquire an elite status. They gain respect and recognition by their attitude, learnedness, and personal conduct. An example was Amin M. Farooqi, whom the author met during field research in Pakistan in 2002. He was a chartered accountant and had been living in Australia and New Zealand before he decided to spend the rest of his life back in Pakistan, his place of birth, in the service of the movement.[26] While he did not seem to hold a particular position he visibly commanded respect for his learnedness and piety, but obviously also because of his brush with the western world.

SPECIALIZATION AND DIFFERENTIATION

Any bureaucracy tends to develop features of specialization and differentiation. The Tablighi movement is no exception to this rule. Its administration has developed several specialized functions and approaches. This specialization can also be seen as an expression of its modernity. While the Tablighis regard themselves as egalitarian they have devised distinct methods to deal with elite groups in society. The latter are still considered very important for the success of the movement, especially in South Asia where local elites wield considerable command over the masses. The Tablighi Jama'at distinguishes between general and special preaching (*umumi gasht* and *khususi gasht*). While the first is directed at local neighbourhoods in general, the second aims at particular elite groups. For the latter purpose special preaching groups are formed. They are sometimes called *tabqati* jama'ats directed at different 'classes' of society. They specifically target groups such as medical doctors, university professors, landowners (zamindars), industrialists, even prominent professional sportsmen and actors, and also the 'ulama'.[27]

While Ilyas already mentioned the need for special jama'ats this feature seems to have become more pronounced with time passing. As one respondent narrated to the author on his own experience, specialized jama'ats preaching among landowners may even dispense with some of the otherwise essential ascetic attributes. As it would be important to be accepted on an equal level, members of the zamindari jama'at would be allowed to travel in their own car and they would even carry their own, special food. The group would consist of highly qualified and educated members; otherwise, the doors of the landed estates would remain closed to them.[28]

The same specialization is reflected in convening smaller congregations for select audiences beside the general ijtima'. As mentioned above, regular meetings are held for the 'trusted comrades' (puranon ka jor) attended by those who have done the four-month 'grand chilla'. A ten-day camp for them is a regular feature of the Raiwind congregation schedule in Pakistan. It consists of a three-day ijtima', a five-day preaching tour out in groups, and a concluding two-day ijtima'.[29] Such select congregations are also convened for special 'classes' of society, such as the industrialists, the educationists, medical doctors, or students.[30]

GUIDANCE AND CONTROL

Mission conformity and uniformity is established through a variety of ways, as the Tablighi Jama'at has spawned an elaborate system of guidance and control. Specialized task groups or jama'ats act in this capacity at the congregations (ijtima'). Some are on organizational duty (khidmat), helping with preparations such as installing a sound system; others ushering people in and out. Performing various kinds of service duties in the shape of khidmat is a central obligation of all followers, as it is part of the six mission goals and will meet with a reward (thawab) in the hereafter. A special kind of khidmat is offered by the guards patrolling the campus of the larger Tablighi centres such as in Raiwind and the congregation grounds. They can be easily recognized by the long sticks they are carrying, usually a cane. At the national centre in Raiwind a more formal depart-ment performing security duty is to be found. Known as the *sho'ba-e paihra*, control is more detailed in it and extends also to enforcing religious duties, especially prayer attendance in congregation. As the Raiwind centre is populated at any time by 5–7 thousand Tablighis, laxity and indulgence are feared. Special guards see to it that nobody misses the congregational prayer sessions. They apply the cane occasionally so that the lines of the praying are drawn straight.[31]

Another group, *ikhtilat* (communication, interaction), performs some sort of 'agitational' duties within the movement. Its members are usually well-trained and alert to engage other Tablighis in meaningful discussions so that nobody remains idle. Yusuf had pointed out how important it was to keep members busy at all times. The ikhtilat people are particularly active at congregations where they give information or motivational talks to individuals and groups when they seem lost or disinterested. They also ensure that people listen during the long hours of bayan and do not talk among themselves of private matters.

The formation of special leadership jama'ats guiding other, mainly travelling, jama'ats is an interesting and hitherto little-known feature. Two different types have been reported from Pakistan: the support or assistance group (*nusrat ki* jama'at) and the centre group (*markaz ki* jama'at). Assistance is provided 'on the job' by doing tabligh work together with those being supervised. The support group gives guidance to those who prepare for a seven or twelve month foreign preaching tour while they are still in the country performing a first round of preaching travel to familiarize themselves with the task and with each other. They are also formed and sent for some weeks to aid and motivate the twelve-month groups walking on foot across the country (*paidal ki* jama'at). The centre groups are formed to assist local and regional units, also councils, by dividing time between preaching and holding council with local preachers. Their task is to sort out local leadership problems or issues of orientation or mission consistency. They are not formed through public calls for volunteers but by invitation on behalf of the Tablighi elders. Eligible candidates would be usually drawn from the 'old comrades'.

FINANCES AND DONATIONS

Such a huge movement with a multi-tier decision-making apparatus can obviously not run without expenses. As the basic work of tabligh where it is carried out by the travelling preaching groups within the vicinity and even within the confines of one country can apparently run on nominal resources, it should not be surprising that it is largely self-financed by intending preachers. The cost for transport in India and Pakistan is still low if travel is undertaken by bus and even by rail. Expenses for food are deliberately kept down, as the Tablighis strive not to exceed the means of the poorest participant. Those giving more time to the movement by sitting on the councils, forming part of leadership groups, or living as resident full-timers at one of the centres tend to be from a middle-class or self-employed background where family connections and private businesses are mobilized to finance their living in whole or part.

Yet still the congregations as well as the centres, particularly the national headquarters, seem to require resources beyond the means of member self-financing. Here the movement has to rely on donations, the collection and utilization of which is largely withheld from the public eye and from most Tablighis. From the various interviews it can be deducted that a large part of these donations comes in kind. Congregations primarily rely on the voluntary offerings by local businesses and administrations sympathetic to their cause. They provide food at nominal prices, sound systems, tents, and transport; local governments arrange for security, health, and fire and emergency services. The same holds true for the national headquarters, where items such as food and also the land, which they utilize, seem to be donated, notably by local landowners in the tradition of landed Muslim patronage of religious institutions.

A certain need for cash transactions still exists if only to repair or extend facilities and buildings, or pay for some of the foreign preaching groups travel cost. Respondents argue that these cash donations are made as *hadiya*, or pious gifts.[32] To establish consistency with mission goals, gifts are accepted only from those who have contributed to the cause of the movement or are doing so. This rule also applies to travelling preachers regarding whether or not to accept food offerings on the road. Donors may either have spent time on preaching, which is the most preferred contribution, or as mothers and fathers, may have provided the movement with several actively serving members from their offspring. Reportedly there is a long waiting list of willing donors to be accepted as few are considered worthy doing so. Since the movement pretends it has no offices, it does not seek legal registration or tax-exemption and its accounts are neither made public nor scrutinized, at least in South Asia as far as is known.

FOREIGN TOURS

A review of the bureaucratic features of the movement would be incomplete without looking at the ways in which foreign preaching tours are organized and conducted, giving the movement the global reach that has attracted so much attention. The foreign tours are initiated on much the same basis as the local ones, either by receiving a formal demand or request from local Muslims (taqaza) or by attracting the attention of Tablighi elders that Muslims of this region are in serious need of religious reformation. However, the financial demands generated by a foreign trip or *berun* jama'at make participation selective where faraway destinations require at least a costly air ticket.[33] In any case, participation in this foreign travel has become an attractive and coveted 'career goal'. Its mobilizing effect is obviously used also by the leadership. Particularly for long trips lasting more than seven months a careful and drawn-out selection process has to be navigated where intending travellers have to qualify. Respondents related that candidates have to meet a minimum of conditions before being eligible for foreign travel. They have to first complete a grand chilla, two year-long preaching tours (*salana*), and they have to be married. Strict rules stipulating that a minimum time has to elapse before becoming eligible again for a foreign trip also apply.[34] Also preachers of little means may participate if they succeed in getting the money, for which they sometimes even borrow money, sanctioned in this case as serving a religious cause provided no interest is charged. Occasionally, this may get followers into deep debts against which the councils carefully caution. Donations may also be forthcoming from wealthy members to sponsor deserving poor followers. But permission has to be granted by a higher-standing council, often at the national level, where the donor's moral, religious, and financial credentials are reviewed. Another condition is that first-grade dependent relatives must give their formal consent so that no ailing parents or hungry children are left behind. As mentioned above, a preaching group heading abroad will undergo formal training and coaching at home for a couple of weeks. Where ten to fifteen men have to spend twenty-four hours together daily, characters may not match, creating problems, as has happened in the past. After their return they will also go together on local missions before the trip is considered complete. The groups going on foreign tours also report in-between through letters (karguzari), some of which have been published. They appear to be a naïve reflection of the cultural conflict into which Muslims from a thoroughly Islamized background in Pakistan or India are thrust when meeting with secularized and largely adapted Muslims in the West. Britain is a notable exception where islands of strong religious commitment by local Muslims can be found and Deobandi institutions flourish.

It is unclear to what extent the prospect of going out with a berun jama'at may have a corrupting influence on the movement as it becomes the subject of favouritism, which could be derived from some hints by respondents. Conversely, foreign preachers from the West coming to the subcontinent are often driven by romantic notions to find the true religious spirit in the homelands of the movement. An increasing number of visiting preachers from Asian, African, and Arabic countries, among which Malaysia and Indonesia seem to stand out, are anxious to learn and emulate the mobilizing effects of the movement for their own Muslim societies, where reformism increasingly targets the diversity of religious practices and Muslim lifestyles. Many visiting preachers learn some Urdu, in the process contributing to its spread as a global lingua franca of the movement. While translations of the main works exist in all major languages, their style is often arcane, formulaic, and marked by migrant speaking habits. Yet the deliberate usage of local languages for Islamic discourse and preaching marks the movement out and explains some of its success in spreading out.[35]

The social and cultural barriers between various segments of the global movement are exemplified in the special treatment which arriving foreign Tablighis receive in the subcontinent. Their accommodation at congregations and at the big centres is usually privileged. At Pakistan's Raiwind a special berun kamra or foreign guest hall exists, which is partially air-conditioned. Also hygienic conditions are better, with separate washing and toilette arrangements. At the national congregations, foreign participants appear to be virtually segregated from local followers as their separate tents are closed to locals. Foreign groups and visitors are assigned separate levels at the huge concrete centre at Nizamuddin, Delhi. They are usually always accompanied, getting all the speeches translated at their place, and almost never join the main auditorium in front of the speakers.

Examining the movement at close range, it seems that its bureaucratic features threaten to take on a life of their own. The movement appears to be more strictly regulated in Pakistan than in India, an assessment also shared by some respondents. To some extent, the bureaucratic transformation seems to be a product of the enormous growth of the movement, which generated considerable demands on leadership, guidance, uniformity, conformity, motivation, and control. The Tablighis have apparently moved from a fringe phenomenon to the mainstream of Muslim society in South Asia. Through this, they have attracted a more heterogeneous following. The growing representation of wider sections of Muslim society in its ranks has brought many middle-class concerns into the movement. Social networking has apparently intensified, aimed at opportunities in business, education, or arranged marriages. Political opportunities are tested with the implicit association of the Tablighi Jama'at and its stalwarts. None of this, however, has been proven to be the deliberate policy of the leadership of the movement. On the contrary, it tries to stem the tide of social and political opportunism by more elaborate and rigid regulation. The dynamics of growth may, therefore, be the major explanation for the emergence of a 'faith bureaucracy'. At the same time, its rules and procedures provide a 'steel frame' for the movement, allowing it to maintain its consistency and coherence when spreading across countries, cultures, and continents. They attest to its 'modernity', even though it deliberately relies on pre-modern forms of communication such as walking and personal oral talk. This 'skeleton modernity', however, remains ambiguous. It does not allow assumptions about the political and social values or activities of its members. Those can be progressive or conservative, active or passive, radical or moderate. Viewing the Tablighi Jama'at as a 'faith bureaucracy' allows insight into its functioning hitherto unavailable. It does not allow making an assessment about the forms and directions of its contributions to society and politics, which primarily are informed by the multitude of—sometimes conflicting—concerns of its rank and file members.

NOTES

1. 'We have not formed a new organization for this work, nor is there any office for it, nor register, nor fund; this is the work of all Muslims, we have also not created a separate group (party) in any traditional way' (Hasani 1982: 750).

2. Culture is understood here as a unique profile and combination of universal aspects of human behaviour and not as reflecting eternal or permanent essential features.

3. Details can be provided on request by the author.

4. In very conservative and traditional Muslim majority areas such as the tribal belt bordering the North-West Frontier Province of Pakistan, the turnout will reach much higher figures though. This observation is owed to Albrecht Kraft who regularly travels in the area.

5. For the 2000 congregation, see *Dawn*, 5–7 November 2000; for Bangladesh, see Agence France-Presse (AFP), 'Muslims stream into Bangladesh for the 34th Biswa Ijtema', dateline 29 January 2000.

6. Interview at Aligarh Muslim University, 13 December 2001.

7. This refers to the Puritanism of the concept of *islah*, a movement for Qur'an-based reform of behaviour that emerged in Egypt at the end of the nineteenth century and spread to the whole Islamic world.

8. Respondents at Aligarh on 12 December 2001, and Lahore on 9 and 15 November 2002.

9. The letter was written by Maulana Yusuf for a jama'at departing to the Hijaz for performing *'umra* (Hasani 1982: 765–82).

10. In Pakistan, zonal (halqa) councils are also formed, combining several local centres for extra leadership and guidance.

11. My interviews at the Bhopal congregation, 5–7 January 2002. The Amir of Pakistan's Tablighi Jama'at is Hajji Abdul Wahhab (b. 1928).

12. Cf. his farewell message and instructions at a congregation near Calcutta as printed in Hasani (1982: 783–91).

13. Interview at Lahore, 13 November 2002.

14. Interview at Lahore, 4 November 2002.

15. Interviews at Raiwind Markaz, 12 December 2002.

16. Respondent at Bhopal Ijtima', 4 January 2002.

17. Interview with Hamid Khan, Lahore, 31 October 2002, speaking about his own experience with his son.

18. Interview at Lahore, 22 October 2002. Cf. the memoirs of an old Mewati comrade of Muhammad Ilyas from the founding days of the movement, Rahim Bakhsh (1995).
19. Cf. the memoirs of an old Mewati comrade of Muhammad Ilyas from the founding days of the movement, Rahim Bakhsh (1995).
20. A significant number of Mewatis migrated to Kasur District in Pakistan at partition and their Tablighi representatives attend the congregations in force.
21. Interview at Lahore, 22 October 2002.
22. My interviews at Lahore in October–November 2002.
23. Interview at Lahore, 19 November 2002.
24. Interview at Nizamuddin, Delhi, 20 November 2001.
25. Interview with Jamshed Khan, long-time participant, although not a regular, at Lahore on 30 October 2002.
26. Interview at Lahore, 5 November 2002.
27. Interview at Lahore, 22 October 2002.
28. Interview at Lahore, 4 November 2002.
29. Interview at Lahore, 30 October 2002.
30. While annual student ijtima' are a regular feature of the Indian Tablighi Jama'at, the same could not be verified for Pakistan.
31. As observed during a visit to the Raiwind Markaz, 12 December 2002.
32. 'Hadiya—a donation made from piety or out of thanks-giving, rather than need (not maintenance, repair etc.). Usually a carpet, plaque or KISWA KIDMA-LI-LLAH service for Allah.' http://members.tripod.com/-wim_canada/glossaryh.html, accessed 7 November 2002.
33. One respondent from Pakistan estimated the cost of participation in a berun jama'at to be around Rs 100,000 and of a paidal jama'at around Rs 10,000. Interview at Lahore, 22 October 2002.
34. According to one respondent from Pakistan, you have to do 3 + 1 + 1 chillas before you can go on berun jama'at, and again before you go on the next one. Lahore, 22 October 2002.
35. Prominent examples are the state of Gujarat in India and Indonesia where the local language dominates the Tablighi discourse and literature of the movement.

BIBLIOGRAPHY

Anwarul Haq, M. (1972), *The Faith Movement of Mawlana Muhammad Ilyas*, London: Allen and Unwin.
Bakhsh, Rahim (1995), *Tablighi Jama'at ke tarikhi halat: malfuzat-o-maktubat*, n.p.
Faridi, I. (1997), *Irshadat wa maktubat-i Hazrat Maulana Shah Muhammad Ilyas Dihlawi*, Lahaur: Makki Daru'l-kutub.
Faust, Elke (2007), 'Die Jama'at at-Tabligh als Teil und Gegenstuck der politischen islamischen Bewegung. Untersuchungen in Marokko', in Dietrich Retz (ed.), *Sendungsbewbutsein oder Eigennutz: zu Motivation und Selbstverstandnis islamischer Mobilisierung*. Berlin: Arabisches Buch, pp. 55–78.

Fuchs-Heinritz, Werner, Rüdiger Lautmann, Otthein Rammstedt, and Hanns Wienod (eds), (1994), *Lexikon zur Soziologie*, 3rd rev. edn, Opladen: Westdeutscher Verlag.

Hasani, M. (1982), *Sawanih Hazrat Maulana Muhammad Yusuf Kandhalawi*, Lakhna'u: Maktaba Darul-'ulum Nadwatu'l-'Ulama'.

Jeffery, Patricia and Amrita, Basu (eds) (1999), *Resisting the Sacred and the Secular: Women's Activism and Politicized Religion in South Asia*, New Delhi: Kali for Women.

Malik, Jamal (1997), *Islamische Gelehrtenkultur in Nordindien: Entwicklungsgeschichte und Tendenzen am Beispiel von Lucknow*, Leiden: Brill.

Marshall, Gordon (ed.) (1994), *The Concise Oxford Dictionary of Sociology*, Oxford: Oxford University Press.

Masud, M. K. (2000), *Travellers in Faith: Studies of the Tablighi Jama'at as a Transnational Islamic Movement for Faith Renewal*, Leiden: Brill.

Mayaram, S. (1997), *Resisting Regimes: Myth, Memory, and the Shaping of a Muslim Identity*, New Delhi: Oxford University Press.

Metcalf, Barbara D. (1982), *Islamic Revival in British India: Deoband, 1860–1900*, Princeton: Princeton University Press.

Metcalf, Barbara, (1999), 'Women and Men in a Contemporary Pietist Movement: Piest Movement; the Case of the Tablighi Jama' at.' in: Jeffery, Patricia, and Amrita Basu (eds), *Resisting the Sacred and the Secular: Women's Activism and Politicized Religion in South Asia*, New Delhi: Kali for Women.

Sikand Yoginder, S. (2002), *The Origins and Development of the Tablighi Jama'at (1920–2000): A Cross-country Comparative Study*, Delhi: Orient Longman.

Weber, Max (1972), *Wirtschaft und Gesellschaft*, Tübingen: Mohr.

Zainuddin, S. (2001), 'Some Aspects of Society and Culture in a Religious Movement among Muslims: A Case of Tablighi Jama'at in Orissa', Dissertation, Department of Sociology, Jamia Millia Islamia, New Delhi.

Zakariya, M. (1994), *Faza'il-e A'mal*, New Delhi: Idara Isha'at-e Diniyat.

5

Bengal in Karnataka's Religious Reform Movement

A Case Study of the Ramakrishna Math and Mission, 1890–1947

MARUTI T. KAMBLE

VIVEKANANDA IN KARNATAKA

Religion as a social variable occupied a significant place in the regeneration of modern South Asia in the nineteenth and twentieth centuries. The nineteenth century was the century of the Indian Renaissance. Bengal was the heart of this renaissance and the religious movements that emerged out of it were the life-blood. There was a saying that if Bengal caught cold, India sneezed. Calcutta was the metropolis of the British Empire in India. Hence, Bengal was much closer to the western impact than any other region in India. The religious movements that began in Bengal in the nineteenth century gradually spread to interior parts of India and became national in character. Karnataka too did not escape the influence of the religious movements of Bengal. At the receiving end as far as Indian Renaissance was concerned, Karnataka's religious renaissance became the product of Bengali influence. Bengali literature, religion, and other aspects of culture acted as a role model to Karnataka in the nineteenth century. This chapter examines the impact in Karnataka of the religious movement of Swami Vivekananda, acting in the name of his guru, Ramakrishna Paramahamsa.

Popularly known in Europe and America as the 'cyclonic monk of India and patriot saint of India', Vivekananda (1863–1902) was intellectually well-equipped at the time of his contacts with Karnataka between

1892 and 1993. He was familiar with Indian traditions as well as Western intellectual traditions, in particular with the dominant ideas of the European intellectual tradition. Apart from these influences, the most dominant impact on his mental make-up came from his guru, Ramakrishna Paramahamsa (c.1834–86). Vivekananda thus declared the impact of Ramakrishna on himself: 'I met Ramakrishna Paramahamsa with whom I lived for a long time, and under whom I studied. All that I am endowed with is owing to my master Shri Ramakrishna' (Majumdar, 1999).

At the time of Vivekananda's arrival in Karnataka, the political, economic, social, and cultural conditions there were not encouraging, similar to elsewhere in India. Karnataka was politically disintegrated during the lifetime of Vivekananda and continued to be so even long after his demise. The British colonial construction had left Karnataka and the Kannadigas in fragments and divisions, such as Bombay Karnataka, Madras Karnataka, Coorg, Hyderabad, and the Wodeyars' kingdom of Mysore. In other words, some regions of Kannada-speaking people were under the direct colonial administration and attached to the Bombay and Madras presidencies. The Nizam of Hyderabad had controlled Kannada-speaking areas called Hyderabad Karnataka. The Hindu ruling dynasty, the Wodeyars, controlled a vast region of southern Karnataka. The cities of Bangalore and Mysore existed in this kingdom during the colonial period. Economically fragmented, Karnataka was generally agrarian and backward. A socially rigid caste system with practices related to untouchability widely and firmly prevailed. Tradition ruled the cultural life of Kannadigah, in this fragmented area. Vivekananda undertook a whirlwind tour of Karnataka in the last decade of the nineteenth century and sowed the seeds of the Bengali renaissance. Vivekananda's travels in Karnataka began on 15 October 1892, when he arrived in Belgaum. He had with him a letter of introduction from the Personal Secretary of the Raja of Kolhapur to the father of G. Bhate, who has recounted his childhood memories of Vivekananda's visit to Belgaum (Purushottamananda 1992: 7–8). Bhate was a traditional Marathi individual who was surprised when he met Vivekananda in his house because Vivekananda was in many ways different from other Indian monks (sannyasis). He was very much impressed by the vast learning of Vivekananda (Purushottamananda 1992: 7–8). When Vivekananda entered the Bhate household, he found the then youthful G. Bhate engaged in studying Panini's famous grammar in Sanskrit, entitled

Astadhyayi. The boy was finding it difficult to repeat the portions by heart. Vivekananda smiled at him. The boy was astonished when Vivekananda recited the difficult portion of *Astadhyayi.*

Vivekananda gradually became the centre of attraction in the Bhate family. Many pandits and political leaders as well as common people came to Bhate's house to see Vivekananda (Purushottamananda 1992: 7–8.) They were impressed by his openness as well as his sense of humour. The pandits of Belgaum engaged Vivekananda in various kinds of philosophical, religious, and social debates. Vivekananda never lost his temper when the debate got heated (Purushottamananda 1992: 6).

While Vivekananda was in Belgaum, an executive engineer came to see him. The engineer was considered to be the most learned man in Belgaum. Outwardly he appeared like a loyalist to Hindu tradition, but in his mind he was a sceptic. He drew Vivekananda into religious debates, claiming that religious rituals in Hinduism were useless and, because of their antiquity, were being practised mechanically. Vivekananda exposed the hypocrisy of the engineer, telling him that mere learning was useless. What was needed was inner religious experience. God's existence could be comprehended only when people gained experience beyond the knowledge of the senses (Purushottamananda 1992: 10).

Vivekananda was anxious to tell people of the significance of Hinduism as a living tradition and Vedanta as a great ideology for the entire world, and that the ideas of Hinduism and Vedanta were relevant not only to India but also to the modern world. In this way, the Belgaum experience was of great value to Vivekananda.

Vivekananda also met Haripada Mitra, a forest officer, through the Bhate family. Mitra was well educated and intelligent but had lost faith in God and religion. According to him, all monks were cheats. He argued with Vivekananda on various topics relating to religion, philosophy, and social problems. Gradually Haripada Mitra was attracted by the dynamic personality of Vivekananda. He was particularly impressed by the fact that Vivekananda disliked money and Vivekananda's saying that mere accumulation of money and power would not bring happiness and that devotion is the root of all faith. Haripada Mitra became the disciple of Vivekananda, who later stayed in Mitra's house for a few days. People crowded into the house of Haripada Mitra to see and hear Vivekananda. When Vivekananda told Haripada Mitra that he had to go to Rameshwaram after visiting several places on the way, Haripada Mitra begged Vivekananda to be his guru and give him *diksha.* Haripada Mitra and his wife were given formal discipleship. He pressed Vivekananda to accept a railway ticket to Goa. During his contact with Haripada Mitra, Vivekananda revealed his knowledge of English literature, including the works of Charles Dickens. The impact of Vivekananda on Haripada Mitra was so deep that later on, Haripada Mitra wrote a long reminiscence about his contact with Vivekananda. In this way, Vivekananda's visit to Belgaum was seminal in the history of renaissance of the region of Karnataka. The visit helped to awaken the people of Karnataka to their Hindu heritage with particular reference to Vedanta (Purushottamananda 1992: 10; cf. His Eastern and Western Admirers 1983: 61).

Vivekananda passed through Dharwad on his way from Goa to Bangalore. The city of Bangalore, in the Wodeyars' kingdom of Mysore, was emerging as a cosmopolitan city in south India, when Vivekananda visited it in 1892. Here he met, and became the guest of, Dr Palpu, a medical officer from Kerala. Dr Palpu belonged to one of the most backward castes of Kerala, whose occupation was toddy-tapping. In spite of his merit, Dr Palpu could not get a job in Kerala because of caste discrimination in the traditional Kerala society. Hence, he had migrated to Bangalore and had secured a job. Vivekananda learnt of the peculiar and dangerous caste system in Kerala through Dr Palpu who described the sufferings of fishermen and other low castes in Kerala. The upper castes kept the Shudras at a distance like a contagious disease but, once a low caste man was baptized by a Christian priest, he was acceptable to the upper caste Hindu. Astonished at this, Vivekananda asked Dr Palpu: 'Why do you people go to Brahmins with all humility? Why don't you select your own leader who is well educated and follow his directions? If you do this many of your problems will be solved' (Purushottamananda 1992: 29). Dr Palpu took this advice seriously. He ultimately found in Narayana Guru in Kerala an appropriate leader of the backward classes. In the course of time, Narayana Guru became the most respected teacher saint of the oppressed castes of Kerala.[1] On the advice of Vivekananda, Dr Palpu spent a part of his income and devoted much of his time in the service of the poor in his own caste. In this way, the meeting between Dr Palpu and Vivekananda at Bangalore was a landmark in the history of the Ramakrishna movement in Karnataka.

The meeting between Vivekananda and K. Sheshadri Iyer at Bangalore may be termed as one of the important landmarks in the early life of Vivekananda. K. Sheshadri Iyer was Dewan of Mysore (1893–1901) and a very learned man. Sir William Hunter, the eminent English scholar and historian, described Sheshadri Iyer thus: 'He gave his head to Herbert Spencer and his heart to Parabrahman' (Gundappa 1971). Sheshadri Iyer was a grand synthesis of East and West. Though he was a great devotee of Hindu tradition, he never neglected modern Vedanta, and was closely associated with the theosophical movement of Annie Besant. He had close contact with the pontiff of Sringeri Math, originally founded by Shankaracharya in Karnataka in the eighth century. Sheshadri Iyer was responsible for the modernization of Mysore State by constructing irrigational dams, and by providing electricity and modernizing education. In this context, Sheshadri Iyer's meeting with Vivekananda was like a meeting of two great minds, one from Bengal and another from Karnataka (Gundappa 1971: 42, 60).

Sheshadri Iyer quickly realized that the young monk was not an ordinary person. He invited Vivekananda to stay at his house in Mysore as a personal guest of the Dewan (Somanathananda 1994: 154–6). Vivekananda was introduced to a number of scholars and eminent personalities in Mysore. Later on, Sheshadri Iyer introduced the monk to Chamaraja Wodeyar, the Maharaja of Mysore, who invited Vivekananda to his palace as his personal guest. Vivekananda remained in Mysore palace for a few days, which were memorable not only in the life of the Ramakrishna movement in Karnataka but also in the life of Vivekananda. Below are recorded a few incidents in Mysore palace related to Vivekananda.

Chamaraja Wodeyar, in the open court before the courtiers, asked Vivekananda, 'what do you think of my courtiers?' Vivekananda replied, 'Maharaja, I feel that your heart is good. Unfortunately you are surrounded by ... flatterers.' Chamaraja Wodeyar had never expected such a straightforward answer. He further asked Vivekananda, 'No Swamiji, at least our Dewan is not such person. I have got full confidence in him. He is an intelligent person'. To this Vivekananda replied, 'My dear Maharaj, Dewan loots the wealth of Maharaja and gives it to the British agents' (Purushottamananda 1992: 33). Vivekananda after all had seen many Dewans in his life. Chamaraja Wodeyar was in fix. He did not want to continue the conversation. He took Vivekananda to a private room and told him that such open talk would lead to the creation of enemies and even might act as a threat to his life. Vivekananda replied sharply saying that an honest monk should not hesitate to utter a truth even at the cost of his life. He had done just that (Somanathananda 1994: 32–3). This shows Vivekananda's strong personality, even before a Maharaja.

During the course of a conversation in Mysore, Vivekananda discussed the Qur'an with Abdul Rehman Saheb, a Muslim legislator of the Mysore Assembly. Abdul and others who had gathered at the time were astonished at the deep knowledge of the Hindu monk about the holy book of the Muslims. Vivekananda resolved many of Abdul Rehman's doubts about the Qur'an (Somanathananda 1994: 34). While staying in Mysore palace, Vivekananda also had an opportunity to meet a musician from Austria with whom he discussed Western music, much to everyone's surprise (Somanathananda 1994: 34). On another occasion, he met an electrical engineer who was in charge of the electrification of Mysore palace. The conversation turned to the topic of electricity. Even on this subject, Vivekananda revealed his exceptional knowledge (Somanathananda 1994: 34).

During a seminar on Vedanta conducted in Mysore palace, over which Dewan Sheshadri Iyer presided, famous pandits participated and the deliberations were in Sanskrit. Even after the long discussion, a consensus was not arrived at. Then Sheshadri Iyer asked Vivekananda to express his opinion. Vivekananda got up and explained in simple Sanskrit the meaning of Vedanta. The scholars appreciated Vivekananda's knowledge of Hindu philosophy (Somanathananda 1994: 34–5).

Chamaraja Wodeyar asked Vivekananda in front of the Dewan what he could do for him. Vivekananda advised the Maharaja to do two things: (i) to modernize the State of Mysore and (ii) to protect the cultural heritage of India. Chamaraja Wodeyar was touched by the ideas of Vivekananda, especially his love of India. The Maharaja of Mysore expressed his desire to provide money to enable Vivekananda to go to America and to cover all his expenses. Vivekananda rejected the offer, probably because he wanted to go to Rameshwar and complete his tour of India (Somanathananda 1994: 34–5).

When time came for Vivekananda to leave Mysore, Chamaraja Wodeyar was deeply unhappy. He requested Vivekananda to stay with him in the palace for a few days, but Vivekananda decided to leave Mysore. Then the Maharaja desired to keep something in memory of Vivekananda and recorded Vivekananda's voice on a gramophone. The Maharaja also wanted to worship the feet of Vivekananda, as was the Hindu custom in showing respect to monks and gurus, but Vivekananda did not allow the Maharaja to do *padapuja*. At the time of departure from Mysore, Dewan Sheshadri tried to push a bundle of notes into Vivekananda's pocket but the latter refused and said, 'If you are really interested in doing something, buy me a railway ticket' (Purushottamananda 1992).

Dewan Sheshadri Iyer purchased a second-class railway ticket and gave a letter of introduction to Dewan Shankaraiah of Travancore, Cochin state. Thus, Vivekananda left Mysore and Karnataka by train. This in brief is the interaction of Vivekananda with the Kannadigas from various strata of society, from the Maharaja to the common man (Somanathananda 1994: 36).

Vivekananda was so impressed by the personality of Chamaraja Wodeyar that he wrote a letter to him from Chicago in USA on 23 June 1894:

Sri Narayana bless you and yours. Through your Highness' kind help it has been possible for me to come to this country. Since then I have become well known here and the hospitable people of this country have supplied all my wants. It is a wonderful country and this is a wonderful nation in many respects. No other nation applies so much machinery in their every day work as do the people of this country. Everything is machine. Then again they are one-twentieth of the whole population of the world. There is no limit to their wealth and luxuries. Yet everything here is so dear. The wages of labour are the highest in the world; yet the fight between labour and capital is constant.

Nowhere on earth have women so many privileges as in America. They are slowly taking everything into their hands; and strange to say, the number of cultured women is much greater than that of cultured men. Of course, the higher geniuses are mostly from the ranks of males. With all the criticism of the westerners against caste, they have a worse one—that of money. The almighty dollar, as the Americans say, can do anything here.

No country on earth has so many laws, and in no country are they so little regarded. On the whole our poor Hindu people are infinitely more moral than any of the westerners. In religion they practise here either hypocrisy or fanaticism. Sober minded men have become disgusted with their superstitious religion and are looking forward to India for new light. Your Highness cannot realise without seeing how eagerly they take in any little bit of the grand thoughts of holy Vedas, which resist and are unharmed by the terrible onslaughts of modern science...

...One such high, noble-minded, and royal son of India as your Highness can do much towards raising India on her feet again and thus leave a name to posterity which shall be worshipped. (Vivekananda 1964, Vol. 4: 361f.).

Another letter written from Chicago on 23 June 1894, to Rao Bahadur Narasimhachar, who was an eminent archaeologist of Mysore State, illustrates Vivekananda's continuing connection with Karnataka intellectuals. The text of the letter is given below:

Dear Sir,

Your kindness to me makes me venture to take a little advantage of it. Mrs. Potter Palmer is the chief lady of the United States. She was the Lady President of the World's Fair. She is much interested in raising the women of the world and is at the head of a big organisation for women. She is a particular friend of Lady Dufferin and has been entertained by the Royalties of Europe on account of her wealth and position. She has been kind to me in this country. Now she is going to make a tour in China, Japan, Siam and India. Of course, she will be entertained by Governors and other high people in India. But she is particularly anxious to see our society apart from English official aid. I have on many occasions told her about your noble efforts in raising the Indian women, of your wonderful College in Mysore. I think it is our duty to show a little hospitality to such personages from America in return for their kindness to our countrymen who came here. I hope she will find a warm reception at your hands and be helped to see a little of our women as they are. So to that, she wants to work apart from all to ameliorate the conditions of women all over the world. This would also be helping me a great deal in this country. May the Lord bless you!

Yours for ever and ever
Affectionately,

Vivekananda
(Vivekananda 1964, Vol. 6: 256–7)

Thus Vivekananda's visit to Karnataka in 1892 inspired many educated men in Belgaum, Dharwad, Mysore, and Bangalore, including Chamaraja Wodeyar and Dewan Sheshadri Iyer. It is said that Vivekananda, while he was in Mysore, addressed a public gathering at Sadvidya Pathasahala (Anon. n.d.: 77).

Vivekananda attended the World's Parliament of Religions in Chicago in 1893. Glowing reports of Vivekananda's performance appeared in Indian newspapers. Many people in India, not least in Karnataka, felt uplifted at the reported success of Vivekananda in Chicago in expounding Hindu religion and culture. A meeting was arranged in Belgaum in August 1894 to thank the people of the United States for the reception recorded to Vivekananda in Chicago and other places. Sheshadri Iyer presided over the meeting, which was held at Central College, Bangalore. Sheshadri Iyer, in the course of his speech, referred to Vivekananda as 'Paramahamsa', for whom life is indeed one of struggle not for his own existence, but for the immortal existence of others. The Swami has nothing to gain and no (particular) country to serve—wide world is his country and his home (Anon. n.d.: 77).

DEVELOPMENT OF THE RAMAKRISHNA MOVEMENT IN KARNATAKA

Vivekananda's travel and interaction in Karnataka resulted in the starting of the Ramakrishna movement in that region. We may briefly describe the development of the institutions, which heralded socio-religious reforms. In fact, it took seven years after the public knowledge of Vivekananda's memorable tour of the United States and other European countries before a beginning could be made to promote the Ramakrishna Mission in Mysore State. The initial momentum it received after Vivekananda's return to India, and its steady progress in the decades following his passing away, make a long story. It is a story that spans nine decades of silent, determined work in the face of many odds. It merits recapitulation in this context because of the contribution of Karnataka to the cause whose aim has been the material and spiritual uplift of the nation. The contribution of Karnataka to this national movement continues. It commenced in Bangalore and Mysore and now encompasses several towns and rural communities. Some leading devotees of Bangalore made a modest beginning as early as 1901, a year before Vivekananda passed away.

Several distinguished men, including V. P. Madhava Rao (Senior counsellor of the Government of Mysore who subsequently rose to be the dewan to the State), J. Devaraje Urs (Chief Commandant, Mysore State Troops), M. A. Narayana Iyengar (Tutor of Yuraj of Mysore who later joined the Ramakrishna Order of Monks under the name of Swami Srivasananda), C. G. Narasimhachar (Co-editor, *Brahmavadin*), and P. Palpu (Health Officer, Bangalore City) started the Vedanta Society in Bangalore in a small rented building situated in the Cantonment Areas. While still in service and many years before he became a monk, Narayana Iyengar had met Vivekananda in 1897 in Madras. Later in 1899, he visited Belur Math along with Amin-ul-mulk Mirza M. Ismail (who later became the dewan of Mysore) when the Vedanta Society was started in 1901. Iyengar was made its President. In 1903, when Swami Ramakrishnananda was invited to Bangalore, this institution got permanent footing with Iyengar's substantial help. Iyengar was thus instrumental in the establishment of the Ashrama and Mission at Basavanagudi, Bangalore. In 1911, when the Holy Mother, Sarada Devi, visited the city during her sojourn in south India, he was given initiation by her. In 1924, he was inducted into the order as a monk by Swami Shivananda, a direct disciple of Ramakrishna. It was again Swami Srivasananda's efforts that later saw the establishment of Ramakrishna Ashrama in Ootacamund and Mysore.

The objective with which the Vedanta Society was started in Bangalore Cantonment continues to remain unchanged to this day, whether the activities are directly handled by the Ashrama or are managed by devotees of the Ramakrishna movement in Karnataka. It would be pertinent to know what exactly its objects were as approved by Vivekananda. They were:

- To promote the study of Vedanta free from all sectarian bias.
- To popularize its fundamental tenets among the public through lectures, study circles, and publications of inexpensive books in English and Indian languages.
- To undertake social welfare works designed to help the poor, relieving the sick, and those in distress to natural calamities.
- To promote the cause of general education and the social uplift of women.
- To inculcate among the people high ethical and social values both by precepts and examples.
- To popularize Sri Ramakrishna's teachings based on his own experience of the fundamental unity of all religions.

Even before the Bangalore centres in Basavanagudi and Ulsoor were built, periodic meetings, *bhajan*s, and lectures by learned monks and disciples were held in various parts of the city. The promoters of the movement, who were distinguished citizens, appealed to the Maharani Regent Mysore for help to open an ashrama. In 1903, on 17 July to be exact, Swami Ramakrishnananda, head of the Madras centre visited Bangalore and had an interview with His Highness Sri Krishna Raja Wodeyar. His frequent visits to Bangalore and the learned lectures he delivered in various places in the city, together with the visits and lectures of other senior monks such as Swami Somananda, Swami Chidananda, Swami Satananda, Swami Nischayananda, Swami Atmananda, and others helped to strengthen public demand for a permanent ashrama and mission in the city. Regular religious classes were conducted by Swami Atmananda in the city, cantonment, and Vivekananda Ashrama, Ulsoor, which was consecrated in 1906. It was formally dedicated to the memory of Vivekananda on 17 November 1907. Public enthusiasm for the Ramakrishna movement was demonstrated with great fanfare on 3 August 1906, when Swami Abhedananda visited Bangalore. The Mayo Hall was bursting with enthusiastic crowds when the Vedanta Society, Vivekananda Society, and Vivekananda Reading Room, Ulsoor presented addresses of welcome to him, and he was taken in a torch-procession to the Vivekananda Ashrama, Basavanagudi. On 20 August 1906, the corner-stone of the Ramakrishna Mission Ashrama, Basavanagudi was laid by Swami Abhedananda. The Ulsoor Ashrama owes its existence to the spontaneous and unstinting help given by T. P. Arunachalam Pillai, a staunch disciple of Vivekananda. It served as a quite beautiful retreat. Today, the Ulsoor Ashrama, built on what was originally a five-acre plot of land acquired from P. Venkata Rangam for Rs 800 in 1926, is a refuge for monks who have retired from active work. Lay disciples continue to visit the Shrine during prayer time and on the birthdays of Sri Rama-krishna, Holy Mother, and Swami Vivekananda and listen to lectures. It was in 1909 that Swami Brahmananda formally declared open the Ramakrishna Ashrama on Bull Temple Road in the presence of the Dewan of Mysore, Swami Ramakrishnananda, and other monks, K. P. Puttanna Chety, Sister Deva Mata, and many other distinguished guests. Vivekananda's staunch disciple, Alasinga Perumal, passed away on 11 May 1909. In 1911, the Bangalore Ashrama was sanctified by the visit of the Holy Mother who stayed there for nine days on her way to Rameshwaram. Among the well-known Mission *sadhu*s who stayed periodically at the Bangalore Ashrama were Swamis Yatishwarananda, Ambikananda, Gokulananda, Suddhananda, Dhyanananda, Mahim-ananda, Anantananda, and others. In its formative stages, the Bangalore Ashrama derived great help and inspiration from all of them. The list of the learned people and volunteers who have helped to build this magnificent institution and make it a major spiritual centre is too long to recapitulate.

It was a turning point in the history of Bangalore Ashrama when Swami Yatishwarananda took charge of the centre. He added to it a temple with a prayer hall. With his towering spiritual personality and sympathetic understanding of human problems, he was able to attract large numbers of devotees and guide many spiritual aspirants. He helped the Ashrama to become one of the most prestigious centres of the Ramakrishna Order.

Among the earliest activities of the Bangalore Ashrama was the starting of the Sri Ramakrishna Students Home in Shankarapuram extension of

Bangalore in August 1919. It began on a modest scale with thirteen student inmates who were provided free board and lodging, besides religious and moral instruction. Later, in 1925, the Students Home was shifted to Vishveshwarapurum. It is now run by a private management, but the Ashrama has its own Students' Home, housing ninety students. About two decades ago, the Ashrama became involved in rural uplift activities and the transformed village of Shivanahalli is a glowing tribute to the success it has achieved.

The Ramakrishna Ashrama was opened in Mysore on 11 June 1925 by Swami Siddheswarananda in a small rented house near Marimallappa High School. A little later it was shifted to a more spacious building in Krishna Murthipuram, again on rent. It was only in 1931 that the Ashrama was shifted to Vanivilas Mohalla after the city Municipality had gifted two acres of land on the advice of H.H. the Maharaja.

Srivasananda was responsible for the initiative taken by a group of devoted public men, such as Banumaiah, H. C. Dasappa, K. H. Ramaiah and others, to start the Ramakrishna Ashrama in 1925. Among other distinguished enthusiasts were some local intellectuals, academics, and scholars, such as A. R. Wadia (Head of the Department of Philosophy in Maharaja's College), V. Subramaniya Iyer, a scholar, and N. Kasturi besides a few others. Swami Ranganathananda (later the President of the Ramakrishna Order) joined this Ashrama as a *brahmachari* in 1926. Karnataka poet laureate K. V. Puttappa stayed in the Ashrama under the care of Swami Siddeshwarananda for thirteen years. In 1932, a Students' Hostel was started in V. V. Mohalla in a small house donated by a devotee named Rangachar, and the first warden of this hostel was Swami Chinmatrananda. The hostel began with barely half-a-dozen students, but in about ten years more students joined the hostel. It was in 1937, during the centenary celebration of Ramakrishna, that the foundation for the temple and a prayer hall of the Ashrama was laid. In 1939, a study circle was started in which monks, brahmacharis, and local academics participated. It lasted until 1942.

These modest efforts blossomed into regular institutions of learning only after 1941 when Swami Shambhavananda from Ponnampet assumed charge of the Mysore Ashrama as its President. This was a turning point in the history of the Mysore Ashrama. He took up the construction of the Ashrama's temple with public donations and added to it a complex of rooms, including a library and reading room for the public. The earlier study circle was revived in 1949, which continued till 1953. In 1950, a spacious prayer hall was constructed and a hostel for the students was opened by Rajgopalachari, the then Governor-General of India.

This was the humble beginning of the now well-known educational institution called Sri Ramakrishna Vidyashala, a residential high school with a composite junior college. The story of the Ramakrishna Vidyashala is a saga of dedication, struggle, and achievement. In the three decades during which Swami Shambhavananda was the President of the Mysore Ashrama, epochal changes were affected in its educational activities. He acquired sixty acres of land from the Railways and the Municipality adjoining the Students' Hostel, and today the campus comprises seventy acres of beautiful gardens with a number of playgrounds, a stadium, swimming pool, and gymnasium, besides assembly halls, and a well-stocked library and reading room for the students. The swimming pool was inaugurated in 1957 by Prime Minister Jawaharlal Nehru. To the residential school was added in 1961 the Pre-University section, together with new accommodation for the resident students. Since then the Ramakrishna Vidyashala has maintained very high standards in teaching and student performance in the curriculum, sports, and other extracurricular activities. It has one of the finest science laboratories of which any Pre-University college can boast. This premier educational institution has over 350 students now. Although the admission is always on merit and students have to pay for boarding and lodging, a number of poor students who make the grade at the time of admission are accommodated practically free of cost or on very nominal charges.

RAMAKRISHNA INSTITUTE OF MORAL AND SPIRITUAL EDUCATION (RIMSE), MYSORE

One of the dreams of Swami Shambhavananda was to start an institution exclusively for the promotion of moral, social, and spiritual values by imparting special training to teachers. A suitable plot of land adjacent to the Vidyashala campus was accordingly acquired with the help of the Mysore City Improvement Trust Board. Special retreats conducted by the Mysore Ashrama since 1965 for the benefit of students and young people had proved the utility and need for a regular institution. The vision of Swami Shambhavananda stands concretized in a beautiful building designed by the well-known Bombay architect D. R. Chowdhari of Gregson Bartly and King. The building comprises 150 rooms, a spacious hall, kitchen and stores, Shrine and prayer hall, meditation centre, library, office and guest rooms, a small theological museum, and an auditorium that can accommodate 300 persons. This is the only institution of its kind with a BEd College providing moral instruction as a compulsory subject. It runs an in-service diploma course of two months for higher secondary school teachers deputed by the Government of Karnataka. In addition, the RIMSE located in Mysore organizes general retreats for the public and special retreats for students and other young people. It was the hard and pioneering work of Swami Harshananda, who was the first head of the institution, which gave definite shape to this unique institution as it stands today. In 1968, Morarji Desai laid the foundation stone of the building, which was completed in 1974 at a cost of Rs 30 lakhs with donations from the Union and state governments and philanthropists. It was opened by Swami Vireswarananda, then President of the Ramakrishna Math and Ramakrishna Mission.

The Mysore Ramakrishna Ashrama has a publication section. It was Swami Somanathananda who built up this section, which at present has more than 150 titles in Kannada. Swami Somanathananada contributed the largest number of these books, including translations and original works on the life and teaching of Ramakrishna. The Ashrama is also publishing works on the Upanishads, Bhagavadgita, and other scriptures, besides the translations of various treaties on Vedanta, which have mostly been produced by Swami Adidevananda and Swami Harshananda. These publications help in the dissemination of ideas of the Ramakrishna–Vivekananda movement, which has resulted in a large number of recruits to the Ramakrishna Order. In this connection, it is necessary to acknowledge the contribution of great Kannada litterateurs such as K. V. Puttappa, T. S. Venkannaiah, A. R. Krishna Shashtry, Prabhu Shankara, G. S. Shivarudrappa, and others who have been instrumental in spreading the message of Ramakrishna and Vivekananda through their writings and speeches.

Ramakrishna Ashrama, Mysore, under the able leadership of Swami Sureshananda, has established a Rural Development Wing and has been working for tribal development in Boodipadaga village of Chamarajanagar taluk. Ever since the inception of the programme, it has widened its spectrum of activities in tune with the needs of the tribal people, with financial assistance from the Government of Karnataka and devotees and well-wishers of the Ashrama. The project has undertaken the following programmes: agriculture, with modern methods of cultivation, a soil conservation scheme, electrical fencing, sericulture, horticulture, and self-employment under cottage industries. These programmes have yielded appreciable results and have helped the tribals to improve their economic lot.

SRI RAMAKRISHNA SHARADASHRAMA, PONNAMPET, KODAGU DISTRICT

The foundation stone of this centre was laid in 1927 by Swami Nirmalananda. The first President of the Ashrama was Swami Shambhavananda, a visionary who brought into being the two unique institutions in Mysore city, namely the Vidyashala and the Ramakrishna Institute of Moral and Spiritual Education. Inspired by the lives and teachings of Vivekananda, A. Kalamayya, K. G. Chengappa, and A. M. Muthappa of Ponnampet took the lead in establishing this ashrama. Kalamayya donated three acres of prime land on which the institution now stands. The building was inaugurated by Swami Nirmalananda in 1927. Now the Ponnampet Ashrama maintains a small hospital, which caters to local patients. It also conducts prayers and discourses for the benefit of the people of Kodagu.

RAMAKRISHNA ASHRAMA, MANGALORE

This Ashrama was started from humble beginnings in a rented house at Falnir in June 1947 under the Holy Mother's Trust. Next year it was shifted to a more spacious building in Urva. It functioned there until October 1951 under the guidance of Swami Vimalananda. A permanent site for the Ashrama measuring about seven acres, along with the Students' Home for boys, was acquired with the help of M. Keshava Pai. Under the guidance of Swami Adidevananda, the charitable dispensary was started in 1955. The Swami Vivekananda Memorial Building was constructed in 1963 to accommodate 50 students of Balaka Ashrama, which provides free board and lodging facilities, stationery, and clothing. There is a shrine for prayer, as well as library and a reading room.

Apart from these centres of the Ramakrishna Order, there are some private centres maintained by devotees drawing inspiration from the main body of the Order, such as the Ramakrishna Ashrama of Kollegal, Davangere, and Sirsi. A special mention may be made of Sri Sharadadevi Andha Vikasa Kendra of Shimoga, which imparts education to blind children. The person behind this institution is A. Padmanabhan who has dedicated himself to the cause of the blind.

RAMAKRISHNA SEVA SANGHA, MYSORE

An event of considerable significance for admirers of Vivekananda's life and achievements was the Youth Convention held in 1980 by the Ramakrishna Math and Mission at Belur. Several young men from Mysore who attended this convention felt inspired to contribute to the betterment of common people in their own state. This was the origin of the Ramakrishna Seva Sangha in 1981. The three guiding stars of this memorable voluntary effort were Swami Harshananda (one-time President of the Bangalore Ashrama), Swami Somanathananda (ex-President of the Mysore Ashrama), and Swami Sureshananda (who later became President of the Mysore Ashrama). Thereafter, voluntary work of two kinds was planned: (i) villages situated in tribal belts and (ii) the outlying extension of Mysore city.

The first category of work is progressing in Bettadabeedu (Heggada-devanakote Taluk) where free medical aid, and supply of medicines, educational aids to the local school is provided by volunteers. Medical camps are held every Sunday and more than 2,000 patients have been treated so far. Free house sites have been distributed to more than 30 families and bank loans have been secured to help local farmers to improve agriculture.

The Ramakrishna Seva Sangha, Mysore, has acquired from the City Improvement Trust Board one-and-half-acres of land in Ramakrishna Nagar on which a kindergarten-school and an outpatient charitable dispensary have been started for the benefit of the people of this new extension. There are now over sixty children studying in the school, which has a small building of its own. The Sangha also organizes the sale of literature concerning Ramakrishna and Vivekananda.

A notable achievement by Dr Balasubramanyam, a young medical doctor, along with a team of other young doctors, has been a remarkable service to the education, health, and environment of Brahmagiri, a small village of tribals who were displaced by the Kapila River project. Today the Vivekananda Youth Centre has blossomed into a hospital and a school, largely from public donations and help from the state government. Swami Sureshananda, President of the Ramakrishna Ashrama, Mysore, is the guiding spirit behind these activities.

VIVEKANANDA GIRIJANA KALYANA KENDRA (VGKK), BR HILLS

This organization is dedicated to the ideal of 'service of God in Man'. It was originally started by H. Sudarshan, who in 1977, inspired and motivated by Vivekananda's call for service of the poor, has ceaselessly worked ever since. His area of service now extends to Yalandur,

Chamarajanagar, and Kollegal taluks of Karnataka and also to Satyamangala taluk of Tamil Nadu. The project covers an area of about 60 km radius and serves a tribal population of 20,000. The initial object of VGKK was curative health, but gradually it grew into an integrated tribal development project, which covers health, education, community organization, cottage industry and educational training, agriculture, housing and co-operatives. Now this huge philanthropic institution stands as a testimony to the undaunted courage, perseverance, and service-mindedness of H. Sudarshan, the moving spirit behind this project (Anon. n.d.: 77).

Besides the above institutions and persons who started the Rama-krishna movement in Karnataka, we may briefly outline here the intellectuals, scholars, and poets of Karnataka who popularized the ideas of Ramakrishna and Vivekananda in Karnataka. Among them, mention may be made of K. V. Puttappa (pen-name Kuvempu), Professor Prabhu Shankara, C. D. Narasimhiah, and B. Sheik Ali. K. V. Puttappa, one of the greatest literary figures of modern Karnataka, was a disciple of Ramakrishna Ashrama, Mysore, and the recipient of the Gnana Peeth Award. A Vice-Chancellor of Mysore University, he wrote biographies of Ramakrishna and Vivekananda in Kannada and also made a com-parative study of Basaveshwara, the twelfth-century revolutionary saint of Karnataka, and Vivekananda (Mysore State Level Committee 1967: 251–61).

Prabhu Shankara is another disciple of Ramakrishna Ashrama and played an important role in the Ramakrishna movement in Karnataka. An expert on Shaivism and Veerashaivism, he was a Professor of Kannada in Mysore University. After retiring, he was appointed as visiting Professor of the Vivekananda Chair instituted by the University of Mysore. He has published a biography of Vivekananda in English (Shankara 2001).

B. Sheik Ali is an eminent historian of Karnataka. He was professor of History in the University of Mysore and also Vice Chancellor of Mangalore and Goa Universities. He has analysed the historical concepts of Vivekananda (Anon. n.d.: 44–6). C. D. Narasimhaih was Professor of English in the University of Mysore. A distinguished scholar of English literature, he has analysed the writing of the Vivekananda from the point of view of literary perspective (Anon. n.d.: 47–52). D. M. Nanjundappa, an eminent economist of Karnataka and Professor of Economics and Vice Chancellor of Karnataka University and Bangalore Universities, on the other hand, has analysed Vivekananda's teachings from the perspective of economic development (Anon. n.d.: 61–5). This is not an exhaustive list of Karnataka scholars on Vivekananda and the Ramakrishna movement. There are a large number of works in Kannada dealing with the subject. Mysore city has adopted the names of Ramakrishna, Vivekananda, Sharada Devi, and the famous disciple of Ramakrishna Movement, namely Kuvempu (K. V. Puttappa), in various new areas of the city. This shows the people's awareness of the teachings and the role of the Bengali saint in the Renaissance and religious movement.

CONCLUDING REMARKS

From the above, a few general conclusions may be drawn. As Bengal was the heart of Indian Renaissance in the nineteenth century, and Calcutta was the capital of British colonialism, East met West in Bengal. Subsequently, a deep impact was made in the interior parts of India by Bengali intellectuals, saints, and reformers, among whom, Vivekananda is outstanding. Vivekananda's interaction with Karnataka resulted in several socio-religious reforms. His meetings in Karnataka during his travel in the region covered all strata of society, from Maharaja to Dewan, from executive engineer to forest officer, from householders to pandits, from humble beings to aristocrats. Chamaraja Wodeyar and Dewan Sheshadri Iyer came under the magnetic personality of the monk from Bengal. Vivekananda was partly responsible for the modernization and preservation of ancient tradition in Mysore. The Ramakrishna movement in Karnataka has little of the recognition that is usually associated with similar movements. In Karnataka, progress of the movement has always been modest but steady. The Ramakrishna movement in Karnataka has gradually taken into its fold the educational, health, social, and economic problems of the community in selected areas. Its strength lies in its steady expansion. The Ramakrishna movement in Karnataka owes its progress to the devotion and hard work put in by monks and householders alike to give life to Vivekananda's hopes. Lastly, the Ramakrishna movement has attracted leading academics from the universities of Karnataka, many of whom have become active in the movement. They have contributed to the development of literary movements in Kannada language and represent various disciplines of knowledge. In this sense, the Ramakrishna movement in Karnataka is mostly middle-class, educated, and with an orientation towards practical Vedanta. In short, socio-religious reforms in Karnataka owe much to the influence of nineteenth-century Bengal, channelled through Vivekananda and subsequently through the Ramakrishna Math and Mission.

NOTE

1. Dr Palpu and Sree Narayana Guru are also discussed in Chapter 8 of this book.

BIBLIOGRAPHY

Anon. (1992), *Padasparsha Souvenir—1892–1992 Swami Vivekananda's Mysore Visit Centenary,* Mysore: Ramakrishna Ashrama.
Anon. (1926), *The Ramakrishna Math and Mission Convention,* Belur, Howrah-Bengal: The Math.
Diwakar, R. R. (1967), *Karnataka through the Ages,* Bangalore: Karnataka Government.
Gundappa, D.V. (1971), *Gnapaka Chitrashale,* Vol. IV, Mysore: Kavyalaya.
His Eastern and Western Admirers (1983), *Reminiscences of Swami Vivekananda,* Calcutta: Advaita Ashrama.
Majumdar, Ramesh Chandra (1965), *Swami Vivekananda: A Historical Review,* Calcutta: General Printers and Publishers.
Mysore State Level Committee (1967), 'Basaveshwar and Vivekananda as Social Reformers', in *Mysore State Level Committee for 8th Centenary Celebrations of Basaveshwara Commemoration Volume,* Bangalore: Mysore State Level Committee for 8th Centenary Celebration of Basaveshwara 1967-Commemoration, pp. 251–61.
Swami Purushottamananda (1992), *Kannada Neladalli Vivekananda,* Bangalore: Ramakrishna Math.
Shankara, P. (2001), 'Spiritual Realization in Shaivism', *Prabuddha Bharata,* Vol. 106, No. 10, pp. 511–15.
Swami Somanathananda (1994), *Swami Vivekananda Jeevan Charitre,* Mysore: Shri Ramakrishna Ashrama.
Swami Vivekananda (1964), *The Complete Works of Swami Vivekananda* (Mayavati Memorial Edition), Vols 4 and 6, Calcutta: Advaita Ashrama.

Part Two
Responding to Colonial Modernity

6

How Favourable is Puritan Islam to Modernity?

A Study of the Ahl-i Hadīs in Late Nineteenth/Early Twentieth Century South Asia

MARTIN RIEXINGER

Based on observations in North Africa, Ernest Gellner (1981: 5ff., 58ff., 170) argued that '... [t]he severe discipline of puritan Islam may be in fact compatible with, or positively favourable to modern social organisation.' According to him, the break with intercessionary Sufism places the burden of salvation on the individual believer who has to fulfil his religious duties meticulously, which forces him to systematize his life in a way the Calvinists in Early Modern Europe had done according to Max Weber's 'Protestantism/capitalism' thesis. Gellner, therefore, alleges that Puritan Islam encourages the decline of the belief in miracles, and thus 'disenchants the World'. Furthermore, he sees an affinity between the puritan lifestyle and urbanity: 'Only urban life provides a good base for the puritans—because their rigorism requires literacy' (Gellner 1981: 147).[1] According to him, the counterpart of puritan Islam—intercessionary Sufism dominated by Sufi sheikhs—is rooted in rural society.

Gellner's thesis was favourably received not only in studies on Islamic fundamentalism in general (Riesebrodt 1990: 38) but also in literature on Islamic movements in South Asia, although not always with explicit reference (for example, Robinson 1997, 2000a; Nasr 2001: 44f.).[2] This chapter will question the applicability of this thesis to developments in South Asian Islamic communities on the basis of results gained from research on the Ahl-i Hadīs in the Punjab under British rule. For this purpose, three aspects, namely social background, religious teachings, and social ethics, are taken into consideration.

HISTORICAL BACKGROUND

The Ahl-i Hadīs are one of the Sunni schools of thought in South Asia. Their emergence can be traced back to the puritan trend initiated by Shāh Walīyullāh Dihlawī (1703–63). However, the Ahl-i Hadīs proper did not come into being before the mid-nineteenth century. Based on the teaching of Walīyullāh, his grandson Shāh Ismāʿīl Shahīd (b. 1779) and the military leader Sayyid Ahmad Barelwī (b. 1786?) formed the religious-cum-political movement *tarīqa-yi muhammadīya*. Their military actions against the Sikhs on the Afghan borders, which ended with their defeat in 1831, are not central to the issue currently under discussion. More important in the religious context is the fact that, before starting military operations, the *tarīqa-yi muhammadīya* undertook a collective *hajj*. Some of its members did not return to India immediately. Instead they travelled to Yemen in order to study under the renowned *ʿālim* and politician Muhammad b. ʿAlī al-Shawkānī (1760–1834) whose religious teachings betray the influence of the doctrines of the Andalusian Zāhirī Ibn Hazm (994–1064) and the Damascene neo-Hanbalite Ibn Taymīya (1263–1328) (Haykel 2003: 127ff.; Riexinger 2004: 108ff.). Al-Shawkānī's teachings reinforced the tendency away from Hanafism and the *madhhab*-system in general (see below), which had already been initiated by Walīyullāh. Furthermore al-Shawkānī's anti-Sufism applies to rituals and teachings. Therefore his influence caused Sufi metaphysical concepts, which were still of central importance for Walīyullāh and the *tarīqa-yi muhammadīya* (Gaborieau 2000), to disappear gradually among the Ahl-i Hadīs. Al-Shawkānī's attitude towards Sufism resembles those of Muhammad b. ʿAbd al-Wahhāb (1703–93) but are slightly less radical (Haykel 2003: 127ff.). This did not keep their Muslim opponents, the Arya Samaj, and the colonial authorities from polemically labelling the Ahl-i Hadīs as Wahhabīs.

Whereas the majority of Sunnis believe that every Muslim is bound to follow (*taqlīd*) one of the four schools of law (*madhhab*, pl. *madhāhib*), the Ahl-i Hadīs do not accept their authority. Furthermore they do not acknowledge analogical reasoning (*qiyās*) as source of law and some of them even reject the authority of the consensus of scholars (*ijmāʿ*). Instead they urge an exclusive orientation on the primary sources of Islamic law, the Qur'an and the Hadīth, the unmediated word of God and the Prophet, hence their designation as 'followers of the Prophetic tradition'. They assert that the legal scholar has to base his judgements on proof texts from those two sources (*ijtihād*) and that he is obliged to explain them to the laymen (*'ammī*) who address him with a request.[3]

The practical outcome of these seemingly fundamental differences in legal theory is rather meagre though: most of the differences concern matters of ritual and purity.[4] Nevertheless these issues often led to clashes with the Hanafi majority (Metcalf 1982: 286ff.; Riexinger 2004: 164ff.). However, some particularities are of greater social significance. First, some of their ritual practices stress the equality of believers. This holds good in particular for their demand that even in villages a congregational prayer with a sermon (*khutba*) has to be held on Fridays (*al-jum'a fī l-qurā*). Furthermore the sermon has to be held not in Arabic but in the local vernacular in order to enhance the religious understanding of the laymen. The Ahl-i Hadīs do not accept the principle of *kafā'a*, which by prohibiting the marriage of a man of lower social status was used to legitimize the persistence of caste-like structures among South Asian Muslims. Second, certain legal doctrines strengthen the position of women. The Ahl-i Hadīs reject *talāq al-bid'a*, that is the repudiation of a wife by exclaiming the formula on one occasion and not during a period of three months. In addition, they make it easier for a wife to buy herself out (*khul'*) of a dysfunctional marriage by seeking the mediation of a scholar and by forfeiting her dowry (*mahr*) (Riexinger 2004: 161f., 425ff.).

In concordance with other Islamic puritan reform movements between the eighteenth and twentieth centuries, the Ahl-i Hadīs abhor mystical practices implying the adoration of someone else other than God—like the ascription of God-like attributes to the Prophet and the veneration of saints and their graves—as deviation from monotheism. This set them in opposition to the dominant mystically inspired piety among South Asian Muslims.

The Ahl-i Hadīs first found their following in Delhi, Bengal, Bihar, and the Benares area. From the 1880s onwards the Punjab emerged as a further important stronghold, with Amritsar surpassing all older centres except Delhi in importance.

SOCIAL BASE

The Ahl-i Hadīs are an obvious case to challenge received wisdom on the social background of Islamic puritanism. Existing studies tend to characterize them as an upper-class sect (be it aristocratic or capitalist) with strong urban roots (Metcalf 1982: 198, 268).[5] This opinion gained plausibility from another cliché: the description of their Sufi opponents, the Barelwīs, as representatives of a backward and moribund, rural 'folk'-Islam (Smith 1946: 320).

The available data urge caution. With regard to the Punjab, a variety of sources (census publications, biographical literature, articles in contemporary magazines, and intelligence sources) show that the Ahl-i Hadīs indeed found their following in the more urban tracts of the province. However, it was often not in the administrative and commercial centres themselves but in their rural surroundings that the first people converted to their teachings. In certain 'Ahl-i Hadīs villages', this community formed the majority of the Muslim population. Some of these places, especially Bhojian (*tehsil* Taran Taran, district Amritsar) and Lakhoke (district Ferozpur), developed into important centres of religious instruction from which a sizeable number of scholars emerged (Riexinger 2004: 189ff., 199ff.).[6] In the recent decades, this does not seem to have changed considerably. A survey of religious scholars active in the 1980s shows that most of them originate from the urbanized tracts of the Punjab but from villages or small towns in these areas (Yusuf 1989).

Data from other regions corroborate the results of the observations in the Punjab. With regard to Bengal, British observations on the 'Hindustani fanatics' show that so-called Wahhābīs who flocked to the *mujāhidīn* of Chamarkand on the Afghan border after World War I were predominantly of rural origin (Baha 1979: 142ff.). In the UP, the *qasba*s Mau Nath Banjan, Sahaswan, and Basti, which rather resembled villages, brought forth a number of Ahl-i Hadīs scholars that surpasses or almost equals that of Benares, one of their centres. In reverse it is noteworthy that major 'modern' cities like Allahabad and Kanpur with their strong entrepreneurial population were anything but Ahl-i Hadīs strongholds. The majority of the Muslims there practised a rather unpuritan 'folk' Islam.[7] In Bombay, India's commercial centre and most 'modern' city of the country, the Ahl-i Hadīs were strikingly weak.[8]

The question whether the Ahl-i Hadīs developed something of a particular 'work-ethic' or 'spirit of capitalism' that would set them apart from other Muslims is impossible to answer with regard to the period of time under discussion, although empirical research on the respective attitudes of contemporary Ahl-i Hadīs would of course be very interesting. But it would seem that this issue was not of particular importance for their '*ulamā*', who, unlike Calvinist theologians in Early Modern Europe, did not bother to write elaborate treatises on this subject. They admonished their followers to abstain from extensive spending on weddings and religious holidays and from indulging in frivolous pleasures such as smoking, fireworks, or going to see movies.[9] This 'innerworldly ascetism' (Weber 1920: 192f.) might indeed have been favourable to the accumulation of capital among the Ahl-i Hadīs, if a particular kind of conspicuous spending had not been widespread among them, namely, extensive donations for missionary purposes.[10]

Quite a number of Ahl-i Hadīs fit perfectly the popular image of a 'sect of shopkeepers' completed by urban professionals and officials. An intelligence survey on 'Wahhabis of note' dating from 1876 identifies 12.7 per cent of prominent Ahl-i Hadīs as traders and manufacturers, 7.4 per cent as officials, 5.7 as teachers, 1.9 as professionals, and 0.4 per cent as lawyers.[11] *Thekedārs* often appear as benefactors financing the building of mosques and religious schools (*madrasa*, pl. *madāris*).[12] The *Anjuman Ishā'at ul-Islām*, a short-lived organization of Ahl-i Hadīs scholars and laymen formed by Muhammad Husayn Batālwī at Lahore in 1880, comprised several officials and secular teachers, two thekedārs, a wholesale trader, and a lawyer.[13] The leading committee of the Ahl-i Hadīs congregation in Peshawar, which consisted mainly of migrants from Delhi and the Punjab, was dominated by traders and manufacturers (Khānpurī 1985: 160, 165ff.).

Such singular observations seem to support received wisdom describing puritan religiosity as an essentially urban upper-class phenomenon. However, a crosscheck suggests that the correlation of the puritan/Sufi dichotomy with the urban/rural and the upper-class/lower-class dichotomy is less convincing. Liebeskind (1998: 282ff., 304f.) has analysed the membership of the two councils controlling the administration of north Indian *darar*s. Their social composition would perfectly fit the clichés about the Ahl-i Hadīs membership because they consist of officials, professionals, entrepreneurs, and traders. The fact that quite a number come from faraway places indicates a strong vertical and horizontal mobility. It is far from surprising that, whenever non-scholars are integrated into religious activities, those with a high social standing and professional experience in talking will prevail. The simple fact that laymen played a greater role among the Ahl-i Hadīs than in other Islamic groups may account for the fact that among them such notables are more visible. With regard to the role of traders in puritan

Islamic movements it is necessary to stress that not only ideological but also practical aspects account for their involvement. As a mobile group, tradesmen are more likely to come into contact with religious ideas other than those in their regional setting. Hence they may play a decisive role when puritan Islam takes roots, whereas their importance may decline later.[14]

To sum up, even if the background of the Ahl-i Hadīs might in general have been more urban and wealthier than that of other Islamic schools of thought, the exceptions are so important that the designation as urban upper-class movement conceals central components. In reverse, the same applies to the Barelwīs.

THE AHL-I HADĪS AND SECULAR EDUCATION IN THE PUNJAB

In one respect the Ahl-i Hadīs showed more affinity to modernity than the adherents of other Sunni schools of thought. Many well-to-do lay members and some scholars played a leading role in the local Muslim associations for the promotion of welfare and secular education (*anjumans*). The outstanding figure among the *'ulamā'* was Sanā'ullāh Amritsarī (1868–1948), the son of poor Kashmiri immigrants whose brothers had risen from rags to riches in the textile business. He often spoke at the annual gatherings of the *Anjuman-i Himāyat-i Islām* in Lahore and actively supported the *Anjuman-i islāmīya* in his hometown. Often he criticized the disdain of many religious scholars for secular education. The lawyer Ilāhī Bakhsh Malwādā, a friend of Sanā'ullāh and headman of the Arain-*birādarī* in Lahore, was a leading member of the Anjuman-i Himāyat-i Islām and later formed the Anjuman-i islāmīya in Hoshiarpur after being transferred to an official post there.[15] Salmān Sulaymān Mansūrpūrī (1867–1930), another lawyer with a sound religious education and a close associate of Sanā'ullāh, often turned up as speaker at anjuman gatherings (Riexinger 2004: 177). Sanā'ullāh's closest collaborator, the scholar Ibrāhīm Mīr Siyālkotī was among the founding members of the Anjuman-i islāmīya in his hometown.[16] The affinity of parts of the Ahl-i Hadīs with these educational associations even found its architectural expression. In the 1920s, the Ahl-i Hadīs of Lahore consciously erected their *Masjid-i mubārak* on the site adjoining the Islamia College founded and directed by the Anjuman-i Himāyat-i Islām.[17] Based on these examples, it might be tempting to infer that the Ahl-i Hadīs were positively inclined towards secular education. As the following section will show, this is only half of the truth.

RELIGIOUS TEACHINGS: HOW 'DISENCHANTED' WAS THE
WORLD VIEW OF PURITAN MUSLIMS IN BRITISH INDIA?

A conflict that arose among the Ahl-i Hadīs from 1902 onwards shows
that the relation between puritan Islam and modernity was very
ambivalent. To understand this, one has to take theology into account,
and in particular the exegesis of the Qur'an, which is an important aspect
of Islam that those who stress the affinity of puritan Islam seldom consider.

In 1902, Sanā'ullāh Amritsarī, editor of the magazine *Ahl-i Hadīs*,
published a commentary on the Qur'ān in Arabic, which immediately
provoked angry reactions from his colleagues. They reproached him for
his method as well as for the content. Sanā'ullāh did not take into account
the exegetical traditions (*ahadith*) that the majority of the Ahl-i Hadīs
scholars saw as indispensable for the interpretation of the Qur'an.[18] This
method did allow him to rationalize several reports of miracles, some of
them in the same manner as Sayyid Ahmad Khān, but this was not the
main bone of contention. The most disputed issue was that Sanā'ullāh
did not interpret the phrase '*thumma stawā 'alā l-'arsh*' (verse 7:54 *et al.*)
in the sense that God is actually sitting (down) on the throne. Instead he
explained these words as an attribute of God's power and sovereignty.
Thus Sanā'ullāh reopened one of the oldest theological debates (on the
relevance of the question of *istiwā*) in the history of Islam.[19]

In fact, the question may be old but that it gave rise to a new
controversy in India around 1900 has something to do with the social
background of the Ahl-i Hadīs and the general socio-cultural setting of
British India. For an analysis, two aspects mentioned before have to be
considered: individual responsibility in puritan Islam and its attraction
for some members of the secularly educated elite. The demand of the
Ahl-i Hadīs that legal judgements have to be based on the two primary
sources of Islamic law and not on the legal handbooks of the Hanafi
school of law implies that the *muftī* has to explain the relevant proof
texts to the laymen asking for a religious ruling (*mustaftī*). This elevates
the status of the laymen. It is most likely that such an attitude appealed
to those who due to their social status and their expertise in other fields
expected to be taken seriously in matters of religion, a group of people
among whom we may expect to find the well-educated laymen in the
anjumans.

But here emerges the problem. For most Ahl-i Hadīs scholars the
primacy of the Qur'ān and the Hadīth is not restricted to law and ethics

but also shapes their theology and hence their world view in general. The contentious question 'does God sit on the throne?' shows this problem clearly. The anthropomorphist interpretation of the Ahl-i Hadīs in the Hanbalī tradition implies the so-called 'Sunna-cosmology' based on the exegetical Prophetic traditions.[20] In this concept, the idea of a compact heaven on which God's throne is to rest is combined with the idea that the sun bows down before the throne of God and the belief that lightning and thunder are caused by the angel Ra'd who drives the clouds like a shepherd drives his flock.[21] The world view of Hanbalī theology held by Sanā'ullāh's opponents was the most conservative in the history of Islamic thought. Around 1900 it simply represented an embarrassment for someone who had encountered during his secular education that the earth revolves around the sun and that the sky is not a dome but simply an optical appearance caused by refraction. Furthermore it was an embarrassment for those like Sanā'ullāh who confronted adherents of other religions in public disputations (*munāzaras*), especially the Arya Samaj who picked on traditional Islamic cosmology with delight (Amritsarī 1916: 39). With his commentaries on the Qur'an, Sanā'ullāh explicitly addressed this class of *ta'līm yāftas*, for whom he wanted to provide an alternative to outdated interpretations on the one hand and the more radical modernism of Sayyid Ahmad Khān on the other.[22]

But for most of the Ahl-i Hadīs scholars, the accommodation of Qur'anical statements to world views promoted by secular institutions of learning was not a primary concern. What counted for them was the fact that the issue of 'istiwā' has been for centuries the shibboleth that marked the difference between exponents of literalist and anthropomorphist interpretations and advocates of a more rationalist approach entailing the allegorical interpretation of verses relating to God's attributes. Following their foremost role model, Ibn Taymīya, those Ahl-i Hadīs frequently indulged in polemics against such *jahmī* and *mu'tazilī* 'heretics', terms with which they also denounced Sanā'ullāh (Ghaznawī n.d.; Khānpurī n.d.).

The issue even affected the organization of the Ahl-i Hadīs. In 1906, Sanā'ullāh began to organize the 'All India Ahl-i Hādīs Conference', which convened for the first time in 1912. In this association he let laymen play an important role. His intention was to diminish the influence of the majority of 'ulamā' who were hostile to him (Riexinger 2004: 513). The dispute was finally settled at the Islamic World Conference in Mecca 1926 by the moderation of 'Abd al-'Azīz Ibn Sa'ūd, ruler of the Hijāz and Najd, king of Saudi Arabia from 1928 onwards. He himself had to come to grips with similar problems in his realm when he tried to push through moderate reforms in the educational sector against the resistance of the Wahhābī 'ulamā' (Wahba 1964: 48ff.; Steinberg 2002: 291ff.).

The second theological issue that tore Ahl-i Hadīs apart in the early twentieth century was the question of miracles. The stress the majority of scholars put on the affirmation of the reports of miracles in the Qur'an and the Hadīth contradicts the assumption that the world view of puritan Muslims is really 'disenchanted'. Against this one might argue that, whereas puritan Islam does affirm reports of miracles in the Qur'an, it at least diminishes the importance of the supernatural for the present. But even this is not the case. The Ahl-i Hadīs ascribe to their most pious members *qabulīyat-i duʿā*. This term means that their prayers were accepted by God with particular favour. Thus those scholars could bring about unexpected healing and economic success with God's help. Hence their social role does not differ too much from Sufi sheikhs.[23]

Another example shows that theological considerations on miracles affected the attitude of certain Ahl-i Hadīs towards modern science and education in general. Muhammad Husayn Batālwī, who originally was a supporter of activities to advance secular education among Muslims, later became increasingly conservative and rejected 'un-Islamic' teachings propagated in modern schools. In particular, a chemistry textbook provoked his anger. He denounced it for presenting the *'necharī* point of view' by stating that natural laws produce water from hydrogen and oxygen. Muhammad Husayn instead defended the classical Sunnī doctrine according to which there are no natural laws but only God almighty who governs and creates the world in every moment. Hence the regularity of events is a divine grace but not an unchangeable rule.[24]

In the field of theology the core of the issue becomes apparent. The strict orientation towards the Hadīth instead of secondary interpretations, which appealed to those with a secular education in the field of religious law, leads to the most embarrassing results for these social groups, if applied to the exegesis of the Qur'an. Thus the affinity of puritan Islam with modernity in one field created severe problems in another. Furthermore, it becomes obvious at this point that parallels between Calvinism and puritan Islam should be drawn with considerable caution. Calvin did not propagate literalism but he argued that the Scriptures should be read allegorically in case their literal interpretation implied conflicts with scientific findings (Hooykaas 1972: 111ff.).[25]

THE IMPACT OF A NEW ALLY

From the mid-1920s onwards there was one issue that united the divided Ahl-i Hadīs: the state that was to become Saudi Arabia in 1928. Before and during World War I, most leading Ahl-i Hadīs denied any affinity with the Wahhābīs and the Āl Sa'ūd in order to stress their loyalty to British rule.[26] This consideration diminished in importance from 1919 onwards when many leading Ahl-i Hadīs joined the Khilafat Movement and the Indian National Congress. Thus political impediments could not keep them any more from applauding the success of a like-minded movement when the Wahhābī–Sa'ūdī alliance under the later king 'Abd al-'Azīz drove the pro-British Hāshimīs from the Hijāz.

Both Sanā'ullāh and his opponents travelled to the Islamic World Conference in Mecca in 1926 and forged those strong organizational ties, which have gained considerable strength during the following eight decades. The fact that the only political issue able to unite the Ahl-i Hadīs was their support for a country with a pre-modern social fabric and political structure hardly supports the notion of the affinity between puritanism and modernity. To the contrary, especially after 1947, the growing influence of Saudi Wahhābism on the Ahl-i Hadīs weakened those aspects in the teachings of the Ahl-i Hadīs that are favourable to modernity. Even if there might still be certain modernists with an Ahl-i Hadīs background, there is no scholar today who is particularly committed to the reconciliation of inherited Islamic doctrines with science.

SOCIAL ETHICS

Robinson (1997: 118), though generally favourable to Gellner's thesis, expresses reservations with regard to the burden the meticulous fulfilment of duties heaps on men and, even more, on women. The fact that individual responsibility does not necessarily imply individual liberty is exemplified by the rather restrictive regulations promoted by the Ahl-i Hadīs scholars. Even Sanā'ullāh—generally more open-minded than other 'ulamā'—expressed his disdain for liberal Western legal thought, which restricts punishments to acts bringing about worldly harm to others, and urged a strict implementation of morality by state agencies with the help of the physical punishments decreed by the Qur'an (hadd, pl. hudud).[27]

The attitude of the Ahl-i Hadīs maulwīs to the women's question hardly provides evidence for an inclination to modernity. In apologetical contexts Ahl-i Hadīs scholars stressed that their regulations regarding divorce were more practical and more favourable to women than those of the Hanafīs. However, they never bothered to develop a systematic approach to improve the status of women, and, therefore, clung to other doctrines that were less favourable than those of the Hanafīs, for example, the demand that all women, including those who have already had intercourse (*thayyiba*), need a guardian (*walī*) for concluding marriage. With regard to one issue there was a connection between the puritanism of the Ahl-i Hadīs and the status of women: their rejection of non-Islamic customary laws, which had been officially acknowledged by the colonial authorities in the Punjab in 1872 (Gilmartin 1988b). Ahl-i Hadīs scholars such as Muhammad Husayn and Sanā'ullāh continually rallied against these regulations, which deprived daughters of all their inheritance rights.[28]

Although certain regulations proposed by the Ahl-i Hadīs were more favourable to women, the attitude of their scholars clearly ranks among the most conservative ones in South Asian Muslim society in general. At a time when Muslim women began to enter the public sphere, the Ahl-i Hadīs maulwīs insisted that they should confine their activities to domestic affairs. Most of them shunned even modest attempts to improve the status of women under the Anglo-Muhammadan Law. This is exemplified by their reaction to the 'Child Marriage Restraint', or 'Sarda Bill', which was discussed from 1928 and finally became law in 1930. The proposal, which was not brought forth by the government but by secular-minded Hindus and Muslims, put up the minimum age for marriages to fourteen years for girls and eighteen years for young men (Forbes 1996: 85ff.). The majority of scholars denounced this as unlawful infringement on religious rituals and beliefs. A few scholars including Sanā'ullāh dared to oppose such a view. He argued that it was indeed permissible under religious aspects to reform practices like child-marriage, which bring about harm under contemporary circumstances. Because of this attitude even some of his closest associates parted ways with him and expressed their disdain in malicious polemics.[29]

However, the conservative attitude of the scholars contrasts with the fact that a number of Ahl-i Hadīs laymen made considerable efforts to improve the educational standard of Muslim women. Rashīd ul-Khayrī (1868–1936), scion of an old Ahl-i Hadīs family in Delhi, started a career as publisher and author. In his novel as well as in his magazine '*Ismat*' he argued for a better education of women. At the same time he was a leading lay member of Ahl-i Hadīs organizations and he wrote in Sanā'ullāh's magazine, 'Ahl-i Hadīs', in order to explain his aims to religious

scholars (Khayrī 1964; Minault 1998: 129ff.). Another friend of
Sanāʾullāh, ʿAbd ul-Haqq ʿAbbās (d. 1960), founded the *Madrasat ul-
Banāt* in his hometown Jullundhur. Thus he intended to break the
duopoly held by Christian missionaries and Aryas in the field of education
for girls.[30] Unfortunately sources documenting the reaction of religious
scholars to their activities have not turned up as yet. But at least in the
case of Rashīd ul-Khayrī the deviation from strict Ahl-i Hadīs norms is
unmistakable. Whereas the scholars opposed the depiction of humans in
general, he illustrated the cover of his magazine with unveiled women.[31]

CONCLUSION

The thesis that puritan Islam is particularly favourable to 'modernity' is
a generalization that conceals important aspects (Eaton 2000).[32] The
systematization of everyday life in the sense of Weber's 'inner-worldly
asceticism' can clearly be observed, but its practical relevance has to be
evaluated in comparison with two other aspects of puritan Islam: its
mythological world view and its restrictive social ethics. Certain adherents
of puritan Islam managed to adapt themselves to modernity by discarding
the latter two aspects. In this context it is noteworthy that some leading
modernists, including Sayyid Ahmad Khān, hailed from a Ahl-i Hadīs
background and used to pray in their fashion (Riexinger 2004: 167ff.).
Nawwāb Muhsin ul-Mulk and Deputy Nazīr Ahmad may be cited as
further examples (Metcalf 1982: 273, 282ff.; Siddīqī 1971: 41ff.). But
these figures do not represent a general tendency. The religious leadership
rejected their views.[33] The fact that with the Taliban the most 'anti-
modernist' movement in recent Islamic history emerged out of the puritan
tradition of South Asian Islam, though not from the Ahl-i Hadīs but
from the Deoband school, reminds us of the double-faced potential of
this religious tendency.

    The thesis of a positive inclination of puritan Islam to modernity was
based on a simplistic adaptation of Weber's 'Protestantism–capitalism'
thesis, which was based on the equation of puritan Islam with Calvinism
in spite of certain important differences in the religious teachings.
However one should not throw out the baby with the bathwater. Weber
saw religion as one important but relatively independent factor
determining social change. As such it interacts with aspirations of other
kinds and material factors (Riesebrodt 1990: 10, 24ff., 250f.), sometimes
in a smooth manner, sometimes in conflict. Whereas some of their
adherents try to adapt these doctrines to other factors, others will attempt

to mould the world according to their precepts. Furthermore, Weber taught to give pre-eminence to the analysis of concrete historical phenomena over the application of theories and he did not doubt that the outcome of doctrines might be quite different from intentions. Obviously, this approach is much more promising than black and white functionalism or theories that seek the social formations and interests behind the camouflage of religious teachings. The schematic application of his theses will lead to wrong conclusions. Combined with a sharpened focus on the particular aspects of certain traditions and their interaction with contexts, Weber's ideas may still help to reach deeper insights into the developments of Islamic societies.

NOTES

1. On urban arrogance and middle-class bias, see also Gellner (1981: 163).
2. See also below with special reference to the Ahl-i Hadīs.
3. Al-Shawkani (n.d.: 37, l. -13ff.). '*Ijtihād* of the laymen means asking for a proof.'
4. The most important ones are that the Ahl-i Hadīs keep their hands to the ears while bowing down during prayer (*raf' al-yadayn*) and their earlier prayer times.
5. Metcalf stresses, however, that her thesis is preliminary and should be taken with caution. See also Robinson (1997: 111, 127, 130, 133f.), Malik (1989: 355ff.; 1997: 212ff., 279f.), and Reetz (2001: 302).
6. For Bhojian, see Ansari (1984). For a list of *madaris* in the Punjab, see Naushahrawi (1970: 172ff.). Further important examples are Zira (district Ferozpur), Kot Kapora (Faridkot state), Sauhadra (district Gujranwala), Mamun Kanjan (district Lyallpur) and Badhwana Khas (district Jhang).
7. Naushahrawi (1970) lists 51 Ahl-i Hadīs scholars from Delhi, 35 from Mau Nath Banjan, 18 from Benares, 15 from Sahaswan, 10 from Basti, plus 6 from neighbouring villages. Kanpur did not bring forth a single Ahl-i Hadīs scholar of note, Allahabad only four. For the strength of *sajjāda nashīn*s and *ta'ziya*-brotherhoods in Allahabad, see Bayly (1975: 79ff.).
8. The small congregation there mainly consisted of migrants from the Punjab, *Ahl-i Hadīs*, 27 January 1922, p. 7f.
9. Fātāwā-yi sana'iya 195, 797; *Ahl-i Hadīs*, 18 January 1924, p. 5; Bhatti (1998: 401f.).
10. According to Hamilton (1996: 101), the same was true for English non-conformists in the eighteenth century. Therefore he urges caution with regard to this argument.
11. According to Hardy (1964), 21.9 per cent of the Ahl-i Hadīs propagandists were maulwis, and 13.8 per cent were farmers. The fact that 30 of the 63 farmers listed hailed from the Ferozpur district further elucidates how strongly the Ahl-i Hadīs were rooted in the rural Muslim population of this particular area.

12. *Police Abstract of Intelligence—Punjab* 1886, p. 224; *Police Abstract of Intelligence—Punjab* 1895, p. 62; Salafi (1994: 84f.); Bhatti (1996: 169; 1998: 401ff.).

13. *Ishā'at us-Sunnat*, Zamīma (appendix) to Vol. III. fasc. 12 (December 1880), 1ff. This magazine published by Muhammad Husayn Batālwī from Lahore since 1877 is one of the earliest, if not the earliest, magazines worldwide dedicated to the propagation of a specific Islamic doctrine.

14. With regard to this aspect, it is worth drawing attention to the spread of 'Wahhabism' in Bamako (Mali) since 1945. This development, which has been analysed by Amselle (1987), does bear striking resemblance to the emergence of the Ahl-i Hadīs in India although it took place in a completely different context. Due to the fact that it occurred one century later, it is much better documented. Merchants were flocking to Wahhabism because they could afford to perform the hajj and hence came into contact with this movement. On the ideological level it enabled them to delegitimize the leadership of the *marabouts*, the West African equivalent of the *pir*s. The more Wahhabism spread, however, the more socially diverse the movement became. With regard to secular education they seem to have exposed an equally ambivalent position like the Ahl-Hadīs, and during the struggle for independence they too have been split between supporters of the colonial order and nationalists.

15. *Police Abstract of Intelligence—Punjab* 1886, p. 210; *Ahl-i Hadīs*, 18 December 1908, p. 11.

16. *Police Abstract of Intelligence—Punjab* 1912, p. 501.

17. *Ahl-i Hadīs*, 5 May 1922, p. 12.

18. Sana'ullah usually refers to parallel verses instead, hence the title *Tafsīr al-Qur'an bi-kalām ar-Rahmān*, 'commentary on the Qur'an with the Merciful's own words'.

19. On the history and relevance of the question of istiwā', see van Ess (1991ff., Vol. iv: 407ff.).

20. This world view has been systematized in a popular tract by the Egyptian scholar as Suyuti (1445–1505). See Heinen (1982) and Radtke (1992).

21. Such beliefs were elaborated upon by one of their early exponents Siddīq Hasan Khān (1834–90), consort of the Begum of Bhopal (Riexinger 2004: 132f.). Certain Ahl-i Hadīs defended such ideas well into the 1930s (Riexinger 2004: 382ff.).

22. *Māhwāri Risāla-yi Anjuman-i Himāyat-i Islām*, February/March/April 1897, p. 15f.

23. Rasūl (n.d.: 99ff.). This biography of an early Ahl-i Hadīs scholar, Ghulam Rasūl, from the village Qila Mahian Singh near Gujranwala contains reports of dozens of *karāmāt* like a Sufi hagiography.

24. *Ishā'at us-sunnat* xxii, p. 39ff. (*ca.* 1907).

25. For the very 'enchanted' world view of the leading puritan thinker of Islam, see Krawietz (2002).

26. In fact, there were contacts between the Wahhabīs and the Ahl-i Hadīs before 1914, but they were functioning the other way round. Wahhabi scholars came to study at Ahl-i Hadīs madaris in India. A publishing house in Delhi belonging to members of the Ghaznawi clan from Amritsar printed the works of Muhammad b. 'Abd al-Wahhab for the first time in 1894 (Riexinger 2004: 524f.).

27. In this pamphlet dating from his loyalist phase (first publication 1902) he calls for corporal punishment for extramarital sex by mutual agreement (*zinā bil-'amd*) and theft according to the Qur'anic teachings (Amritsarī 1948: 11ff.).

28. *Ishā'at us-Sunnat* iii, p. 114; Amritsarī, Tafsīr-i sanā'i, vol. v, p. 178f.; *Ahl-i Hadīs,* 13 July 1923, p. 4.

29. *Ahl-i Hadīs,* 20 September 1929, p. 13; 15 November 1929, pp. 1–9, 15.

30. 'Ubayd ul-Haqq (n.d.); Minault (1998: 250ff.). The Madrasat ul-Banāt was one of only four Muslim colleges whose pupils were examined by the Punjab University. See Salamat (1997: 387 n.142).

31. See the covers reproduced in Minault (1998: 141). On the attitude of the Ahl-i Hadīs scholars to depicting humans, see Riexinger (2004: 430).

32. Eaton (2000). Two case studies deserve interest in this context. Gaborieau (1993: 141ff.) shows that in Kathmandu the rich Muslim traders are associated with the veneration of shrines, whereas poor migrants tend to follow puritan Islam in opposition. In his sociological study on the South East Asian puritan Islamic movement 'Kaum Muda', Peacock (1978) demonstrates that the rural adherents of this group exposed the most puritan value system, but also the lowest inclination to entrepreneurial ethics and modern education.

33. To the question whether Muslims should utter the formula '*Rahimahu Llāh*' (may God have mercy with him) after mentioning the late Sayyid Ahmad Khān, Sanā'ullāh answered, yes, for two reasons: on the one hand he continued to pray regularly, on the other hand he is in dire need of divine mercy. *Ahl-i Hadīs,* 29 April 1910, p. 5, 17 May 1910, p. 5.

BIBLIOGRAPHY

ARCHIVAL SOURCES

Police Abstracts of Intelligence (Punjab).

HISTORICAL MAGAZINES

Ahl-i Hadīs, Amritsar, 1904–47.
Ishā'at us-sunnat, Lahore, 1874–*ca.* 1920.
Māhwārī Risāla-yi Anjuman-i Himāyat-i Islām, Lahore, 1884 ff.

BOOKS AND ARTICLES

Ali, Imran (1988), *The Punjab under Imperialism 1885–1947,* Princeton: Princeton University Press.

Amritsari, Sana'ullah (1348 AH.), *Tafsīr-i Sanā'ī*, Amritsar: Sana'i Barqi Pras.

―――― (n.d.), *Fatāwā-yi sanā'īya*, Sargodha: Maktaba-yi sanā'īya.

―――― (1902), *Tafsīr al-Qur'an bi-kalām ar-Rahmān*, Amritsar: Sana'ī Barqī Pras.

―――― (1916), *Bā'is-i surūr dar mubāhasa-yi Jabalpūr*, Lahore: Tājuddīn.

―――― (1948), *Islām aur British lā'*, Karachi: Maktaba-yi Shu'ayb.

Amselle, Jean Loup (1987), 'A Case of Fundamentalism in West Africa: Wahhabism in Bamako', in Lionel Caplan (ed.), *Studies in Religious Fundamentalism*, Basingstoke: Macmillan, pp. 79–94.

Ansari, 'Abdul'azim (1984), *Tazkira-yi 'ulamā'-i Bhojiyāñ*, Qasur: 'Umar Fāruq Bhojiyani.

Baha, Lal (1979), 'The Activities of the *Mujāhidīn* 1900–1936', *Islamic Studies*, Vol. 18, pp. 97–168.

Bayly, Christopher A. (1975), *The Local Roots of Indian Politics: Allahabad 1880–1920*, Oxford: Oxford University Press.

Bhatti, Muhammad Ishaq (1996), *Nuqūsh-i 'azmat-i rafta*, Lahore: Maktaba-yi quddūsīya.

―――― (1998), *Bazm-i arjumandāñ*, Lahore: Maktaba-yi quddūsīya.

Buehler, Arthur F. (1998), *Sufi Heirs of the Prophet: The Indian Naqshbandiyya and the Rise of the Mediating Sufi Shaykh*, Columbia: University of South Carolina Press.

Eaton, Richard M. (1985), 'Approaches to the Study of Conversion to Islam in India', in Richard C. Martin (ed.), *Approaches to Islam in Religious Studies*, Tuscon: University of Arizona Press, pp. 106–23.

―――― (2000), '(Re)imag(in)ing Otherness: A Postmortem for the Postmodern in India', in Richard M. Eaton, *Essays on Islam and Indian History*, New Delhi: Oxford University Press, pp. 133–55.

Forbes, Geraldine (1996), *Women in Modern India*, (New Cambridge History of India; Vol. 2, section iv), Cambridge: Cambridge University Press.

Gaborieau, Marc (1993), 'The Transmission of Islamic Reformist Teachings to Rural South Asia', in Elboudrari Hassan (ed.), *Modes de transmission de la culture réligieuse en Islam*, Cairo (Publications de l'Institut Français d'Archéologie Orientale: Textes arabes et etudes islamiques; 31), pp. 119–57.

―――― (2000), 'Sufism in the First Indian Wahhabi Manifesto: *Sirātu'l mustaqīm* by Ismā'īl Shahīd and "Abdu'l Hayy" ', in Muzaffar Alam, Françoise Delvoye and Elboudrari Hassan (eds), *The Making of Indo-Persian Culture: Indian and French Studies*, New Delhi: Oxford University Press, pp. 149–64.

Gellner, Ernest (1981), *Muslim Society*, Cambridge: Cambridge University Press, 1981.

Ghaznawi, 'Abdulwahid (n.d.), *Ma'ārij ul-wusūl ilā anna 'ilm al-Qur'ān wa 'amaluhu qad bayyanahu r-rasūl*, n.p., n.e., (*ca.* 1900).

Ghaznawi, Sayyid Abu Bakr (ed.) (1994), *Dā'ud Ghaznawī*, Lahore: Maktaba-yi salafīya.

Gilmartin, David (1988a), *Empire and Islam: Punjab and the Making of Pakistan* (Comparative Studies in Muslim Societies; no. 7), London: Tauris.

——— (1988b), 'Customary Law and Sharī'at in British Punjab', in Katherine Ewing (ed.), *Sharī'at and Ambiguity in South Asian Islam*, Berkeley: University of California Press, pp. 43–62.

Hamilton, Richard F. (1996), *The Social Misconstruction of Reality: Validity and Verification in the Scholarly Community*, New Haven and London: Yale University Press.

Hardy, Peter (1964), 'Wahhābīs' in the Punjab, 1876', *Journal of the Research Society of Pakistan*, Vol. 1, No. 2, pp. 1–7.

Haykel, Bernard (2003), *Revival and Reform in Islam: The Legacy of Muhammad al-Shawkānī*, Cambridge: Cambridge University Press.

Heinen, Anton (1982), *Islamic Cosmology. A Study of as-Suyūtīs al-hay'a as-sanīya fī l-hay'a as-sunnīya* (Beiruter Texte und Studien; 27), Stuttgart: Steiner.

Hooykaas, Reijer (1972), *Religion and the Rise of Modern Science*, Edinburgh: Scottish Academy Press.

Khanpuri, 'Abdulahad (n.d.), *Kitāb ut-tauhid S-Sunna Fīradd Ahl il-ilhād wa l-bid'a*, Lahore: Gulzār-i Hind (*ca.* 1925)

Khanpuri, Muhammad 'Abdullah (1985), *Tazkira-yi 'ulamā'-i Khānpur*, Lahore: Al-Maktaba as-salafiya.

Khayri, Raziq ul-(1964), 'Sawānih-i 'umrī-yi 'allāma Rashīd ul-Khayrī', *'Ismat*, 'Sālgira nambar', July.

Krawietz, Birgit (2002), 'Dschinn und universaler Geltungsanspruch des Islam bei Ibn Taimiyya', in Rainer Brunner, Monika Gronke, Jens Peter Laut, and Ulrich Rebstock (eds), *Islamwissenschaften ohne Ende: Festschrift für Werner Ende zum 65. Geburtstag* (Abhandlung für die Kunde des Morgenlandes; LIV, 1) pp. 251–61, Würzburg: Ergon-Verlag.

Liebeskind, Claudia (1998), *Piety on its Knees: Three Sufi Traditions in South Asia in Modern Times*, New Delhi: Oxford University Press.

Malik, Jamal (1989), *Islamisierung in Pakistan 1977–84: Untersuchungen zur Auflösung autochthoner Strukturen* (Beiträge zur Südasienforschung; no. 128), Stuttgart: Steiner.

——— (1997), *Islamische Gelehrtenkulur in Nordindien: Entwicklungsgeschichte und Tendenzen am Beispiel von Lucknow* (Islamic History and Culture; Studies and Texts; 19), Leiden Boston and Cologne: Brill.

Metcalf, Barbara (1982), *Islamic Revival in British India: Deoband, 1860–1900*, Princeton: Princeton University Press.

——— (1987), 'Islamische Reformbewegungen', in Wolfgang Schluchter (ed.), *Max Webers Sicht des Islam: Interpretation und Kritik*, Frankfurt/Main: Suhrkamp (Stw; 638), pp. 241–55.

Minault, Gail (1998), *Secluded Scholars: Women's Education and Muslim Social Reform in Colonial India*, New Delhi: Oxford University Press.

Nasr, Seyyed Vali Reza (2001), *Islamic Leviathan: Islamic and the Making of State Power*, Oxford: Oxford University Press.

Naushahrawi, Abu Yahya Imam Khan (1970), *Hindūstān meñ Ahl-i-Hadīs kī 'ilmī khidmāt*, Chicha Watni: Maktaba-yi nazīrīya.

———— (1971), *Tarājīm-i'ulamā'-i Ahl-i-Hadīs-i Hind*, Lahore: Subhānī Akedemī and Lyallpur: Markazi Jam'īyat-i Talaba-yi Ahl-i Hadīs.

Peacock, James L. (1978), *Muslim Puritans: Reformist Psychology in Southeast Asian Islam*, Berkeley and Los Angeles: University of California Press.

Peters, Rudolph (1987), 'Islamischer Fundamentalismus: Glaube, Handeln, Führung', in Wolfgang Schluchter (ed.), *Max Webers Sicht des Islam: Interpretation and Kritik*, Frankfurt/Main: Suhrkamp (Stw; 638), pp. 217–41.

Radtke, Bernd (1992), *Weltgeschichte und Weltbeschreibung im mittelalterlichen Islam*, (Beiruter Texte und Studien; no. 51), Stuttgart: Steiner.

Raskl, 'Abd ul-Qadir (n.d.), *Sawānih-i hayāt-i Hazrat ul-'allāma Maulānā Ghulām Rasūl sākin-i Qil'a Mahiyāñ Singh*, Lahore: Maktaba-yi nu'mānīya and Gujranwala: Fazl Buk Dapo.

Reetz, Dietrich (2001), 'Kenntnisreich und unerbittlich: Der sunnitische Radikalismus der *Ahl-i Hadīth* in Südasien', in Dietrich Reetz (ed.); *Sendungsbewußtsein oder Eigennutz: Zu Motivation und Selbstverständnis islamischer Mobilisierung*, Berlin: Das Arabische Buch, pp. 79–105,

Riesebrodt, Martin (1990), *Fundamentalismus als patriarchalische Protestbewegung: Amerikanische Protestanten (1910–1928) und iranische Schiiten (1961–1979) im Vergleich*, Tübingen: Mohr.

Riexinger, Martin (2004), *Sanā'üllāh Amritsarī und die Ahl-i Hadīs im Punjab unter britischer Herrschaft*, (Mitteilungen zur Sozial- und Kulturgeschichte des islamischen Orients; No. 13), Würzburg: Ergon-Verlag.

Robinson, Francis (1997), 'Religious Change and the Self in Muslim South Asia Since 1800', in Francis Robinson (ed.), pp. 105–21 (Originally *South Asia*, Vol. 20).

————, 'Secularization, Weber and Islam', in Francis Robinson (ed.), pp. 122–37.

———— (ed.) (2000), *Islam and Muslim History in South Asia*, New Delhi: Oxford University Press.

Salafi, Munir Ahmad (1994), *Maulwī 'Abdulmannān Wazīrābādī*, Lahore: Faran Akedami.

Salamat, Zarina (1997), *The Punjab in 1920's: A Case Study of Muslims*, Karachi: Royal Book Company.

Sanyal, Usha (1996), *Devotional Islam and Politics in British India: Ahmad Riza Khan Barelwi and his Movement 1870–1925*, New Delhi: Oxford University Press.

Schluchter, Wolfgang (ed.) (1987), *Max Webers Sicht des Islam: Interpretation und Kritik*, Frankfurt/ Main: Suhrkamp, (Stw; 638).

al-Shawkani, Muhammad b. (n.d.), 'Alī, *Al-Qaul al-mufid fi adillat al-ijtihād wa t-taqlīd*, Cairo: al-Idāra al-tibā'a al-munīrīya.

Siddiqi, Iftikhar Ahmad (1971), *Maulwī Nazīr Ahmad*, Lahore: Majlis-i taraqqī-yi adab.

Smith, Wilfred Cantwell (1946), *Modern Islam in India; A Social Analysis*, London: Gollancz.

Steinberg, Guido (2002), *Religion und Staat in Saudi-Arabien: die wahhabitischen Gelehrten 1902–1953* (Mitteilungen zur Sozial- und Kulturgeschichte des islamischen Orients; No. 9), Würzburg: Ergon-Verlag.

'Ubayd ul-Haqq (n.d.), *Bānī-yi madrasa 'Abd ul-Haqq 'Abbās kī zindagī aur Madrasat ul-Banāt kīlānī par ek nazar*, n.p.

van Ess, Josef (1991 ff.), *Theologie und Gesellschaft im 2. Und 3. Jahrhundert der Hidschra: Eine Geschichte des religiösen Denkens im frühen Islams*, Berlin: Springer, 6 vols.

Wahba, Hafiz (1964), *Arabian Days*, London: Barker.

Weber, Max (1920), *Versammelte Aufsätze zur Religionssoziologie*, Tübingen: Mohr.

Yusuf, Muhammad, *Tazkira-yi 'ulamā'-i Ahl-i Hadīs*, Sialkot: Jāmi'a-yi ibrāhīmīya, 3 vols, (1989 ff.).

7

Continuity and Change in Women's Roles in Indo-Muslim Society Seen through Female Members of the Tyabji Family*

DANIELA BREDI

WESTERN CHALLENGE AND INDO-MUSLIM RESPONSE

In the Muslim world, perhaps even more than elsewhere, women are often construed as identity symbols and cultural borders. In South Asia, where Islam is the reference culture for the peoples of Pakistan and Bangladesh and a big minority of the people of India, Muslim women have been taken by many as guardians of Islamic identity and as a bulwark of the Islamic model of society, often in defence against, as well as in opposition to, an 'other' identified not only with the West, but also with Hindus.[1] This came about in the course of a process begun within the context of Islamic revival in the nineteenth and twentieth centuries, when Indo-Muslims, confronted with the challenge of the West and Hindu revival and competition, felt in danger of absorption and loss of visibility.

Cultural challenges as well as socio-economic and, a little later, also political pressures may be held responsible for the elaboration of a model of woman that should respond to the needs of the times. For the first time since the arrival of Islam in the Indian subcontinent, polygyny, repudiation, and veil were openly discussed, in the attempt to obviate the relative advancement of Western societies and the perceived need of reform of Muslim societies, inextricably connecting women's role to the issues of nationalism and political reform. In British India, the various communities that made up Indian society gave different responses to the challenge of modernization. In fact, even the components of each community elaborated different responses, especially to the connection between culture and the question of women's role and rights—more precisely, between the culture of the colonized and the oppression of women as it was construed by colonizers for their purposes (Ahmed 1982: 127–43).

The model role elaborated by neo-traditional reformers and taken up by contemporary Islamist thinkers is exemplified in the monumental work of Ashraf 'Ali Thanawi, the famous Deoband 'alim converted in extremist to the Pakistan movement. His *Bihishti Zewar,* still a best-seller in Urdu bazaars, was meant to propagate reformist teachings among women. That a Deoband intellectual felt the need to address women in spite of belonging to a current of thought hostile to Westernization, indicates that he was convinced that there were not fundamental differences between the potential of men and women for personal and religious realization. To the woman, he attributes the same potential for rational discrimination and moral behaviour as the man. Therefore, her first duty consists in knowing her place in family and society—knowledge to be acquired through education. An educated woman acquires respectability because she speaks standard Urdu, follows scripturalist religion, is an efficient manager of the household, brings up well-bred children, and performs her duties towards every member of the family. Education, instead of weakening the veil as an institution (seclusion), strengthens it, because an educated woman is able to communicate with the outside world without being compelled to go out of her home. The model Muslim woman, theoretically the equal of the Muslim man as far as religion is concerned, should acquire elementary capacities in religious knowledge and education, in order to increase her influence in the community at large and in the family in particular (Thanawi 1954; Metcalf 1990: Book 1, 24–30).

Another branch of modernism and reformism—represented by Mumtaz 'Ali, Sayyid Ahmad Khan's collaborator and the author of *Huquq un Niswan,* Chiragh 'Ali, and Amir 'Ali—favoured women's education but not the institution of the veil, which they considered un-Islamic and a mark of backwardness. Their proposals were an expression of the socio-economic developments that brought about the creation of a new, Westernized elite, willing to stand as equal to the colonial masters, accepting the Western ideas and ways necessary to be recognized as 'modern'. They legitimized female education and the discarding of *purdah* in Islamic terms, trying to make change acceptable in the eyes of the community (Mumtaz 'Ali 1898; Chiragh Ali 1883; Ali 1922; Minault 1985: 295–322). Both currents were modernizing, both pretending to be in continuity with Islamic tradition and advocating change at one and the same time. They differed in their attitude towards the West: critical acceptance and collaboration for one, refusal and confrontation for the others.

The question of women's role and rights (education among them) was taken up by men in the middle of the attempt at renewal caused by the challenge of the West, and did not arise in opposition to men, but was functional to their vision. By the end of the nineteenth century, educated Muslims gradually became reconciled to the idea of educating their women. The main obstacle was that formal education had to be acquired in Western-style schools—essentially missionary schools, whose medium was English and whose purpose was, basically, conversion. Muslim men, themselves members of the Indo-Muslim élite, accepted Western education only instrumentally, after the great upheaval of 1857, as the only means to get a share in the economic and political fields in a world where the rules were made by the British (Hasan, M. 1998; Lelyveld 1978; Manzoor 1998). Women of their class were not supposed to get jobs or to fend for themselves in the outside world, and so these men could not conceive of educating them, exposing them to cultural contamination. The more so because they usually equated education with emancipation and were not inclined to allow women to escape male control. Therefore, if Muslim women had to be educated, at least this should happen in a sound Muslim environment. The establishment of Muslim schools for girls was crucial in making acceptable women's education, and even so the process was quite slow. First of all, Muslim men had to be convinced that they needed educated women in order to bring about a renewal of their society and to meet the challenge of modernization (Bredi 1999: 64; Minault 1999: Ch. 5).

From 1904 to 1911 several girls' schools were established in Bombay, Calcutta, Aligarh, Lahore, Karachi, Patna, and elsewhere and, at the same time, various magazines and journals for women began to be circulated. In Lahore itself, there were three, *Akhbar-i Niswan, Sharif Bibi,* and *Tahzib-i Niswan*. They were mainly men's enterprise, but soon women began to take an active part in them as writers and members of the editorial staff. It was the first time in India that women were addressed as a group and were encouraged to speak and write for themselves. In terms of figures, however, this growth was quite slow: in 1911, only two Muslim women in 1,000 got an education and, although their number doubled in the following ten years, the percentage remained at a discouraging 0.4 per cent. In 1924, there were 137,800 educated Muslim women, and only 3,940 (slightly less than 3 per cent) had received a modern education (Mumtaz and Shaheed 1987: 40). The Fyzee family, a branch of the extended Tyabji clan, was among the pioneers of women's education, taking the bold step of sending abroad the three sisters Atiya, Zohra, and Nazli for further education. We consider below the circumstances that made this possible.

THE TYABJIS

The Tyabji clan was founded in the first decades of the eighteenth century by a Gujarati Bohora Muslim, Bhoymeeah, a fairly successful petty trader who migrated from Cambay to the prospering city of Bombay. His son, Tayyib, established a career in trade, selling the wool his mother spun, and ended up being one of the great Bombay merchant princes. His trading firm enlarged its connections in China and Europe, but for the following generation commerce lost its vital importance as more and more members of the family entered the Indian Civil Service and appeared on British benches and were called to the Bar. The two most outstanding personalities of this period were Badruddin and Abbas Tyabji, both of whom were politically committed to Indian nationalism and were called to the Bar after they finished their studies in England (Tyabji 1952). This rapid ascent was due to the conditions prevailing in Bombay in those times.

In fact, Bombay came to new fervour with the British Raj. Many immigrants from the nearby areas were attracted to it and the city's multicultural character received a fresh stimulus. As Bombay became the main trading centre in western India, especially Parsi and Muslim trading sects like the Bohoras and the Khojas tried their fortune in the flourishing harbour. The newcomers saw in the developments brought about by the British a chance to improve their economic and social conditions, and more than one literally went from rags to riches. A new élite grew in Bombay that was eager to collaborate with the British in order to get posts and the riches of the former Maratha rulers, and was ready to adopt the British values of liberalism, utilitarianism, and Weberian ethics. With no tradition as landowners, the majority of the merchant princes (*shetias*), who made their fortunes in the nineteenth century, were free from the cumbersome feudal values, and the Ryotwari settlement introduced in this area by the British prevented them from investing their capital in land and turning away from trade. So, surplus of capital and the demand for diversification of activities led to a concentration on other ventures such as banking, attempts at industrialization, and politics. Along with their importance, the shetias' awareness of a common interest grew stronger. The merchant princes of Bombay, like their homologues in Calcutta, founded the first associations, giving life to a phenomenon that determined the features of early Indian politics. Initially, they were set up to open more possibilities to the emerging élite and to assure a greater influence in the municipal administration. Later on, as the merchants got support from the intellectuals educated in British universities, they could allow themselves to do without the traditional ideological patronage, but their loyalties did not go to open groups of common interest and education only, but continued to go to closed groups like castes and sects as well. Parallel to the trend towards a more dynamic social order of the Western type, there was a new felt need to define religious identities. Modernization and colonialism stimulated the definition of formal membership criteria as individuals became more self-conscious and, in times of transformation, questioned their identity and challenged the power of religious authorities. Further, the introduction of British law and the establishment of British courts required increasingly precise legal definitions of religious groups (Dobbin 1972: 31, 46; Markovits 1995: 26–9; Masselos 1974: 22; Wright 1976: 227).

Tayyib, a Sulaimani Bohora, became part of the élite of his sect, marrying Mulla Meher 'Ali's daughter, and, due also to his economic success, he rose to the rank of Mulla and acted as 'Amil of Bombay. His reformist attitude, which led him to send his sons to England for education while the majority of the Muslims were still hostile to Western education, was tolerated by his religious group, a small community that surely valued the support offered by a rich and influent clan, and innovations were accepted without much opposition. In fact, Badruddin Tyabji Jr describes the position held by his family in the community as 'rather special and privileged'. In other words, they fulfilled the social claims on them but, as far as religious doctrines and practices were concerned, they enjoyed great liberty of interpretation (Futehally 1994: 7–10; Tyabji Jr 1971: 13). The high level of modernization that presently distinguishes Sulaimani Bohoras is probably due to some extent to the Tyabjis' influence.

Economic success and the material opportunities the Tyabjis offered to the members of their community, in terms of employment and education, made the Tyabjis very influential. In Badruddin's personal papers there are several letters of introduction and a resolute intervention in favour of posts in the British administration reserved for Muslims (Tyabji, letter dated 28 May 1888). It does not seem a coincidence that the second generation, with Badruddin and Camruddin, established the Anjuman-i Islam—an institution designed to improve the educational standard among the Muslims. Badruddin held modern education as the remedy for all the ills of society. His success with this and other initiatives was due in great part to the emerging Bombay élite, which formed an alliance of interests across religious divisions and supported him in municipal affairs. After the return of Telang, Mehta, and Tyabji from their studies in England, they started a serious attack against the traditional oligarchs who still were in control of the political associations, municipality, and press. The trend of relying on interreligious organizations, in the case of the Tyabjis, grew not only out of a new Westernized outlook, relegating religion to the private sphere, but as well out of the necessity to find a background wider than the Sulaimani group. Badruddin was aware of the problem of being a member of a small Shiite group and was willing to win over the support of the Sunni Muslim majority, showing his all-Muslim point of view. It was for this purpose that the Anjuman-i Islam held its first public meeting in favour of the Khilafat Movement, and that he never lost a chance to pose as an all-Muslim leader (Tyabji 1952; Tyabji, letter dated 8 September 1888; Education Commission 1882: 6). Badruddin must have been a perfect example of a modernized Muslim. Though he adopted some English values and habits, he did so only after critical reasoning. He was punctilious over religious duties such as prayer and fasting, and did not drink alcohol. But he rejected certain outward Muslim customs he did not think to be a necessary part of faith, like the visiting of tombs or purdah (Futehally 1994: 63, 76; Tyabji's testament, 24 November 1905).

In Badruddin's times, women were increasingly becoming the symbols of the reformers' hopes and fears. The idea of a model woman, corresponding to a new interpretation of the world and the requirements of a new kind of society, was elaborated. For the new, modernizing Bombay élite, which was undergoing a process of embourgeoisement, the new economic situation required different values similar to those of Victorian England, and the discarding of customs that were outside British comprehension. Purdah, once a mark of 'ashrafization', social ascent, was now seen as a sign of backwardness, and education, piety, and modesty were adopted as parameters for the woman of the new élite (Metcalf 1990: 12). Purdah undoubtedly was given up for practical needs connected with socialization with English and Parsis, and the desire to keep up with them, but this step was justified with arguments typical of Muslim modernism.

It is not surprising that Bibi Rahat un-Nafs, Badruddin Tyabji's wife, looks like an example of the nineteenth-century, ideal Muslim woman. She studied Gujarati, Urdu, and Persian, read historical novels, acquired basic medical notions useful within domestic walls, and listened to Badruddin translating for her the great classics of English Literature. In this way, she could fulfil her role in maintaining social relations with Bombay's ladies, attending zenana parties in which she mixed with British and Indian women of different creeds (Tyabji 1952: 23). She embodied the woman to whom Mumtaz 'Ali looked forward in his Huquq un Niswan.

The speech in favour of schools for Muslim girls that Badruddin delivered at the session of the Mahomedan Anglo-Oriental Educational Conference in 1903 found many opponents, but was nothing new for his times. He attributed Muslim backwardness to the purdah system and women's lack of education, and said that the Qur'anic ideals of modesty and decency had nothing to do with seclusion, so promoting one of the favourite arguments of nineteenth-century Muslim reformers (Tyabji 1952: 323). The idea that women had the power and the duty to safeguard the tradition and the morals of the family and of the society was also an innovative approach, because women had not been regarded historically as the guardians of virtue and tradition. Classical Islamic discourse saw the feminine element not as a warrant of morality, but as a factor leading to licentiousness and lack of self-control (Ait Sabbah 1982: 203–4). On the contrary, modernists such as Mumtaz 'Ali and Chiragh 'Ali saw these faults as the effects of seclusion and attributed certain feminine characteristics, which they did not deny, to lack of education and zenana life. Badruddin, a typical exponent of this current of thought, tried to reconcile Islamic discourse with his acquired Western ideas in a process of negotiation, translation, and naturalization of European notions.

The approach to women's engagement in social activities underwent the same process. Initially, Muslim modernists did not give up the idea of the division of the world into a male and a female sphere, but extended the limits of the feminine sphere to comprise social work outside domestic walls (Minault 1999: 267). Implicitly, in so doing, they eliminated the barriers between home and the external world, and made the first step towards a society without distinct spheres. Bibi Rahat un-Nafs' involvement in the Ladies Branch of the National Indian Association is an example of this trend.

What distinguishes Badruddin for the most part from the Muslims of his times is his radical attitude in favour of a change in women's conditions. Generally, his generation's Muslim intellectuals, who wrote about women and for women, were in favour of private education or schools safeguarding the observance of purdah (Minault 1999: 5). Badruddin moved a step forward, sending his daughters to Western schools and encouraging them to discard the veil. Moreover, he not only underlined the necessity of a better education for women, promoting their moral perfection, but claimed for them a right to enjoyment. In one of his papers, dated 1872, he criticized purdah while deploring the absence of Muslim ladies at a party of Governor General Northbrook, defining it as *zulm*, 'tyranny', denying women every enjoyment in life (*Akhbar Book* 25). It seems quite consequential that with him the purdah practices of the clan became next to non-existent. In 1894, one of his nieces, Mrs 'Ali Akbar, and his daughter, Mrs 'Abbas Tyabji, went to England where they discarded the veil altogether. In 1898, another niece, Lady Hydari, attended unveiled a large mixed gathering at Jamsetji Tata's residence.

The marriage behaviour of members of the Tyabji clan has also been very liberal, beginning with Badruddin's brother, Camruddin, who married an Iranian Twelver Shiite girl, and continuing in the following generations, when Hamida Tyabji was permitted to marry a Hindu, Prabodh Mehta, without consulting the *Hazrat* of the Sulaimanis, and asking instead the opinion of Mahatma Gandhi and Maulana Azad (Karlitzky 2001: 82).

THREE TYABJI LADIES BETWEEN TRADITION AND CHANGE

The ladies belonging to the Tyabji clan were among the first Muslim women to get an English education and to attend English style schools and universities in England. For them, as for their brothers and cousins, a stage abroad was deemed an essential part of education. Once back home, they were not likely to resume purdah and went out of the domestic sphere, getting involved in social and political activities (Shah 1998). Among them, three examples have been selected as paradigms of the different results brought about by the process of modernization, each showing some continuity with traditional culture as well as a degree of change and detachment from the past.

Salima, born Latifi, wife of Faiz Tyabji and daughter-in-law of Badruddin, embodies the 'reformed' Muslim woman. In reading the letters she wrote to her fiancé Faiz at the beginning of 1900, one comes to know how she imagined their life:

I have a sudden desire to tell you the plan which I have formed for our married life, will you tell me yours? It is simply this: the first three years are to be spent at Somerset [the patriarchal villa that was the residence of the Tyabjis since Badruddin's time] and trying to please mother, father, brothers and sisters. After pleasing and satisfying them at least they have got a tolerable wife for their darling son we will take a nice house in Bombay and, only then, shall we begin our plan about helping the poor, and not until then (Karlitzky 2001: 82).

From this one can see that the patriarchal house, where the enlarged family lived together, is not taken as the only possible residence any more. But the woman's role as wife and support for her husband is not questioned. In fact, Salima assures her future husband that she is preparing to become a good administrator of the family budget, studying domestic economics: 'It will be my duty to try and help you, for I am going to be a Model Wife'. (Salima Tyabji to Faiz Tyabji, 25 August 1900).

Salima's words seem to echo those of her father-in-law Badruddin about purdah when she writes:

... look here, you left your love but you have something in return though perhaps you will say not much. You have got nice society, you are working to distinguish yourself and be a great man while I, poor girl, have lost my lover for what: to stay at home and learn all sort of nonsense. Surely God never made me to stay in a sort of Purdah. I want to go out, to make friends, to help people, to ride, to see places and oh so, so many things. ...How I hate to go everywhere in a closed carriage and not enjoy myself (Salima Tyabji to Faiz Tyabji, 4 October 1900).

After marriage, Salima was active socially and politically, acting outside domestic walls and was the main force behind the establishment of the Anjuman-i Islam Mahim Girls' School in 1941, but never went beyond the tasks that the 'enlightened' Muslims thought suitable for a woman: charities and social work, possibly for the benefit of women and children. Even her appointment as a member of the Municipal Legislative Council in the 1930s cannot be considered a break away from the generally accepted schemes, because in the two years she sat in the Council she never intervened on a matter that was not directly related to women. As a representative of the Muslim League she spoke for financing women's handicrafts, for training and controlling nurses and midwives, and other issues connected with women, in particular Muslim women (Bombay Legislative Assembly Debates, 1937, Vol. 1, 31 September 1937; Vol. 3, 25 February 1938).

Atiya Fyzee, daughter of Hasan 'Ali Fyzee and Amir un-Nissa Tyabji, born in Istanbul in 1887, went on a scholarship to London in 1906 and visited Germany, France, Italy, China, and Japan. She compiled a book on music that was published from London and had Iqbal and Shibli Nu'mani among her admirers. Married to a painter, Fyzee Rahamin, she migrated with him to Pakistan in 1947 at the invitation of Jinnah. While in London she met Iqbal, who would exercise a deep and lasting influence over her. In the book written by her about him, published in Bombay in 1948, she describes their first encounter in these words:

For the first of April, 1907, Miss Beck sent me a 'special invitation'—to use her own expression—to meet a very clever man by the name of Muhammad Iqbal, who was specially coming from Cambridge to meet me. This caused me a little amusement as I had never heard of Iqbal before, and as I was used to getting such invitations from various Indians in London, it did not rouse more than passing curiosity....' (Fyzee Rahamin 1969: 12).

Actually, at that time Atiya was quite well known in India, having contributed, as had her sister Zohra, several articles to the magazine *Tahzib un-Niswan*, to which she sent accounts of her travels in Europe, published in weekly instalments (Minault 1999: 12). On being introduced to Iqbal, she asked him why he wanted to meet her, and he replied:

'You have become very famous in India and London through your travel diary and for this reason I was anxious to meet you'. I told him 'I am not prepared to believe you that you took the trouble to come all the way from Cambridge just to pay me this compliment, but apart from this jest, what is the real idea behind this object?' (Fyzee Rahamin 1969: 12)

This lively exchange left Iqbal a little baffled, but later on they became close friends. Iqbal was fascinated by the culture of this unusual woman, with whom he could discuss philosophers like Nietzsche and Plato, talk about Western and Eastern poetry, and argue about politics and economics. She went to see him in Heidelberg, following Professor Arnold's advice, remembering that Iqbal said to her: 'If you wish to

increase your understanding in any branch of learning, Germany should
be your goal.' She described him in Heidelberg as 'so unlike of what I
had seen him in London, Germany seemed to pervade his being, and he
was picking knowledge from the trees he passed by and the grass he trod
upon' (Sabir 1999).

After returning to India, Atiya and her sisters served as vocal and
visible champions and generous patrons of women's education, together
with Sultan Jahan Begum of Bhopal. Iqbal was back in India in 1908
and kept up a busy exchange of letters with Atiya—seldom was there any
letter of Iqbal without a poem or some verses in it. Atiya says: 'I had also
invited him to Janjira on behalf of Their Highness the Nawab Saheb and
Begum Saheba [her sister Nazli] of Janjira.' Iqbal, however never went
there, 'in spite', in his words, 'of a strong almost irrepressible desire'.
Atiya was naturally angry about this, especially because they had probably
planned to marry,[2] and Iqbal wrote to her in 1909:

You say I have no regard for your wishes!! This is indeed strange for I always
make it a point to study your wishes and to please you in any way I can. But
sometimes, of course, such a thing is beyond my power. The force of my own
nature impels me in a different direction (Sabir 1999).

Their affair lasted till December 1911, and in 1912 Atiya married Fyzee
Rahamin. The Iqbal–Atiya correspondence continued but for a short
pause at the time of Atiya's marriage, and their friendship ended only
with the death of Iqbal after forty years (Sabir 1999).

Atiya's behaviour was certainly extremely free for her times: she mixed
with men, went with them sightseeing and dining, was ready to share life
with a man like Muhammad Iqbal, who, though a great thinker and a
wonderful poet, came from a very different social background and was
in quite unstable financial conditions. She was a type of woman quite
inconceivable and unpalatable to ordinary Indo-Muslim men. She put
aside roles and limits imposed on women and adopted a new feminine
model, unencumbered by barriers between private and public, men's and
women's spheres. Though this development was linked undeniably to
the assimilation of Western customs and culture, and for her came about
almost naturally, it has to be said that, for most Muslim women, it was
politics that give them the opportunity to express their abilities to organize
and to act for themselves, blurring the line dividing the males' domain
from that of the females. Recall that it was during the Khilafat Movement
that Bi Amma, 'Ali Brothers' mother, addressed for the first time an
audience of men and later threw her veil off (Mumtaz and Shaheed 1987:

42–4). Atiya played her part in this respect as protagonist of a sensational event at the meeting of the Muhammadan Educational Conference in Aligarh in 1925, which is described in a letter to Sayyid Husain Bilgrami by a friend prophesying the demise of purdah:

...You know what Atiya Begum of Bombay did at the Educational Conference at Aligarh. She with some other Muslimahs cared nothing of our Sadrus Sudoor's strong protest but came up openly and got up on the dais unveiled and delivered a strong speech demanding equal rights with men to go about on God's earth freely and openly... (Minault 1999: 268–9).

Atiya Fyzee's personality, however, was quite complex. Alongside her attitudes, which suggested a rupture with Indian and Muslim tradition and which might lead one to consider her a champion of change, there was the firm desire to maintain a strong link with Islamic culture, a continuity she thought necessary in order to preserve Muslim identity. On the one hand, she bitterly criticized Indo-Muslim society. In the last lines of her book on Iqbal, probably thinking also of the social constrictions that compelled him not to marry her, she writes:

Even as I write I am conscious of one or two instances of Indian girls of delicate and refined temperament with the intellectual capacity of reaching the desired height, who are marked out for such sacrifice [of mental degradation], only because the family wishes her to be married to someone, to get rid of her, their one concern is that she would be held respectable before such society. Her own life has no value; all that matters to the elders is to satisfy the curiosity of the unthinking herd. Having seen Iqbal's tragedy I am appealing to my community to take this as a warning, and think seriously before interfering with young lives. (Fyzee Rahamin 1948: 87–8).

On the other hand, in spite of her harsh opinion on Muslim society, Atiya Fyzee remained strongly linked to Islamic culture, and was firmly convinced of the importance of religion not only at a personal level, but also at social and political levels. Her sense of belonging transcended the limits of her Sulaimani community, and she recognized herself in the enlarged Muslim community and the Great Tradition of Islam. In politics, she outspokenly supported Muslim separatism and, after Partition, she moved to Pakistan with the hope of building the nation-state of the Indo-Muslims. She was disappointed, anyway, by the limited interest Pakistanis showed in Islam as the basic foundation of the new-born state. In a speech she delivered on the occasion of the Prophet's birthday, she underlined the importance of Islamic ideals and regretted the lack of enthusiasm of the Pakistani people for this festivity (Fyzee Rahamin 1948: 2). Her elder cousin Badruddin's political stance might induce one to think that Westernization had as a corollary a secularized concept of politics, but Atiya's position contradicts this inference. Certainly, her closeness to Iqbal and her brother-in-law, the Nawab of Janjira, had a remarkable influence on her on this respect.

Raihana, born in 1901 from Amina, Badruddin's eldest daughter, and 'Abbas Tyabji, was no less endowed with a striking personality. Her father, a loyalist converted to nationalist politics and Gandhism after Jallianwala Bagh, allowed her to become an ardent follower of the Mahatma and to devote herself completely to spiritual life. Her mother, an ardent Gandhian herself, although she felt hurt when Raihana increasingly took to wearing simple dresses and shunning the elaborate clothes she made for her, accepted her daughter's choices of life, as she accepted, even with initial difficulty, the marriage of Hamida, another of her daughters, to a Hindu (Lukmani n.d.: 4–5). Raihana lived for long periods in Gandhi's ashram, composing poems and songs for him. Gifted with a beautiful voice, she used to sing *bhajans* to Gandhi and other leaders. She considered Gandhi her confidante and mentor and carried on a frequent correspondence with him in Gujarati and Urdu. Her independent mind and autonomy come out clearly from a letter of Gandhi in response to her father's complaints about Raihana, where he writes: 'If I were you, I would either let her have her way ungrudgingly and joyously or give her a separate house and maintenance and let her have her way' (Gandhi 2000–1: Vol. 58, 437).

Raihana went so far as to adopt a Hindu style of life and to write a story about an encounter with Krishna, entitled *The Heart of a Gopi*. In its introduction one may discern her mystical inclinations, when she says:

Step after step I understood that this was not a diary but the revelation of God's path towards my soul, which was ready to spiritual awakening. It starts with hearing a name and goes on with a curiosity that changes into attraction in a short time. Then the encounter with a real Bhakta (like Radha Darshan) takes place and, finally, a sensation of his presence is born and becomes more and more intense, a deep desire to unite directly with Him (Tyabji 1941: 11).

While Atiya looks like a result of the mixing of Islamic and Western cultures, Raihana represents a point of contact between Islam and

Hinduism in a time when communal tension was dangerously growing in India. Bhakti, with its passionate devotion, eclecticism, and rejection of the scripture and ritual could be, as in the case of Kabir, a bridge between Islam and Hinduism, a way to blend these two religious ideologies. Bhakti devotees may be seen as a product of the encounter between Islamic, Sufi, and Ismaili concepts and Hindu ideas based on the Bhagavadgita, their communities being caste-free and with a strong initiatory character (Ahmad 1964: 140–52). Perhaps, Raihana was doing no more than following to the extreme the way indicated by Ismaili teachings, in which there is an inclination to syncretism. Undoubtedly, her Shiite Ismaili background and cultural heritage must have had some influence on Raihana, but her personal experiences seem more likely to have had a major weight.

In fact, Gandhi was a most welcome visitor of Raihana's parents, a great friend of her father, 'Abbas Tyabji, who was one of his staunch supporters and followed him to the end in his Civil Disobedience campaign. The dense correspondence with Mahatma Gandhi and the long periods she stayed in his ashram, where she settled down permanently on the death of her parents, lead us to think that Gandhi and his ethics had an overwhelming influence on her. Persevering to lead an active life, propagate *khadi*, and picket foreign shops, she became a prominent figure in the Gandhian circle, a trustee of the Kasturba Gandhi Memorial Trust, a member of the Rashtra Basha Prachar Samiti, and a member of the committee running the Hindustani Pracharak Madrasa School. More than her activities in the political and social fields, she gave her most valuable contribution to the cause of a united India with her religious eclecticism and spiritual fusion (*jugalbandi*) with Gandhi (Shah 1998: 19). In Raihana's case, as in Atiya's, one can see elements of continuity—syncretism as an Ismaili trend and devotion of mystical kind in the Bhakti and Sufi tradition—as well as of change—the prevailing of the Indian over the Muslim identity, the choice of a style of life that her parents found difficult to accept in spite of their open-mindedness and political orientation.

CONCLUSION

In conclusion, one can note that, let alone Salima, not even Atiya or Raihana ever reached a breaking point with their family. They could defy social conventions and were able to participate in the public sphere because they were members of a rich and influential family belonging to the élite class. They occupied an unassailable position in society and had no need to bow to the dictates of their community. Therefore, the continuity appears to be in terms of reliance on the family group, while the elements of change consist in the relation of the family with community and cultural tradition. In fact, the Tyabji clan, due to the particular conditions of Bombay in British times, reacted to challenges and stimuli coming, not from within the small Sulaimani community, but from the enlarged Muslim and Indian society. Its members, men and women alike, assumed their clan and not their sect as a focus of group solidarity, gaining a great amount of freedom in establishing relations with other Muslims, members of other Indian communities and Westerners (Karlitzky 2001: 81–90). Western ideas and usage, from the use of forks and knives to the education of women and the abandoning of purdah, were absorbed with little or no trauma and were easily reconciled with religious culture, enabling the Tyabji chan to be products and producers of change without the ugly corollary of the crisis of identity that usually goes with it.

Salima, Atiya, and Raihana, as members of the privileged élite, did their part in serving the cause of the Indo-Muslim community as they perceived it, each in her own way, and probably never thought of themselves in terms of 'boundaries'. The class they belonged to and the times they lived in, though requiring from them commitment and responsibility, preserved them from 'suffering' modernity. This problem, on the contrary, confronts a great number of Muslims of present times, who sense the magnitude of the economic, political, socio-demographic, and cultural problems in societies whose traditional structures are shattered, and whose problems are now related to those of an ever shrinking world. In this context, the role of women acquires an increasing significance as a symbol of the struggle of Islam to maintain indigenous values and 'cultural authenticity' as voiced by radical Islamists, no matter how high the price is for Muslim women (Khan 1994: 90).

ACKNOWLEDGEMENT

This article was first published in *Annals of CaFoscari*, Vol. XLII, No. 3, Eastern Series 34, University of Venice, 2003, pp. 223–41.

NOTES

1. This development was not unique to Muslims. In India, Hindus also construed woman as border and boundary, especially in the aftermath of Partition. See

Menon and Bhasin (1998), Hasan, M. (2000), and Hasan, Z. (1994).

2. According to Mohammed Usman, Iqbal loved Atiya as a person, perhaps once wishing to marry her but later thinking this impossible. Masood ul-Hassan writes that Iqbal and Atiya had decided to marry during 1907–8 (Sabir 1999).

BIBLIOGRAPHY

Ahmad, Aziz (1964), *Studies in Islamic Culture in the Indian Environment*, London: Oxford University Press.

Ahmed, Leila (1982), *Women and Gender in Islam*, New Haven and London: Yale University Press.

Ait Sabbah, Fatna (1982), *Femme dans l'incoscient musulman: désir et pouvoir*, Paris: Le Sycomore.

Akhbar Book, Private Archive of Qays Tyabji, Bombay.

Ali, Sayed Amir (1922), *The Spirit of Islam*, London: Christophers.

Badruddin Tyabji Private Papers, New Delhi: National Archives of India.

Bombay Legislative Assembly Debates, Mumbai: Maharashtra State Archives.

Bouhdiba, Abdelwahhab (1975), *La sexualité en Islam*, Paris: Presse Univérsitaire de France.

Bredi, Daniela (1999), 'Muhammad Iqbal sulla questione femminile', *Rivista degli Studi Orientali*, vol. 73, No. 1–4, pp. 53–68.

Chiragh Ali, Moulvi (1883), *The Proposed Political, Legal and Social Reforms in the Ottoman Empire and Other Mohammedan States*, Bombay: Education Society's Press.

Dobbin, Christine (1972), *Urban Leadership in Western India (Politics and Community in Bombay City, 1840–1885)*, London: Oxford University Press.

Education Commission 1882, *Badruddin Tyabji's evidence and Anjuman-i-Islam Memorial*, New Delhi: National Archives of India.

Futehally, Laeeq (1994), *Badruddin Tyabji*, New Delhi: National Book Trust.

Fyzee Rahamin, Atiya Begum (1948), 'Academy of Islam celebrates Prophet's Day', *Dawn*, Karachi, 19 January.

——— (1969), *Iqbal*, Lahore: Aina-i Adab.

Gandhi, Mohandas Karamchand (2000–1), *Collected Works of Mahatma Gandhi*, New Delhi: Publications Division, Ministry of Information and Broadcasting, Government of India.

Hasan, Mushirul (1998), *Knowledge, Power and Politics: Educational Institutions in India*, New Delhi: Lotus Collection.

———, (ed.) (2000), *Inventing Boundaries: Gender, Politics and the Partition of India*, New Delhi: Oxford University Press.

Hasan, Zoya (ed.) (1994), *Forging Identities: Gender, Communities and the State*, New Delhi: Kali for Women.

Karlitzky, Maren (a.a.2000–01), 'Il clan Tyabji—una famiglia Bohra Sulaimani nel periodo del nazionalismo indiano', unpublished thesis, University of Rome "La Sapienza".

Khan, Nighat Said (1994), 'Reflections on the Question of Islam and Modernity', in Nighat Said Khan, Rubina Saigol, and Afiya S. Zia (eds), *Locating the Self: Perspectives on Women and Multiple Identities*, Lahore: ASR Publications, pp. 168–70.

Lelyveld, David (1978), *Aligarh's First Generation: Muslim Solidarity in British India*, Princeton: Princeton University Press.

Letters of Salima Tyabji to Faiz Tyabji, Private Archive of Qays Tyabji, Bombay.

Lukmani, Yasmeen (n.d.), 'The Tyabji Women in the Independence Movement', (unpublished paper), University of Mumbai.

Manzoor, Ahsan (1998), 'Education, Culture and Westernisation: Sir Syed and the M.A.O. College', *Islam in the Modern Age*, Vol. xxix, No. 2, pp. 117–34.

Markovits, Claude (1995), 'Bombay as a Business Centre in the Colonial Period: A Comparison with Calcutta', in Sujata Patel and Alice Thorner, *Bombay: Metaphor for Modern India*, Bombay: Oxford University Press, pp. 26–46.

Marsot, Afaf Lutfi al Sayyid (ed.) (1979), *Society and the Sexes in Medieval Islam*, Malibu, Ca.: Undena Publications.

Masselos, Jim (1974), *Towards Nationalism Group Affiliations and the Politics of Public Association in the 19th Century Western India*, Bombay: Popular Prakashan.

Menon, Ritu and Kamla Bhasin (1998), *Borders and Boundaries: Women in India's Partition*, New Brunswick, N.J.: Rutgers University Press.

Metcalf, Barbara Daly (1990), *Perfecting Women: Maulana Ashraf Ali Thanawi's Bihishti Zewar*, Berkeley: University of California Press.

Minault, Gail (1985), 'Sayyid Mumtaz 'Ali and Huquq-i Niswan: an advocate of women's rights in Islam in the late 19th century', *Islamic Culture*, Vol. 59, No. 4, October, pp. 295–322.

—— (1999), *Secluded Scholars*, New Delhi: Oxford University Press.

Mumtaz, Khawar and Farida Shaheed (1987), *Women of Pakistan*, London: Zed Books.

Mumtaz 'Ali (1898), *Huquq un Niswan*, Lahore: Dar ul-Isha'iat-i Panjab.

Sabir, Ghulam (1999), 'Kirkegaard and Iqbal', available at *http://www.allamaiqbal. com/publications/journals/review/october99/3htm*

Shah, Shireen (1998), 'The Tyabji Women and the Indian National Movement', Paper prepared for the Seminar on Comparative World History, Homewood: Hopkins University, 17 February.

Thanawi, Ashraf 'Ali (1954), *Bihishti Zewar*, Lahore: Shaikh Ghulam Ali and Sons [1905].

Tyabji, Badruddin Jr (1971), *The Self in Secularism*, New Delhi: Orient Longman.

Tyabji, Husain B. (1952), *Badruddin Tyabji: A Biography*, Bombay: Thacker and Co.

Tyabji, Raihana (1941), *The Heart of a Gopi*, Bombay: Vora.

Wright, Theodore P. Jr (1976), 'Muslim Kinship and Modernization: The Tyabji Clan of Bombay', in I. Ahmad (ed.), *Family, Kinship and Marriage among Muslims in India*, Columbia: South Asia Books, pp. 217–38.

8

New Religious Movements and their Interpretation of Ancient Scriptures

Two Texts on Feminine Divinity
(*Devimahatmya*[1] and *Saundarya Lahari*)

HILTRUD RÜSTAU

RELIGIOUS MOVEMENTS AND THE SCRIPTURES

When analysing religious movements it is important to ask how traditional texts are being interpreted by various movements. Sacred writings may function differently for different members of the tradition, and sometimes scriptures get interpreted in a way that is 'unconcerned with what a text meant in the original author's (or authors') historical context' (Minor 1986: 1). Consequently, religious movements can be comprehended more adequately, if one looks at the texts a particular movement refers to and the way in which these texts are understood.

Living a religion means reassessing time and again traditional values. Each generation has to make its own tradition anew. Religious scriptures function by allowing later generations to bring their concerns to the text (Coburn 1991: 3). This is particularly true of Hinduism where it seems to be of special importance. It is claimed that, in the *smritis*, the *shruti* tradition has been adjusted again and again to the changed conditions of life. In the course of the development of Hinduism almost every new religious or philosophical movement took pains to prove that it adhered to tradition by referring to the commonly recognized scriptures. Thus, since Shankara (ninth century), in Vedanta philosophy it has been a general practice to establish one's own views by commenting upon three fundamental texts, or the *Prasthana Traya* (the *Brahma Sutras*, the main

Upanishads, and the Bhagavadgita). In the middle ages, the translation of important scriptures into the vernaculars was often connected with an individual commentary (for example, Jnanadeva's *Jnaneshwari* at the end of the thirteenth century in Maharashtra).

Since the nineteenth century a new tendency has emerged, namely, to comment upon sacred texts in English in order both to prove the equality of Hinduism with Christianity and also to meet the demands of Western admirers of Hinduism and the Indian English-educated middle classes. Of course, such commentators have intentionally interpreted these widely recognized texts according to their own views, thereby adding more authority to them, as did Gandhi in his interpretation of the Bhagavadgita. Mention could be made here also of Ram Mohan Roy's and Aurobindo's translations of the main Upanishads, Swami Vivekananda's lectures on Patanjali's *Raja Yoga*, and Tilak's and Radhakrishnan's translations and commentaries on the Bhagavadgita, to give only a few of the most outstanding names. In short, we observe a commonly shared endeavour on the part of different contemporary religious thinkers and movements in Hinduism to adjust the ancient scriptures to the ideological requirements of their time by simultaneously offering new interpretations and providing evidence of the movement's conformity with the so-called eternal wisdom.

The ongoing discussion of feminist theology projects Hinduism as the only world religion in which the Absolute can also be viewed as feminine. There exist several sacred texts in which, according to common understanding, Devi, the Goddess, is praised as the Absolute. In order to contribute to a better understanding of Hindu religious movements, two commentaries on two different texts have been selected for a detailed analysis. The intention here is neither to offer literary criticism of these two texts or their commentaries, nor to analyse how in general Hindus today look at these texts. It is rather an inquiry into some aspects of philosophical theology from the point of hermeneutics, focusing on the connection between the exegesis of a certain text and the gender question. Inevitably, it will not be possible to do full justice to the complexity of the philosophical content of the two commentaries or to deal comprehensively with the gender question as raised in connection with the two texts.

The *Devimahatmya* has been commented on by Pravrajika Vivekaprana from the Sarada Math, which is the sister organization of the Ramakrishna Math. Its headquarters is located in Dakshineshwar, West Bengal. Sarada

Math has existed as an independent feminine monastic organization since 1959. Pravrajika Vivekaprana is a senior *sannyasini* of this Math. She hails from an Urdu-speaking area of India with a Pathan family background, and has been the Secretary of the Ramakrishna Sarada Mission in Delhi where she worked also as a teacher in the school attached to it. She has been invited repeatedly to the United States of America (USA) and different European countries to give lecture tours. At present, she lives partly in Pangot, near Nainital in Uttaranchal, where she supervised the construction work for an Advaita Ashram inaugurated in October 2003. The analysis of her comments on the *Devimahatmya* is based on oral sources only, that is, on the records of seven lectures given by Vivekaprana in Sacramento, USA, in the summer of 1999 to a women's group, and on lectures delivered during a seminar in Bindweide, Germany, 20–3 September 2001, which were attended by the author of this chapter.[2]

The *Saundarya Lahari* has been commented on by Dr Nataraja (Nataraja Guru, 1895–1973). He was the second son of Dr Palpu (1863–1950) who, together with Sri Narayana Guru,[3] was the co-founder of the Sree Narayana Dharma Paripalana Yogam (SNDP), which was established in 1903 in Trivandrum. Dr Palpu was the first Izhava to receive a modern medical education, including further training in Europe, but was denied a job in the governmental health system of the Princely State of Travancore because of his caste background.[4] That is why he shifted to the state of Mysore where he became a respected health officer. His son Nataraja (like his other sons and daughters) received a modern western education. He studied geology, zoology, and educational psychology in Madras and passed the MA examinations. The heroes of his youth were Swami Vivekananda, Rabindranath Tagore, and M. K. Gandhi. He knew by heart Vivekananda's speech delivered in Chicago and parts of Tagore's *Gitanjali*. Through the family links with Sri Narayana Guru, Nataraja came into closer contact with him and in 1922 became his disciple. Nataraja tried in vain to get a job and started a *gurukula* in Fernhill, Nilgiris. As this experiment failed, he went to Europe for further training supported by Sri Narayana Guru. In the years between 1928 and 1933, Nataraja taught Science and English at a Quakers' School in Geneva, simultaneously working on his PhD thesis on the 'Personal Factor in the Educative Process' to be submitted at the Sorbonne in Paris. In 1933, he got his doctorate and went home, but again he failed to get an occupation commensurate with his qualification. Since he was not on good terms with either the SNDP, a cultural and social organization that to his mind had become 'a closed, static and tribal organisation' (Nataraja 1989: 261), or with the Sree Narayana Dharma Sangham, the organization of the ascetic followers of Sri Narayana Guru, he stayed again in Fernhill with the exception of the time spent on some casual jobs.

As Nataraja had participated in the World Conference for Peace through Religion in 1932 in Geneva, after the end of World War II he was invited to participate in the World Conference of Religion in New York in 1948. The paper he read was dedicated to his guru, Sri Narayana, and his teaching of 'One race (or caste), one religion, one god (or goal) for men', included the demand for the world's unity, for tolerance and peace. Afterwards he stayed for a longer period in the USA, lecturing, studying, and also starting a gurukula.

One of Nataraja's close friends for many years of his life was Garry Davis, with whom he shared the ideal of a World Government, being a natural consequence of his Guru's teaching of the unity of humanity. Davis (b. 1921) had given up his US-citizenship and called himself a world citizen. In 1951, Nataraja attended the Constituent Assembly of the Peoples (of the world) in Geneva before he travelled back to India. On his return he was received in triumph. The sannyasins of the Dharma Sangham recognized him in public as the successor of Guru Narayana. Nataraja again concentrated all his endeavours on the gurukula movement. He founded the East–West University of Brahma Vidya, where between 1956–60 Garry Davis studied and got an MA in 'geo-dialectics', a subject newly developed by Nataraja. In response to Davis' demand, Nataraja drafted a 'National Memorandum on World Government'. In 1956, Nataraja officially took *sannyasa* according to the ritual prescribed in the *Narayana Upanishad*.

From 1948 Nataraja divided his time between travelling around the world in response to invitations from various esoteric circles, from south Indians living abroad, from friends made through the Quakers' College etc., and organizing classes, lectures, conferences, and functions at different centres of the Sri Narayana movement and at gurukulas founded in many places in South India. He repeatedly made lecture tours to South East Asia, Europe, Australia, and USA. In 1968, he spent some time in Brussels at the Yoga Institute of Andre Van Lyzbeth (author of *Tantra: The Cult of the Feminine*) who calls Nataraja his guru.[5]

Nataraja played an important role in making his Guru internationally known (Rolland 1931: 166 seq.). Among other things, he translated Narayana's poems into English and published his biography.[6] But Nataraja's publications also include several books explaining his own philosophical views (for example, *An Integrated Science of the Absolute*, Vols I–III, *Vedanta Revalued and Restated*, and *Dialectical Methodology*).

Nataraja's views were influenced above all by Guru Narayana and also by Swami Vivekananda. He admired Mahatma Gandhi but kept a critical distance, mainly because of Gandhi's inconsistency with regard to the caste system. Already during his time as a student at the Teachers' Training College, Nataraja had been keen to gather all possible information about modern thinking on educational reform, as pedagogics was one of his favoured fields of interest throughout his life. He mentions Rousseau (especially the *Social Contract*), Voltaire, Tolstoy, Thoreau, Ruskin, Carlyle, Marx, Engels, Quesney, St Simon, Comte, and Emerson among others as those who had inspired him (Nataraja Guru 1989: 613). The structuralism of Eddington and Bergson attracted him very much, which he saw already developed in the Upanishads and revalued and restated by Kalidasa and Shankara as well. The philosophical heritage of India was known and highly respected by Nataraja, but it was only after his return from Europe in 1933 that he started to study it more thoroughly. He translated the Bhagavadgita and wrote a commentary on it; furthermore he undertook studies in Ramanuja and Shankara and knew Kalidasa quite well, but mainly he illustrated his own concepts by pointing at contemporary Western scientific and philosophic discourses. He participated in yoga conferences and started to lecture on yoga only in the last decade of his life, most probably because of the interest people in the West showed in this topic, although it seems that he himself had practised yoga since much earlier.

One characteristic feature of Nataraja's personality was his global outlook. Following his journeys abroad, he was able to develop further Narayana's famous saying of 'One caste, one religion, one god for men' into an active endeavour for strengthening peace and harmony in the world. Repeatedly, he organized and participated in international peace conferences. Throughout his whole life, he stressed the demand for equality, criticizing the caste system justified in ancient Hindu scriptures.[7]

Nataraja called himself an Absolutist, defined as 'one who regulates his life with the Absolute as his norm of reference', one who did not make compromises and was characterized by honesty and earnestness.

Advaita Vedanta with its statement 'You are That'—you are the
Absolute—according to Nataraja (1989: 682) corresponded to the
outlook 'which could be described as absolutist', that is, a view in which
all rival antinomian categories were abolished. He did not call this Absolute
Brahman, a term he very rarely used exclusively, but *tao*, and connected
with a deterministic and optimistic world view. Everything in the world
is connected within structures derived from the tao or the Absolute.
Sometimes he used for these references or relations the term *maya* but
without casting any doubt upon the reality of the world, only to name
these invisible, and in their totality, unknowable relations. Thus, maya,
according to him, is the indeterminate uncertainty in all phenomena as
the eternal game of nature in the sense of 'maybe, maybe not' (Nataraja
1989: 454).

Towards the end of his life, in the years between 1968 and 1973,
Nataraja worked on the English translation and the commentary of the
Saundarya Lahari, which was published posthumously in 1988 by the
East–West University of Brahmavidya, Srinivasapuram, Varkala.

GLORY OF THE GODDESS: SOME REMARKS ON THE
DEVIMAHATMYA

The *Devimahatmya* plays an important ritualistic role in Hinduism. In
Devi temples, especially at Navaratra in autumn when the Durga Puja is
celebrated with great pomp, it is read or recited in the public or at home,
very often by paid professionals. In the northern part of India at Durga
Navami during the time of the spring equinox, the text is also read in
temples, homes, and in public. Although the Sanskrit version in its totality
can be understood only by a minority, and the number of people knowing
the scripture by heart is dwindling, its myths are known by everybody.
Various places in the Himalaya region of Uttaranchal are directly
connected with these myths.[8] In this region these myths are at least as
popular as the stories of the Mahabharata and the Ramayana. In the
early nineteenth century, H. H. Wilson called the Devimahatmya one
of the most popular works in the Sanskrit language (Coburn 1988: 59),
which holds true 150 years later: 'The text is among the handful of best
known religious documents in contemporary India...' (Coburn 1991:
149).[9]

The *Devimahatmya* (fifth/sixth century CE) is the 'first comprehensive
account of the Goddess to appear in Sanskrit' (Coburn 1988: 84). It
gives evidence of a very special feature of Hinduism. Whereas the

replacement of female by male gods did occur in India as elsewhere in the civilized world, in India the goddess reappeared in contrast to all the other cultures (Chakrabarti 2001: 167). In the *Devimahatmya*, we are confronted with the continuation of an old non-Vedic or pre-Vedic religious tradition, which was revitalized or, to be more precise, was adapted by the Brahmanical elite. Accordingly, the *Devimahatmya* can be regarded correctly as the culmination of the synthesis of the non-Vedic character of the goddess and her Brahmanical transfiguration (Chakrabarti 2001: 170), or, to put it in another way, as proof of her successful integration into the Brahmanical Hindu pantheon. And, what matters most, the *Devimahatmya* 'created the goddess, in which form she is still conceived and worshipped' (Chakrabarti 2001: 170).

The *Devimahatmya* is a narrative discourse with a frame story and an account of three glorious deeds of the goddess, combined with hymns in her praise. A king and a merchant both had lost everything and were deceived by their own kith and kin. They met each other by chance in the forest. Together they went to a sage to ask him why they still were attached to their people notwithstanding of their betrayal. Answering their question, the sage told them about the cause of their delusion, Mahamaya, the goddess, defined by the sage as being eternal and the creatrix of the universe. To describe her further, the three episodes are related by the *rishi*. The first of the glorious deeds is linked to Yoganidra— the sleeping force due to which Vishnu sleeps on Shesha, the cosmic snake. Entreated by Brahma, she withdraws herself out of Vishnu so that he awakes and is able to fight the demons Madhu and Kaitabha. These two demons had come into being out of Vishnu's ear-wax and had threatened to kill Brahma, the father of all beings. In the second story the demon Mahishasura had become the lord of the world, having been victorious in the war between gods and demons. Thrown out from heaven, the gods became very angry. The concentrated force of their anger took shape in a female form, the Devi, upon whom each god bestowed his weapon. She fought the demons, killed Mahishasura in his buffalo shape, and reinstalled the gods in heaven.

In the first story, Yoganidra, the devi sitting in Vishnu's eyes, seems to be subordinated to him, and she contributes to the rescue of the world only by leaving him and by bewitching the demons. In the second story, two different views are possible: either the goddess is produced by the force of anger of the male gods and has thus to be understood as their *shakti*, or her manifestation in a female form happens due to the wrath of the gods, whereas in reality she is the eternal, invisible Absolute manifesting herself in a human form out of sympathy with the suffering gods. Thus, any commentary on this episode has to take sides with regard to the question of whether she was in existence before the gods made her appear or was called into being by their force. The third story is very clear about the supremacy of the goddess. Again two demons, Shumbha and Nishumbha, had gained sovereignty over the three worlds. Deprived of all their privileges and expelled out of the heaven, the gods remembered the Devi and asked for her assistance. After a long and fierce fight described in great detail she was victorious. After each episode the goddess is praised in beautiful hymns.

But the *Devimahatmya* is not merely a story book or a poetic work. It also represents a mantra, that is the actual embodiment of the divine presence. As a part of the *Markandeya Purana*, it belongs to the smriti complex, but it is dealt with in the ritual as if it were a Vedic hymn, that is, as belonging to the *shruti*. The *Devimahatmya* 'is in a sense the "Bible" of the Devi-worshippers' (Desai 1968: 149). At the Durga Puja, it is recited by including two groups of *anga*s, that is appendages or subsidiary texts, the first three of which are ritually always chanted before the recitation of the *Devimahatmya*, whereas the latter three are optionally recited at the end. These texts were added in the fourteenth century (Kali 2003: 30).

The *Devimahatmya* is commonly divided into three unequal parts according to the three episodes, and at the beginning of each of these episodes a goddess, understood as a manifestation of Devi, the great goddess, is invoked. These invocations (or meditations, *dhyana*s) of Mahakali, Mahalakshmi, and Mahasarasvati were incorporated into the text between the ninth and twelfth centuries to signal the beginning of a new episode (Kali 2003: 29). The three goddesses traditionally meditated upon are each identified with one of the three *guna*s. These strands, constituents or basic energies of the primal goddess, describe the three cosmic aspects of shakti, and their interaction creates the physical universe. Each of the three manifestations of the goddess described in the *Devimahatmya* is connected with one of these three gunas.

Many different comments upon the *Devimahatmya* have been written over the course of time. The three episodes of the Devi's heroic fights have been explained quite differently. Myths can be analysed not only within studies of the history of a specific religion. They can also be taken as illustration of 'elusive truths that are difficult to express by more conventional means, precisely because it ventures beyond the realm of fact and into the realm of meaning. Open to multiple interpretations, a myth is valuable as a window through which one's experience of the world can be understood' (Kali 2003: 14).

Only a few examples of different interpretations of the *Devimahatmya* will be mentioned here. Sociologist Veena Das analyses the text from the point of view of the connection between gods and demons on the one hand and the goddess and the demons on the other, for which she sketches three different levels according to the three episodes in connection with the three gunas. The first episode is connected with *tamas*, the delusion. The second one represents *rajas*, the creative energy, used for the destruction of the evil forces. At the third level, representing *sattva*, the goddess absorbs the evil so that the male element becomes stainless again. This concept of the absorption of tamas and rajas by sattva is a deviation from the common understanding of the internal relationship of the gunas. Veena Das comes to the conclusion that, in order to restore the universal order, a total separation of the gods from the demons, who had been at first connected (see the ear wax), is necessary. In contrast to this, the female element, having been at first without connection to the demons, has to absorb the demonic element to restore the world order: Kali drinks the blood of one of the demons (because out of every drop of blood a new demonic fighter arises). Finally, Kali is taken back into Devi out of whom she had come into being in the course of the fight: in the beginning of the *Devimahatmya* the demons came out of Vishnu and at the end were taken back by Devi. Veena Das finishes her paper with the surprising remark: 'Thus, a woman may be seen as the ensnaring maya of ignorance and delusion, the formidable shakti or power, and the auspicious Sati, the devoted wife whose asceticism protects her husband. Movements between these three facets of the feminine provide the rich contextual variation which is the stuff of male–female relations in Indian society' (Das 1985: 32). It is true, the Devi in the *Devimahatmya* is the personification of maya, she is a heroine, a terrific fighter. Furthermore, she is praised as a mother and described as a beautiful virgin, but she is definitely not the consort or devoted wife or spouse of any of the male gods. She is not the shakti of Shiva, but she herself possesses shaktis, who joined her in the fight and whom she drew back into herself afterwards.

Swami Chinmayananda also based his commentary upon the *Devimahatmya* on the triadic relationship between the three gunas.[10] According to him, this text has to be seen as an allegory. Everywhere the struggle between the three gunas for preponderance is going on. There is also a constant battle within ourselves between the higher and the lower, the negative and the positive. 'The heroes of this battle are sculptured out and given names, forms and qualities, and their battles are dramatised through stories, allegories, parables, and so on by the Rishis for perception by the grosser minds' (*Glory of the Mother* 1991: 15). The *Devimahatmya*, according to Chinmayananda, is the description of the development of the Self, within which finally the realm of the gunas will be transcended. The three episodes of the goddess have been told to illustrate this process. The first episode at the level of tamas (Kali is invoked first) shows the fight against wrong values in order to get internal peace. The second episode at the level of rajas means the invocation of positive values; it is the constructive phase. At the third level, determined by the guna of sattva, we reach the victory over the senses, the mind, and the ego-ness and gain the consciousness of identity with the divine: I am god, illustrated by the third episode, the culmination of which is the tenth day of Durga Puja when the goddess of wisdom is celebrated (*Glory of the Mother* 1991: 7).

The *Devimahatmya* has been interpreted mainly according to the *Shrividya*, that means *shakti tantrism*, interwoven with the '*vedic dharma*', the mainstream Hinduism as it is shaped by the Brahmanic elite. There is only one reality, thought of as feminine and as shakti, the creative energy, that is, the Goddess, who is identical with the supreme Brahman. The Shrividya-Philosophy is non-dualistic, like Advaita Vedanta, but with the difference that the ultimate reality is understood as feminine. By force of her own power the Goddess assumes a binary form out of which everything really develops: the world is real. And that is the second decisive difference from Shankara's Advaita Vedanta. In Shankara's view, the absolute is the non-dual Brahman, eternally unchangeable and of absolute reality, whereas the empirical world is only relatively real—like the snake whose reality vanishes when recognized as a rope. The development of the phenomena of the empirical world appears only to be real (*vivarta vada*). In contrast to this, the Shrividya stresses the actual transformation of the Absolute as the cloth is a real transformation of the thread (*parinama vada*) without limiting the absolute reality. The unchanging one somehow transforms itself into the ever-changing many while simultaneously remaining one and unchanging.

According to Shrividya non-dualism, Devi creates, sustains, and dissolves the cosmos. She is the limitless consciousness and also the primal matter, *prakriti*, and the primordial energy. The goddess is *mahamaya*, the omnipotent power through whose veiling magic the world of phenomena comes into being with suffering, rebirth, etc. She is also *mahavidya*, the eternal wisdom, by the grace of which finally the veil of ignorance is lifted and redemption is reached. The *Devimahatmya* is the first text known to us in which such an understanding has been articulated in Sanskrit.

Devadatta Kali, although not Indian, nevertheless comments upon the *Devimahatmya* 'from within', that is from the point of *Shakta* philosophy.[11] His translation and interpretation of the text is also evidence of academic scholarship. He too understands the three episodes as an allegory of the outer and internal experience. The demons, according to him, symbolize both the outward disorder and inwardly the ego-based ignorance of the human being. The gods, including the Devi, represent light and truth. The destructive forces of the Devi are seen in the three reports of battle, whereas her protective quality has been stressed in the hymns following them.

In the first battle, the evil forces within us are destroyed. For Kali this first story (of tamasic power) already establishes the Devi as the ultimate power in the universe, upon whom the gods are dependent (Kali 2003: 16). She is the supreme reality who manifests as the universe (Kali 2003: 161). The divine mother is the one who projects the many. The *adya shakti*, the primordial power, is devoid of all duality, meaning that Shiva and Shakti are one. The Absolute is called Shiva when experienced as the unchanging ground of existence and Shakti when experienced as the dynamic power of becoming. The second story (of rajasic power) demonstrates, according to Kali, that the Devi is subordinate to none of the gods. Their powers, which coalesce into the one supreme female form, are but facets of the goddess' own individual energy. Thus Kali answers the question whether Devi is derived from the male gods in the negative; she is the sovereign of all gods, the supreme mother of the gods. The goddess intervenes in the world to destroy evil (Kali 2003: 165). This story is interpreted as symbolizing the conquest of the ego-based attachment (Kali 2003: 22). But it contains also the request for sufficient prosperity along with positive virtues (Kali 2003: 32). According to Kali, the Devi here teaches us how to live in the world.

During the battle of the third story (of sattvic power), Devi sends Shiva as her messenger to the demons, which convincingly gives evidence of her supremacy. At the end of this story, the sense of attachment, symbolized by the demon Nishumbha, and also the ego as personified by Shumbha, are overcome, the veil of individual nescience is torn, and the infinite consciousness can be realized (Kali 2003: 29). The goddess alone is capable of granting liberation (Kali 2003: 165). Just like Swami Chinmayananda, so too Kali understands the tenth day of the Durga Puja as the commemoration of the great and total victory, that is, the realization that the individual soul is one with the divine (Kali 2003: 165). This story teaches how the fetters of rebirth, of *samsara*, can be broken to pieces (Kali 2003: 161). Devadatta Kali in his interpretation underlines the Shakta view of the goddess as being superior to and independent of the male gods.

THE *DEVIMAHATMYA* AS UNDERSTOOD BY
PRAVRAJIKA VIVEKAPRANA

Due to the popularity of the *Devimahatmya* in India, women in the West interested in Vedanta wanted Pravrajika Vivekaprana to explain this text to them. Vivekaprana did not give an exegesis of the text as such but analysed it from the point of view of what it meant for women. Until now, this question has not been taken into account by other known commentators, so Vivekaprana's lectures broke new ground. In general, the *Devimahatmya* is correctly understood as a text for men worshipping the female divinity. We can recognize this, for example, from stanza 22 (respectively stanza 25) of the second part of the ancillary texts *Argalastotra* ('The Stopper'), which is chanted before the formal recitation of the *Devimahatmya* and begins: 'Grant me a wife, pleasing to the mind, who follows my inclination, born of a good family, who helps in crossing this difficult ocean of existence' (Coburn 1991: 181).[12] Also verse 12 of the *Kilakastotra* ('The Bolt'—against misuse of the *Devimahatmya*) includes women solely from the view of men: 'Whatever qualities are seen to exist among women-folk, having a long-lived husband, and the like, all that is by her grace' (Coburn 1991: 183). In the first appendage, the *Devyah Kavacam* ('The Armour'), the goddess is asked for the protection of all that is precious to the male head of a family: stable, herds, children, wife, wealth, virgin daughter, as the order is given in the text (verses 42, 43; cf. Kali 2003: 193).

L. Bennett (1983: 264), who did field research in Nepal in the 1980s, noted: 'One striking feature of the Candi is the fact that it is read and heard almost exclusively by men.' She reported that women are specifically forbidden to recite the *Durga Kabac* (*Kavacam*, that means the first of the three appendages) because of its power as a mantra and the possible harm caused by mispronouncing it. She stated: 'Most women [in the villages of her field studies] had never heard the text read and knew the myths only vaguely ... though ... all expressed great respect for Durga's powers' (Bennett 1983: 264). She concluded her remarks on the *Devimahatmya* with the observation that men were much more involved in the worship and mythology of Durga than women. Navaratri to her mind was an exclusively male affair. 'Durga represents perhaps a predominantly male perception of women that women themselves only partially share' (Bennett 1983: 269).[13] From this, it would seem to be of special interest to analyse how the *Devimahatmya* has been interpreted from the point of its meaning for women. And more than this, Vivekaprana expressed her opinion that this text was especially meant for women.

According to Vivekaprana, the *Devimahatmya* belongs to the sacred books of the Hindus—together with the Bhagavadgita, the Upanishads, and the *Bhagavatapurana*. In summarizing her interpretation, mention may be made of the following points:

* Vivekaprana expressed her firm conviction that in this text the final cause of the universe is declared to be feminine. According to her, this book is the presentation of the feminine power of the universe: 'Devi is the primary energy which is superconscious and manifests itself in the universe and in our human experience as well.' The Devi is understood to be identical with Vishnu and Brahman respectively. That is, the Devi is Brahman, she is neither the spouse nor the consort or wife or even the shakti of a male god. She is the Absolute, the Mother of the Universe, the first cause of everything. But as there is no life without duality, without antagonism, she must be the cause both for good and evil, for enjoyment and delusion. She releases from transmigration but creates also delusion by maya, her magic power. She is cruel and she is compassionate.[14]
* In contrast to the general view, in order to understand the *Devimahatmya* as a text upon which the worship of the Goddess by men is based, Vivekaprana emphasized that this book contains a special message for women. It 'leads you back, to your own core' because it contains the idea of a tremendous power, feminine by nature. And

like the feminine divinity, women are also able to fight. According to their nature as women, they are strong and powerful. They possess the power of maya, though they have forgotten it.

• Vivekaprana saw a special kind of bhakti taught in the *Devimahatmya*, because it teaches how to relate oneself to the power that is the final cause of everything. In case of a man, this relationship is that between a child and his mother, whereas in case of a woman it is the relationship of identification: 'I am the Goddess, I am Kali.' Vivekaprana underlined as one peculiarity of this kind of bhakti that Devi in this text is the source of knowledge and belief. Devi, when approached at the end of the story by the two despairing persons, did not talk about guilt, and did not make reproaches. She did not threaten or punish. She did not ask anything or point at something done wrongly. In short, she fulfils wishes and forgives everything—in contrast to 'father religions', and even in contrast to other Indian texts of *jnana* or bhakti, she is really the loving Mother without any criticism of her devotees.

• Vivekaprana interpreted the Devi's fight with the *asuras* as teaching that male arrogance will be crushed when they do not accept the idea of feminine power being the most valid power on earth. She also gave the reason why this is so: the woman is most powerful when she is a mother. Vivekaprana substantiated this traditional Indian view in an original manner through the idea of evolution. Evolution to her meant life that consists in permanent embodiment. But embodiment needed motherhood. Any struggle for survival would be impossible without motherhood. It was the intention of creation to bring forth creatures and for this the mother principle was needed. Therefore, motherhood was not one factor among many, Vivekaprana said, but the basic background of life, the life force as it is manifested in women specially. So when Devi in the *Devimahatmya* says 'Everything comes out of me', this can be superimposed on life as such in the shape of motherhood. The mother principle manifests itself in the body of every woman. Vivekaprana took the stories of the *Devimahatmya* as proof that, when it looks upon itself as the mother of the species, feminine power is stronger than the masculine power. Today, Vivekaprana noted, women were protesting against their limitation to be physical mothers or objects of pleasure only. They felt exploited by men. But the woman must learn to understand herself not as victim, otherwise she really becomes a victim. The way out for which they were searching today is dangerous, Vivekaprana said. Instead of thinking of motherhood, by stressing 'I am a woman' women demanded the right to be equal with men. This idea had also gained ground in Indian culture, which, according to Vivekaprana, traditionally was determined by the view: You are a mother. Women were copying men, and, according to Vivekaprana, that would not lead to any of the goals they sought but would bring about only confusion and destruction of the social texture. So, in short, Vivekaprana repeated her opinion of the present feministic discussion we have dealt with elsewhere (see Rüstau 2003; Vivekaprana 2002: 85–91).

It has to be mentioned here that in the Hindu scriptures traditionally it was not, strictly speaking, motherhood that was stressed in the first place, but wifehood, *stridharma*, the total subordination of women under male dominance. To confine the role of women to motherhood, as Vivekaprana appears to do, would be to reduce one half of human individuals to being just a means to an end—that is, producing and nourishing, etc. the future generation but not being an end in itself. Nobody today confines the male gender's role to fatherhood. Nevertheless, it has to be remembered here that Vivekaprana understands motherhood in a broader sense, not confined to biological motherhood only (cf. Rüstau 2003: 164).

• However, motherhood, according to Vivekaprana, should not be seen as the final point of the women's development: The aim could not be just to imitate the men. Women had to do everything for the human species. But more than this: women were not competitors to men in society because 'they have to travel within', as she said. Then women were no challenge to men. The women's battle was directed at achieving superiority over men not in the sense of physical or intellectual power. Men stood for aggression, for war and destruction, whereas the image of the woman was that of a victim. But the time had come, according to Vivekaprana, to show that women are better than anyone else through the use of the tremendous energy that is in her by becoming aware of the awareness we live in. What is really needed, she said, was the spiritual 'consciousness that I am more than that'. In the sense of being the very mother principle, the woman has to proceed to the principle of *atman*, pure consciousness, because the mother principle is rooted in some other principle, namely the knowledge that I am the atman, I am beyond motherhood and masculine power and even more than a human being. The *Devimahatmya*, according to Vivekaprana, was teaching the lesson that women can reach this goal. According to the responsibility given to women by evolution, they had to produce babies. But, when looking more deeply into the universe, women recognize that freedom can be the only goal. So they realize: 'I am the principle (*atman*), not a woman or a man.' Since it is the responsibility of women to have in mind the future of the next generation, they have the task of bringing back reason to humankind, that is, to make men (and women) aware of the Advaitic point of view: *aham brahmasmi*, I am Brahman.

Generally the stories of the *Devimahatmya* were being taken symbolically by Vivekaprana as images to meditate upon. She interpreted the frame story of the merchant and the king, who were still attached to those who had betrayed them, as teaching one of the most important stories of the book. The *rsi* to whom these two people came by chance demonstrated convincingly through several similes that these are not just problems of two peculiar people but universal problems shared by many others. Furthermore it was shown that we are not isolated; there exists only one unit and we are basically identical with it. Our individual energy is part of the universal energy. This universal energy is the cause why, notwithstanding all disappointments, we are attached to the world. It is mahamaya, to be translated as ignorance, illusion, magic, Mother, or Goddess being totally feminine. Though maya was a paradox and could not be translated, it did not mean illusion in the sense that the world is not real, Vivekaprana said.

The first episode is taken as an illustration of the unity of the world: everything develops out of the same unit of awareness, here called Vishnu. Without the feminine Yoganidra no movement is there; she is infinitely powerful and the source for everything existing. According to Vivekaprana, the second story is of especial importance, because it requests us to fight, to be active. The buffalo demon (Mahishasur) is depicted here as the image of evil, of animality, and of strength. Whereas in the second story the Devi appears at the instance of the male gods, in the third story there exists no male power anymore to which the goddess is subordinated. Vivekaprana's explanation of this story is that in the universe, as also within every human being, there is a dualism of good and evil, and we have to learn to live with antagonisms. Like the goddess who at first, called by the male gods, did not know who she was, women in our time have to discover their power. Men had made the universe their own and considered everything, even women, as their property. But Kali-Devi got furious when the demons tried to take her as their property, seeing her only as an object of their cravings. Also women today feel themselves exploited, and they have a right to fight against being looked at only as an object. But the fight should be done in the proper way.

Vivekaprana also mentioned the ancient Indian belief that control of sexuality gives tremendous power, which was used by Gandhi as a weapon against the British, as she said. According to her, *brahmacarya* was taught in this third story, taken as the source of the strength of the goddess.

In Vivekaprana's interpretation of the *Devimahatmya*, the main emphasis was put on the women's role as mother, admonishing women not to ask to catch up with men but to overtake them in the field of spirituality. In general, Vivekaprana's interpretation can be seen as an expression of women's growing self-confidence. As she remarked elsewhere: 'Men have said to women all over the earth, in every single country, that they were not intelligent enough to rise to the ultimate level of abstract thinking. This is the greatest insult possible' (Vivekaprana 2002: 91). Today women have proved already that they were as intelligent as men— but that was not enough to solve human problems. What is needed today, in Vivekaprana's opinion, is to reach the next level—that of spirituality, including a new responsibility of women. Elsewhere, following Sri Ramakrishna, she calls this feminine spiritual energy *vidya*-shakti as representing the subliminal goal of the modern woman. Sri Sarada Devi, Sri Ramakrishna's wife, has to be understood, according to Vivekaprana, as a manifestation of that power (Vivekaprana 2004: 37). She came 'to show the feminine side of that beneficent energy, which helps human beings to evolve' (Vivekaprana 2004: 36). Vivekaprana expresses her firm belief that 'it is possible for women to come out of their weakness and confusions ... and lift society to higher levels of evolution by their love and encouragement' (Vivekaprana 2004: 46). Her interpretation of the *Devimahatmya* has to be understood within this framework.

THE FLOOD OF BEAUTY: THE *SAUNDARYA LAHARI*

The *Saundarya Lahari* is later than the *Devimahatmya* by some hundred years. It is a *stotra*, a devotional hymn in praise of the goddess, and not a work of instruction or a report of divine deeds. Traditionally, Shankara is thought of as having been its author, although Indologists (both Western and some Indians too) have cast some doubt on this, as for example, Norman W. Brown, translator and editor of the *Saundarya Lahari* (Brown 1958: v). Commonly it is mentioned together with the *Sri Lalita Sahasranama Stotram*, the *Sivananda Lahari,* and other stotras as belonging to the apocryphal Shankara tradition. In general, the *Saundarya Lahari* is said to be one of the most central texts of *shakta tantrism*.[15]

The *Saundarya Lahari* is as popular in the south of India as the *Devimahatmya* is in the north. It has often been commented upon, and there are many translations into modern Indian languages and into English as well. It is said that reading the text can only help to understand it intellectually, whereas for real understanding or the real adoration of the goddess initiation by a teacher of the authentic tradition is needed. The text consists of 100 verses, but there exists a discrepancy between the first part (verses 1–41) and the following 59 verses. According to a myth, the first 41 verses are said to have been of divine origin, whereas the remaining 59 verses were composed by Shankara after their first version had been wiped off by Ganesh (or torn by Nandi).

Similar to the *Devimahatmya*, the *Saundarya Lahari* forms a basic part of *Shrividya* doctrine, which teaches the worship of the supreme being (Brahman) in its aspect of shakti, that is, the prime creative energy, symbolized in the *shricakra* and connected with its triangle of concepts (mantras, *yantra*, and *tantra*) and yogic practices. According to the philosophical view, the *Saundarya Lahari* based upon this non-dual supreme reality has within itself an internal polarity, a distinction without difference (Tapasyananda n.d.: 4). It is a unity of two distinct entities, that is of being (Shiva) and will (Shakti), out of which the empirical world of the multiple phenomena develops. The unity changes in a real sense into the world of multiplicity. So the phenomenal world is real, and is not born only out of ignorance, a wrong superimposition on the absolute Brahman in the sense of maya.

There have long existed two different schools for interpreting the *Saundarya Lahari*, although there seems to be no doubt about the supremacy of Shakti or Devi, according to the text. In the Samaya school, Shiva and Shakti are looked upon as equal (*sama*). Shiva and his Shakti, as the two aspects of Brahman, are ultimately the same. They are of equal value, complementing each other. In the Kaula school, the Devi holds the supreme position among the gods. Being identical with Brahman, she represents the dominant factor, whereas Shiva is secondary to her. It is beyond the scope of this analysis to determine to which of the different schools of shakta tantrism this text belongs, to the *samaya marga* or to the *kaula marga*. As there are inconsistencies within the text, one could point to evidence for both the positions.

In the first part of the text, Devi's supreme and all embracing character as shakti or feminine power is dealt with, personified as the divine mother. She lives in union with Shiva in the shricakra, which she also is. We are vaguely informed about mantra and yantra, the sound and the geometrical diagram symbolizing the goddess, to be meditated upon for realizing the final aim, that is, identity with the goddess. According to the common interpretation, the *Saundarya Lahari* contains the esoteric teaching of spiritual devotion, meditation, and yoga practices with the help of yantras and mantras, so that knowledge of the real nature of the absolute can be gained and finally the aim of merging into the Absolute can be realized. Within this framework also other philosophical and ritual aspects of the Shakta cult are dealt with.

The Devi is described as the personified supreme principle of the universe, being second to none, that is, she is identical with Brahman. She comprises the feminine and the masculine principle. Together with Shiva she creates the cosmos by exercising her power to produce change; just by opening her eyes and by closing them, she dissolves it. Without her, Shiva is not even able to move. But simultaneously she is Shiva's devoted and faithful wife. In the 59 verses of the second part, the beauty of the goddess is described in an impressive poetical way from head to toe, leaving out no part of her body. Whereas in the *Devimahatmya* the goddess is mainly praised because of her heroic deeds, these 59 verses of the *Saundarya Lahari* are a eulogy to an extraordinary beautiful female, seen from the male point of view. Like the *Devimahatmya*, the *Saundarya Lahari* is also a religious text meant for the male's worship of the female divinity. See, for example, *Saundarya Lahari*, verses 13, 18: 'The happy one who successfully meditates on the beauty of the goddess can subdue all women, and by her grace even the ugliest man will be irresistible to every woman!'

SAUNDARYA LAHARI: THE UPSURGING BILLOW OF BEAUTY OF SHANKARACARYA ACCORDING TO NATARAJA GURU

Nataraja's comments and explanations are based not only on the Indian philosophical heritage but also on a profound knowledge of European culture in its complexity of philosophy, literature, and science in past

and present, taking into consideration the Zeitgeist of the late 1960s
with, for example, the Beatles and the so-called drop-out generation of
the 'flower-children'. We will concentrate on one aspect only: how
Nataraja perceives the goddess, knowing that in doing so we shall not be
able to do full justice to the highly demanding text.

Nataraja came by chance across the Malayalam translation of the
Saundarya Lahari by Kumaran Asan. Kumaran Asan (1873–1924), who
was the first of Narayana's disciples (and was later to become a famous
Keralite poet). He was sent by his guru to Calcutta for Sanskrit studies
in one of the Ramakrishna Mission's institutions. After his return,
Kumaran Asan translated the *Saundarya Lahari* into Malayalam, most
probably on the suggestion of Sri Narayana Guru. Since Nataraja was
quite familiar with Shankara's main works, he could not believe that
this staunch Advaita Vedantin had really composed this stotra for the
benefit of the Keralite 'Kaulins' (that is, the kula marga, claiming the
supremacy of the goddess) as Kumaran Asan had put it (Nataraja 1988:
2). Very proudly Nataraja stressed that he was the first to recognize the
true meaning of the *Saundarya Lahari* as representing pure Advaita
philosophy, and that by his comment he wanted to save this precious
contribution to Advaita Vedanta (Nataraja 1988: 329). Simultaneously,
being a convinced Advaitin or Absolutist, he rejected strongly the
common opinion according to which this text belonged to the Mother
worship or Shakta cult. In his view, the text had nothing to do with
Shakta cults as such (Nataraja 1988: 123) because in Shaktism primacy
was given to Parvati over Shiva, which according to Nataraja meant
dualism. His declared aim was to extinguish 'the error of dualism'
(Nataraja 1988: 49).

Nataraja also did not agree with W. N. Brown's doubts about whether
Shankara was the author of the *Saundarya Lahari* (Brown 1958: v).
Leaving no doubt about Shankara's authorship, Nataraja's translation and
commentary are determined to prove that the *Saundarya Lahari* contains
pure Advaitic philosophy rather than being a *tantra shastra.* Furthermore,
it was not at all a text of worship but a philosophical treatise (Nataraja
1988: 187). As the Absolute was characterized by *sat* (being), *cit* (wisdom),
and *ananda* (bliss), ananda 'could easily be equated to the high value of
Absolute Beauty' (Nataraja 1988: 26). He called *saundarya* the objective
aspect of appreciating the Absolute, whereas ananda had to be seen as
the subjective aspect (Nataraja 1988: 3). According to Nataraja no visible
goddess was directly envisaged in any of the verses. Independently of any

anthropomorphically conceived notions of the goddess, these verses expressed only an overwhelming sense of sheer Absolute Beauty, which is difficult or even impossible to express verbally (Nataraja 1988: 12).

But Nataraja could not avoid a circular argument: he declared that such an appreciation of beauty by an author like Shankara must necessarily belong to the context of the Absolute. And since Shankara was the author, the text had to be understood as advaitic. And because the poem was a masterpiece of *advaita,* no other than Shankara could be the author (Nataraja 1988: 215). Nataraja's main point is that in this poem Shankara had adopted a non-verbal, proto-linguistic approach to philosophy by using the spiritual wisdom of his time and revaluating anterior positions (Nataraja 1988: 7). That means, according to Nataraja, that Shankara had used the non-verbal linguistic medium to restate his message of Advaita Vedanta for which he always stood (Nataraja 1988), whereas the majority of his other works (with the exception of the *Sivananda Lahari*), were written in the metalinguistic form. Metalinguistically it is called the Absolute, protolinguistically it is Beauty, Nataraja said. The necessary linguistic elements or symbols were taken by Shankara from mythology— as modern science derived its language from mathematics. Since it was a hard task to give a real or tangible content to the notion of the Absolute being, otherwise empty for ordinary human understanding, the Absolute in this poem was called Beauty, a value that can be experienced by everybody. But because Beauty had to be given some visible form and, as one could not think of beauty without the form of a woman coming into it, the exploration of the advaitic philosophy was dressed in a mythological language (Nataraja 1988: 13).[16] The widespread belief in the Goddess was taken up. The description of her beauty was meant by Shankara to be understood symbolically and had to be understood as the exploration of the bliss of Brahman. The eternal union of male and female is understood by Nataraja as representing the absolute value of Beauty (Nataraja 1988: 50), but 'It is neither a God nor a Goddess that is given a unilateral importance here. It is an absolute neutral or normative value emerging from the cancellation or neutralization of two factors, named Siva and Shakti respectively, that is noticeable consistently throughout this composition' (Nataraja 1988: 28). So, according to Nataraja, the doctrine of the *Saundarya Lahari* was philosophically the same as Shankara had elaborated in all his other great commentaries, although here it was presented in a visible and colourfully real, protolinguistic form (Nataraja 1988: 46).

In order to remove any doubt about Shankara's authorship of this poem, Nataraja tried his very best to remove any identification of the Goddess with the Absolute in the sense of shrividya. The inseparable and complementary unity of Parvati and Shiva, although only of symbolical value, in Nataraja's view is characterized by the dominance of Shiva, who is understood as the positive counterpart of his negative and dynamic aspect on the ontological level, represented by Parvati (Nataraja 1988: 79). Shiva is explained as being the symbol of the Absolute, 'the Absolute of absolute' (Nataraja 1988: 248), whereas Parvati, although the personification of the absolute Beauty, is the 'relative Absolute' or the negative existential principle to which all activity belongs. Her sentiments, as depicted in the poem, remain just human and nothing more (Nataraja 1988: 249). But, although she is called the negative principle, because of her activity the world, maya, created at her insistence, is real: 'Nothing should be explained away as being not real or merely mental' (Nataraja 1988: 85). It is the common picture of the relationship between the female and the male that is drawn here. Parvati, although being a Goddess but nevertheless belonging to the so-called weaker sex, is capable of attaining the same as her husband by means of her direct affiliation to him (Nataraja 1988: 81). Parvati, as representing the eternal Feminine, is subordinated to Shiva, the representative of the eternal Masculine (Nataraja 1988: 233). She caused the world to come by insistence, but she will not take the initiative (Nataraja 1988: 168). This is the opposite to verse 1 of the poem where it is said: 'If Siva is united with Sakti, he is able to exert his powers as lord, if not, the god is not able to stir ...' (Brown 1958: 48; cf. 'Otherwise, He is incapable even of movement', Tapasyananda n.d.: 27).[17]

Nataraja did not recognize any special message for women in this poem. It was also beyond his imagination to understand the Absolute as feminine, notwithstanding the beautiful poems praising the Goddess composed by Guru Narayana. Nataraja also did not establish any linkage between his interpretation and the thinking about women in society, although otherwise his comments give evidence of his world-affirming, optimistic world view. The bliss of male and female unity in matrimonial life is the only allusion to real life that we come across in his commentary. Elsewhere he summarized his understanding of the *Saundarya Lahari* in the following way: 'The word Saundarya Lahari ... suggests both the intoxication resulting from beauty as well as a general overwhelming upsurge of the aesthetic sense in the contemplation of the Absolute Self.

... Ethics, aesthetics and penetrating metaphysical analysis meet here in the upsurging of the sense of beauty within the contemplative as understood here by Shankara' (Nataraja 1989: 553).

THE SARADA MATH AND THE SREE NARAYANA DHARMA SANGHA AND THE WOMEN'S QUESTION

When we try to summarize the results of our analysis, the first point to be mentioned is that one can also come across interpretations of the *Devimahatmya* that are similar to Nataraja's comment on the *Saundarya Lahari*.[18] Speaking about religion, the cult of goddesses is as popular in Kerala as it is in West Bengal, and both the regions are known to be major centres of the Shrividya cult. What has to be underlined is the time difference of *ca* 30 years between the two commentaries. Since Nataraja finished his work, studies in feminist theology have come into vogue or, to put it more generally, since then a new approach to the gender question has come to the fore in social sciences. The so-called Zeitgeist plays a decisive role in how a text is being interpreted at a particular time.

However, there are some more differences to be taken into consideration. There is, firstly, the difference between the founder figures of the two religious movements under discussion, Swami Vivekananda and Sri Narayana Guru. Both were genuine humanitarians and as such very much interested in female improvement. Whereas Swami Vivekananda always stressed the necessity of promoting women in such a way that they would be able to improve their conditions themselves, Narayana also did a lot for a real betterment in the life of the women; see his endeavour for education in general, for hygienic improvement, for religious enlightenment, etc. But his followers continued to view women as still being more or less objects who needed support and not as subjects capable of changing their life themselves. It is difficult to say what Narayana himself had in his mind.[19]

We also have to take into consideration the difference between the experiences of the ordinary middle-class Bengali living in the capital of colonial India, together with the additional experiences Vivekananda gathered in the advanced countries of the West, and those of the low-caste Keralite from a Princely State with his rural background. Thus Swami Vivekananda had already turned the switches in favour of the foundation of a women's order of ascetics, which after a long time finally came into being. Strengthening women's self-confidence was always his declared aim, although, as we have seen in the case of Vivekaprana, it primarily identified the women as mothers who must be accorded an active role in society. Vivekananda was able to recognize the discrepancy between the worship of female divinities and the actual situation of women in the society. For example, he quoted in March 1894 a verse of the *Devimahatmya* in a letter to one of his brother disciples: 'You are the Goddess of Fortune ... The Goddess who resides in all beings as power', continuing 'And look at our girls, becoming mothers below their teens!! Good Lord! ... our degradation is due to our calling women "despicable worms", "gateways to hell" and so forth' (Vivekananda 1990: Vol. 6, 252 seq.). Vivekaprana, being part of this tradition and being a female ascetic herself, was invited by women in the USA and in Germany to lecture on the *Devimahatmya*. Therefore, she could comment very easily on this text by making evident a special message for women.

The tradition to which Nataraja belongs appears different.[20] The SNDP provided many possibilities for the participation of women in public life but, for example, there is at present no woman on its board of fourteen officials. The picture in the past was not different. Women's questions are dealt with in the Youth and Women's Organisation of the SNDP. It might be significant that women and youth have been grouped together. In the Headquarters of the Sree Narayana Dharma Sangham at Sivagiri, the sannyasis are very reluctant to talk to women according to personal experience. In the 1960s, the Sannyasini Devika Amma founded the Sivagiri Sree Narayana Dharmasodari Matom in Varkala. But after her death in 1980 long legal proceedings with the Sree Narayana Dharma Sangham were needed to maintain its independence. In the meantime its headquarters have shifted to Thiruvananthapuram. Only very few women were initiated as sannyasinis by ascetics of the Sree Narayana Dharma Sangham, as for example, the Swamini Jnanamayi Indra Devi by the second guru of the Fernhill Gurukula, Nitya Chaitanya Yati. She later ran her own independent gurukula.

Nataraja himself respected female scientists in the West and admired famous women like Joan of Arc or heroines like Dante's Beatrice or Rousseau's Heloise. Indian women like Kumaran Asan's widow supported him financially and he maintained friendly relations with Sarojini Naidu and her sisters, and also with a good number of Western ladies devoted to him and his gurukula movement. He even admitted a woman into his gurukula, although subsequently he came to recognize this as a mistake (Nataraja 1989: 482). He recognized that the woman 'can be deified on a par with the Absolute itself' (Nataraja 1989: 482—where he mentioned in this connection the Upanishadic story of Indra and Uma). Yet, in his autobiography, he again and again expressed his opinion that 'women's reason works in reverse of the manner in which a man's reason works', so conflicts were unavoidable when they came together to solve any problem. Both the sexes, therefore, had to be kept strictly apart in an ashram (Nataraja 1989: 481). He repeated the often used cliché of the fickleness of a woman's mind, quoting Manu as well as Shakespeare and drew the conclusion, 'To a woman freedom, according to the Sannyasa way of life, is unthinkable', since women always would need the steadying influence of a man. He said that even in the Bhagavadgita womanhood and death had been put together, by pointing at verse X.34, (Nataraja 1989: 482). Women were made to give birth and nourishment by their bodies, determined by emotion and instinct, whereas men's bodies were made to be active (Nataraja 1989: 498).

In addition to the traits of his world view, Nataraja personally did not come into contact with the popular devotional worship of a personalized god, not to speak of a goddess, because of the family surroundings of his childhood and the way he was educated. In contrast, Vivekaprana lives in a religious atmosphere where Ramakrishna is worshipped together with Swami Vivekananda and Sarada Devi, Ramakrishna's wife. In the annual calendar of religious ceremonies within the institutions of the Sarada Math and the Ramakrishna Sarada Mission, the celebration of Durga Puja plays a prominent role. But all these indications cannot be taken as the sole key to the way in which Nataraja interpreted the *Saundarya Lahari*. It was for him of decisive importance to uphold Shankara's authorship of the text, because he was proud of Shankara, as well as of his Guru, Narayana, as two great Keralites. Thus he wanted to understand this text as authored by Shankara and for this it had to be explained as an advaitic text. The reason why he placed so much stress on Shankara's authorship of the 'enigmatic' text, as he called the *Saundarya Lahari*, was not only that by this his own views could be backed by the most important authority in Indian philosophy. There was something more that resulted from his social self-identification as belonging to the original inhabitants of Kerala. In verse 75, the author of the *Saundarya Lahari* calls himself 'the Dravidian child', which according to Nataraja had to be understood as a reference to the proto-Aryan culture of the author. Nataraja confessed that, by scrutinizing this text, 'I began to be aware of a new and all-absorbing advaitic approach to spiritual progress, having its locus not in the Aryan North, but in the Dravidian South' (Nataraja 1989: 635). Nataraja thus took the expression 'Dravidian child' as indicating that Shankara 'did not belong to the context of Vedic, Aryan or even Brahmanical orthodoxy', something that he saw also affirmed by the legend connected with his mother's funeral when Shankara was treated like an outcast. So Nataraja guessed that Shankara 'must have been born to a south Indian non-Aryan woman, so as to justify his reference to himself as a Dravida Sisu (child of the Dravidian culture by race of birth)' (Nataraja 1989: 668).

Shankara's philosophy, according to Nataraja, had to be taken as proto-aryan monistic or Absolutist philosophy, 'aryan' here understood as meaning 'noble, honourable' and not necessarily belonging to the Vedic group, whom he regarded as interlopers and intruders from other lands who came and exploited the people through their theocratic set-up (Nataraja 1989: 474). This can be taken as an additional reason why he tried his very best to deny the *Saundarya Lahari* the status of a eulogy of the Goddess.

Both Vivekaprana and Nataraja quite naturally interpreted the two scriptures in terms of their own philosophical outlook. Whereas Vivekaprana stressed the *Devimahatmya* as a text of immense religious importance, Nataraja laid stress on his findings of the great philosophical value of the *Saundarya Lahari*. Both the authors expressed their opinion of having found the true meaning of the text under discussion, namely that the *Devimahatmya* was meant for women and that the *Saundarya Lahari* contained a pure advaitic philosophy in a non-verbal proto-linguistic language. Both the texts have been understood by the two interpreters as teaching non-dualism (Advaita Vedanta respectively 'absolutism'). Although the *Devimahatmya* and the *Saundarya Lahari* are commonly used for worshipping the goddess in the bhakti sense, this element played only a negligible role in Vivekaprana's interpretation, and it was rejected in Nataraja's commentary, as was also observed in the study on different modern interpreters of the Bhagavadgita (Minor 1986: 226).

NOTES

1. Also *Sri Durgasaptasati*, Seven Hundred Verses to Sri Durga.
2. Most probably these lectures will be published, as have her other lectures; for example, in *Samvit*, the bi-annual journal of the Sri Sarada Math. See also Pravrajika Vivekaprana (2002, 2004).
3. On Sri Narayana Guru, see also Rüstau (2002).

4. The Izhavas (Ezhavas) formed the largest group of untouchables in Kerala, by profession toddy tappers, but also astrologers and physicians of the low-caste people among which they ranked highest.

5. *Tantra: The Cult of the Feminine*, York Beach, Maine: Samuel Weiser, 1995, first Indian edition, Delhi: Motilal Banarsidass, 2001.

6. *Life and Teachings of Narayana Guru*, Fernhill: East–West University Publication, rev. edn., 1990.

7. In this connection, Nataraja (1989: 606) raised some doubts about Vivekananda's claim of Hinduism being based on toleration in his famous Chicago speech.

8. See, for example, Kali Shila (Guptakashi district) and Kasar Devi (Almora district) in Uttaranchal.

9. Together with the Bhagavadgita and works of Bankim Chandra Chattopadhyaya, the *Devimahatmya* or *Candi*, as it is called in Bengal, had been ascribed by the British a prominent place among literature favouring terrorism. James Campbell Ker (1973: 48–51) wrote in his confidential report on political trouble in India in the years between 1907 and 1917: 'Two religious books that found a prominent place in the literature of the revolutionaries were the Bhagwat Gita and Chandi.... The book called Chandi ... relates how the gods ... created ... the goddess Durga, to destroy the demons.... The destruction of the demons is a regular metaphor in Indian revolutionary literature, the gods being the people of India and the demons the English, and this accounts for the great popularity of the book in these circles.'

10. Swami Chinmayananda (1916–93) was a disciple of Swami Sivananda, the founder of the Divine Life Society. In 1953, Swami Chinmayananda founded the Chinmayananda Mission which is administered today by the Chinmayananda Mission, Trust in Mumbai. Its present head is Swami Tejomayananda.

11. Devadatta Kali (David Nelson), like Christopher Isherwood and Aldous Huxley, is a disciple of Swami Prabhavananda (1914–76), founder of the Vedanta Society of Southern California.

12. Kali (2003: 205) in his commentary on this stance recommends: '...if the reciter is a married woman or a celibate monastic, "wife" may be replaced by either "husband" or "companion".'

13. Although it is true that the *Devimahatmya* in principle is meant for male worship of the female divinity, it is doubtful whether this observation of Bennett more than twenty years back can be generalized with regard to the change of time and place. So during the Durga Puja in 2003 in the Himalaya region of Uttaranchal, at least as many women were involved as men, as could be observed in temples and around. In a shrine in the Badrinath temple compound dedicated to Krishna and Arjuna, Durga in the shape of Urvashi was also worshipped and two men, together with one lady, were reciting the *Devimahatmya*. They even asked the author a female foreigner, to join them and take a seat in the shrine.

14. We are reminded of Swami Vivekananda's (1990: Vol. III, 421) conviction that there is not a God '...you make the reservoir of all good qualities only. You cannot have two Gods, God and Satan; you must have only one and dare to call Him good and bad.'

15. Swami Tapasyananda (n.d.: 2) calls it a fundamental text of the Shakta cult. Similarly, Kinsley (1987: 137, 141f.) speaks of it as '... perhaps the most famous hymn praising the Devi', where the great Gods are depicted as her servants.

16. This was not understood in an abstract way only, as could be supposed in the case of an ascetic. This is demonstrated by the following episode: during his stay in Honolulu he saw women going barefooted, 'with their waists and navels exposed to view. This region of the women's body has intrigued me personally and has been the object of my meditation and study, especially since the day it dawned on me that Shankara, the great advaitic philosopher, pointedly referred to it in his famous composition called *Bhaja Govindam*...'. He said that he had found the same hints in the *Saundrya Lahari* (Nataraja 1989: 635).

17. See also Nataraja's translation of verse 1: '...this God does not know even how to pulsate ... (Nataraja 1988: 45).

18. Personal discussion with Smarajit Chakravorty (Kolkata), summer 2001 in Berlin.

19. In a booklet published in 1972 by the Sivagiri Sree Narayana Dharmasodari Matom, Varkala, it was said: 'The Dharmasodari Matom is an organisation of women founded on the lofty ideals of Sree Narayana Guru who wanted to establish a separate institution for women in the above name, to work for the all-round improvement of the condition of women in this country. The Guru could not materialise his ambition in his lifetime. So, we devotees of that great Reformer, thought it our duty to start this organisation in the manner envisaged by the Guru. We started this organisation on the 19th December 1967' (*Thus Spake Sree Narayana Guru* 1972: 19). But there is no evidence given for his intention of founding a women's math. In the early 1990s, legal proceedings were instituted by the Sree Narayana Dharma Sangham against the Dharmasodari Matom. The land on which the headquarters of the Matom were erected was claimed to be the property of the Sangham and it was demanded that the women vacate the land.

20. Today it manifests itself chiefly in the three above-mentioned organizations: the SNDP, founded in 1903 for propagating Narayana Guru's views and supporting religious and social reforms; the Sree Narayana Dharma Sangham, registered in 1926, is an organization of ascetics, and its aims are the propagation of Narayana's message and the training of sannyasin disciples at the Brahma Vidyala; and the Narayana Gurukula, which was started in 1923 and officially opened in 1956 by Dr Natarajan. It is organized according to the ancient *guru–shishya parampara sampradaya*, the hierarchical succession of the guru by the disciple. The Gurukula concentrates on research, religio-philosophical publications, and teaching. An international East–West University of

Brahmavidya, affiliated to the Gurukula, was officially established in 1974. Nataraja Guru was succeeded by Nitya Chaitannya Yati (d. 1999). The present head is Swami Muni Narayana Prasad.

BIBLIOGRAPHY

Bennett, L. (1983), *Dangerous Wives and Sacred Sisters: Social and Symbolic Roles of High-caste Women in Nepal*, New York: Columbia University Press.

Brown, C. Mackenzie (1974), *God as Mother: A Feminine Theology in India (A Historical and Theological Study of the Brahmavaivarta Purana)*, Hertford, Vermont: Claude Stark and Co.

Brown, W. Norman (ed. and trans.) (1958), *The Saundaryalahari or Flood of Beauty*, (Harvard Oriental Series, Vol. 43), Cambridge, Mass.: Harvard University Press.

Chakrabarti, Kunal (2001), *Religious Process: The Puranas and the Making of a Regional Tradition*, New Delhi: Oxford University Press.

Coburn, Thomas B. (1988), *Devi Mahatmya: The Crystallization of the Goddess Tradition*, Delhi: Motilal Banarsidass, [1984].

—— (1991), *Encountering the Goddess. A Translation of the Devi-Mahatmya and a Study of its Interpretation*, Albany: State University of New York Press.

Das, Veena (1985), 'The Goddess and the Demon. An Analysis of the *Devimahatmya*', *Manushi*, Vol. 30, Nos 5 and 6, pp. 28–32.

Desai, Nileshvari Y. (1968), *Ancient Indian Society, Religion and Mythology as Depicted in the Markandeya-Purana*, Baroda: Faculty of Arts, The M.S.University of Baroda.

Gandhi, M. K. (1989), *The Bhagavadgita*, New Delhi and Bombay: Orient Paperbacks.

Glory of the Mother, Bombay: Central Chinmaya Mission Trust, 1991, 1994.

[Swami] Jagadiswarananda (trans.), *Devi Mahatmyam (Glory of the Divine Mother) 700 Mantras on Sri Durga*, Mylapore, Madras: Sri Ramakrishna Math, n.d. [1953].

Jnanadeva (1989), *Bhavartha Dipika Otherwise Known as Jnaneshwari: Commentary on the Bhagavadgita*, Ramchandra Keshav Bhagwat (trans.), Madras: Samata Books.

Kali, Devadatta (David Nelson) (2003), *In Praise of the Goddess: The Devimahatmya and its Meaning*, Berwick: Nicolas-Hays, Inc.

Ker, James Campbell (1973), *Political Trouble in India 1907–1917*, Delhi: Oriental Publishers.

Kinsley, David (1987), *Hindu Goddesses: Visions of the Divine Feminine in the Hindu Religious Tradition*, Delhi: Motilal Banarsidass.

—— (1997), *Tantric Visions of the Divine Feminine: The Ten Mahavidyas*, Berkeley: University of California Press.

Minor, Robert N. (ed.) (1986), *Modern Indian Interpreters of the Bhagavadgita*, Albany: State University of New York.

Nataraja Guru (trans. and commentary) (1988), *Saundarya Lahari: The Upsurging Billow of Beauty of Sankaracarya*. Srinivasapuram and Varkala: East–West University of Brahmavidya.

—— (1989), *Autobiography of an Absolutist*, Varkala: Gurukula Publishing House.

—— (1990), *Life and Teachings of Narayana Guru*, Varkala: Narayana Gurukula Foundation.

Rambachan, Anantanand (1994), *The Limits of Scripture: Vivekananda's Reinterpretation of the Vedas*, Honolulu: University of Hawaii Press.

Rolland, Romain (1931), *The Life of Ramakrishna*, Mayavati: Advaita Ashrama.

Rüstau, Hiltrud (2002), *Continuity and Discontinuity in Modern Indian Philosophy: The 'Avarna' Advaitin Narayana Guru'*, in J. Heidrich, H. Rüstau and D. Weidemann (eds), *Indian Culture: Continuity and Discontinuity: In Memory of Walter Ruben (1899–1982)*, Berlin: Trafo Verlag.

—— (2003), '"The Hindu Women's Right to Sannyasa": Religious Movements and the Gender Question: The Sri Sarada Math and the Ramakrishna Sarada Mission', in A. Copley (ed.), *Hinduism in Public and Private*, New Delhi: Oxford University Press, pp. 143–72.

Sastri, Subramanya S. and T. R. Srinivasa Ayyangar (trans.), (1937), *Saundarya-Lahari of Sri Samkara-Bhagavatpada*, Adyar, Chennai: The Theosophical Publishing House.

Sreenivasan, K. (1989), *Sree Narayana Guru: Saint Philosopher Humanist*, Trivandrum: Jayasree Publications.

Subramanian, V. K. (ed. and trans.) (1977), *Saundaryalahari of Shankaracarya*, Delhi: Motilal Banarsidass, n.d.

[Swami] Tapasyananda (ed. and trans.), *Saundaryalahari of Sri Sankaracarya*, Mylapore, Madras: Sri Ramakrishna Math.

Thus Spake Sree Narayana Guru, (1972), Compiled by Sanyasini Devaki Amma, Varkala: The Sivagiri Sree Narayana Dharma Sodari Matom.

[Swami] Vivekananda (1990), *The Complete Works of Swami Vivekananda*, Vols III and VI, Calcutta: Advaita Ashram.

[Pravrajika] Vivekaprana (1999), A series of 7 Lectures on the *Devimahatmya*, given in Sacramento during August/September, unpublished tapes.

—— (2002), *A Challenge for Modern Minds*, Albany: Sri Sarada Society.

—— (2004), 'Talks on Sri Candi', in Amalaprana Pravrajika (ed.), *Eternal Mother*, Dakshineswar, Kolkata: Sri Sarada Math, pp. 36–46.

9

The Swami and the Artist
The Use of Indian Art in Swami Vivekananda's Apologetics

GWILYM BECKERLEGGE

INTRODUCTION

While imprisoned in Ahmadnagar Fort, Jawaharlal Nehru had both the
time and good reason to reflect on his cultural inheritance as British rule
over India came to a close. In the resulting *My Discovery of India*, his
disclaimer, 'I know nothing about art, eastern or western, and am not
competent to say anything about it' (Nehru 1960: 204), sits in the midst
of a lengthy apologia in defence of Indian art. The reason for this is
probably to be found in his observation that 'Indian art is...intimately
associated with Indian religion and philosophy...' (Nehru 1960: 203).
Europeans, Nehru (1960: 204) explained, had generally regarded forms
of Indian art as 'degraded' versions of the Graeco-Buddhist art of
Gandhara, the one style they admired because of its affinity to the world
of ancient Greece (see Guha-Thakurta 1995: 83). He went on to contrast
hostile European commentators with more appreciative judgements, and,
in particular, that of E. B. Havell, Superintendent in turn of the Madras
School of Arts and, between 1896 and 1906, the Government School of
Art in Calcutta (Nehru 1960: 205). With Ananda Coomaraswamy, Havell
is said to have 'pioneered an "Indian defence" in reaction against the
insidious "Western bias" that had so far dominated the European view of
Indian art' (Guha-Thakurta 1992: 146; cf. Guha-Thakurta 1995: 76–
80). Bhupendranath Datta (1993: 220), however, has stated in his
biography of his famous brother, Swami Vivekananda (1863–1902),
that the arguments of Havell and Coomaraswamy were anticipated by
Vivekananda's defence of Indian art, and that Vivekananda inspired the

passionate interest in Indian art displayed by his disciple, Sister Nivedita.[1]
From the time of Vivekananda, defence of Indian art became part of a
more general apologetic advanced on behalf of Hinduism.[2]

Vivekananda has been hailed as the source of an influential expression
of Hinduism, as an educator, and a thinker who restored Hindu self-
confidence, nourishing the roots of the nationalist movement. He is said
to have shaped modern forms of the Bengali language (for example, Brekke
2002: 42ff.). According to his biographers, he excelled in the performing
arts even as a child, being blessed with a fine singing voice, and became
a commanding orator. Bhupendranath Datta (1993: 219–28) recalled
specifically that Vivekananda's talents as a painter, as well as a singer
and actor, were also put to use in dramatic performances. This emphasis
is not generally evident in later appreciations of Vivekananda, even in
those emanating from the Ramakrishna Math and Mission, the movement Vivekananda founded. There are many parallels drawn between
the hagiographic accounts of the childhoods of Vivekananda and
Ramakrishna, but it is not generally suggested that Vivekananda shared
his master's flair for painting and modelling, an aptitude known to
Vivekananda (1989: Vol. V, 259, 373).

Mitter's (1994: 228) observation that 'references to art abound' in
the records of Vivekananda's conversations is potentially misleading. Such
references are far from extensive, particularly when measured against
Vivekananda's recorded reflections on matters generally recognized as his
major concerns. *Prabuddha Bharata*, a journal instigated by Vivekananda,
does appear to echo Bhupendranath Datta when it asks 'Who else could
be the best judge of art than Swami Vivekananda, whose mastery over
the world's history, culture, philosophy, art, literature, and a thousand
other subjects were unparalleled?' (cf. His Eastern and Western Disciples
1989: Vol. I, 447). By way of an answer, the journal links together almost
verbatim Vivekananda's 'grand ideas' about art from the nine published
volumes of his *Collected Works* to form a short narrative article (Swami
Vivekananda 2002: 64). This modest collation hardly conveys an
impression of Vivekananda's continuous engagement with this subject.
Yet, Vivekananda's reported judgements on Indian art will be the subject
of this chapter.

This chapter does not set out to offer another or rival account of the
recent history of Indian art.[3] Instead, it traces the relationship between
Vivekananda's statements about Indian art and his more extensive
theorizing about the Hindu religious tradition. These statements provide

another perspective on Vivekananda's position within late nineteenth-century Hinduism, and more particularly within the process of the intensive interaction between Indian and Western intellectual, religious, and aesthetic traditions, which provided the backdrop to his mission and which to some extent he consciously mediated.

Transformations of Indian art, which were taking place in much the same period as Vivekananda's reformulation of Hindu religious ideas, have attracted a degree of dismissive comment comparable to that directed against 'Neo-Hinduism', the category within which Vivekananda is often placed. This is hardly surprising. So many aspects of Hindu aesthetic, intellectual, social, and spiritual life—art, literature, philosophy, politics, and religion—were undergoing significant modifications at much the same time as a result of the impact of European thinking and technological innovation in a context marked by British dominance.[4] Often cited is the disparaging observation passed in 1886 by Trailokyanath Mukharji of the Indian Museum in Calcutta who noted that the 'ancient style of painting' had given way in Bengal to cheap lithographic prints (Mukharji 1886: 1), referring in 1888 to 'foul-smelling oleographs' (quoted in Inglis 1995: 51). According to Guha-Thakurta (1995: 63), the sense of a present decline from past glory was 'sharply etched in the emerging Bengali discourse on art and aesthetics'. This 'recurrent motif of a fall from a prior golden age', a distant classical past that offered itself to the present as a source of renewal, was closely linked to current concerns with national regeneration and progress (Guha-Thakurta 1995: 63). A more recent commentator, Bharati (1971: 87; cf. 1970: 268), identified the 'radical decline of aesthetic perception in modern India' as one of the modifications of traditional' Hinduism, referring to 'a loss of traditional acumen in the arts and their appreciation'. The ramifications of Bharati's argument become fully apparent when one takes into account his general profile of the religious dimensions of the 'Hindu Renaissance', which are presented as substantially shaped by Western influence and similarly exhibiting a lack of rigour when compared with earlier Hindu religious thought and practice.[5]

Studies of Hindu devotional pictures ('god posters') frequently acknowledge that such works are often dismissed, whether simply on grounds of taste as 'kitsch' (Smith 1995: 24), or more tellingly as 'degenerate and as a threat to what was distinctive and culturally precious in Indian art' (Inglis 1995: 52). This sense of loss of value and cultural distinctiveness (here clearly implying continuity with 'the past') finds many parallels in unsympathetic characterizations of what has variously been labelled 'modern', 'Renaissance', or 'Neo-' Hinduism (see Beckerlegge 2000: 52–4). A preoccupation with cultural distinctiveness surfaced constantly in public debates about the directions taken by Indian art during the period surrounding Vivekananda's life.

CHANGING STYLES OF INDIAN ART[6]

The subject matter, style, and function of both painting and sculpture continued to be intimately linked in the minds of many nineteenth-century Hindus to religious purposes, and in particular to the production of religious iconography and the construction of temples (cf. Topsfield 1979: 35). This, of course, was the way in which many European observers first encountered Hindu painting and sculpture, undoubtedly influencing their judgements on Hindu art.

The eclectic style of Mughal painting had already absorbed certain European elements, but the increasing presence of Europeans in India and their adoption of the role of patrons of Indian artists resulted in a richer fusion of influences. Subject matter, style, and modes of production and dissemination were all transformed. British tastes, for example, encouraged the increasing secularization of the subjects chosen by painters and modellers as they strove to capture the 'exotic' scenes and artefacts of everyday life. 'Company artists' frequently worked alongside mapmakers and others involved in compiling historical and geographical accounts of India's past and present. European techniques relating to perspective, shading, and the use of watercolours and oils were rapidly assimilated by Indian artists, as was the pursuit of naturalism, a tendency reinforced by the advent of photography. European painters, lured to centres like Calcutta by rich clients, gave lessons to the wealthy and took Indians as assistants, thus further enhancing familiarity with these techniques. Some of these students looked to develop careers as professional artists, in a manner comparable to that of their European counterparts. Conscious of their status as 'artists', they distanced themselves from traditional forms of art, now held to be 'crafts'. Wealthy Bengali families began private collections of European art and supported public exhibitions to promote the appreciation of 'fine art', as distinct from decorative 'crafts', in which the 'higher forms' were by then assumed to be European.

In 1854, the Government School of Art was established in Calcutta to provide training for middle-class 'artists'. This School initially attempted to promote Western-style art while fostering vocational skills (see Guha-

Thakurta 1995: 64–7). When Havell adopted the policy of excluding the teaching of European art from the School, following his appointment as Principal in 1896, students protested and the Jubilee Art School was formed subsequently by Ranadaprasad Das Gupta to ensure the continuation of the teaching of European, academic art. This protest was linked to nationalist suspicions that to prevent Indian artists from studying European artistic techniques would prejudice their careers and impede the development of artistic endeavour in India.

Mitter (1994: 283) notes that, although later reversed, Havell's policy, 'deepened the rift between cultural nationalists and political activists.' While the latter wished to rid India of British rule but not reject Western innovations, here including what were held to be the 'scientific' conventions of European painting, the former devoted themselves to exploring Indian cultural uniqueness rather than to the acquisition of political power. For some, the recovery and promotion of the core of this 'uniqueness' implied the eventual achievement of self-determination as a condition necessary for this uniqueness ultimately to flourish without hindrance. The distinctively 'Indian' quality in a work of art was frequently attributed to its 'spirituality' and 'idealism', expressed through extra-naturalistic symbolism. The wider use of the terms 'spirituality' and 'idealism' was part of an increasingly well-established apologetic discourse constructed by Indian authors, including Vivekananda, who contrasted these 'Indian' qualities with Western 'materialism' and 'realism'. It may be compared to the distinction drawn by nineteenth-century Japanese intellectuals, during the turmoil of Japan's encounter with the West, between Western science and Eastern moral values (for example, Sakuma Shozan, quoted in Tsunoda 1958: 96ff.). Similarly, the emphasis placed by Vivekananda and others on Indian spirituality was designed to assert at least India's equality with, if not its superiority over, the West, and to bind India more closely to a sense of being of the East and all this now implied about its values. For many, this 'Indian' and 'Eastern' character was to be found pre-eminently in the paintings of Abanindranath Tagore and his disciples.

Havell's partnership with Abanindranath Tagore was another outcome of the decision to reform the curriculum of the School of Art, which fostered the growth of the 'national' art movement in Bengal, known as the New Calcutta School or the Neo-Bengal School. Its *swadeshi* ideology was seen to represent nationalist political aspirations. After its influence had spread more widely throughout India as Abanindranath's students

became artists and teachers, it later was simply, if inaccurately, referred
to as the Bengal School. It drew upon classical literature and earlier periods
of Indian history for its subject matter and techniques, including the
work of Mughal and Rajput painters. Under Abanindranath's influence,
however, it also reached out far more widely to absorb not just the
Western principles and techniques in which he had been trained prior
to falling under Havell's influence but increasingly Chinese and Japanese
artistic traditions. Guha-Thakurta (1992: 5) makes an observation about
a tension at the heart of this 'renaissance' of Indian painting that, if
suitably recast, could easily be found in critical discussions of the religious
achievements of the 'Hindu Renaissance': 'The idea of an "Indian"
aesthetic that could be *recovered* and *reconstructed* from the past must be
pitted against the fundamental process of colonial education and *severance
with tradition* that produced modern Indian art' [emphasis added]. The
problems inherent in attempting to categorize such an experiment are
well illustrated in Mitra's judgement on the genius of the Bengal School,
'…at its worst, eclectic rather than single-notedly derivative or revivalist.
If anything was revived, it was the urge to find a new idiom for the art of
a resurgent India' (Mitra 1990: 262).

The meeting ground for so-called 'high art' and 'bazaar art', according
to Guha-Thakurta (1990: 152), was the colour print. Although the quest
for status as an 'artist' had involved a conscious distancing from the work
of the 'craftsman' and the bazaar as a commercial outlet, this was where
some of those schooled in the no longer fashionable traditions of Mughal
painting sought employment. 'Company artists' and practitioners of
European-style 'high art' also found that 'bazaar art' provided a lucrative
subsidy for their other interests. Consequently, the displacement of
Mughal courtly art by European aesthetic ideals and techniques was
paralleled by no less rapid and far-reaching changes in the art of the
bazaar, dubbed by Guha-Thakurta (1990: 152) as 'Westerization from
below'. Here too, the tastes of the new British patrons brought about
shifts to more secular subject matter and the techniques of European
drawing and painting began to modify traditional practice, for example,
that of the Kalighat *patuas* (see Gupta 1990: 139–42).

An extensive mass market was created once lithography had been
brought to Calcutta in the 1820s. It rapidly displaced the use of woodcuts,
which had provided the illustrations for cheap books and prints (see, for
example, Neumayer and Schelberger 2004: 17–34). Lithographic prints
shaped a new form of popular, Hindu devotional art that has survived to

the present day. In 1878, the Calcutta Art Studio, then recently founded by a breakaway group from the School of Art, established a chromolithographic press. This was the first of many such presses that served a steadily expanding, profitable, and durable market. Some of these were based in Europe and fed by pictures brought from India, which were then exported back to the Indian market. The prints from these presses portrayed Hindu deities and scenes from the popular devotional stories in a manner that combined traditional Hindu iconographic conventions with European techniques and modelling. The technique of chromolithography was thus established in Calcutta some years before Raja Ravi Varma's more famous press on the other side of India in the area of Bombay (Gupta 1990: 145). It was Ravi Varma, with a German collaborator, however, whose oleographic press and distribution system succeeded in creating an all-India market for his devotional prints.

Familiar with the techniques of Indian courtly painting and European oil painting, Ravi Varma drew on the subject matter of Hindu mythology but portrayed in accordance with conventions borrowed from the genre of European history painting. He thus presented the viewers of his pictures with 'the conjunction of the realistic and the totemic' (Blurton 1988: 57), in contrast with the 'Hindu mytho-pictures' of the Calcutta Art Studio in which '...realism itself suffered much dilution in mingling with conventional iconography' (Guha-Thakurta 1990: 153). Rabindranath Tagore recalled from his childhood the impact of these oleographs when they began to circulate in Bengal (quoted in Mitter 1994: 180). Ravi Varma's prints achieved their height of popularity in Calcutta during the 1890s. The discussion they provoked around the current preoccupations with their 'Indian' and 'aesthetic' qualities and the quality of the printing technology '...gave rise to a new distinction between the print as "art" and the print as "bazaar" picture or religious oleograph' (Guha-Thakurta 1990: 155). Like Abanindranath Tagore, Ravi Varma was held by some of his admirers to have expressed something quintessentially 'Indian' through his representation of India's past, while utilizing influences, techniques, and materials in a thoroughly contemporary manner. Within a year of his death in 1906, however, supporters of the 'national' Neo-Bengal School rejected Ravi Varma's work as 'unspiritual' and 'hybrid' (Mitter 2001: 177).[7] As Pinney (2004: 60–1) notes, a retrospective of Ravi Varma's work in 1993 re-ignited the debate about his standing and legacy, leading Pinney to conclude that 'Ravi Varma emerges as ... a space in which conflicting histories and aspirations are invested.'

Having been acclaimed for capturing something quintessentially 'Indian', Ravi Varma's work, according to Desai (2002: 12), has played a crucial role in 'the construction of the hegemonic culture of the Indian bourgeoisie'.[8] This 'hegemonic culture', defined by its elites on the basis of a shared, upper-caste, Hindu patriarchal outlook, became the culture of India's ruling class, which embraced 'the modernization of Hinduism, its bourgeoisification and nationalization' (Desai 2002: 22). Desai (2002: 11) identifies two processes within the construction of this 'hegemonic culture': the modernization of Hinduism from the period of the Bengal Renaissance to the rise of the *Sangh Parivar*, and the accompanying nationalization of Hinduism. If Ravi Varma was 'central to the changes in India's culture and indeed the emergence of Hinduised Indian culture' (Desai 2002: 11), Vivekananda's role in the modernization of Hinduism and creation of a religion for the bourgeoisie was no less significant.

In the period after 1897, Vivekananda was at the height of his fame and popularity in India. Vivekananda died in 1902 and thus never saw the flowering of the Bengal School. Even before Vivekananda's return to Calcutta in 1897 after his first journey to the West, however, Havell's determination to 'Indianise' the curriculum of the School of Art in Calcutta had fanned a public controversy about the character and quality of Indian art in relationship to European-style art. The remainder of the chapter will be devoted to examining Vivekananda's statements about Indian art not just within the familiar framework of his ideas about the relationship between India and the West, and within this his defence of Hinduism, but also mindful of the independent but not unrelated debate then taking place about the 'recovery' of Indian art.

VIVEKANANDA ON ART EAST AND WEST

Vivekananda's undergraduate studies in Calcutta favoured history, philosophy, and literature. It is not clear whether aesthetics or the history of art fell within the fold of his eclectic interests at this time to the extent that social theory undoubtedly did. Vivekananda's biographers maintain that art was a subject, along with many others, discussed by the young members of the Baranagore Math (His Eastern and Western Disciples 1989: Vol. I, 205). Later in his life, Vivekananda (1989: Vol. V, 361–2) emphasized that a trained ear and eye and deeper study are necessary to understand music and painting, and implied that he had imposed this discipline on himself but without indicating the circumstances. In the year before his death, his interest in art was still sufficient for him to have made time to read about it in the *Encyclopaedia Britannica* (Vivekananda 1989: Vol. VII, 206).

After the death of Ramakrishna, Vivekananda travelled extensively throughout India (particularly 1889–93) and made two extended visits to the United States and Europe (1893–97 and 1899–1900). During his travels, he viewed collections of art in libraries, museums, and exhibitions, and went to historic locations, such as places of worship or other religious activity, where examples of a country's artistic achievements were to be found (for example, His Eastern and Western Disciples 1989: Vol. I, 393, 395, 398). On arrival in Chicago at the end of July 1893, where he would shortly speak at the World's Parliament of Religions, Vivekananda marvelled at the displays of machinery and the arts brought together from many countries at the World's Fair (His Eastern and Western Disciples 1989: Vol. I, 400). The World's Parliament of Religions was actually held in the newly built Art Institute of Chicago. Once the Parliament was over and before embarking upon a lecture circuit, Vivekananda remained in Chicago and 'visited museums, universities, schools and art galleries, trying to comprehend the spirit of Western life. Gazing at some work of art, or studying some signal engineering or architectural achievement, his thought would leap in admiration of the greatness of the human mind' (His Eastern and Western Disciples 1989: Vol. I, 447, cf. Vol. II, 538).

During his second stint in the West, Vivekananda saw a collection of paintings by Dutch masters in Vienna, making specific observations on the characteristics of the Dutch 'style' (Vivekananda 1989: Vol. VII, 389), and visited Constantinople and Athens. In Paris, he repeatedly went to the Louvre (Vivekananda 1989: Vol. VII, 402–4), and exhibitions that formed part of the Paris Exposition of 1900 (His Eastern and Western Disciples 1989: Vol. II, 538). These experiences and his quest to penetrate the 'spirit' of different cultures shaped his attempts to understand the relationship between East and West (for example, 'The East and The West' in Vivekananda 1989: Vol. V, 441–537, and 'Memoirs of European Travel' in Vivekananda 1989: Vol. VII, 297–404). The majority of Vivekananda's references to Indian art date from 1893 when he began to construct the theoretical platform from where he would assert the value of India's contribution to a world in which both the East and the West had need to learn and to take from each other.

Vivekananda's statements on art can be divided into general, often sweeping, references and discussions of particular works, artists, or movements. The former category includes unequivocal assertions of the supremacy of India's cultural achievements over those of the West, which were characteristically directed at Western audiences. Speaking about 'India's Gift to the World' in New York in 1895, Vivekananda (1989: Vol. II, 510–13) asserted the foundational nature of India's contribution to ethics, arts, sciences, and literature, and outlined the ways in which 'the earliest cradles' of these forms of knowledge and creativity in India prefigured many later advances in Europe. Similar themes occur in a reported lecture, 'The Vedanta Philosophy or Hinduism as a Religion', delivered in Los Angeles in December 1899 (Vivekananda 1997: 499). In a talk entitled 'Arts and Sciences in India', given in Oakland in March 1900, Vivekananda invited his listeners to compare India and England in the Elizabethan period, and to appreciate how 'enlightened' Indians were during this period when England was undergoing a 'dark age'. In poetry, music, drama, and art (explicit reference is made to sculpture), India 'led' the way. He added the rider, however, 'Whatever is done now is merely an attempt at imitation' (Vivekananda 1989: Vol. IV, 196–7). This is a point to which we shall return. At this stage, however, we should note the extent to which Vivekananda evidently felt it necessary or strategically useful to present his defence and promotion of Hinduism, understood as a religion, within a style of apologetics that encompassed a range of India's intellectual and creative traditions, including art.

Close discussion of both painting and sculpture was prompted by Vivekananda's travels in Europe and in particular by his encounters with ancient Greek art in Paris and Athens. In his 'Memoirs of European Travel', composed during his second journey to the West, 1899–1900, Vivekananda identified three stages of Greek art, stating categorically that the first stage (Mycenaean) 'engaged itself in merely copying Asiatic art'. 'Greek art proper', which followed this and was divided by Vivekananda (1989: Vol. VII, 402) into 'archaic' and 'classic' Greek art, gave up 'its Asiatic tinge'. Its hallmark was 'exact imitation of nature. The difference between Greek art and the art of other countries consists in this, that the former faithfully delineates the living phenomena of natural life' (Vivekananda 1989: Vol. VII, 402). Further dividing classic Greek art into the Attic and Peloponnesian schools, Vivekananda (1989: Vol. VII, 403) noted that certain exponents of the Attic school 'completely divorce art from religion and keep it restricted to the delineation of merely human life', while the latter school established the principle that 'the proportion of the human body must be faithfully reproduced in art'.

In an undated note, Vivekananda (1989: Vol. V, 258) compared what he presented as the characteristic of Greek art, its imitation of nature, with that of Indian art, which is to 'represent the ideal, the supersensual'. Here again, we find Vivekananda, although less baldly, preparing the ground on which to assert the supremacy of Indian art over Greek art, the East over the West, in keeping with the general thrust of his apologetics. Thus, he asked 'what glory is there in merely imitating nature?' (Vivekananda 1989: Vol. V, 258). In this passage, however, he revealed a preoccupation with what lies at the heart of Indian art, 'its secret', which, as we saw earlier in this chapter, was central to the debate provoked by the transformation of Indian art, and painting in particular, during the nineteenth century. If exact imitation of nature may be said to be the distinguishing quality of Greek art, for Vivekananda the distinguishing quality of Indian art was its capacity to penetrate to the ideal, to the 'supersensual'. Thus he wrote, 'So Art must be in touch with nature—and whenever that touch is gone, Art degenerates—yet it must be above nature' (Vivekananda 1989: Vol. V, 258). For that reason, just as the Greeks' faithful delineation of living phenomena can lead to the mere 'imitation' of nature, so too India's preoccupation with representing the 'supersensual' can lead to degeneration through failing to represent the natural adequately.

Vivekananda's insistence that works of art should keep in touch with nature while being above it serves his overall apologetic purpose. It also strongly suggests that he was not untouched by the tension experienced by other Indian intellectuals of his age between acknowledging what naturalism could bring to a composition, implying at that time the use of the techniques of European-style art, and seeking to preserve and promote a uniquely Indian artistic perception. If this passage does illustrate Vivekananda's broad familiarity with, and use of, contemporary critical perspectives on Indian art, it may be possible to clarify the allusion in the following judgement: 'The Indian tendency, on the other hand, to represent the ideal, the supersensual, has become degraded into painting grotesque images' (Vivekananda 1989: Vol. V, 258). At the most general level, this could be read as a comment about a perceived trend in artistic skill and expression, possibly tinged by *advaitin* sympathies that did not place concrete imagery (the *murti*) at the heart of the religious life. It could also be applied more narrowly to the state of Indian religious art before the growing impact of naturalism during the nineteenth century, culminating in Ravi Varma's presentation of Hindu mythological themes within the conventions of European history painting. More specifically again, it could refer to the reassertion or perpetuation of traditional forms of Hindu religious iconography in the popular art of the kind produced by the Calcutta Art Studio and similar presses in which realism was typically 'diluted' by the perpetuation of traditional conventions.

In a conversation reported to have taken place just prior to his second journey to the West, Vivekananda (1989: Vol. VII, 272) placed great emphasis upon the need for artists to strive for historical accuracy, for 'What good is it to paint a picture if the details are wrong? … The truth must be presented, otherwise the picture is nothing.' This attitude was consistent with other statements made by Vivekananda relating to matters of historical accuracy, although he imposed limits on the extent to which historical research could intrude into areas of religious belief. History could not prove or disprove the central truths of religion but it could dispel 'wrong ideas born of ignorance'. He was critical of religious groups that would tolerate untruths in order to spread their message, and declared 'But our duty should be to convince ourselves of the truth, to believe in truth only. Such is the power of superstition, or faith in old traditions without inquiry into its truth, that it keeps men bound hand and foot' (Vivekananda 1989: Vol. IV, 105–6). Vivekananda had been invited to comment on a picture of Krishna addressing Arjuna on the battlefield and, in addition to taking exception to the accuracy of the representation of an ancient Indian chariot, criticized the way in which Krishna had been depicted. Typically, to make the point to his listener, Vivekananda (1989: Vol. VII, 273) took up the pose and demeanour that he thought should have characterised the portrayal of Krishna; an image of 'Activity combined with firmness and serenity'.[9] In passing, he made this more general observation, 'In these days, our young men who go in for painting are generally those who were unsuccessful at school, and who have been given up at home as good-for-nothing; what work of art can you expect from them?' (Vivekananda 1989: Vol. VII, 272). These scathing comments may imply that Vivekananda (1989: Vol. VII, 272) would have viewed artists as equally lax in their adherence to accuracy and truth.

It would be wrong to assume that historical accuracy can be taken for granted in paintings produced consciously within the genre of European history painting, but Vivekananda's response to his friend's painting of Krishna might lead one to conclude that he would have been sympathetic to portraits produced in this style. In fact, it has been suggested that Vivekananda had great respect for the work of his contemporary, Raja

Ravi Varma (1848–1906), widely regarded as the greatest Indian exponent of this style at that time. His oil paintings, eagerly sought by members of the Indian aristocracy and the British ruling class in India, won prizes in both India and abroad and, as was noted above, made an indelible mark on popular Hindu devotional art when turned into prints. He created for 'an average Indian' the 'mental picture' of their popular deities through his recreation of 'the ancient world of myths and legends enshrined in the "Puranas"' (Pillai 1981).

SWAMI VIVEKANANDA AND RAJA RAVI VARMA:
REPRESENTATIVES OF INDIA

When Ravi Varma heard of the forthcoming Columbian Exposition to be held at Chicago in 1893, he felt 'As the country's premier artist, it was his duty...to represent India' (Venniyoor 1981).[10] His religious scruples, however, prevented him from crossing the sea and he sent a series of ten canvases to convey the life of India in both its diversity and underlying unity. According to Sen (2000: 83), Vivekananda who, of course, did attend the Exposition in person is known to have visited an exhibition of Ravi Varma's paintings at Chicago. Sen cites this as evidence that Vivekananda held Ravi Varma in higher regard than he did Indian artists in general. Venniyoor (1981: 33) is more tentative, merely suggesting that Vivekananda 'must have seen the works of his compatriot too'. The Kerala Arts and Literary Association (n.d.), on the other hand, claims that the best accolade Ravi Varma received came from Vivekananda, having seen the former's work at Chicago. Unfortunately, the judgement attributed to Vivekananda was delivered some years earlier and was unrelated to Ravi Varma's exhibition at Chicago.

Venniyoor (1981: 33) holds out the possibility that the Swami and the artist were personally acquainted when he notes that some of Ravi Varma's biographers have claimed that Ravi Varma played host to Vivekananda at Bombay, a claim apparently corroborated by Ravi Varma's cook. According to Venniyoor (1981: 33), moreover, one of the earliest photographs of Vivekananda in the south of India was taken by Aswati Tirunaal, a young prince of Travancore whose relative and mentor was none other than Ravi Varma who, Venniyoor suggests, presumably arranged this. This photograph was in all probability one taken in Trivandrum in December 1892, showing Vivekananda seated in the garb of a *sannyasi* (His Eastern and Western Disciples 1989: 333). The name of the photographer is usually given as Prince Martanda Varma. It was the habit of the royal house, however, to take additional names according to the stars under which they were born, Tirunaal (Thirunal) being a title of respect for the royal family (Allen 1984: 24). There is no evidence to suggest that Vivekananda and Ravi Varma had met previously or that they actually met during the former's nine-day stay at Trivandrum. This seems unlikely because Ravi Varma is said to have been busy during December 1892 at his own home at Kilimanoor, some 40 kilometres from Trivandrum, painting five canvases for exhibition in Chicago (Venniyoor 1981: 30). What is certain is that Vivekananda was acquainted with Ravi Varma's work by this time.

Ravi Varma produced his first commissioned work in 1870. His reputation as a painter of studies of Indian women grew and prizes followed as his work was exhibited in India and Europe. When he decided to represent India at Chicago in 1893, he chose to do so through ten studies of women intended to encapsulate India, which Desai (2002: 23) contends actually depicted a self-idealization by the high-caste, propertied elite in which women were conformed to Brahmanical norms. Significantly, although these paintings were awarded two prizes and this was much heralded in India, they were displayed in the ethnographic section at the Columbian Exposition, not in the fine arts pavilion, and thus were never entered in the catalogue of fine arts exhibits. It cannot be assumed, therefore, that Vivekananda saw these pictures in Chicago as part of his wider visiting of art galleries. If he did see them, their setting as exhibits in an ethnographic collection, where they were praised for 'giving careful attention to the detail of costume and articles used in the social and ceremonial life' may well have affected his reception of them (Neumayer and Schelberger 2004: 45). For whatever reason, there is no reference made to these exhibits or their painter in the general accounts of Vivekananda's appearance at the Parliament and his time in Chicago. Vivekananda, however, had seen other examples of Ravi Varma's work several months before his visit to Trivandrum at the end of 1892.

It was Ravi Varma's novel portrayals of scenes from India's literary tradition that created the 'real breakthough' into a 'totally new kind of religious and illustrative painting ... which catapulted the fame and career of the artist' (Guha-Thakurta 1986: 175). In 1881, he received one of his most important commissions, when he was invited by the Gaekwad of Baroda to produce five paintings on religious and puranic themes. This was followed in 1888 with a larger commission for fourteen paintings of scenes from the Mahabharata and Ramayana, which would be displayed in the Durbar Hall of the Gaekwad's new palace, Lakshmi Vilas (see Desai 2002). They were exhibited first at Trivandrum and then taken by the artist in 1891 via Bombay, where they were again exhibited, to Baroda and their ultimate but less accessible location in the Gaekwad's palace. The level of popular interest aroused by the brief, public display of these pictures convinced Ravi Varma that there was a hunger in India for religious pictures of this sort, prompting him to establish his own press. According to Guha-Thakurta (1986: 186), this decision was also shaped by Ravi Varma's abhorrence of the standard of popular religious prints then already being produced and circulated in Bombay.

Writing about his fleeting visit to Baroda in a letter of 26 April 1892 to one of his supporters, Haridas Viharidas Desai (Dewan of Junagadh), Vivekananda (1989: Vol. VIII, 286) declared, 'Of course, I have seen the Library and the pictures of Ravi Varma, and that is about all worth seeing here.' Vivekananda did not identify any of the paintings he had seen, which is perhaps surprising in one with a reputed interest in art, and so it is uncertain whether these included examples of portraiture or religious (puranic) painting. By this time, however, Ravi Varma had produced a substantial body of work including examples of the portraits, regional depictions of Indian women, and mythological subjects for which he was becoming increasingly famous. Vivekananda's brief comment is often cited in evaluations of Ravi Varma's standing in the eyes of other Indians and, as noted above, has on occasion wrongly been reported as a judgement uttered by Vivekananda at Chicago. As with Vivekananda's judgement, quoted above, on the tendency in India to paint 'grotesque images' (Vivekananda 1989: Vol. V, 258), his terse judgement on Ravi Varma is open to more than one interpretation. It could be taken as an acknowledgement of the superior quality of Ravi Varma's work, or as a less flattering concession that Ravi Varma's work was merely the best of what was on display.

Vivekananda referred to Ravi Varma in a far less ambiguous manner in 'The East and The West', his reflection on his second visit to the West in 1899–1900 and thus written towards the end of his life. Commenting on the practice in Europe and America of collecting works of art, Vivekananda made the plea that some effort be made in India to preserve what would otherwise be lost. Having stated that Indians were less skilled than Europeans in painting and sculpture, he observed, 'By imitating the Europeans we at the utmost can only produce one or two Ravi Varmas among us!' The thrust of this comment is made plain in his claim that the work of the *patua*s of Bengal was 'far better', adding 'The paintings of Ravi Varma and others make one hide one's face from shame! Far better are those gilded pictures of Jaipur and the Chalchitra [frames over the images of deities] of the goddess Durgâ that we have had from old times' (Vivekananda 1989: Vol. V, 476; cf. Vol. V, 174).

Vivekananda died at the height of Ravi Varma's popularity and some years before the rise of the Neo-Bengal School with its more consciously nationalist expectations of art. The seeming ambivalence, if not outright contradiction, in Vivekananda's judgements on Ravi Varma, therefore, is unlikely to have been a simple consequence of Vivekananda being carried along by a sweeping sea change in public opinion. He may, of course, have reached the same verdict independently and somewhat earlier. Bhupendranath Datta, as we noted, made a similar claim about his brother anticipating the stance adopted by Havell and Coomaraswamy. It is possible, however, to make sense of Vivekananda's views about Ravi Varma within the overall framework of his apologetic statements about Indian art and its relationship to European-style art. As suggested at the outset of this chapter, this may lead in turn to a fuller appreciation of the complex attitudes that Vivekananda brought to his major task as a cultural mediator, recasting Hindu religious ideas and practices.

IMITATION AND DEGENERATION

Criticism of 'imitation' recurs repeatedly throughout Vivekananda's judgements on art and his view of the relationship between Indian and European art during his own time. To summarize, just as Vivekananda (1989: Vol. I, 3) trumpeted Hinduism as 'the mother of religions' in his first address at the World's Parliament of Religions', so too he asserted that India once 'led' the way in its artistic accomplishments (Vol. IV, 196f.), providing the earliest 'cradle' of art (Vol. II, 510), which was one of India's gifts to the world. Consequently, he was able to declare that the Greeks had 'copied' Asiatic art, bringing to it their own distinctive skill of faithfully 'imitating' nature (Vivekananda 1989: Vol. VII, 402). In the process, as we have seen, he believed that the Greeks progressively lost the Asiatic quality, then supremely evident in Indian art, of going beyond the mere 'imitation' of nature in order to represent the 'supersensual' (Vivekananda 1989: Vol. V, 258). Since this early exchange, however, Vivekananda (1989: Vol. V, 258) recognized that the technical skills of painting and fidelity to detail had greatly advanced in European-style painting, while 'The Indian tendency ... to represent the ideal, the supersensual, has become degraded into painting grotesque images.' Vivekananda (1989: Vol. IX, 376) identified a similar degeneration in sculpture, which he attributed to the influence of popular forms of worship in India. This loss of vision and vitality had resulted in Indian artists 'imitating' both the former glories of Indian art and also European art (Vivekananda 1989: Vol. IV, 196–7). Talking with Ranadaprasad Das Gupta, the founder of the Jubilee Art Academy, in 1901 about art in India and the West, Vivekananda bemoaned a contemporary lack of artistic originality, which he attributed in part to reliance upon models produced through photography. In contrast, 'The ancient artists used to evolve original ideas from their brains and try to express them in their paintings' (Vivekananda 1989: Vol. VII, 202). He asserted, 'As in Western countries paintings like those of former times are not produced now, so in our country also, attempts to give expression to original ideas in art are no longer seen.' He concluded that he held the same to be true of the work produced by Ranadaprasad's own school, suggesting 'It would be well if you try to paint the objects of everyday meditation of the Hindus by giving in them the expression of ancient ideals' (Vivekananda 1989: Vol. VII, 203).

There is much in Vivekananda's apologia for Indian art that mirrors his more familiar defence of the Hindu religion, which he also believed had suffered a decline, largely because of a self-interested religious leadership and increasing preoccupation with 'don't touchism' (the minutiae of caste observance) (Vivekananda 1989: Vol. V, 226). What is striking in both these strands of his more comprehensive vision of India's relationship to the West is his eagerness to bring about change in certain areas by drawing upon Western knowledge and expertise, and the tension this creates as he wrestles to contain this influence and to maintain that it contributed no more than a relatively modest fillip to the regeneration of India's own artistic and religious life. The model he placed before his Indian followers was that of Japan.

Vivekananda visited Japan *en route* for Chicago in 1893. In contrast to China, which he found to be as 'mummified' as India, the Japanese seemed '… now to have fully awakened themselves to the necessity of the present times', and he commented upon the organization of the Japanese army, and engineering and industrial achievements (Vivekananda 1989: Vol. V, 7, 9). He also noted that 'The modern rage for progress has penetrated even the priesthood' (Vivekananda 1989: Vol. V, 9–10). This brief and partial encounter with the impact of Meiji policy upon late nineteenth-century Japan was to bring forth an indictment of present conditions in India. Vivekananda reproached 'young India' for sitting under an 'ever-increasing load of crystallised superstition', which prevented people from travelling abroad for fear of loss of caste and so discovering the achievements of the Japanese. Compared to the Japanese, Indians were 'vain talkers' and a 'race of dotards' consumed with a passion for discussing the untouchableness of this, that and the other 'with all humanity crushed out of you by the continuous social tyranny of the ages'. Rather than addressing the realities of India's situation, Vivekananda (1989: Vol. V, 10) depicted 'young India' as 'repeating undigested stray bits of European brainwork'.

By 1901, Vivekananda was in contact with the Kakuzo Okakura (1862–1913), the Japanese art scholar and Pan-Asian theorist who, like Havell in India, had attempted to ban instruction in Western art. Okakura's subsequent battles fostered alliances with Indian sympathizers (see Guha-Thakurta 1995: 84–5). There were plans that Vivekananda should again visit Japan with Okakura's help (Vivekananda 1989: Vol. V, 164–5; Vol. IX, 176). Both Josephine MacLeod, Vivekananda's American supporter, and Vivekananda himself assisted Okakura during his first visit to India in 1902 to study Buddhist art (Vivekananda 1989: Vol. V, 174–5; Vol. IX, 176–8, 186). Okakura's ideas about a Pan-Asian civilization, shortly to be published in his *Ideals of the East* (1903), had much in common with Vivekananda's own appreciation of a cultural unity marked by a keen spiritual awareness, which had been fostered by the pervasive influence of India through the medium of Buddhism. For Vivekananda, early Buddhism was nothing other than a development within Hinduism that had been turned into a distinct religion by followers who misunderstood their teacher's message. Okakura in his own way acknowledged a debt to India, the home of Buddhism, and thus the source of powerful artistic, aesthetic, and spiritual ideals (Guha-Thakurta 1992: 168). Okakura believed, however, that Japan alone of all the Asian countries had succeeded in absorbing and channelling, while yet withstanding, the force of Western influence to create its own 'modern renaissance'. Vivekananda had come to a similar view of the achievements of Meiji Japan as early as 1893.

If Japan provided Vivekananda with an Asian model to place before his followers when attempting to galvanize them into modernizing the social organization of Hinduism, it also figured in his urgings that Indians should assimilate Western knowledge without falling prey to the dangers of cultural 'indigestion'. This in his view was the great accomplishment of the Japanese and one to be emulated (Vivekananda 1989: Vol. V, 372).[11] In a highly topical conversation just prior to Okakura's visit to India, Vivekananda was asked by a disciple about the value of Indians visiting Japan. In his answer, Vivekananda (1989: Vol. V, 372) repeated the image of the cultural indigestion rife among Indians that he had used when describing Meiji Japan in 1893. His questioner then ventured to praise Japanese art as something 'which is their own and beyond imitation' (Vivekananda 1989: Vol. V, 372). Vivekananda seized upon this as a sign of the greatness of Japan but quickly attributed this to the fact that the Japanese were Asians, a trait they shared with Indians. The next question proved to be ill-judged for Vivekananda was then asked whether English art was as good, which led him to heap scorn on his questioner. Unlike Europeans who had been trying to infuse art into their life since coming into contact with Asia, Vivekananda declared that 'The very soul of Asia is interwoven with art...art is, with us, a part of religion'. This was to be found in domestic religious rituals, everyday utensils, and even in the decoration of farming buildings. Such signs are entirely lacking in the West where instead the ideal of utility had been prized above all (Vivekananda 1989: Vol. V, 373–4).[12] Bowing to the influence of the West, India had now grasped this same quality to a 'ridiculous' degree, whereas 'what we need is a combination of art and utility', as sought by the Japanese (Vivekananda 1989: Vol. V, 374).

Drawing together Vivekananda's comparative analyses of Indian, European, and Japanese styles of art, his major ideas can be set out as follows:

	East/India	West/European
Beginnings	Earliest cradle of art	Copiers of Asian art
Secret	Penetrating the supersensual	Faithful delineation of living phenomena
Quality	Originality	Imitation
Development	Degeneration to the grotesque	Technical skills
The Ideal	Art/religion in life	Utility
The Present	Degeneration, imitation of Western art and earlier styles of Indian art, lack of originality	Imitation of earlier Western art, lack of originality

Vivekananda's prescription for Indian artists was to find inspiration in 'something which is their own and beyond imitation' (Vivekananda 1989: Vol. V, 372). This is what had happened in Japan where 'you find a fine assimilation of knowledge, and not its indigestion, as we have here'. The Japanese 'have taken everything from the Europeans, but they have remained Japanese all the same, and have not turned European' (Vivekananda 1989: Vol. V, 372). Like Japan, India should return to the spiritual roots of its art, intertwined with the religious preoccupation with the 'supersensual'. Thus, when Vivekananda offered practical advice to the despondent Ranadaprasad Das Gupta, it was to capture the blissful and terrible aspects of Kali in a painting, offering his own poem, *Kali the Mother*, as a stimulus. It is reported that, although Ranadaprasad started this painting the next day, it was never completed nor shown to Vivekananda (Vivekananda 1989: Vol. VII, 203–4).

REACTING TO RAVI VARMA: A CONCLUSION

Vivekananda's two explicit judgements on Ravi Varma's work were separated by an interval of some seven years. It would be possible to read the second and more negative statement as indicative of a change of mind on Vivekananda's part as his own ideas about art developed as a result of his extensive travels. Ravi Varma was just beginning to establish a national reputation when Vivekananda saw his work at Baroda in 1892. Perhaps Vivekananda's earlier verdict was coloured by his initial response to a newly fashionable artist, or perhaps Ravi Varma failed to live up to whatever promise Vivekananda then saw in his work. All of these suggestions, however, fail to give due weight to the ambivalent and possibly grudging tone of Vivekananda's first opinion.

It seems unlikely, moreover, that the ambivalent and negative qualities apparent in Vivekananda's brief but telling judgements on Ravi Varma can be explained satisfactorily as anticipations of the painter's fall in popular esteem immediately after his death. Nevertheless, it is evident that Vivekananda's evaluation of Ravi Varma's work was greatly shaped by an all-embracing determination to maintain the unique nature of India's spiritual and artistic gifts to the world. To this extent, Vivekananda's subordination of the artist's work to an over-arching imperative was little different from the more vehement rejection of Ravi Varma, which was soon to follow, by Sister Nivedita and critics sympathetic to the Neo-Bengal school such as Havell and Coomaraswamy. Both rested upon essentialist notions of 'Indianness', which located this in a certain view of Hindu culture. While Vivekananda judged the artist on his expression of India's spiritual vision, the Neo-Bengal school looked for an embodiment of India's nationalist aspirations in his art. Although these two concerns were closely linked in the minds of many, the ways in which individuals respectively ranked these could dictate significantly different priorities and goals. Sister Nivedita's ultimate severance from the Ramakrishna movement might be cited as a case in point.

The positive note in Vivekananda's reaction to Ravi Varma's painting in all probability sprang from recognition of the painter's technical skill and a degree of sympathy for the naturalist depictions that were a hallmark of Ravi Varma's art. Ravi Varma's 'naturalistic' depiction of deities and heroic figures, although realistic, was hardly productive of attention to historical detail, given that his religious subjects were largely drawn from the *puranas*, and amounted more to a re-mythologization. He did avoid, however, what Vivekananda dubbed the 'grotesque', producing 'respectable' and 'modern' versions of Hindu myths—a 'visual version of the teachings of groups such as the Brahmo Samaj' (Blurton 1988: 56). This would have chimed well with Vivekananda's persistent concern to present an account of Hinduism, including the life and teaching of his *guru*, which did not offend the sensibilities of a Western audience.

Ravi Varma may have kept 'in touch' with nature, thereby meeting one of the criteria Vivekananda employed in his judgements on art, but ultimately was included by Vivekananda with other painters who 'make one hide one's face from shame'. The reason for this is that Ravi Varma failed to measure up to Vivekananda's other criterion of 'originality', being classed merely as the best of those who had 'imitated' European-style artists (Vivekananda 1989: Vol. V, 476). In fact, although Vivekananda's verdict on Ravi Varma at Baroda in 1892 has been seized upon as evidence of approbation, its concession that Ravi Varma's pictures were 'about all worth seeing here' could be regarded as entirely consistent with Vivekananda's later words, if one accepts that Vivekananda never regarded Ravi Varma as more than the most accomplished of a generation of artists who had imitated Western painting (Vivekananda 1989: Vol. VIII, 286).

Many of Vivekananda's most bitter criticisms were directed at Hindu religious and social reformers whose alienation had led them to turn against their own tradition (for example, Vivekananda 1989: Vol. III, 219; Vol. V, 217). His scorn for them was matched in his less frequent references to Indian artists who had copied Western styles. Yet, in matters of religion, social organization, as well as art, it is beyond question that

Vivekananda was himself critical of much of what he saw in India, pressed for selective change, and was willing to find the impetus for change outside India, not least in the West, even while downplaying the significance of this. As Jones (1989: 67) has observed, 'He [Vivekananda] feared that the negative stereotype of the educated Bengali, as proclaimed by English-men, might indeed be true, for there is a remarkable similarity between the two visions of Bengalis, his own and that of the foreign conqueror.'

The challenge Vivekananda faced both at a personal and institutional level (once he created the Ramakrishna Math and Mission) was to find appropriate exemplars and models to put primarily before Hindus, which would lend support to the changes he wished to promote by legitimating them as consistent with the essentials of Hinduism. His respect for Japan was an extension of this tactic, enveloping India and Japan within the unity of Asia/the East. In the realm of religion, Vivekananda's presentation of Ramakrishna, his formulation of Practical Vedanta, and many organizational features of the Ramakrishna Math and Mission centred upon the role of the sannyasi all sprang from this need. At a personal level, Vivekananda was willing to identify himself with 'awakened', 'revived', or 'purified' Hinduism, but less comfortable with notions of 'modern' or 'Neo-' Hinduism (Beckerlegge 2000: 54–61). He remained conscious of his caste status and accusations that he was not a true sannyasi and that his version of Hinduism was a Western import. His rejection of others' attempts to stimulate change in India by drawing upon Western ideas and practices may well have been an attempt to reinforce in the minds of his followers and critics, and possibly in his own mind, his insistence that Hinduism itself would provide the solutions to current problems. There is little evidence to suggest that Vivekananda recognized in any significant sense a common cause with other contemporary movements working for religious change within Hinduism. This is more than apparent from his negative comments at various times on Brahmos and Theosophists (Vivekananda 1989: Vol. III, 207–8; Vol. VIII, 477–8), and he was no less dismissive of Anagarika Dharmapala's reformulation of Sri Lankan Buddhism.

Both Raja Ravi Varma and Swami Vivekananda felt called to represent India in their different ways on the world stage provided by the Columbian Exposition in 1893. Rising to prominence when they did in their respective fields where they secured a degree of international recognition, it was inevitable that they would have been hailed as heroes in a climate of growing nationalist self-consciousness.[13] It is no less understandable that those who saw them as working towards the same goal of reviving Hindu India's self-respect should have assumed that they would have mutually admired and supported each other's achievements, although one was a sannyasi and the other a commercially-minded artist. Indeed, Vivekananda had sprung from the social class that had shown such an avid interest in Ravi Varma's depiction of Hindu India and its past.

There is more than enough evidence of Vivekananda's general interest in art to understand why he should have taken the trouble to pass comments on Ravi Varma's work in 1892, even if he had no prior acquaintance with Ravi Varma. The artist's growing reputation at the time might have been sufficient reason in itself. Yet, we have no way of knowing whether Vivekananda was attracted to the exhibition at Baroda specifically by the prospect of viewing Ravi Varma's work, or whether this was nothing more than fortuitous. It would seem, however, than once placed within the context of Vivekananda's apologetic treatment of Indian art, his judgements on Ravi Varma could never have been wholly positive. The delicate balancing act performed by those who openly put Western techniques and knowledge to use in their attempts to reshape Hindu tradition according to their own lights not infrequently led their critics to accuse them of abandoning or diluting their heritage. Vivekananda had faced such charges and had levelled them against others in his turn. Few individuals, it would seem, managed to achieve in his eyes the balanced assimilation of Western influence that he so admired at a national level in Japan. As this chapter has hinted, it is more than possible that Vivekananda's perspective on a contemporary who was also engaged in cultural mediation between India and the West, in a field other than but historically linked to religion, brought to the surface the ambivalence that he felt about his own role.

NOTES

1. Nivedita's work is discussed in Guha-Thakurta (1992: 167–75) and Mitter (1994: 254ff.).
2. For comment on Sri Aurobindo's response to attempts by some eminent European scholars to trace Indian literary and artistic achievements back to European, usually Greek, predecessors, see Chapter 10 in this volume.
3. This study forms part of the author's ongoing exploration of attitudes to iconographic symbolism in the Ramakrishna Math and Mission and recent Hinduism more generally. See Beckerlegge (2000: Ch. 6); 2001; 2004a). Beckerlegge (2004b) is currently being prepared for publication and will contain a detailed examination of iconographic representations of Vivekananda.

4. See Chatterjee (1995) for discussion of the application of academic disciplines, including the study of art, in colonial Bengal.
5. In less polemical vein, Basham (1975: 492) has noted that the '…tradition of Indian painting seems also to be lost', having been replaced by 'applied painting' (illustrations and greetings cards) and 'international painting'.
6. More comprehensive, specialist accounts of the changes that took place in styles of Indian art during the period of British rule are to be found in Guha-Thakurta (1992) and Mitter (1994).
7. For a sympathetic account of this criticism, see 'Postscript' in Venniyoor (1981: 66–82). See also Guha-Thakurta (1992) and Mitter (1994).
8. I am grateful to Radhika Desai, University of Victoria, for permission to refer to her unpublished paper.
9. Vivekananda brought this same assertive confidence to the poses he struck when being photographed. See Beckerlegge (2004a).
10. This sense of responsibility invites comparison with the sense of national mission felt by intellectuals and writers in Meiji Japan, for example, Natsume Soseki (Eto 1965: 603).
11. Some Japanese intellectuals of the period would have challenged this judgement. See, for example, the judgement of the novelist Soseki (quoted in Reischauer and Craig 1979: 210). The alienation of the Japanese was a major theme in Soseki's writing.
12. Sri Aurobindo (1994: 1) begins *The National Value of Art* with the same sentiment.
13. For an examination of the use of Vivekananda in the later *sangh parivar*, see Beckerlegge (2003).

BIBLIOGRAPHY

Allen, Charles (1984), *Lives of the Indian Princes*, London: Century Publishing.
(Sri) Aurobindo (1994), *The National Value of Art*, (6th edn), Pondicherry: Sri Aurobindo Ashram.
Babb, Lawrence A. (1981), 'Glancing: Visual Interaction in Hinduism', *Journal of Anthropological Research*, Vol. 37, No. 4, pp. 387–401.
Basham, Arthur L. (1975), 'Conclusion', in A. Basham (ed.), *A Cultural History of India*, Oxford: Clarendon Press, pp. 487–500.
Beckerlegge, Gwilym (2000), *The Ramakrishna Mission: The Making of a Modern Hindu Movement*, New Delhi: Oxford University Press.
———— (2001), 'Hindu Sacred Images for the Mass Market', in G. Beckerlegge (ed.), *From Sacred Text to Internet*, Aldershot: Ashgate in association with The Open University, pp. 57–116.
———— (2003), 'Saffron and *Seva*: The Rashtriya Swayamsevak Sangh's Appropriation of Swami Vivekananda', in A. Copley (ed.), *Hinduism in Public and Private: Reform, Hindutva, Gender and Sampraday*, New Delhi: Oxford University Press, pp. 31–65.

———— (2004a), 'Iconographic Representations of Renunciation and Activism in the Ramakrishna Math and Mission and the Rashtriya Swayamsevak Sangh', *Journal of Contemporary Religion,* Vol. 19, No. 1, pp. 47–66.

———— (2004b), 'Approaching the Ramakrishna Math and Mission through its Iconography', Paper presented at the Spalding Symposium on Indian Religions, Oxford, March, (unpublished).

Bharati, Agehananda (1970), 'The Hindu Renaissance and its Apologetic Patterns', *Journal of Asian Studies,* Vol. 29, No. 2, pp. 267–87.

———— (1971), 'Hinduism and Modernization', in R. F. Spencer (ed.), *Religion and Change in Contemporary Asia,* Minneapolis: University of Minnesota Press, pp. 67–104.

Blurton, T. Richard (1988), 'Tradition and Modernism: Contemporary Indian Religious Prints', *South Asia Review,* Vol. 8, No. 1, pp. 47–69.

Brekke, Torkel (2002), *Makers of Modern Indian Religion in the Late Nineteenth Century,* Oxford: Oxford University Press.

Chatterjee, Partha (ed.) (1995), *Texts of Power: Emerging Disciplines in Bengal,* Minneapolis and London: University of Minnesota Press.

Datta, Bhupendranath (1993), *Swami Vivekananda Patriot-Prophet: A Study* (2nd rev. edn), Calcutta: Nababharat Publishers.

Desai, Radhika (2002), 'Seeing is believing: Raja Ravi Varma, Baroda and Hindutva', unpublished Paper presented at the European Conference on Modern South Asian Studies at the University of Heidelberg.

Eto, Jun (1965), 'Natsume Soseki: A Japanese Meiji Intellectual', *The American Scholar,* Vol. 34, pp. 603–19.

Guha-Thakurta, Tapati (1986), 'Westernisation and Tradition in South Indian Painting in the Nineteenth Century: The Case of Raja Ravi Varma (1848–1906)', *Studies in History* No. 2 (NS), pp. 165–95.

———— (1990), 'Art in Old Calcutta: The Melting Pot of Western Styles', in Sukanta Chaudhuri (ed.), *Calcutta: The Living City,* Vol. 1: *The Past,* Calcutta: Oxford University Press, pp. 146–55.

———— (1992), *The Making of a New 'Indian' Art,* Cambridge: Cambridge University Press.

———— (1995), 'Recovering the Nation's Art', in P. Chatterjee (ed.), *Texts of Power: Emerging Disciplines in Bengal,* Minneapolis and London: University of Minnesota Press, pp. 63–92.

Gupta, Radha Prasad (1990), 'Art in Old Calcutta: Indian Style', in Sukanta Chaudhuri (ed.), *Calcutta: The Living City,* Vol.1: *The Past,* Calcutta: Oxford University Press, pp. 137–45.

His Eastern and Western Disciples (1989), *The Life of Swami Vivekananda,* 2 Vols (6th edn), Calcutta: Advaita Ashrama.

Inglis, Stephen R. (1995), 'Suitable for Framing: The Work of a Modern Master', in L. A. Babb and S. S. Wadley (eds), *Media and the Transformation of Religion in South Asia,* Philadelphia: University of Pennsylvania Press, pp. 51–75.

Jones, Kenneth W. (1989), *Socio-religious Reform Movements in India* (Cambridge History of India III, 1), Cambridge: Cambridge University Press.

Kerala Arts and Literary Association (n.d.), *Raja Ravi Varma*, available at *http://website.lineone.net/~kala_uk/rajaravi.htm*, accessed 10 May 2002.

Mitra, Tarun (1990), 'Art and Artists in Twentieth-Century Calcutta', in Sukanta Chaudhuri (ed.), *Calcutta: The Living City*, Vol. 2: *The Past*, Calcutta: Oxford University Press.

Mitter, Partha (1994), *Art and Nationalism in Colonial India, 1850–1922*, Cambridge: Cambridge University Press.

——— (2001), *Indian Art*, Oxford: Oxford University Press.

Mukharji, Trailokyanath (1886), 'The Art Industries of Bengal', *Journal of Indian Art*, January, pp. 1–4.

Nehru, Jawaharlal (1960), *The Discovery of India*, London: Meridian Books.

Neumayer, Erwin and Christine Schelberger (2004), *Popular Indian Art: Raja Ravi Varma and The Printed Gods of India*, New Delhi: Oxford University Press.

Pillai, R. Balakrishna (1981), 'Preface' in E. M. J. Venniyoor, *Raja Ravi Varma*, Trivandrum: Government of Kerala.

Pinney, Christopher (2004), *'Photos of the Gods': The Printed Image and Political Struggle in India*, London: Reaktion Books.

Reischauer, Edwin O. and Albert M. Craig (1979), *Japan: Tradition and Transformation*, Sydney, London, and Boston: George Allen & Unwin.

Sen, Amiya P. (2000), *Swami Vivekananda*, New Delhi: Oxford University Press.

Smith, H. Daniel (1995), 'The Impact of "God Posters" on Hindus and Their Devotional Traditions', in L. A. Babb and S. S. Wadley (eds), *Media and the Transformation of Religion in South Asia*, Philadelphia: University of Pennsylvania Press, pp. 24–50.

Topsfield, Andrew (1979), 'Painting', in R. Skelton and M. Francis (eds), *Arts of Bengal*, London: The Whitechapel Art Gallery, pp. 34–56.

Tsunoda, Ryusaka W.M. Theodore de Barry and Donald Keene (1958), *Sources of Japanese Tradition*, Vol. 2, New York and London: Columbia University Press.

Venniyoor, E. M. J. (1981), *Raja Ravi Varma*, Trivandrum: Government of Kerala.

(Swami) Vidyatmananda (1977), 'The Photographs of Sri Ramakrishna', *Vedanta Kesari*, Vol. 63, No. 9, pp. 263–75.

(Swami) Vivekananda (1989), *The Complete Works of Swami Vivekananda*, 8 Vols, Mayavati Memorial Edition, Calcutta: Advaita Ashrama.

——— (1997), *The Complete Works of Swami Vivekananda*, Vol. 9, Calcutta: Advaita Ashrama.

——— (2002), 'Art as Adoration', *Prabuddha Bharata*, Vol. 107, No. 1, pp. 56–64.

10

Shades of Orientalism[1]
Paradoxes and Problems in Indian Historiography

PETER HEEHS

INTRODUCTION

Now that 'orientalism' has become an academic buzzword, it may be useful to recall its former meanings. From the mid-eighteenth to the late-twentieth century, the term was applied to the study of the languages, literatures, and cultures of the Orient. In his 1978 book, *Orientalism*, Edward Said (1991: 3f.) acknowledges this ordinary (but by then obsolete) meaning and adds two others: 'a style of thought based upon an ontological and epistemological distinction made between "the Orient" and (most of the time) "the Occident" and "a Western style" for dominating, restructuring, and having authority over the Orient'. It is with the third sort of orientalism that Said chiefly is concerned. 'Orientalism' in this sense is a discourse about the Orient as the 'other' of Europe, which confirms Europe's dominant position. Said studies the works of scholars who instantiate this discourse but he is less concerned with particular individuals than with the body of European discursive practices in regard to 'the Orient' that generate a self-affirming account of what it is (essentially inferior to Europe, and so on) (Said 1991: 94). One of his more controversial contentions is that all European orientalists of the colonial period were consciously or unconsciously complicit in the aims of European colonialism.[2]

Said's theory has been criticized by scholars who study oriental cultures—now referred to as Indologists, Sinologists, Asian Studies specialists, and so forth—on several counts. Many object to his indiscriminate lumping together of different types of orientalism. Denis Vidal

(1997: 14–15), for instance, insists that colonial orientalism of the nineteenth century and the sort of orientalism highlighted by Said are 'two entirely different things'. The orientalism of the nineteenth century itself had two sides, one scholastic, the other romantic, and 'Said's definitions cannot account for' this distinction. Thomas Trautmann reminds us that British champions of Indian languages and culture (called 'Orientalists') were opposed by government proponents of English education (called 'Anglicists'), and notes that 'the Saidian expansion of Orientalism, applied in this context, tends to sow confusion where there was once clarity' (Trautmann 1997: 23).[3] David Ludden (1993: 252) distinguishes 'colonial knowledge', which generated authoritative facts about colonized people, from other forms of orientalism, some of which were explicitly anticolonial. Rosane Rocher (1993: 215) spells out the consequences of Said's conflations: 'Said's sweeping and passionate indictment of orientalist scholarship as part and parcel of an imperialist, subjugating enterprise does to orientalist scholarship what he accuses orientalist scholarship of having done to the countries east of Europe; it creates a single discourse, undifferentiated in space and time and across political, social and intellectual identities.' The irony is that the Saidian analysis of orientalist discourse is itself an orientalist discourse—one that 'sometimes appears to mimic the essentializing discourse it attacks', as James Clifford (1980: 210) puts it.[4] This essentializing of orientalist scholarship might be excused if it resulted in a transformed view of oriental and occidental societies. But to Said, the Occident is always the dominant partner, determining the terms of the oriental response. As a result the very orientals who are meant to be the beneficiaries of the Saidian analysis are again denied agency and voice.[5]

At one point in his presentation, Said (1991: 206) does distinguish between what he calls latent orientalism, 'an almost unconscious (and certainly an untouchable) positivity' of ideas about the Orient, and manifest orientalism, 'the various stated views about Oriental society, languages, literatures, history, sociology, and so forth'. This allows him to acknowledge the possibility of varying expressions of orientalism while retaining his core concept. For, he asserts, 'whatever change occurs in knowledge of the Orient is found almost exclusively in manifest Orientalism; the unanimity, stability, and durability of latent orientalism is more or less constant'. The changes in the forms of manifest orientalism are froth on the surface; the underlying truth of latent orientalism is the same. If this is so, the paradox remains. The concept on which Said and his epigones base their critique of the essentializing of 'the Orient' is itself an essential category.

Despite the criticisms levelled against Said by specialists in the literature that comprises his material, his theory has gained currency both inside and outside the academy, with the result that 'orientalism' is now applied loosely to any unflattering Western attitude about the East. In what follows, I return to scholarly discourse properly speaking. Acknowledging the utility of Said's 'orientalism' as a critical tool, I enlarge and historicize the concept by examining various forms of oriental knowledge. Said's area of interest was Middle Eastern orientalism; I confine myself to Indian. I begin by distinguishing six 'styles' of orientalist discourse about India. These, it should be clearly understood, are heuristic categories, not essential types. Three belong to the colonial era, and three to the postcolonial era.[6] There were also, of course, numerous indigenous discourses about what Europeans call 'the Orient' in precolonial times.

Limitations of space prevent us from doing more than identifying typical exponents of each style and citing illustrative passages. This should be enough to serve the immediate purpose, which is to show that there are many shades of orientalism. The next step is to show that the exponents of these styles interact with one another in various ways. This is accomplished by examining the life and works of the nationalist orientalist Sri Aurobindo, showing how his approach took form in the matrix of colonial orientalism and how it has been criticized or appropriated by postcolonial orientalists of various sorts. Such scholars stress Aurobindo's nationalistic premises but miss the broader import of his arguments. The value of his work and the work of other scholars of the Orient depends more on the quality of their scholarship than on their political or religious assumptions.

PRECOLONIAL DISCOURSES

If the European idea of the Orient is a European invention, the Orient itself is not. Even Said (1991: 5) is obliged to 'acknowledge it tacitly'. Long before Vasco da Gama landed in Calicut in 1498, the peoples of South Asia created modes of self- and world-representation that owe nothing to European notions. (It is necessary to mention this obvious fact, since reductive orientalists who push theory to extremes are sometimes inclined to forget it.) Many of these systems of discourse are preserved in texts or methods of practice or both. One example (among hundreds) is the Shaiva Siddhanta school of early medieval India, whose

STYLES OF ORIENTALIST DISCOURSE

Era	Style	Approximate period	Examples
Precolonial	0. [various]	Before 1750	*Kamikagama* (?seventh century)
Colonial	1. Patronizing/ Patronized	1780–1947 (and after)	Jones, *Institutes of Hindu Law or the Ordinances of Menu* (1794); Ram Mohan Roy, *Translation of an Abridgement of the* Vedant (1816)
	2. Romantic	1800–1947 (and after)	F. Schlegel, *Über die Sprache und Weisheit der Indier* (1808); Sarda, *Hindu Superiority* (c. 1906)
	3. Nationalist	1850–1947 (and after)	Nivedita, *Aggressive Hinduism* (1905); Aurobindo, *A Defence of Indian Culture* (1918–1921)
Postcolonial	4. Critical	1947 to present	Thapar, *Interpreting Early India* (1992); Trautmann, *Aryans and British India* (1997)
	5. Reductive	1978 to present	Inden, *Imagining India* (1990); Chatterjee *et al.*, *Texts of Power* (1995)
	6. Reactionary	c.1980 to present	Rajaram and Frawley, *Vedic Aryans and the Origins of Civilisation* (1995)

rituals are still performed in south India. The *Kamikagama* (?seventh century CE) and related texts present a systematic and coherent view of the Divine, the world, and the human being, and detail practices that 'not only sought to bring the agent personally into relation with God and to transform his or her condition, but also collectively engendered the relations of community, authority, and hierarchy within human society' (Davis 1991: 6). Far from being influenced by Western discourse, such precolonial societies were oblivious of it. 'There is', as intellectual historian Wilhelm Halbfass (1988: 437) writes, 'no sign of active theoretical interest, no attempt to respond to the foreign challenge, to enter into a "dialogue"—up to the period around 1800'.[7]

THREE STYLES OF COLONIAL ORIENTALISM

Patronizing/Patronized Orientalism

European visitors to India between 1500 and 1750 published their observations in travel narratives, missionary polemic, and so on, but serious European oriental scholarship may be said to have begun towards the end of the eighteenth century. Two landmarks are the formation of the Asiatic Society of Calcutta in 1784 and the publication of Charles Wilkins' translation of the Bhagavadgita the following year. The preface to this volume by Governor-General Warren Hastings contains a passage that is archetypally 'orientalist' in the Saidian sense: 'Every accumulation of knowledge, and especially such as is obtained by social communication with people over whom we exercise a dominion founded on the right of conquest, is useful to the state.' But Hastings also demonstrates a real, though patronizing, appreciation of Hindu culture. He notes, for instance, that the Brahmans' 'collective studies have led them to the discovery of new tracks and combinations of sentiment, totally different from the doctrines with which the learned of other nations are acquainted: doctrines, which . . . may be equally founded in truth with the most simple of our own.' In a similar vein, the iconic orientalist William Jones (1807: 89f.) writes in the preface to his translation of the *Manu Smriti* that this code is 'revered, as the word of the Most High, by nations of great importance to the political and commercial interests of *Europe*', who ask only protection, justice, religious tolerance, and 'the benefit of those laws, which they have been taught to believe sacred, and which alone they can possibly comprehend'. With British rule established, patronizing Europeans taught their language to patronized Indians, some of whom made important contributions to English-language scholarship. Ram Mohan Roy (1772–1834), who produced a number of translations and expositions of Sanskrit texts, notes in the introduction to one that he had undertaken the work 'to prove to my European friends, that the superstitious practices which deform the Hindoo religion have nothing to do with the pure spirit of its dictates!' (Roy 1999: 3).

Romantic Orientalism

British orientalism during the colonial period was obviously connected, if not invariably complicit, with British imperialism. Germany had nothing to do with imperialism in India, yet Germany took the lead in Sanskrit studies in the nineteenth century, a fact that impels Trautmann

(1997: 22) to ask: 'How does Said's thesis help us to understand' this? One of the first German Sanskritists was Friedrich von Schlegel, whose *Über die Sprache und Weisheit der Indier* (1808) is a glorification of the religion and philosophy of the 'most cultivated and wisest people of antiquity' (in Halbfass 1988: 76). The work of Schlegel and other orientalists helped in the development of German Romanticism, of which Indophilia was a major strand. Writers like Goethe and Schopenhauer were influenced by Sanskrit literature, and published positive assessments that helped offset the largely negative British view. Indian scholars were delighted to reproduce such European praise. *Hindu Superiority* by Har Bilas Sarda (first published *c*. 1906) is a catalogue of out-of-context encomiums by writers from Strabo to Pierre Loti, to which Sarda adds his own *obiter dicta*, for example, 'The Vedas are universally admitted to be not only by far the most important work in the Sanskrit language but the greatest work in all literature' (Sarda 1917: 177).

Nationalist Orientalism

Towards the end of the nineteenth century, educated Indians began turning from the imitative Anglophilia of the previous generation to a renewed interest in their own traditions. Around the same time the national movement got off to a slow start. In this climate a nationalist style of orientalism took root. Sister Nivedita (Margaret E. Noble, 1867–1911), a disciple of Swami Vivekananda (1863–1902), gives an explicitly nationalistic turn to her writings on India. 'The land of the Vedas and of Jnana-Yoga has no right to sink into the role of mere critic or imitator of European Letters', she writes in *Aggressive Hinduism*. 'The Indianising of India, the organising of our national thought, the laying out of our line of march, all this is to be done by us, not by others on our behalf' (Nivedita 1973: 492, 500). Nivedita's friend Aurobindo Ghose insists even more firmly on the necessity of judging Indian culture by Indian standards. The career of this scholar, revolutionary, and mystic is discussed in some detail below.

THREE STYLES OF POSTCOLONIAL ORIENTALISM

Critical Orientalism

Nationalist scholarship was prominent during the years of the freedom movement (1905–47) and the first two decades after the achievement of Independence. During the 1950s and 1960s, historians trained in

Western methods and working within Western theoretical frameworks began to produce empirical studies of all periods of India's past. More recently, critical scholarship has turned its attention to historiographical issues. Romila Thapar (1992: 1), for example, investigates how 'both the colonial experience and nationalism of recent centuries influenced the study, particularly of the early period of [Indian] history' in her *Interpreting Early India*.

Reductive Orientalism

As we have seen, Saidian interpretations of orientalism and the Orient are themselves orientalist discourses. As Ludden (1993: 271) puts it, they inhabit 'a place *inside* [emphasis added] the history of orientalism'. Saidian treatments of Indian history and culture began to appear within a decade of the publication of *Orientalism*. One of the first was Ronald Inden's *Imagining India* (1990; preceded by Inden 1986). His stated aim is to 'make possible studies of "ancient" India that would restore the agency that those [Eurocentric] histories have stripped from its people and institutions' (Inden 1990: 1). But by insisting that Hinduism, the caste system, and so forth, were constructions of European orientalists, he tends rather to deny Indian agency and give a new lease on life to Eurocentrism (Inden 1990: 89, 49, 58, etc.).

Reactionary Orientalism

In recent years a loose grouping of scholars, many with degrees in scientific disciplines but without training in historiography, have sought to restore India to its ancient glory by rewriting its history. This revisionism is necessary because, 'as a consequence of a century and a half of European colonialism, and repeated extremely violent onslaughts [by Muslims and Christians] going back nearly a thousand years, Indian history and tradition have undergone grievous distortions and misinterpretations'. This critique is directed against nineteenth-century European orientalists as well as contemporary writers who 'assumed that the fashionable theories of the age in which they were brought up—theories like Marxism—represented universal laws of human history' (Rajaram and Frawley 2001: xvf.).

A BRITISH-TRAINED INDIAN NATIONALIST

In the table given above, nationalist orientalism occupies a pivotal place, midway between the precolonial and early colonial discourses on one side and the three forms of postcolonial practice on the other. In this section, I examine the life of a nationalist writer, showing how his style of orientalism emerged in a scholarly environment dominated by patronizing and romantic orientalists and a political environment in which loyalism and moderate dissent were giving way to extreme forms of nationalism. Aurobindo Ghose (known as Sri Aurobindo, 1872–1950) is often spoken of as a typical nationalist scholar, but his career was in some respects unique. Raised in England with no knowledge of the culture of his homeland, he was destined for a position in the colonial civil service but instead became a revolutionary politician. After a decade of literary and political activity he retired to French India to practise yoga, embodying, in the eyes of his admirers, the spiritual tradition that, according to reductive orientalists, was an invention of colonial orientalism.

Aurobindo's father was a British-trained physician who was active in local government in Bengal. Frustrated in his attempts to enter the Indian Medical Service and shunted here and there by the bureaucracy, he resolved that one or more of his sons would become members of the Indian Civil Service (ICS). Sent to England at the age of seven, Aurobindo won scholarships to St Paul's School, London, and King's College, Cambridge, and passed the ICS entrance examination in 1890. At Cambridge he received a thoroughly 'orientalist' introduction to the culture of his homeland. He read about India's past in books like Elphinstone's *History of India* and Mills's now-notorious *History of British India*. He learned Bengali (the 'mother-tongue' his father had forbidden him from speaking) from an Irishman unable to read the novels of Bankim Chandra Chatterji. His teachers of Sanskrit and Hindustani also were European, as was his lecturer in Hindu and Muslim law (Final Examination of Candidates 1892: 6, 10). By the time he left Cambridge in 1892, his Greek and Latin were good enough to win prizes, but his Sanskrit was so sketchy that when he first read the Upanishads, it was in the English translation of the Oxford orientalist F. Max Müller.

We get a glimpse of Aurobindo's attitude towards patronizing orientalism in a passage he wrote a decade later in reply to a passage in Müller's preface to the *Sacred Books of the East*. 'I confess it has been for many years a problem to me, aye, and to a great extent is so still', Müller (1981: xii) wrote, 'how the *Sacred Books of the East* should, by the side of so much that is fresh, natural, simple, beautiful, and true, contain so much that is not only unmeaning artificial and silly, but even hideous and repellent.' Aurobindo's reply was ironic in the great tradition of British irony:

Now, I myself being only a poor coarse-minded Oriental and therefore not disposed to deny the gross physical facts of life and nature...am somewhat at a loss to imagine what the Professor found in the Upanishads that is hideous and repellent. Still I was brought up almost from my infancy in England and received an English education, so that I have glimmerings. But as to what he intends by the unmeaning, artificial and silly elements, there can be no doubt. Everything is unmeaning in the Upanishads which the Europeans cannot understand, everything is artificial which does not come within the circle of their mental experience and everything is silly which is not explicable by European science and wisdom (Aurobindo 2001: 164).

In India, Aurobindo mastered Sanskrit and Bengali and began to translate literary classics—the poems of Vidyapati, portions of the Mahabharata and Ramayana, some works of Kalidasa—into elegant Victorian English. He also wrote essays on various Sanskrit authors, in some of which he twitted the opinions of European orientalists. 'That accomplished scholar & litterateur Prof Wilson'—H. H. Wilson, first Boden Professor of Sanskrit at Oxford—was, Aurobindo noted around 1900, 'at pains to inform' his readers that the mad scene in Kalidasa's *Vikramorvasiyam* was nothing compared to the mad scene in *King Lear*, but rather 'a much tamer affair conformable to the mild, domestic & featureless Hindu character & the feebler pitch of Hindu poetic genius. The good Professor might have spared himself the trouble' since there was 'no point of contact between the two dramas'.[8] The European condemnation of Indian drama as sapless was 'evidence not of a more vigorous critical mind but of a restricted critical sympathy'. 'The true spirit of criticism', he concluded, 'is to seek in a literature what we can find in it of great or beautiful, not to demand from it what it does not seek to give us' (Aurobindo 2003: 188f.).

Another habit of European scholars that Aurobindo disapproved of was their tendency to trace Indian achievements back to European, usually Greek, predecessors. Where Greek influence was evident, as in the Gandharan school of sculpture, he condemned the work as inferior to 'pure' Indian styles.[9] Europe's literary criteria were not applicable to India. Albrecht Weber's idea that the original Mahabharata consisted only of the battle chapters was a case of 'arguing from Homer'. It was, Aurobindo insisted, 'not from European scholars that we must expect a solution of the Mahabharata problem', since 'they have no qualifications for the task except a power of indefatigable research and collocation. . . . It is from Hindu [i.e. Indian] scholarship renovated & instructed by contact with European that the attempt must come' (Aurobindo 2003: 277, 280).

For all his condemnation of European scholars, Aurobindo admired their textual scholarship and made use of it in his own work. He wrote around 1902 that a student of Gaudapada's *Karikas* could not do better than to start with 'Deussen's System of the Vedanta in one hand and any brief & popular exposition of the six Darshanas [philosophical schools] in the other' (Aurobindo 1972a: 319). However, he felt that European academics could not grasp the full meaning of Indian scriptures. This was due to an essential difference in mentality: the Indian mind was 'diffuse and comprehensive', able to acquire 'a [deeper] and truer view of things in their totality'; the European mind, 'compact and precise', could hope only for 'a more accurate and practically serviceable conception of their parts' (Aurobindo 1972a: 346). Situated between these two 'minds', he was in a position to mediate. His aim as a scholar, as he saw it around this time, was 'to present to England and through England to Europe the religious message of India' (Aurobindo 1972a: 163).

Aurobindo pursued this project between 1902 and 1906 in a series of commentaries on the Upanishads. Between 1906 and 1910, he put most of his energy into the nationalist movement and its revolutionary offshoot. His transformation from quiet scholar to fiery patriot was much remarked on at the time. After his arrest for conspiracy to wage war against the King, a former ICS classmate wrote: 'Fancy Ghose a ragged revolutionary! He could with far greater ease write a lexicon or compose a noble epic' (Dutta 1959: 81f.). During these years he managed to complete a few 'patriotic' translations; but it was not until he retired from politics and settled in French Pondicherry in 1910 that he found time to fulfil his scholarly mission. This was, as he described in August 1912, 'to re-explain the Sanatana Dharma to the human intellect in all its parts, from a new standpoint'.[10] Specifically, he would explain 'the true meaning of the Vedas', outline 'a new Science of Philology', and present the true 'meaning of all in the Upanishads that is not understood either by Indians or Europeans'.[11] He worked steadily at these and related projects between 1910 and 1920, returning to them on and off until his death in 1950.

Struck by Aurobindo's passage from Cambridge classicist to Sanskrit scholar to revolutionary publicist to philosophical yogin, many writers have sought clues in his early life, scripting selected biographical data into explanatory narratives. His disciples find evidences of the future yogi almost from his birth and the stamp of divine election on all his actions. The historian Leonard Gordon (1974: 101, 106) condemns this hagiographical approach, offering instead a jejune pop psychology ('Aurobindo's lifelong obsession with mother figures dates from his childhood', 'It seems to have been the fear of failure rather than God's call or nationalist speeches that kept him out of the ICS'). More sophisticated and fruitful is political psychologist Ashis Nandy's 'enquiry into the psychological structures and cultural forces which supported or resisted the culture of colonialism in British India', in which he contrasts Aurobindo with Rudyard Kipling, the latter 'culturally an Indian child who grew up to become an ideologue of the moral and political superiority of the West', the former 'culturally a European child who grew up to become a votary of the spiritual leadership of India'. Nandy is weakest when dealing with Aurobindo's spiritual life, falling back, like Gordon, on unsubstantiated guesswork ('Aurobindo's spiritualism can be seen as a way of handling a situation of cultural aggression', 'the "exotic" alternative he found to it [revolution] in mysticism was probably the only one available to him'). But his working assumption is both applicable to Aurobindo and germane to the Orientalism debate: 'Colonized Indians did not always try to correct or extend the Orientalists; in their own diffused way, they tried to create an alternative language of discourse' (Nandy 1988: xvi–xvii, 85–100).

Nandy (1988: xvii) admits that his 'use of the biographical data' of his subjects is 'partial, almost cavalier'. As a result he makes some minor but significant errors in regard to Aurobindo's life. For a psychological analysis of a historical figure to be useful, the data must be reliable and the analysis based on a non-reductive theory that takes the subject's personal and cultural values seriously. The following data seem relevant to a study of Aurobindo's style of orientalism. (i) He spent his earliest years in a colonial environment in India (speaking English, attending convent school) and his entire youth in England. (ii) He developed a distaste for English life after a brief period of admiration as a child. By his own (retrospective) account, this was the result of an aesthetic reaction to the ugliness and hurry of life in England,[12] supported by a reading of romantic, anti-industrial poets and critics such as Blake, Shelley, Ruskin, etc. (iii) His education was that of a British literary scholar and civil servant. (iv) He admired the verbal scholarship of orientalists such as Müller, Wilson, and Deussen, but resented their patronizing attitude towards India and things Indian. (v) While still young he became convinced that the British occupation of India was unjust, and that he was destined to struggle against it (Aurobindo 1972b: 3f.). (vi) After his return to India he quickly became re-nationalized through what he later called a 'natural attraction to Indian culture and ways of life and a temperamental feeling and preference to all that was Indian' (Aurobindo 1972b: 7).[13] (vii) At some point he became convinced that the West was in moral and spiritual decline, and that the inherently superior values of India could help the West recover its spiritual balance.

What does this tell us about Aurobindo as an orientalist? One thing that is certain is that he resented the colonial way of writing about the literatures, arts, religions, and societies of India. Well acquainted with the British equivalents, he was comparatively immune to the colonial 'myth' of British cultural superiority.[14] To break the debilitating hold of this myth, which he considered the greatest obstacle to the creation of a revolutionary consciousness, he put forward the opposite myth of Indian superiority in matters of the mind and spirit. This was not in his case simply a strategic move; it sprang from his conviction that in many important respects Indian culture was in fact superior to that of Europe. He shared this feeling with other Indian nationalists, among them B. G. Tilak and M. K. Gandhi.

Indian nationalists' assertions of cultural difference or claims of cultural superiority are seen by recent political philosophers as a reversal of the essentialist premises of colonial orientalism. As Sudipta Kaviraj (2000: 141) puts it: 'Orientalism—the idea that Indian society was irreducibly different from the modern West . . . gradually established the intellectual preconditions of early nationalism by enabling Indians to claim a kind of social autonomy within political colonialism.'[15] I would put it the other way around: one of the ways the nationalists asserted their claim of cultural and political autonomy was by deliberately reversing the terms of orientalist discourse. The problem, for the historian, is whether this reversal, this alternative discourse, has opened the way to a more accurate account of the Indian past. In studying Indian history, is Indocentrism necessarily better than Eurocentrism?

FIVE PROBLEMS AND AN ASSORTMENT OF SOLUTIONS

Among the topics Aurobindo touched on in his Indological writings are five problems that are still actively debated by students of Indian history: (i) the significance of the Vedas, (ii) the date of the Vedic texts, (iii) the

Aryan invasion theory, (iv) the Aryan-Dravidian divide, and (v) the idea that spirituality is the essence of India. This section sketches the outlines of these problems, and summarizes Aurobindo's solutions along with those of other orientalists of the colonial and postcolonial periods. Taking his nationalistic approach as the primary point of reference, we show how his views took shape in a particular historical matrix (of which the biographical factors discussed in the previous section were only one strand) and how they have been criticized and in some cases appropriated by postcolonial writers. Disentangling what is of lasting value in his work from what belongs to his era, we show that both his critics and admirers miss out on his enduring contributions. If the views of other orientalists were subjected to a similar triage, it might be possible to approach the five problems, and others, with a better chance of finding satisfactory solutions.

THE SIGNIFICANCE OF THE VEDAS

In the Hindu tradition, the hymns of the Vedas occupy an unusual place. On the one hand they are regarded as Divine Revelation, uncreated and the source of all truth. On the other, they are treated as crude sacrificial formulas, meant to propitiate gods who reward their worshippers with welfare, progeny, and so on. Patronizing orientalists, interested only in the ritual interpretation, studied the Vedas as interesting relics of primitive humanity. Romantic orientalists gave their attention not to the hymns (the *karmakanda* or 'action part' of the Vedas) but to the Upanishads (the *jnanakanda* or 'knowledge part'), which deal among other things with mystical knowledge. Aurobindo too was at first interested only in the Upanishads, accepting passively the ritual interpretation of the hymns. Later he theorized that the hymns present, in symbolic form, the same knowledge that subsequently was given intellectual expression in the Upanishads. According to his theory, the hymns are concerned outwardly with gods and sacrifices but inwardly with the attainment of divine knowledge and bliss. Their language is deliberately equivocal, having at the same time a ritual and spiritual significance (Aurobindo 1998).

Incompletely worked out, mystical in intent, Aurobindo's theory has found few takers among academic orientalists. Dutch Sanskritist Jan Gonda (1975: 244) asserts that Aurobindo goes 'decidedly too far in assuming symbolism and allegories'. Indian philosopher S. Radhakrishnan (1941: 70) writes that it would be unwise to accept his theory, since it 'is opposed not only to the modern views of European scholars but also to

the traditional interpretations of Sayana and the system of Purva-
Mimamsa'. While Aurobindo's followers of course endorse his reading,
only one, T. V. Kapali Sastry (1977–92), founds his exposition on an
independent study of the Sanskrit texts and commentaries.[16] The others
simply base their assertions on Aurobindo's authority (for example, Joshi
2001; *Rigveda Samhita* 1998).

Most critical scholars of the postcolonial period follow the lead of
their patronizing predecessors in regarding the Vedas as documents of
great historical and linguistic value but no literary or philosophical interest.
At the other end of the spectrum, reactionary scholars see the Vedas as
repositories of extraordinary wisdom, much of it in advance of modern
science.[17] Few of them have enough knowledge of Vedic Sanskrit to argue
intelligently in favour of this hypothesis. For most the Vedas are just
unchallengeable evidence of the antiquity and superiority of Indian
culture. Reductive orientalists regard this sort of interest in the Vedas as
an expression of a postcolonial nostalgia for origins, with worrisome
applications to the reactionary project of imposing essentialist Hinduism
on the Indian state.

Given the millennia that separate us from the texts, and the paucity
of non-textual supporting materials, it is unlikely that we will ever know
what the Vedas meant to their creators. Reactionary scholars rely on little
but faith when they make their extraordinary claims. It is easy for critical
scholars to undermine these assertions, but their own interpretations
leave much to be desired. Like the readings of an art historian who knows
everything about the provenance, iconography, and formal structure of
a quattrocento painting but nothing about Christian belief and practice
their work seems often to be an empty display of linguistic and historical
virtuosity. Aurobindo's theory accounts in principle for the historical as
well as the spiritual sides of the texts, but in practice he gives almost all
his attention to the latter (Aurobindo 1998: 8, 139).[18] This omission is
the primary weakness of his theory, which to be true must permit both
an inward and an outward reading of every hymn.

THE DATE OF THE VEDAS

Precolonial Indian scholars were for the most part uninterested in the
historical origin of the Vedas, regarding them as eternal and uncreated.
Traditional Indian chronology, which deals in cycles of millions of
years, is not much help in placing the texts in a historical framework.
Documentary Indian chronology begins with the Buddha around 500

BCE. The Vedas predate the Buddha, but by how much? By estimating the rate of change between the language of datable texts and the Sanskrit of the *Rig Veda*, eighteenth- and nineteenth-century orientalists such as William Jones and Max Müller arrived at a date around 1000 BCE.[19] Other scholars (most of them Indian) have tried to push the date back by a couple of thousand years or more. B. G. Tilak (1975a), a scholar and nationalist associate of Aurobindo, proposed a date not later than 4000 BCE and perhaps as early as 6000 BCE. Aurobindo himself showed little interest in the question. In his published writings he accepted provisionally a date of 3,500 years before the present, though he suggested that the actual date might be much earlier.

Modern critical orientalists stand by their colonial predecessors, placing the *Rig Veda* no earlier than 1900 BCE and generally centuries later. They offer linguistic and archaeological data to support this dating but admit that they lack knock-down arguments, since the texts of the Vedas contain no sure dating clues, and accurately dated artifacts cannot surely be correlated to the texts. The one thing that might decide the matter would be the decipherment of the script of the Harappan Civilization ('mature' phases c. 2600 to c. 1900 BCE). First excavated in the 1920s, and so unknown to earlier orientalists, this long-forgotten civilization has become an important battlefield in the contemporary Indian culture wars. It is certain that the Harappan people created one of the most extensive civilizations in ancient Eurasia. But what was their relation to Vedic culture? If the Vedas were composed after the decline of Harappan culture, the claim made by romantic, nationalist, and reactionary orientalists that the Vedas are the primordial sources of Indian civilization fails. Passions in this debate run remarkably high, though few of the participants know enough about linguistics, palaeontology, archaeology, or history to make significant contributions (see Bryant 2002). Very briefly, critical orientalists argue that the differences between the urban Harappan culture and the pastoral culture described in the Vedas are too great for the two to be the same. A familiar argument cites the lack of reliable evidence of the horse in Harappan cities. (The Vedas are filled with references to horses.) Reactionary orientalists read the evidence so as to make the Harappan cities a late efflorescence of Vedic culture. N. S. Rajaram (n.d.), writing on the website of the Vishwa Hindu Parishad, an aggressive sectarian group, asserts without evidence that 'the Vedic and Harappan civilizations were one'. Rajaram also is co-author of a book purporting to show that the language of the

Harappan script is Sanskrit. This decipherment, which has won no acceptance, has been shown to be based in part on doctored evidence (see Jha and Rajaram 2000; Witzel and Farmer 2000). Arguments and counter-arguments on this and related questions fill books, academic papers, Sunday supplement features, and internet newsgroups. The rhetoric reveals the preconceptions and attitudes of the participants. Critical scholars, versed in the primary and secondary literature, lay out impressive data with a show of objectivity but often betray a superciliousness similar to that of colonial orientalists. Their reactionary opponents make up for lack of linguistic knowledge by attacks on their opponents, Max Müller, and the British Empire, and half-informed invocations of nationalist orientalists such as Tilak and Aurobindo (see, for example, Jha and Rajaram 2000; Danino 1999a).

The Aryan Invasion Theory

Aurobindo never referred to the Harappan Civilization, which was excavated after he wrote his major works. He did sometimes speak of an issue related to the Harappan puzzle: the question of the Aryans' homeland. Colonial orientalists theorized that Sanskrit, Greek, Latin, and so on were all descended from an earlier language spoken by a distinct group of people in a fairly compact homeland, who dispersed in various directions. These people were formerly known as 'Aryans'.[20] Much scholarly ingenuity has been expended in the search for their homeland, sites as disparate as India and Scandinavia being proposed. A consensus eventually emerged that the homeland was located in Central or western Asia. The southeastern Aryan tribes were thought to have entered India as conquerors, displacing the earlier Dravidian inhabitants, who spoke languages unrelated to Indo-European. Not long after the formulation of this 'Aryan-invasion' theory, it was recognized that conquering or even migrating 'races' are not required for the dispersion of languages; but the damage had already been done. Taken up by romantic orientalists in nineteenth-century Germany, the hypothetical 'Aryan Race' began a career that even the defeat of Nazism could not end.

Aurobindo (1998: 26) was unconvinced by the Aryan invasion theory, pointing out that Indian tradition, including the texts of the Vedas, makes 'no actual mention of any such invasion'. In one or two drafts not published during his lifetime, he said that the theory was a 'philological myth' foisted on the world by European scholars. He suggested that this and other speculations be brushed aside in order to 'make a tabula rasa of all previous theories European or Indian [bearing on the meaning of the Vedas] & come back to the actual text of the Veda for enlightenment'.[21] But when he came to publish his findings, he simply expressed doubt about the Aryan invasion theory without denying the possibility that an 'Aryan'-speaking people may have entered the subcontinent from the north (Aurobindo 1998: 26, 31, 38). He sometimes spoke favourably of Tilak's hypothesis that the Aryans dwelt originally in the Arctic region and later migrated to India (Aurobindo 1998: 31; cf. Tilak 1975b). For the most part, however, he showed little interest in the historical origins of Vedic culture. This has not prevented reactionary orientalists from enrolling him posthumously in their campaign to destroy the Aryan-invasion theory, which they view as a creation of colonial orientalism meant to transfer the sources of Indian culture to a region outside India. Such writers often cite Aurobindo's manuscript drafts but ignore the more cautious references in his published writings (Gautier 1997: 7f.; Frawley 1998: 8; Danino and Nahar 1996: 39–43; Danino 1999a: 53; Danino 1999b: 44).

Those who campaign against the Aryan-invasion theory are flogging a long-dead horse. Critical scholars abandoned it decades ago in favour of a theory that holds that speakers of Indo-Aryan (the presumed predecessor of Sanskrit) entered the subcontinent in one or more migrations (see, for example, Thapar 1975: 26; 1996: 3–29).[22] The relation between the different branches of the Indo-European family is linguistic; race does not enter into it. (This is a point Aurobindo insisted on as early as 1912.) Critical scholars do maintain, however, that the linguistic distinction between Indo-Aryan and Dravidian languages is valid.

THE ARYAN–DRAVIDIAN DIVIDE

In the late nineteenth century, the distinction between the Indo-Aryan languages of northern India and the Dravidian languages of the South was seized upon by colonial ethnologists, who made it a benchmark in their survey of Indian physical types. The 'Dravidian races', inhabiting south and central India, were depicted as dark, flat nosed, etc., in contradistinction to the 'Indo-Aryans' of the North, who were almost like Europeans (Risley 1908). Linguistic data became the basis of an ethnographic split between two essential types, who were said to be at odds with each other.[23] The Aryan invasion was used to plot this work of historical fiction. The almost-European Aryans pushed the dark, flat-

nosed Dravidians from the fertile plains of the North into southern India.
Isolated texts were cited to support this theory. The word *anasa*, which
occurs once in the *Rig Veda* in a description of the Aryan's enemies, was
taken to mean 'noseless', that is, flat-nosed. This accorded well with the
'racial science' of the era. In 1872, a French writer of popular scholarship
noted that the seers of the Vedas *often* spoke of their 'negro' enemies as
'the noseless ones', thus 'revealing an anthropological characteristic of
great importance' (Lietard 1872: 13).

When Aurobindo arrived in south India in 1910, he was surprised to
discover no radical physical differences between his new neighbours and
people in the north. Eventually he became convinced that 'the [racial]
theory which European erudition started' was wrong, and that 'the so-
called Aryans and Dravidians' were parts of 'one homogenous race'
(Aurobindo 1998: 25, 593).[24] When he began to study Tamil he was
further surprised to find 'that the original connection between the
Dravidian and Aryan tongues was far closer and more extensive than is
usually supposed'. This led him to speculate that 'that they may even
have been two divergent families derived from one lost primitive tongue'
(Aurobindo 1998: 38). He never went so far as to assert that Tamil was
an 'Aryan dialect', but he did question the methodology and conclusions
of European philology, which used meagre data to arrive at grand
conclusions. In this connection, he ridiculed the reading of anasa as
'noseless'. This was, he said, not just bad etymology but also bad ethnology,
'for the southern nose can give as good an account of itself as any "Aryan"
proboscis in the North' (Aurobindo 1998: 26).

Aurobindo's philological research, preserved in hundreds of pages of
notes on Sanskrit, Latin, Greek, Tamil, and other languages, helped
convince him that European comparative philology was overrated. He
liked to allude to a remark by Ernest Renan characterizing philology as a
'petty conjectural science' (cf. Aurobindo 1998: 29, 50; 1972c: 298;
1973: 180).[25] His citation (apparently from memory) was somewhat
inaccurate,[26] though his belief that the philology of the period promised
more than it delivered is one that few today would question.

Modern critical orientalists would agree with Aurobindo that the
ethnological theories of colonial scholars are politically suspect and
scientifically worthless (see Trautmann 1997). They would reject his
idea that the Dravidian languages may have sprung from the same proto-
language as Sanskrit (see Trautmann 1997: 131–64).[27] Reactionary
orientalists distort his views on this matter, turning his cautious

speculations into positive assertions and supporting their rejection of historical linguistics by means of his misquotation of Renan (Danino and Nahar 1996: 42; Nahar *et al.* 1996: 96; Jha and Rajaram 2000: 18; Rajaram and Frawley 2001: xvi, 118).

SPIRITUALITY AS THE ESSENCE OF INDIA

When the culture of India was introduced to Europe, it was made to look predominantly religious. Travellers and missionaries wrote about the country's exotic faiths. Translations of texts such as the Bhagavadgita lent support to the notion that Indians were uniquely preoccupied with spirituality. The stereotype of the 'mystical Indian' was not without its use in a colonial state: otherworldly Indians needed down-to-earth Englishmen to rule over them. The mystical stereotype was confirmed and extended by Romantic orientalists, scholarly as well as flaky. In 1882, the Theosophical Society moved to India, which soon displaced Egypt as 'the source of the ancient wisdom' (Bevir 1994: 756). New forms of traditional religions took shape. Vivekananda (1989: 74), founder of the Ramakrishna Mission, spoke of an India that was chiefly distinguished from Europe by its inherent spirituality. 'That nation, among all the children of men, has believed, and believed intensely, that this life is not real. The real is God; and they must cling unto that God through thick and thin. In the midst of their degeneration, religion came first.'

Aurobindo agreed with Vivekananda that spirituality was the essence of India, but he insisted that it was not the whole of what he called 'the Indian mind'. He begins a key paragraph: 'Spirituality is indeed the master-key of the Indian mind', but goes on to say that India 'was alive to the greatness of material laws and forces; she had a keen eye for the importance of the physical sciences; she knew how to organise the arts of ordinary life. But she saw that the physical does not get its full sense until it stands in right relation to the supra-physical' (Aurobindo 1997: 6). He was aware of the influence of colonial discourse on the formation of this image, and tried to enlarge it beyond Western stereotypes:

European writers, struck by the general metaphysical bent of the Indian mind, by its strong religious instincts and religious idealism, by its other-worldliness, are inclined to write as if this were all the Indian spirit. An abstract, metaphysical, religious mind overpowered by the sense of the infinite, not apt for life, dreamy, unpractical, turning away from life and action as Maya, this, they said, is India; and for a time Indians in this as in other matters submissively echoed their new Western teachers and masters (Aurobindo 1997: 5f.).

In fact, Aurobindo claimed, the Indian spirit comprised 'an ingrained and dominant Spirituality', 'an inexhaustible vital creativeness', and 'a powerful, penetrating and scrupulous intelligence' (Aurobindo 1997: 10). In passages like this he seems practically to slip into the self-laudatory tone of works like Sarda's *Hindu Superiority*. Yet for all his 'defence of Indian culture' (the title of his main work on the subject), he was not blind to the country's limitations. He specifically condemned the 'vulgar and unthinking cultural Chauvinism which holds that whatever we have is good for us because it is Indian or even that whatever is in India is best, because it is the creation of the Rishis' (Aurobindo 1997: 75). He promoted India as aggressively as he did because of the historical circumstances in which he wrote. It would have been self-defeating for this sworn anti-colonialist to be completely even handed in his discussion of Indian culture while European writers were condemning it wholesale.[28]

In the postcolonial period, critical historians have tried to revise colonial depictions of Indian spiritual culture. The results have often been iconoclastic, in part because many of the better writers are Marxist or Left-leaning. The reactionary orientalists' reaction is against this perceived attack on Indian spiritual values (see, for example, Shourie 1988; Rajaram and Frawley 2001; Nahar *et al.* 1996). Reductive orientalists, too, have been hard on the romantic and nationalist views of Indian spirituality. Some of them depict Aurobindo and other nationalist writers as precursors of today's reactionary scholarship as well as of Hindu identity politics (*Hindutva*). Peter van der Veer (1999: 154), for example, says that Aurobindo wrote that 'the Ramayana and Mahabharata constitute the essence of Indian literature. This orientalist notion was foundational for the Hindu nationalisation of Indian civilisation'. There is no such statement in Aurobindo's works, nor is it true that his mature views on Indian spirituality lend support to the monolithic Hindu, anti-Muslim nationalism that van der Veer justly criticizes.[29]

Other reductive writers go farther than van der Veer in reducing Indian spirituality to a construct of colonial-period orientalism. Ronald Inden (1990: 89) writes that European colonial scholars 'constituted Hinduism and brought it into relationship to the religion and science of Europe'. Richard King (1999: 90) seconds this: 'The notion of a Hindu religion. . . . was initially invented by Western Orientalists basing their observations on a Judeo-Christian understanding of religion'.[30] If the intent of such assertions is that the European view of 'Hinduism' as a single religion like Judaism or Christianity is a European invention, there could be no objection, since the statement is tautologically true. If it is suggested that this and other European notions have had a massive impact on Indians' ways of viewing themselves and their beliefs and practices, any objection would be futile, since the intellectual history of India since the seventeenth century gives ample testimony to such influence. But if the meaning is that Europeans created Hinduism *ex nihilo* and that precolonial Indians had no ideas about themselves and their religious practices and beliefs, one would have to be a very orthodox Foucauldian to accept it.

A serious investigation into the formation of cultural ideas in India would have to begin with the precolonial period, that is, the 3,000 years that precede the colonial era. Hundreds of traditions are preserved, to a greater or lesser degree, in texts written in a dozen or more languages.[31] Even a cursory study of the textual, historical, and anthropological data makes it clear that religion played an important role in the lives of the people of the subcontinent as far back as we can go. It follows that an adequate theory of the construction of Indian cultural forms would have to include a critical reading of precolonial religious texts. At present, such theories are far more likely to be based on readings of eighteenth-century British scholarship—or nineteenth-century British fiction. There are practical reasons for this. It is easier to get hold of and understand the novels of Jane Austen than the treatises of Abhinavagupta. Even scholars who read Sanskrit and other subcontinental languages tend to subject Indian discourse to European theory—just as their colonial predecessors did. This is due in part to the continuing fascination with Foucault, in part to the exigencies of contemporary politics. Liberals and Leftists are so afraid of Hindutva and the culture of violence it has spawned that they brand any scholar who tries to examine Indian religion on its own terms as a fascist or fellow-traveller—a phenomenon Arvind Sharma calls 'secular extremism' (in Biswas 2002: 57) and Edwin Bryant (2002: 7) 'Indological McCarthyism'.

PROVINCIALIZING EUROPE?

The principal claims of Said's *Orientalism* are that oriental scholars of the colonial period were all of a piece, and were subservient to the political system that supported them. I have shown that there are many styles of Indological scholarship, and that all of them reflect, in various ways, the political, social, and intellectual concerns of their authors. Patronizing orientalists took the British Empire for granted, and viewed Indian cultural forms from a position of assured cultural superiority. Romantic and nationalist orientalists reversed this bias, the former seeking in India the wholeness Enlightenment Europe seemed to have lost, the latter insisting on the superiority of Indian cultural forms and the consequent need of political independence. Scholars of the postcolonial era are also divided according to their preconceptions. Critical orientalists stress the objectivity of knowledge, seemingly unaware that their views too have political underpinnings. Reductive orientalists base their critique on a specific intellectual foundation, yet claim to be anti-foundationalist. The political concerns of reactionary orientalists are patent, and are defended, if at all, by majoritarian claims and aggressions.

How is one to choose between these conflicting styles when examining a question of historical fact? It should be clear from my discussion of five problems of Indian historiography that the style of orientalism adopted by a given scholar neither guarantees nor precludes good results. What is important is the way the scholar collects and analyses the data and formulates conclusions. In other words, good scholars must practise the traditional scholarly virtues: gathering all available data, remaining open to new findings, and drawing conclusions as dispassionately as possible. These virtues are not the monopoly of critical writers, just as their opposites are not the preserve of nationalists or reactionaries.

This is not to say that the framework within which a scholar works has no effect on his or her practice. Some sets of assumptions are too confining, others are too amorphous, and all have a limited shelf-life. After a time it becomes necessary to challenge the established framework, to look at the data from a different angle of vision.[32] Such a challenge against the framework of traditional (mostly) European orientalism has been mounted for a century or longer by (mostly) Indian orientalists of different styles. Their approach varies greatly in accordance with their preconceptions, but their common objective has been to shift the centre of the debate from Europe to the non-European world—to provincialize Europe, as Dipesh Chakrabarty (2000) puts it.

Chakrabarty writes about this project from a (roughly) Marxist–Foucauldian standpoint, and this gives a postmodern and 'postcolonial' colouring to his presentation. But his aim, as distinct from his theories and methods, is hardly new. Many scholars of the colonial period, and many contemporary scholars with no sympathy for Marx and Foucault, have tried to put Europe in its place. Chakrabarty and his associates have more in common than they would like to admit with nineteenth-century Romantics who saw the Indian 'nation' as possessing a unique essence, with twentieth-century nationalists who insisted that India should be interpreted by Indians, and with twenty-first-century reactionaries who say that only 'Indians' (by which they mean traditionally minded Hindus) have the *adhikara* or capacity to write about India. Chakrabarty (2000: 43) distances himself from such writers, insisting that his provincialization of Europe 'cannot be a nationalist, nativist, or atavistic project'. He also abjures the simple expedient of saying that India lies beyond the reach of European categories and concepts. He is committed 'to engaging the universals—such as the abstract figure of the human or that of Reason—that were forged in eighteenth-century Europe and that underlie the human sciences'. But this engagement, he admits, originates 'from within' the Western intellectual tradition, since 'the phenomenon of "political modernity"' is one that 'is impossible to *think* of anywhere in the world' without invoking certain characteristically European concepts and categories: the state, civil society, and so forth. This puts him in the paradoxical position of trying to provincialize Europe while accepting European modernity as his necessary 'and in a sense indispensable' framework (Chakrabarty 2000: 4f.).

Chakrabarty's project is one of the most sophisticated attempts to arrive at an Indian, or at any rate a not-exclusively-European, way of looking at Indian history, but he builds on foundations that were laid a hundred years ago. Many of his predecessors exhibit great subtlety of thought and are not hobbled, like him, by an excessive reliance on (European) figures such as Heidegger and Marx who, taken at face value, seem to offer little support to his thesis. By way of example, I examine one branch of this lineage, the nationalists of nineteenth- and twentieth-century Bengal.

Any survey of this style must begin with Bankim Chandra Chatterji, who, suggestively in his novels and explicitly in his essays, challenged the right of Europeans to dictate the terms of the colonial encounter. His aim, as Hans Harder puts it, was 'to take the authoritative discussion about Indian culture out of [European] Orientalist hands and back to India' (Harder 1999).[33] Rabindranath Tagore (1918: vi), who assumed Bankim's literary mantle at the end of the century, wrote about this development: 'For some time past a spirit of retaliation has taken possession of our literature and our social world. We have furiously begun to judge our judges.' Around the same time, Bengali authors, artists, academics, mapmakers, and others took up the disciplines that helped the colonial state assert its mastery, making what Chakrabarty's *Subaltern*

Studies colleague Partha Chatterjee (1995: 27) calls 'serious attempts to produce a different modernity'. This move towards literary and cultural autonomy helped pave the way for the emergence of nationalist politics in the first decade of the twentieth century. Political organizer Bipin Chandra Pal wrote in 1906:

The time has come when . . . our British friends should be distinctly told that . . . we cannot any longer suffer ourselves to be guided by them in our attempts at political progress and emancipation. . . . They desire to make the government of India popular, without ceasing in any sense to be essentially British. We desire to make it autonomous and absolutely free from British control.[34]

Aurobindo expanded on this the following year: 'If the subject nation desires not a provincial existence and a maimed development but the full, vigorous and noble realisation of its national existence, even a change in the system of Government will not be enough; it must aim not only at a national Government responsible to the people but a free national Government unhampered even in the least degree by foreign control' (Aurobindo 1972a: 92). Aurobindo subsequently left the political field because he saw that what he was doing 'was not the genuine Indian thing', but only 'a European import, an imitation of European ways'.[35] He wrote in 1920 (the year Gandhi emerged as the leader of the freedom movement) that the country was sure to achieve independence if 'it keeps its present tenor'. What was preoccupying him was what India 'is going to do with its self-determination'. Would she 'strike out her own original path' or forever 'stumble in the wake of Europe'?[36]

One thing that distinguishes the attempt of the nationalists cited above to create 'an alternative language of discourse' or 'different modernity' and the efforts of modern scholars to write the history of India from an Indian point of view is the latter's attitude towards religion. Chatterji, Tagore, Pal, and Aurobindo were all modern in outlook and education, but they all used religious concepts in their writings. Most contemporary Indian historians, reactionaries excepted, reject religious forms of expression as impossible to square with their secular, often Marxist, backgrounds. This lands them in awkward positions when they try to represent the attitudes and ideas of the subaltern groups whose histories they wish to tell. The lower classes in India, broadly speaking, take religious and mythological discourse very seriously indeed. I would need a hundred pages to justify this generalization (it is no more than that), but will content myself with a single anecdote. When a friend of mine, then a member of the Communist Party of India (Marxist-Leninist), was organizing in rural Maharashtra during the 1960s, he was often taken aback, at the end of a lecture on the Marxist theory of History, to be asked what all that had to do with the history of Rama, Sita, and Lakshman. For his listeners the heroes of the Ramayana were a great deal more real than the nineteenth-century German and his theories. Confronted with such attitudes, even the most sympathetic scholar tends to resort to some sort of reductive historicism or 'anthropologism' to fit his human data into his theory. Chakrabarty's mentor Ranajit Guha (1983: Vol. 2, 34), writing about a nineteenth-century insurrection among the Santals (a tribal people of central and eastern India), admits that 'religiosity was, by all accounts, central to the *hool* [uprising]'. He examines with respect the statements of leaders of the hool that they were impelled to revolt by their god (*thakur*). He concludes: 'it is not possible to speak of insurgency in this case except as a religious consciousness', but adds, 'except, that is, as a massive demonstration of self-estrangement (to borrow Marx's term for the very essence of religion)'. The question is whether a student of the insurrection is better off accepting Marx's or the Santals' explanation of the 'essence of religion'. The Santals are a decidedly unmodern South Asian subaltern group. Do the ideas of a metropolitan, atheistic, nineteenth-century European political philosopher, however brilliant, really help us understand them?

It is to Chakrabarty's credit that he does not sweep this problem under the carpet. Commenting on Guha's discussion of the Santals' statements, he writes:

In spite of his desire to listen to the rebel voice seriously, Guha cannot take it seriously enough, for there is no principle in an 'event' involving the divine or the supernatural that can give us a narrative-strategy that is rationally-defensible in the modern understanding of what constitutes public life. The Santals' own understanding does not directly serve the cause of democracy or citizenship or socialism. It needs to be reinterpreted.

Historians may admit that participants in the hool did not view it as a secular event, but there are limits to how far they can go in applying this insight. Ordinarily the notion of divine intervention cannot be admitted to 'the language of professional history in which the idea of historical evidence ... cannot ascribe to the supernatural any kind of agential force except as part of the non-rational (i.e. somebody's belief system)' (Chakrabarty 1998: 20f.; cf. Chakrabarty 2000: 104). But

Chakrabarty is not satisfied with just drawing a line between the non-modern and modern modes of discourse. He wishes 'to raise the question of how we might find a form of social thought that embraces analytical reason in pursuit of social justice but does not allow it to erase the question of heterotemporality from the history of the modern subject'. As he puts it in his conclusion, 'to provincialize Europe in historical thought is to struggle to hold in a state of permanent tension a dialogue between two contradictory points of view' (Chakrabarty 2000: 239, 254).

Chakrabarty has been criticized for giving an opening to religious obscurantism, even for providing aid and comfort to the religious Right. The entry of religious discourse into Indian politics has done the country a great deal of harm, his critics aver. If it is allowed to enter academic discourse as well, would not things become much worse? This line of thought is not without justification. Much of the political and social tension in contemporary India is due to the misappropriation of religious discourse by political parties. Politicians incited people to destroy the Babri Mosque and justified the act by saying that Hindus believed that the mosque stood on the site of a temple that marked the place of Rama's birth. The mosque needed to be destroyed to make way for a glorious temple, the erection of which will usher in the Rama Rajya or earthly Kingdom of Rama. The terms are those of religious discourse, but the methods and motives are political. The anti-mosque movement would never have succeeded without anti-Muslim hatred being whipped up by religio-political organizations such as the Vishwa Hindu Parishad, Rashtriya Swayamsevak Sangh, and Bharatiya Janata Party (BJP).[37] The anti-mosque movement played an important role in the rise to power of the BJP, which controlled the government in New Delhi between 1999 and 2004.

If religion can be put to such perverse use, would it not be better to ban it from intellectual discourse—unless indeed it is rendered harmless by viewing it in the framework of historiographical or anthropological theory? This is what reductive and critical orientalists have tried to do for the last few decades, and they have failed. Now they are being challenged by reactionary 'new historians', who embrace religious discourse but lack training in critical historiography, and so contribute little of value. The same reactionary historians have tried to appropriate the work of nationalist writers like Aurobindo, Tilak, and Gandhi,[38] and critical historians have let this go unchallenged or even helped it along by writing of the nationalists as proto-reactionaries in scholarship as well as in politics (see, for example, van der Veer 1999; Thapar 1975: 13). This is unfortunate both because it misrepresents the positions of the nationalists, and because it fails to make use of those parts of their work that are of lasting scholarly value and that might be of help in establishing the dialogue that is needed to arrive at a viable reinterpretation of Indian history. A return to nationalist orientalism is hardly the way to resolve the outstanding problems in Indian historiography. The approach of the nationalists was a product of their age, and much of it is obsolete. Their essentializing of the Indian soul, for instance, is unjustifiable on historical or anthropological grounds, and politically dangerous. On the other hand, the dissolution of all cultural distinctiveness in the name of political stability, which Said seems sometimes to propose,[39] would also be bad social science and would not provide a solution to our political problems. Writers like Chatterji, Tagore, and Aurobindo laid stress on India's distinctiveness because it seemed threatened by absorption into a universalized Europe. But they were also internationalists who knew and respected Europe and worked for intercultural understanding.[40] Their defenders and detractors lay stress on their essentialism, but they themselves went beyond it, contesting the validity of Eurocentrism without promoting an equally imperfect Indocentrism.

NOTES

1. This chapter was originally presented as a paper at the 17th European Conference on Modern South Asian Studies, held in Heidelberg, in 2002, and subsequently published in *History and Theory,* Vol. 42, May 2003, pp. 169–95. The author is grateful to the members of the Religions Reform Movement panel at the 17th European Conference on Modern South Asian Studies; to Brian Fay and the other editors of *History and Theory;* to Jacques Pouchepadass; and to two anonymous reviewers for their comments and suggestions. The final responsibility is, of course, the author's own.

2. See, for example, Said (1991: 203–4): 'For any European during the nineteenth century—and I think one can say this almost without qualification—Orientalism was such a system of truths, truths in Nietzsche's sense of the word. It is therefore correct that every European, in what he could say about the Orient, was consequently a racist, an imperialist, and almost totally ethnocentric. . . . My contention is that Orientalism is fundamentally a political doctrine willed over the Orient because the Orient was weaker than the West.'

3. This point was made earlier by Kopf (1980).

4. The same point is made by Hourani (1979: 5), Dirlik (1994: 344), Hallisey (1995: 32), Dallmayr (1996: 118), Pinch (1999: 389–407), and Eaton (2000: 69–71).

5. This paradox has been noted by Hallisey (1995: 32), Eaton (2000: 65f.), Doniger (1999: 945), and others.

6. Here and elsewhere, I use 'postcolonial' in its unadorned meaning: 'belonging to the period after the colonial period', that is, with regard to India, 'post-1947'.

7. Halbfass's statement is a generalization and can pass as such, though I would move the date back to 1750 or earlier. Works such as Mirza Shah I'Tesamuddin's (2002) account in Persian of his trip to England in 1765, and Ananda Ranga Pillai's diaries in Tamil, dealing with official and private life in French Pondicherry between 1736 and 1761, show that eighteenth-century Indians were as capable of observing and theorizing about Europeans as Europeans were of them. One might even go back as far as the late sixteenth century, when the emperor Akbar (1542–1605), always curious in matters of religion, interacted with Jesuits from Goa.

8. Manuscript note included in Aurobindo (2003: 202).

9. For a discussion of Swami Vivekananda's response to European claims of Indian indebtedness to Europe's aesthetic and artistic traditions, see Chapter 9 in this volume.

10. A Sanskrit phrase that in classical texts means 'constant duty' or 'invariable law'. In the nineteenth century it was reinterpreted as 'eternal religion' and put forward as an Indian equivalent of the English term 'Hinduism'. Aurobindo used it to signify the 'religion of Vedanta', which he believed to be the supreme expression of the one universal religion. I discuss the history of the term *sanatana dharma* at some length in Heehs (2003a).

11. Undated letter (*c.* August 1912) to Motilal Roy, published in Aurobindo (1973: 433f.).

12. Interview in *Empire*. Calcutta, 9 May 1909.

13. A historian is not obliged to take retrospective assertions like this at face value, but there seems to be less danger in accepting them provisionally, in the spirit of Paul Ricoeur's 'second naïveté' (see Ricoeur 1969: 347–57), than in imposing an alien explanatory framework on them.

14. Pages could be written summarizing how this 'myth' was created and enforced by British law, anthropology, architecture, ceremony, etc., as well as by military force. The most interesting of the recent Foucault-inspired studies of imperial disciplines, such as those in Chatterjee (1995), are concerned with various aspects of this myth-creation. However, such studies give far too much importance to disembodied 'discourse' and too little importance to deliberate personal, political, diplomatic, and military force.

15. Kaviraj here draws on, and cites, Chatterjee (1993).

16. Although Sastry attempts to show the superiority of Aurobindo's interpretation to the 'European' interpretation and to the traditional interpretation preserved primarily in the work of the fourteenth-century ritualistic commentator Sayana, he admits that he has 'generally taken Sayana as his model in regard to word-for-word meaning, grammar, accent, etc.' (Sastry 1977–92: Vol. 4, ix).

17. Typical claims are that the rishis ('seers' of the Vedas) knew about airplanes, atomic energy, and cloning. Such absurdities make it difficult for people to accept that Indian mathematicians and scientists did make some remarkable observations, such as the ratios of the Pythagorean theorem (before Pythagoras) and the revolution of the earth (before Copernicus). It might be added that neither of these observations had generalized scientific or cultural consequences in India.

18. Sastry (1977–92: Vol. 1, 17) argues in Aurobindo's defence that the ritual meaning 'was unimportant with the Rishis as that was intended as an outer cover for guarding the secret knowledge'. This is unconvincing. The ritual meaning and its associated practices are still current after more than two millennia, while Aurobindo's exoteric meaning is not part of the extant indigenous tradition.

19. Müller's linguistic computations, by which he dated the *Rig Veda* to 1000 BCE, are explained in Gonda (1975: 22). William Jones arrived by a different means at a date of *c.* 1200 BCE (Jones, 1807: Vol. 7, 79).

20. The modern word 'Aryan' comes from the Vedic *arya*, which was taken to be the name of the 'race' that composed the Vedas. In modern scholarly literature, the presumed linguistic ancestor of Sanskrit, Greek, Latin, etc. is known as Proto-Indo-European; the presumed people who spoke this language are often called Indo-Europeans.

21. See 'The Gods of the Veda [second version]' in Aurobindo (1984: 136); cf. 'A System of Vedic Psychology: Preparatory' in Aurobindo (1973: 183).

22. The migratory theory appears in all up-to-date textbooks, for example, Kulke and Rothermund (1998: 30).

23. In this connection, see Risley's misreading of a Buddhist bas-relief, which he presents as 'the sculptured expression of the race sentiment of the Aryans towards the Dravidians' (Risley 1908: 5).

24. Aurobindo did, however, acknowledge a difference in culture between the 'Aryans' of the north and centre and the inhabitants of the south, west, and east (Aurobindo 1972c: 278).

25. 'The Secret of the Veda' (manuscript draft) in Aurobindo (1985: 42).

26. What Renan (n.d.: 190) wrote, in an ironic passage of his memoirs, was that if he had not gone to Saint-Sulpice and learned Hebrew, German, and theology, he might have become a natural scientist. As it was, his studies led him to the 'historical sciences, little conjectural sciences, that forever are unmaking themselves as soon as they are made and are forgotten in a hundred years'. There is no special mention of philology. (Renan did important work in many 'historical sciences', philology among them.) The French savant was simply giving expression to the usual longing of the social scientist for the neatness and precision of the natural sciences.

27. See Trautmann (1997: 131–64). One well-published linguist writes that 'it is quite clear that Chukchi-Kamchatkan and Eskimo-Aleut ... are both closer to Indo-European than Afro-Asiatic or Dravidian is' (Ruhlen 1994: 134f.).

28. *A Defence of Indian Culture* was written in reply to William Archer's *India and the Future* (1917), a condescending and primarily destructive critique of Indian life, literature, and art.

29. Van der Veer cites, without page reference, Aurobindo's *Foundations of Indian Culture*, the editorial title under which *The Defence of Indian Culture* and other essays were formerly published. There is no passage in these essays in which Aurobindo writes that the two Sanskrit epics were the essence of Indian civilization. He does say that 'the Mahabharata and Ramayana, whether in the original Sanskrit or rewritten in the regional tongues, brought to the masses by Kathakas—rhapsodists, reciters, and exegetes—became and remained one of the chief instruments of popular education and culture, moulded the thought, character, aesthetic and religious mind of the people and gave even to the illiterate some sufficient tincture of philosophy, ethics, social and political ideas, aesthetic emotion, poetry, fiction and romance' (Aurobindo 1997: 346). The allusion to the translations and dramatic presentations of the epics is interesting, for it is part of van der Veer's argument that the neglect of these popular traditions was one of the errors of 'orientalist' scholarship. The passage in Aurobindo's works that comes closest to van der Veer's paraphrase is this one from a very early essay: 'Valmiki, Vyasa and Kalidasa [the authors, respectively, of the Mahabharata, the Ramayana, and several classical poems and plays] are the essence of the history of ancient India; if all else were lost, they would still be its sole and sufficient cultural history' (Aurobindo 2003: 152). Aurobindo's point here is that the three poets represent what he then regarded as the three main 'moods' of the 'Aryan civilisation', the moral, the intellectual, and the material. Hinduism is not mentioned. As for Indian Islam, see the last chapter of the *Defence of Indian Culture* for Aurobindo's inclusive attitude.

30. It should be noted that Inden and King are serious scholars whose arguments are based on primary research. The nuances and qualifications present in their work are lost when their conclusions are retailed by popular writers, as in this extract from a review of a collection of essays: 'Quite correctly, the contributors argue that the conventional construction of India is a product of orientalist scholarship. Though more marked in the case of Muslims and Islam, European imperialism in general invented the traditionalism that formed the ideological "other" in the orient. . . . [E]ach of these contributors and their positions are by now well known, at least within the charmed circle' (Sethi 1997: 9). The 'charmed circle' in question might concisely be described as a hundred-odd people who went to the same colleges and attend the same parties in south Delhi.

31. One happy result of the trend towards specialization in the study of Indian languages and culture has been the production of a large number of first-class monographs and translations representing a wide variety of traditions. Extracts from and references to many such works are found in Heehs (2003b).

32. I hesitate to use the much-abused word 'paradigm', but what I am referring to here is a paradigm shift of the sort spoken of by Thomas S. Kuhn (1970) in the *The Structure of Scientific Revolutions*.

33. Hans Harder (1999). Harder (2001) elaborates this point.

34. Bipin Chandra Pal, article in a lost issue of the newspaper *Bande Mataram*, quoted in *The Times* (London), 10 September 1906.

35. Letter (Bengali original with English translation) to Barindrakumar Ghose, April 1920, reproduced in Aurobindo (1980: 3).

36. Aurobindo (1972b: 430f.), letter to Joseph Baptista, 5 January 1920.

37. These groups continue to use religious discourse to serve political ends. 'A time has come to bring [Vinayak Damodar] Savarkar's dictum of Hinduising politics and militarising the Hindudom to reality', said Giriraj Kishore (2002), vice-president of the Vishwa Hindu Parishad (VHP), in a speech to members of the Bajrang Dal, the VHP's youth wing, on 30 June 2002, reported in *Hindustan Times*. The sort of 'Hindudom' Kishore had in mind may be imagined by reading accounts of the anti-Muslim pogrom in Gujarat in February–March 2002, in which the VHP and Bajrang Dal played conspicuous roles (see, for example, Kumar and Bhaumik 2002). On 3 September, VHP president Ashok Singhal (2002), speaking of the February–March events, stated in a speech in Amritsar, as reported by the *Indian Express*: 'We were successful in our experiment of raising Hindu consciousness, which will be repeated all over the country now'. After the BJP won the Gujarat state elections by a wide margin in December 2002, VHP leader Praveen Togadia (2002) lauded the organization's workers for helping to bring about the victory, stating at a press conference in Jaipur on 15 December 2002, as reported by *Rediff.com* the same day, that Gujarat had turned out to be 'a graveyard for secular forces' and declaring that 'a Hindu Rashtra [Hindu theocracy] can be expected in the next two years'.

38. The Hindu Right's misappropriation of Aurobindo is discussed in Heehs (2003a).

39. In the first chapter of *Orientalism*, Said (1991: 45) states the 'main intellectual issue raised by "Orientalism"': 'Can one divide human reality, as indeed human reality seems to be genuinely divided, into clearly different cultures, histories, traditions, societies, even races, and survive the consequences humanly?'

40. See, for example, Aurobindo's 'Message to America' (Aurobindo 1972b: 413–16), and Tagore (1931).

BIBLIOGRAPHY

Archer, William (1917), *India and the Future*, London: Hutchinson & Co.

(Sri) Aurobindo (1972a), *The Doctrine of Passive Resistance* (April 1907), reprinted in *Bande Mataram: Early Political Writings—I*, Pondicherry: Sri Aurobindo Ashram Trust.

——— (1972b), *On Himself*, Pondicherry: Sri Aurobindo Ashram Trust.

——— (1972c), *The Hour of God and Other Writings*, Pondicherry: Sri Aurobindo Ashram Trust.

——— (1973), *Supplement*, to the Sri Aurobindo Birth Centenary Library, Pondicherry: Sri Aurobindo Ashram Trust.

——— (1980), letter (translated from Bengali) to Barindrakumar Ghose, April 1920, in *Sri Aurobindo: Archives and Research*, Vol. 4, pp. 1–23.

——— (1984), 'The Gods of the Veda [second version]', in *Sri Aurobindo: Archives and Research*, Vol. 8, pp. 132–79.

——— (1985), 'The Secret of the Veda: Introduction', (manuscript draft) in *Sri Aurobindo: Archives and Research*, Vol. 9, pp. 23–49.

——— (1997), *The Renaissance in India with a Defence of Indian Culture*, Pondicherry: Sri Aurobindo Ashram Trust.

——— (1998), *The Secret of the Veda*, Pondicherry: Sri Aurobindo Ashram Trust.

——— (2001), *Kena and Other Upanishads*, Pondicherry: Sri Aurobindo Ashram Trust.

——— (2003), *Early Cultural Writings*, Pondicherry: Sri Aurobindo Ashram Trust.

Bevir, Mark (1994), 'The West Turns Eastward: Madame Blavatsky and the Transformation of the Occult Tradition', *Journal of the American Academy of Religion*, Vol. 62, pp. 747–67.

Biswas, Soutik (2002), 'A Faith Besieged', *Outlook*, Vol. 42, 8 July, pp. 57–61.

Bryant, Edwin (2002), *The Quest for the Origins of Vedic Culture: The Indo-Aryan Migration Debate*, New Delhi: Oxford University Press.

Chakrabarty, Dipesh (1998), 'Minority Histories, Subaltern Pasts', *Postcolonial Studies*, Vol. 1, pp. 15–29.

——— (2000), *Provincializing Europe: Postcolonial Thought and Historical Difference*, Chicago: University of Chicago Press.

Chatterjee, Partha (1993), *The Nation and Its Fragments*, Princeton: Princeton University Press.

——— (ed.) (1995), *Texts of Power: Emerging Disciplines and Colonial Bengal*, Minneapolis: University of Minnesota Press.

Clifford, James (1980), 'Review-essay of Said's *Orientalism*', *History and Theory*, Vol. 19.

Dallmayr, Fred (1996), *Beyond Orientalism: Essays on Cross-Cultural Encounter*, Albany: State University of New York Press.

Danino, Michel and Sujata Nahar (1996), *The Invasion That Never Was*, Delhi: The Mother's Institute of Research.

Danino, Michel (1999a), *Sri Aurobindo and Indian Civilisation*, Auroville: Editions Auroville Press International.

——— (1999b), *The Indian Mind Then and Now*, Auroville: Editions Auroville Press International.

Davis, Richard H. (1991), *Ritual in an Oscillating Universe: Worshipping Siva in Medieval India*, Princeton: Princeton University Press.

Dirlik, Arif (1994), 'The Postcolonial Aura: Third World Criticism in the Age of Global Capitalism', *Critical Inquiry*, Vol. 20, No. 2, pp. 328–56.

Doniger, Wendy (1999), '"I Have Scinde": Flogging a Dead (White Male Orientalist) Horse', *Journal of Asian Studies*, Vol. 58, No. 4, pp. 940–60.

Dutta, Charuchandra (1959), *Puranokatha Upasanghar*, Kolkata: Sanskriti Baithak.

Eaton, Richard M. (2000), '(Re)imag(in)ing Other²ness: A Postmortem for the Postmodern in India', *Journal of World History*, Vol. 11, pp. 69–71.

Final Examination of Candidates Selected in 1890 for the Civil Service of India, London: Printed for Her Majesty's Stationery Office, 1892.

Frawley, David (1998), *The Myth of the Aryan Invasion of India*, New Delhi: Voice of India.

Gautier, François (1996), *Rewriting Indian History*, New Delhi: Vikas Publishing House.

Gonda, Jan (1975), *Vedic Literature (Samhitas and Brahmanas): A History of Indian Literature*, Vol. I.1, Wiesbaden: Harrassowitz.

Gordon, Leonard A. (1974), *Bengal: The Nationalist Movement 1876–1940*, New York: Columbia University Press.

Guha, Ranajit (1983), 'The Prose of Counter-Insurgency', in Ranajit Guha (ed.), *Subaltern Studies: Writings on South Asian History and Society*, Vol. 2, Delhi: Oxford University, pp. 1–40.

Halbfass, Wilhelm (1988), *India and Europe: An Essay in Philosophical Understanding*, Albany: State University of New York Press.

Hallisey, Charles (1995), 'Roads Taken and Not Taken in the Study of Theravada Buddhism', in Donald S. Lopez, Jr (ed.), *Curators of the Buddha: The Study of Buddhism under Colonialism*, Chicago: University of Chicago Press, pp. 31–61.

Harder, Hans (1999), 'Bankimchandra's Religious Thinking', *IIAS Newsletter*, Vol. 18.

——— (2001), *Bankimchandra Chattopadhyay's Srimadbhagabadgita: Translation and Analysis*, New Delhi: Manohar.

Hastings, Warren (1785), 'To Nathaniel Smith, Esquire', in *The Bhagavat-Geeta or Dialogues of Kreeshna and Arjoon*, trans. Charles Wilkins, London: Printed for C. Nourse.

Heehs, Peter (2003a), '"The Centre of the Religious Life of the World": Spiritual Universalism and Cultural Nationalism in the Work of Sri Aurobindo', in Antony Copley (ed.), *Hinduism in Public and Private: Reform, Hindutva, Gender and Sampraday*, New Delhi: Oxford University Press, pp. 66–83.

——— (ed.), (2003b), *Indian Religions: A Historical Reader of Spiritual Expression and Experience*, New York: New York University Press.

Hourani, Albert (1979), 'The Road to Morocco', *New York Review of Books*, 8 March, p. 5 of online edition. *http://www.nybooks.com/articles/article-preview?article_id =7882*, [accessed 7 November 2007].

Inden, Ronald (1986), 'Orientalist Constructions of India', in *Modern Asian Studies*, Vol. 20, No. 3, pp. 401–46.

——— (1990), *Imagining India*, Oxford: Basil Blackwell.

Jha, N. and N. S. Rajaram (2000), *The Deciphered Indus Script*, New Delhi: Aditya Prakashan.

Jones, William (1807), *Institutes of Hindu Law: or, the Ordinances of Menu*, in *The Works of Sir William Jones*, Vol. 7, London: Printed for John Stockdale and John Walker.

Joshi, Kireet (2001), *The Portals of Vedic Knowledge*, Auroville, India: Editions Auroville Press International.

Kaviraj, Sudipta (2000), 'Modernity and Politics in India', *Daedalus*, Vol. 129, Winter, pp. 137–62.

King, Richard (1999), *Orientalism and Religion: Postcolonial Theory, India and 'The Mystic East'*, London and New York: Routledge.

Kishore, Giriraj (2002), a speech reported in *Hindustan Times*, 1 July, online edition, available at *http://www.hindustantimes.com/nonfram/300602/dlnat55.asp*, accessed 1 July, 2002.

Kopf, David (1980), 'Hermeneutics versus History', *Journal of Asian Studies*, Vol. 39, No. 3, pp. 495–506.

Kuhn, Thomas S. (1970), *The Structure of Scientific Revolutions* [1962], Chicago: University of Chicago Press.

Kulke, Hermann and Dietmar Rothermund (1998), *History of India*, New York: Routledge.

Kumar, Amrita and Prashun Bhaumik (eds) (2002), *Lest We Forget: Gujarat 2002*, New Delhi: World Report.

Lietard, G. (1872), *Les peuples ariens et les langues ariennes*, Paris: G. Masson.

Ludden, David (1993), 'Orientalist Empiricism: Transformations of Colonial Knowledge', in Carol A. Breckenridge and Peter van der Veer (eds), *Orientalism and the Postcolonial Predicament: Perspectives on South Asia*, Philadelphia: University of Pennsylvania Press, pp. 1–35.

Müller, F. Max (1981), *The Upanishads*, Part I. Volume I of *The Sacred Books of the East*. Reprint edition, Delhi: Motilal Banarsidass.

Nahar, Sujata et al. (eds) (1996), *India's Rebirth*, Mysore, India: Mira Aditi.

Nandy, Ashis (1988), *The Intimate Enemy: Loss and Recovery of Self under Colonialism*, Delhi: Oxford University Press.

(Sister) Nivedita (1973), 'Aggressive Hinduism', in *The Complete Works of Sister Nivedita*, Vol. 3, Calcutta: Sister Nivedita Girls' School.

Pillai, Ananda Ranga (1985), *The Private Diary of Ananda Ranga Pillai* (J. Frederick Price, ed.) reprint edition, New Delhi: Asian Educational Services.

Pinch, William R. (1999), 'Same Difference in India and Europe', *History and Theory*, Vol. 38, No. 3, pp. 389–407.

Radhakrishnan, Sarvepalli (1941), *Indian Philosophy*, Vol. 1, London: George Allen & Unwin.

Rajaram, Navaratna S. (n.d.), 'Vedic-Harappan Gallery', available at *http://www.vhp.org/englishsite/hbharat/vedicharappan_gallery.htm*, accessed 6 July 2002.

Rajaram, Navaratna S. and David Frawley (2001), *Vedic Aryans and the Origins of Civilisation: A Literary and Scientific Perspective*, 3rd edn, New Delhi: Voice of India.

Renan, Ernest (n.d.), *Souvenirs d'enfance et de jeunesse*, Paris: Nelson Éditeurs.

Ricoeur, Paul (1969), *The Symbolism of Evil*, Boston: Beacon Press.

Rigveda Samhita, R. L. Kashyap and S. Sadagopan (eds), Bangalore: Sri Aurobindo Kapali Shastri Institute of Vedic Culture, 1998.

Risley, Herbert (1908), *The People of India*, Calcutta: Thacker, Spink & Co.

Rocher, Rosane (1993), 'British Orientalism in the Eighteenth Century: The Dialectics of Knowledge and Government', in Carol A. Breckenridge and Peter van der Veer (eds), *Orientalism and the Postcolonial Predicament: Perspectives on South Asia*, Philadelphia: University of Pennsylvania Press, pp. 215–40.

Roy, Rammohan (1999), 'Translation of an Abridgement of the *Vedant*', in Bruce Robertson (ed.), *The Essential Writings of Raja Rammohan Ray*, Delhi: Oxford University Press, pp. 1–14.

Ruhlen, Merritt (1994), *The Origin of Language: Tracing the Evolution of the Mother Tongue*, New York: John Wiley.

Said, Edward W. (1991), *Orientalism: Western Conceptions of the Orient*, London: Penguin Books.

Sarda, Har Bilas (1917), *Hindu Superiority: An Attempt to Determine the Position of the Hindu Race in the Scale of Nations*, 2nd edition, Ajmer: Scottish Mission Industries Company.

Sastry, T. V. Kapali (1977–92), *Collected Works of T. V. Kapali Sastry*, 12 vols, Pondicherry: Dipti Publications.

Sethi, Harsh (1997), 'Threads of Communalism', *Indian Review of Books*, 16 January–15 February, pp. 8–9.

Shourie, Arun (1988), *Eminent Historians: Their Technology, Their Line, Their Fraud*, Delhi: Asa.

Singhal, Ashok, (2002) '"Wee' ll repeat our Gujarat experiment"', speech in Amritsar, 3 September 2002, reported in the *Indian Express*, 4 September 2002, online edition, available at *http://www.indianexpress.com/full_story.php?content_id =8831*, accessed 6 November 2007.

Singhal, Ashok (2002), speech reported in *Indian Express*, 4 September, online edition, available at *http://www.indianexpress.com/full_story.php?content_id =8831*, accessed 4 September.

Tagore, Rabindranath (1918), 'Introduction', in Sister Nivedita, *The Web of Indian Life*, Bombay: Longmans, Green and Co., pp. v–viii

———— (1931), *The Religion of Man*, London: George Allen and Unwin.

I'Tesamuddin, Mirza Shah (2002), *The Wonders of Vilayat* (translated by Kaiser Haq), Leeds: Peepal Books.

Thapar, Romila (1975), *The Past and Prejudice*, Delhi: Oxford University Press.

———— (1992), 'Ideology and the Interpretation of Early Indian History' [1974], in *Interpreting Early India*, New Delhi: Oxford University Press, pp. 1–22.

———— (1996), 'The Theory of Aryan Race and India: History and Politics', *Social Scientist*, Vol. 24, January–March, pp. 3–29.

Tilak, Bal Gangadhar (1975a), *The Orion or Researches into the Antiquity of the Vedas* [1893], *Samagra Lokmanya Tilak*, Vol. 2, Poona: Kesari Prakashan.

——— (1975b), *The Arctic Home in the Vedas* [1903], in *Samagra Lokmanya Tilak*, Vol. 2, Poona: Kesari Prakashan.

Togadia, Praveen (2002), '"Hindu Rashtra" in two years: Togadia', statement at a press conference in Jaipur on 15 December, reported by *Rediff.com*, 15 December 2002, available at *http://www.rediff.com/election/2002/dec/15guj13.htm*, accessed 6 November 2007.

Trautmann, Thomas R. (1997), *Aryans and British India*, Berkeley and Los Angeles: University of California Press.

van der Veer, Peter (1999), 'Monumental Texts: The Critical Edition of India's National Heritage', in Daud Ali (ed.), *Invoking the Past: The Uses of History in South Asia*, New Delhi: Oxford University Press, pp. 134–55.

Vidal, Denis (1997), 'Max Müller and the Theosophists: The Other Half of Victorian Orientalism', in Jackie Assayag, Roland Lardonois and Denis Vidal (eds), *Orientalism and Anthropology: From Max Müller to Louis Dumont*, Pondicherry, India: Institut Français de Pondichéry, pp. 13–22.

(Swami) Vivekananda (1989), 'My Life and Mission', in *The Collected Works of Swami Vivekananda*, Vol. 8, Calcutta: Advaita Ashrama.

Witzel, Michael and Steve Farmer (2000), 'Horseplay in Harappa', *Frontline*, Issue 17, 30 September–13 October, pp. 1–14.

Contributors

DIEGO ABENANTE Associate Professor of South Asian History, Department of Political Science, University of Trieste.

GWILYM BECKERLEGGE Senior Lecturer in Religious Studies, The Open University.

DANIELA BREDI Associate Professor of History of Islam in South Asia, Faculty of Oriental Studies, University of Rome La Sapienza.

IAN COPLAND Professor of History, School of Historical Studies, Monash University.

PETER HEEHS Archivist at the Sri Aurobindo Ashram, Pondicherry.

MARUTI T. KAMBLE Professor of History, Department of History and Archaeology, Karnatak University.

DIETRICH REETZ Senior Researcher at Zentrum Moderner Orient, Senior Lecturer in Political Science at Free University, Berlin.

MARTIN RIEXINGER Lecturer in Arabic and Islamic Studies, Göttingen University.

HILTRUD RÜSTAU School for Asian and African Studies, Humboldt University, Berlin (retired).

HEINZ WERNER WESSLER Assistant Professor, Department of Indology, Institute for Oriental and Asian Studies, University of Bonn.